Source Material for the Social and Ceremonial Life of the Choctaw Indians

John R. Swanton

Foreword by Kenneth H. Carleton

Published in Cooperation with the Birmingham Public
Library

D1736122

THE UNIVERSITY OF ALABAMA PRESS

Tuscaloosa and London

Originally published by the Smithsonian Institution in 1931 as *Bureau of American Ethnology Bulletin 103.*

2 4 6 8 9 7 5 3 1
02 04 06 08 09 07 05 03 01

∞
The paper on which this book is printed meets the minimum requirements
of American National Standard for Information Science–Permanence of
Paper for Printed Library Materials, ANSI Z39.48-1984.

Library of Congress Cataloging-in-Publication Data

Swanton, John Reed, 1873–1958.
Source material for the social and ceremonial life of the Choctaw
Indians / John R. Swanton ; foreword by Kenneth H. Carleton.
p. cm. — (Contemporary American Indian studies)
"Published in cooperation with the Birmingham Public Library."
Originally published: Washington : U.S. G. P. O., 1931. (Bulletin /
Smithsonian Institution, Bureau of American Ethnology ; 103)
Includes bibliographical references and index.
ISBN 0-8173-1109-2 (pbk.: alk. paper)
1. Choctaw Indians—Social life and customs. I. Title. II. Series.

E99.C8 S9 2001
976.004'973—dc21
2001017102

British Library Cataloguing-in-Publication Data available

CONTENTS

ILLUSTRATIONS

FOREWORD

Kenneth H. Carleton

John Reed Swanton, 1873–1958, is generally considered the father of modern Southeastern American Indian ethnology and ethnohistory (although it was not called that when Swanton was doing it). The majority of his major works are about the Indians of the Southeast. They concentrate on historical documentation of the native peoples using original source material and synthesizing the information in them to study the histories and cultures of the tribes of the Southeast and North America. Swanton was one of the first professional anthropologists to undertake such work at a time when most anthropologists were solely concentrating on ethnographic field work—the frantic documentation of the "disappearing cultures" of the early twentieth century.

He began his professional career when he received one of the first Ph.D.'s in Anthropology awarded in the United States from Harvard University in 1900. Swanton initially conducted some field work among the tribes of the Northwest Coast. The data from this field work comprise most of his earliest publications. Swanton then began his lifelong association with the Smithsonian Institution's Bureau of American Ethnology, where he worked for over forty years. Once there Swanton began his life's work, that of documenting the culture and history of the Southeastern Indians.

Swanton began publishing a series of major volumes on Southeastern and North American Indians, most of which have achieved the status of "classics" in the field, after joining the BAE. The first of these major works was *Indian Tribes of the Lower Mississippi Valley and Adjacent Coast of the Gulf of Mexico,* published in 1911. Other works included such classics as *Early History of the Creek Indians and their Neighbors,* 1922; *Social Organization and Social Usages of the Indians of the Creek Confederacy,* 1928; *Social and Religious Beliefs and Usages of the Chickasaw Indians,* 1928; *Myths and Tales of the Southeastern Indians,* 1929; *Final Report of the United States DeSoto Expedition,* 1939; *Indians of the Southeastern United States,* 1946; and his final major work, *The Indian Tribes of North America,* 1946.

Social and Ceremonial Life of the Choctaw Indians is a work that

compiles both Swanton's own limited field work among the Mississippi Choctaws during at least one trip to Mississippi, during which
he interviewed Olman Comby and Simpson Tubby, and all the historical documentation available to him before the book's publication
in 1931. It was originally published as *Smithsonian Institution Bureau of American Ethnology Bulletin 103*. It has been reprinted in
small editions twice in the recent past, first by the Birmingham Public Library in 1993 and again by the Mississippi Band of Choctaw
Indians in an undated edition in 1995, both of which are now un-
available.

This significant work is a major synthesis of the vast majority of
the known historical descriptions of the Choctaws. While Swanton
did not have access to all of the documents that we have today, he did
have access to most of the major works. These include at least one
major manuscript document, the anonymous *French Relation,* which
he is responsible for originally bringing to light from the Ayer Collection at the Newberry Library and which he translated and published
in 1918; the full French text is reproduced as an appendix in this
work. *Source Material for the Social and Ceremonial Life of the
Choctaw Indians* is still the most extensive work to date on Choctaw
culture and history from the eighteenth to early twentieth centuries.
However, it is about the *source material* for the social and ceremonial life of the Choctaw. Therefore a great deal of attention is given
to describing and reproducing information from original historic
sources. This makes this volume an extremely useful and timeless
resource, since it gives the reader access to at least excerpts of a
majority of the original sources covering the Choctaw. Many of these
sources are quite rare and hard to come by and have either never
been published or have been out of print for decades, if not centuries.
It must, however, always be remembered that the material reproduced in *Social and Ceremonial Life* consists of excerpts selected by
Swanton; only rarely is the complete text of a source quoted. Some of
the more pertinent works have, however, been reproduced in full-
text in *A Choctaw Source Book* (Peterson 1985). It must also be remembered that while Swanton did have access to most of the important sources, today we have access to many to which he did not.

While Swanton does cover many other topics in this work, social
and "ceremonial" are the aspects of Choctaw culture upon which he
concentrates. Therefore there is only minor discussion of such things
as material culture, but these are more extensive than one might
expect given the title of the work. Some of the material culture for
which there is discussion of varying detail includes housing, baskets, clothing, and other objects and tools. At the time this work was
written, the study of archaeology in the Southeastern U.S. was only

really just beginning. The study of the archaeology of the Choctaw themselves was virtually nonexistent and is today still only beginning to be understood. Therefore very little of Swanton's work deals with Choctaw history and culture before sustained European contact occurred with the French settlement of Louisiana in 1699. The main discussion of events before that time deals with Hernando de Soto and his purported contact with the Choctaw. Today most scholars believe that the Choctaw-proper as a group probably did not exist at the time of Soto. While Soto may have encountered groups speaking Choctaw or a Western Muskhogean language, those people were more than likely one or more of the ancestral groups whose remnant descendants confederated before (and during) French contact to become the group that we today know as the Choctaw. (Carleton 1994; Galloway 1995).

The vast majority of this work deals with the social organization, political organization, and "ceremonial" life of the Choctaw. His chapters include such topics as Social Organization, Government, Property, Marriage, War Customs, Burial Customs, and Religion and medicine. These topics are all covered with varying amounts of detail, since there are widely disparate source materials dealing extremely unevenly with many of these aspects of Choctaw culture. Unfortunately the Choctaw have what is probably the poorest body of historical descriptions of any of the major tribes in the Southeast. There was no Adair for them, and despite his many faults, Adair does give some excellent details about Chickasaw culture. The one topic for which there is a plethora of descriptions for the Choctaw is that of funerals. This is, of course, because of the morbid fascination that any Euro-American visitor who witnessed a Choctaw funeral had for their custom of scaffolding the body of the deceased and then the "bone picking" of the remains. Here we have description after description, some of which are very detailed, others of which are not. However, this custom was already falling into disuse by the opening of the nineteenth century, and many of the most detailed accounts of the Choctaw from the first quarter of the nineteenth century have to rely on secondary accounts of this lapsed custom to report on it.

In this work Swanton did an unfortunate and significant disservice to research on the Choctaw by putting forth the idea that the "Absence of pronounced native institutions made it easy for them to take up with foreign customs and usages . . . and [they] became with great rapidity poor subjects for ethnological study" (1931:2). This one statement seems to have killed any interest in future research into Choctaw traditional culture as being completely acculturated and forgotten. This was a complete misunderstanding by Swanton of the Choctaw. He seems to have missed the real point—that the Choctaw do not have large public ceremonies and other major events, nor do they have a very formalized priesthood or other such institutions, not because they had lost them over the years, but rather because they never had them; they really are different from their neighbors. The absence of these institutions did not mean that they were any more susceptible to acculturation and in fact may have made them less so. Since they did not have "significant" "institutions," the failure of which would result in a collapse of the traditional culture, they probably had survived with more of their traditional culture intact than any of the other Southeastern tribes. The only problem with trying to record this traditional culture is that it is much less visible from the outside. Swanton made the same mistake that virtually every European observer made throughout the eighteenth century when they stated that the Choctaw "have no religion." Of course they did. It just was not readily visible to the casual observer; there were no showy Green Corn Festivals for observers to watch. Therefore what Swanton missed was the fact that when he was talking to Olmon Comby and Simpson Tubby in the early 1920s in Mississippi, although they knew little of the structure of the Choctaw in 1800, their worldview was still Choctaw, and a significant portion of their culture was still very much with them, even if changed over the two hundred years since Iberville landed at Biloxi.

This is a major failing on the part of Swanton and affects a number of his interpretations throughout this work. In many instances, particularly where there are limited data available about a particular topic, Swanton makes the assumption that the Choctaw must have been just like the Creeks or Cherokee, with whom he was infinitely more familiar. Sometimes this assumption is correct, but in as many instances it is not. Often Swanton would make a basic statement reflecting what the limited data say, which is often closer to correct in my opinion, and then argue around to an incorrect interpretation. An excellent example of this is his discussion of clans among the Choctaw.

In his discussion of "clans and local groups," Swanton first quotes Adam Hodgson and J. F. H. Claiborne asserting the presence of totemic clans among the Choctaw, and then refutes them effectively. He then says: "Aside from these questionable statements there seems to be nothing to warrant the assumption that totemic groups existed among the Choctaw" (1931:79). In the next paragraph, however, he states: "But even though there were no totemic iksa, it is quite possible that there were nontotemic divisions corresponding to the Chickasaw totemic clans" (1931:79). He then launches into a tortuous discussion of group names gleaned mainly from informants in the early twentieth century and attempts to assert that they represent clans among the Choctaw in the eighteenth century. This has of course led most popular readers to assume that the Choctaw did in fact have a clan system like the other tribes of the Southeast, when in fact his first statement is correct—there were no totemic clans among the Choctaw. Only the moieties, of which Swanton also has a major discussion, existed, and virtually all of the vague references to "clans" can be explained away using solely the moieties, which were misunderstood by the Euro-American observers.

There are other failings of this work. One of the major ones is Swanton's tendency to make statements of fact without supporting references. There are numerous examples of this throughout this work. It is probably the most aggravating aspect of this volume. Another major failing, which reflects the times in which Swanton worked and the prevailing thoughts at the time more than any deficiencies in his scholarship, is the indiscriminate mixing of data temporally. This reflects the outmoded and discredited concept of a "pristine" native society, one in which nothing had changed until European contact. Even though he was fully aware of the amount of culture change that had occurred over the previous three hundred and more years among the cultures of the Southeast, Swanton is still just as likely to use historical data from the 1730s right alongside data from his own field work from the second decade of the twentieth century without regard for the fact that things had changed in two hundred years. This is very problematical. He also sometimes relies too heavily on his or others' twentieth-century informants to try to explain or elucidate institutions and structures that had not existed among the Choctaw for 170-plus years, rather than turning to the contemporary descriptions that are available. Swanton also, in my opinion, fails to give one of his principal sources sufficient credit. That source is Henry S. Halbert, with whom Swanton collaborated in the publication of Cyrus Byington's *Choctaw Dictionary* (*A Dictionary of the Choctaw Language, BAE Bulletin 46,* 1915) as coeditor. Swanton uses a significant amount of Halbert's published and unpublished works throughout this volume. Whether he received the unpublished information from Halbert directly during their collaboration on Byington's dictionary or had access to Halbert's extensive unpublished papers housed at the Alabama state archives is unknown, but Swanton does make extensive use of this enormous body of information throughout *Source Materials.* While Swanton never fails to give a proper attribution of information gained from this source, he rarely mentions in the text, which might be several pages away from the source reference, that it is someone else's data, when presenting the information. He should have made it much clearer that some of what he was presenting was largely Halbert's research, only supplemented by his own work.

Despite the many problems with this volume, it is still a monumental work with much to offer the reader and researcher. It is the most comprehensive work on Choctaw culture and history which exists. Even if someone were to attempt to write an up-to-date culture and history of the Choctaw, much of what would be said would merely repeat what Swanton said in 1931.

Carleton, Kenneth H.
  1994 "Where Did the Choctaw Come From: An Examination of Pottery in Areas Adjacent to the Choctaw Homeland." In *Perspectives on the Southeast: Linguistics, Archaeology and Ethnohistory,* Patricia B. Kwachka, Ed. Southeastern Anthropological Society Proceedings No. 27. University of Georgia Press, Athens.
Galloway, Patricia K.
  1995. *Choctaw Genesis: 1500–1700.* University of Nebraska Press, Lincoln.
Peterson, John H., Jr., editor.
  1985 *A Choctaw Source Book.* Garland Publishing, Inc., New York.

APUSHMATAHA

SOURCE MATERIAL FOR THE SOCIAL AND CEREMONIAL LIFE OF THE CHOCTAW INDIANS

By John R. Swanton

INTRODUCTION

Each of the larger tribes which formerly occupied portions of the Gulf region of our country had its own peculiar characteristics, and this was as true of those known to have belonged to the same linguistic stock as of tribes alien to one another in this respect. One associates with the Natchez a developed solar worship with a temple and perpetual fire, absolutism in government, and tragic funeral rites; with the Creeks a highly developed clan system, a confederate organization second in North America above Mexico to the Iroquois only, striking annual ceremonies, and prowess in war; with the Chickasaw warlike prowess of a still higher order, second to none except perhaps that exhibited by the Iroquois, and a social organization reminiscent of both Creeks and Choctaw. The feeling of a student for the Choctaw, however, might be described as of a powerful indefiniteness. Although during the seventeenth and eighteenth centuries the disparity in numbers between this tribe and the Creeks was probably not so great as it later became, the Choctaw were always, it is believed, the more populous and they appear to have been six or eight times as numerous as the Chickasaw. They lived as near to the French as the Creeks did to the English and much nearer than the Chickasaw. The important relation they bore to French colonial dominion, since they covered the flank of the Louisiana colony and the mouth of the Mississippi, was well recognized, and relations between them and the French, Spaniards, and Americans in succession were constant and intimate. Friends and foes alike testify to their courage, and a modified form of their language had become a trade medium which extended throughout most of the territory of the present States of Mississippi and Louisiana and along the whole of the lower Mississippi River. Yet how poorly press agented were the Choctaw is shown by the fact that this trade language received its name either from the Chickasaw or the little Mobile tribe. The fact of the matter is there were few customs observable among them sufficiently striking to attract the attention of European travelers—little " copy stuff," in other words, such as would interest officers of

1

trading corporations or missionary societies or governmental functionaries back home, or such as could be used to circulate explorers' narratives. Seemingly their unique way of disposing of the dead was the only feature of their lives thought worthy of much publicity, and that is about all that is purely Choctaw which most early writers vouchsafe us.

Although a certain political centralization had been attained it was not so absolute as to have become spectacular or oppressive, and therefore interesting to white men. There were no complicated religious ceremonials to arrest the attention of the foreigner and the intelligence of the native, and it is the general testimony that the Choctaw were less inclined to display their superiority to other people by trying to kill them than is usual even in more civilized societies. The significant things about them are told us in a few short sentences: That they had less territory than any of their neighbors but raised so much corn that they sent it to some of these others in trade, that their beliefs and customs were simple, and that they seldom left their country to fight but when attacked defended themselves with dauntless bravery. In other words, the aboriginal Choctaw seem to have enjoyed the enviable position of being " just folks," uncontaminated with the idea that they existed for the sake of a political, religious, or military organization. And apparently, like the meek and the Chinese and Hindoos, they were in process of inheriting the earth by gradual extension of their settlements because none of their neighbors could compete with them economically. Absence of pronounced native institutions made it easy for them to take up with foreign customs and usages, so that they soon distanced all other of the Five Civilized Tribes except the Cherokee, who in many ways resembled them, and became with great rapidity poor subjects for ethnological study but successful members of the American Nation. It is generally testified that the Creeks and Seminole, who had the most highly developed native institutions, were the slowest to become assimilated into the new political and social organism which was introduced from Europe. The Chickasaw come next and the Cherokee and Choctaw adapted themselves most rapidly of all.

As was said above, the story of the meek makes less exciting reading in the world to-day than the story of the aggressive, but perhaps man killing and large scale appropriation of values will not always appeal to human beings as the noblest objects of contemplation. However, the fact that human interest during the last two centuries has been of this character accounts for the relatively meager amount of material which it has been possible to collect for the present undertaking. While the French have left us two elaborate descriptions of Natchez institutions and activities and a number of shorter ones, I know of but one single effort to describe the Choctaw in a similar manner, and that relatively feeble. It is contained in an unpublished French Relation which I have dated tentatively about 1755, though it is very likely that it was written somewhat earlier. It is one of the many valuable documents in the Edward E. Ayer collection of the Newberry Library, Chicago, a photostat copy of which was obtained by Mr. F. W. Hodge for the Bureau of American Ethnology at the instance of the writer some years ago. That section dealing with the Choctaw I translated into English, and it was published in 1918 as Volume V, part 2, of the Memoirs of the American Anthropological Association. The only other French writer on this tribe worthy of mention is Bossu, who does vouchsafe us some original observations, but is much briefer than his compatriot. The next writer to pay more than incidental attention to this tribe was Bernard Romans, who traveled through the territory now constituting the States of Mississippi and Florida and some other parts of the Southeast in 1770 and 1771. Volume I of his narrative was printed in New York in 1775, but Volume II was never sent to press, apparently, probably on account of the outbreak of the Revolutionary War. Copies of this work are exceedingly rare, but it contains valuable information regarding the Indians of the Gulf area, particularly the Choctaw. Of a much later period and very different in character is "A History of the Choctaw, Chickasaw, and Natchez Indians" by the missionary, H. B. Cushman, printed in 1899. The author presents his material in a rambling and highly emotional manner, but he had lived practically all his life in close contact with the Choctaw Indians and was nearly as well acquainted with the Chickasaw. His material is often of a kind that can not be duplicated. He is our only authority on certain phases of ancient Choctaw life and in consequence it has been necessary to quote him extensively. Mr. Bushnell's little study of the Choctaw of Bayou Lacomb, Louisiana, is the only modern attempt to give an account of any Choctaw band from an ethnographical point of view and is correspondingly valuable.   Henry S. Halbert was a Choctaw enthusiast who derived considerable important information from that section of the Choctaw Indians who remain in the State of Mississippi. On certain special aspects of Choctaw life, such as their former geographical distribution, their migration legends, and their burial customs, his work is unsurpassed. Mention should also be made of the contributions of Rev. Alfred Wright, an early Choctaw missionary, to the Missionary Herald during the years 1828 and 1829, which in particular seem to give us the key to primitive Choctaw religion. The other writers mentioned in the bibliography merely furnish us with details upon special phases of the native culture.

Even more than in my previous papers, I have pursued the policy in this bulletin of constructing a source book for the tribe under discussion. On account of the rapid disappearance of the ancient customs, little can be gathered at the present day that has not already been recorded in a much more complete form. I have, however, added some notes obtained from one of the eastern Choctaw Indians named Olmon Comby and a considerable body of material from another eastern Choctaw, Simpson Tubby, for many years a preacher in the Methodist Church.

HISTORICAL SKETCH

The history of the Choctaw people since they first came to the knowledge of Europeans may be illustrated from many documentary sources and is capable of elaborate treatment. A few salient points are all that the present work calls for.

Halbert has pointed out that the "Apafalaya" chief and river and the "Pafallaya" province mentioned by the De Soto chroniclers Ranjel and Elvas, respectively, evidently refer to the Choctaw, or a part of them, since the Choctaw were known to other tribes as Pansfalaya or "Long Hairs." They were then, it would seem, approximately in the territory in southeastern Mississippi which they occupied when they were again visited by Europeans. There are notices of them in some Spanish documents dating from toward the close of the seventeenth century, and they immediately took a prominent position in the politics of colonizing nations when the French began settling Louisiana in 1699. Like the Creeks and Chickasaw, they were subjected to pressure from the Spaniards, English, and French, especially the two latter nations, each of whom enjoyed the support of a faction. These internal differences eventuated in civil war during which the Sixtowns, Chickasawhay and Coosa Choctaw supported the French interest and were finally successful, peace being made in 1750. The ascendency of the English east of the Mississippi, secured by the peace of 1763, soon tended to allay all remaining internal difficulties. With the passage of the Louisiana Territory into the hands of the United States an end was put to that intriguing by the representatives of rival European governments of which the Choctaw had been victims.

The Choctaw were never at war with the Americans. A few were induced by Tecumseh to ally themselves with the hostile Creeks, but the Nation as a whole was kept out of anti-American alliances by the influence of Apushmataha, greatest of all Choctaw chiefs. (Pl. 1.) However, white settlers began pouring into the region so rapidly that the Mississippi Territory was erected in 1798 and Mississippi became a State in 1817. Friction of course developed between the white colonists and the original occupants of the soil, whose removal to lands farther west was clamorously urged by the settlers and ultimately agreed to by the Choctaw themselves at the treaty of Dancing Rabbit Creek, September 27 and 28, 1830. By this treaty they secured a tract of land along Red River, in the southeastern part of the present State of Oklahoma, to which the bulk of the tribe emigrated in 1831, 1832, and 1833. The first emigrants suffered cruelly, but those who went later sowed their fields promptly and experienced fewer hardships than the Indians of most of the other expatriated tribes. A portion held on in their old territories, though bands of them joined their western kindred from time to time, 1,000 in 1846, 1,619 in 1847, 118 in 1848, 547 in 1849, 388 in 1853, and more than 300 in 1854. A considerable body still remained, numbering 1,253 in 1910 and 1,665 in 1930. In 1855 the Chickasaw, who had at first enjoyed the privilege of settling indiscriminately among the Choctaw, were given a separate territory west of the latter, and an independent government. The history of the Choctaw national government in Oklahoma would constitute an interesting contribution to our knowledge of native American capabilities in the handling of their affairs under a frame imported from abroad. Like the governments of the other four red republics of the old Indian Territory, it is now of course a thing of the past, the Choctaw being citizens of Oklahoma and of the United States.

THE ORIGIN LEGEND

There are two forms of the Choctaw origin legend, and both are suggested in the following passage from Du Pratz, which perhaps contains our earliest reference to it:

According to the tradition of the natives this nation passed so rapidly from one land to another and arrived so suddenly in the country which it occupies that, when I asked them from whence the Chat-kas came, to express the suddenness of their appearance they replied that they had come out from under the earth. Their great numbers imposed respect on the nations near which they passed, but their wholly unmartial character did not inspire them with any lust of conquest, so that they entered an uninhabited country the possession of which no one disputed with them. They have not molested their neighbors, and the latter did not dare to test their bravery; this is doubtless why they have grown, and augmented to their present numbers.[1]

Romans (1771) says:

These people are the only nation from whom I could learn any idea of a traditional account of a first origin; and that is their coming out of a hole in the ground, which they shew between their nation and the Chickasaws; they tell us also that their neighbours were surprised at seeing a people rise at once out of the earth.[2]

---

[1] Du Pratz, Hist. de La Louisiane, II, pp. 216–217. Paris, 1758.
[2] Romans, B., Nat. Hist. of E. and W. Fla., p. 71. New York, 1775.

Adair, a still earlier English writer, does not give a Choctaw migration story distinct from that which he obtained from the Chickasaw.[3] In the latter the Chickasaw, Choctaw, and Chakchiuma are represented as having come from the west " as one people." However, he vouchsafes us our earliest description of the hill of Nanih Waiya, the site of the hole out of which Romans tells us this nation came.

About 12 miles from the upper northern parts of the Choktah country, there stand on a level tract of land, the north-side of a creek, and within arrow-shot of it, two oblong mounds of earth, which were old garrisons, in an equal direction with each other, and about two arrow-shots apart. A broad deep ditch inclosed those two fortresses, and there they raised an high breast-work, to secure their houses from the invading enemy. This was a stupendous piece of work, for so small a number of savages, as could support themselves in it; their working instruments being only of stone and wood. They called those old fortresses *Nanne Yah*, " the hills, or mounts, of God." [4]

As usual, Adair has allowed himself to be carried away by his theory of a Hebrew origin of the American Indians. The "*Nanne Yah*" is actually Nanih Waiya, and, although he has translated the first word correctly, the second certainly has no reference to the Hebrew Yahweh. Most recent authorities, including the noted Choctaw student, H. S. Halbert, spell this name Nanih Waiya. Halbert says:

The adjective *Waiya* signifies " bending," " leaning over," but it is difficult to see the appropriateness of the term as applied to the mound. According to the conjecture of the writer, the term was originally applied to the circular rampart, which the Choctaws may have considered a kind of *bending hill*. And in process of time the name could have become so extended as to be applied to the mound and rampart conjointly, and ultimately restricted to the mound alone, as is now the case in popular usage.[5]

Schermerhorn (1814) tells us that—

An old Indian gave . . . a very rational explication of the [Choctaw] tradition, that they sprung out of the mound between the forks of Pearl River. The banks of these streams are a marsh, and at that time probably formed an impassable ravine. There is an embankment, which served as a fortification from one branch to the other, and which, with the ravines, encloses an area of nearly three miles. He observed to the agent, S. Dinsmore, " that their ancestors, when they arrived in this country, knew not what the inhabitants were; for their own protection, therefore, they cast up this mound, and enclosed and fortified this area, to plant their corn, and as a defence against enemies. This mound served as a place for look-out, to give notice of the approach of invaders. When this was accomplished, they sent out their hunters to see what were the inhabitants of the land. These on their return reported, that they could dwell in safety, that the land was good, and game in abundance.

---

[3] See Forty-fourth Ann. Rept. Bur. Amer. Ethnol., p. 174.
[4] Adair, Hist. Amer. Inds., pp. 377–378.
[5] Pubs. Miss. Hist. Soc., II, p. 224. For another explanation of the name see p. 13.

On this they left their encampment as it may be called, and settled in different parts of the country. From this arose the tradition that they sprung or crept out of the mound." [6]

Dr. Gideon Lincecum, another early authority, accepts the same translation of Nanih Waiya as does Halbert, but adds that the hill was so called because "it leaned toward the creek"; Catlin renders the name "the sloping hill"; Alfred Wright, "the stooping or sloping hill"; Cushman, "the leaning mound." That some physical peculiarity gave rise to the name is probable, but with the lapse of time its exact nature has been lost and it is unlikely that it can be recovered. On the other hand, some plausible suggestions may be made regarding the localization of the origin legend at this place. As intimated above, there are two forms of this story, one treating Nanih Waiya as the point of exit to the upper world of the ancestral Choctaw, the other as their center of distribution after they had immigrated from the west. It is probable that the tradition of a western origin was in part correct, but whether it was so or not the prominence of the hill in Choctaw history is easily accounted for, because (1) it is a conspicuous landmark in the midst of one of the most fertile sections of the old Choctaw country, (2) within a mile there is a considerable cave tending to localize the tradition of a subterranean origin which nearly all southeastern tribes entertain, and (3) the word waiya happens to be very similar to another Choctaw word, waya, which signifies "to bear," "to bring forth." Indeed, Nanih Waya may have been the earlier form, but it is less common to find a term of purely mythic significance etymologized over into a physical description than evolution in the opposite direction. However, we must not forget the statement of Schoolcraft's Chickasaw informant to the effect that the Indians of that tribe called the mounds in their country "navels." As Halbert points out, the spelling "Warrior," which appears on some of our maps instead of Waiya, is a barbarism.

The next description of the mound, or rather the mound system, is by Doctor Lincecum:

I visited this celebrated mound in 1843. I found it a rounded off, oblong square, 200 yards in circumference at its base; 80 feet in height, with a flat space on the top 52 yards in length by 25 yards in width. The whole mound was thickly set with forest trees. 200 yards to the north of it is a lake, which I suppose to be the place whence they carried the earth to construct the mound.

Speaking of the earthen rampart, he continues:

I went all around this earth wall. . . . It seemed to be a complete circle, and from one and a half to two miles in circumference, the southeastern portion

---

[6] Schermerhorn, Report on the Western Indians, in Mass. Hist. Soc. Coll., series 2, vol. II, p. 17.

cutting the bluff of Nunih Waya creek. Many places in the wall were still eight feet in height. The two gaps in the wall had never been filled up.[7]

Prof. Calvin S. Brown has published a brief but very interesting account of the Nanih Waiya earthworks, arranged from the manuscript notes of B. L. C. Wailes, who visited them on the 5th of December, 1854.

I visited the Indian mounds and entrenchment in the fork of Nanawaya and Tallahaya, identified by tradition as the place of origin or the birth-place of the Choctaws, who held it in superstitious reverence as their mother. The height of the principal mound is at least 50 feet; it is a parallelogram with corners rounded by plowing; dimensions 180 or 200 feet east and west by perhaps 100 or 105 [150?] feet north and south.

Some 200 yards to the north of the high mound is a cone covering more extent, but only about 10 feet high. Some small mounds nearly obliterated are between the two large ones.

The wall or entrenchment goes around three sides of the mound and in many places in the woods has trees of 4 feet diameter growing upon it. The height in the most elevated places is near 10 feet, the width 30 or 40 feet; in other places it dwindles away to a slight embankment; in the clear land east of the mounds it can scarcely be traced owing to the constant plowing. Many gaps or gate-ways have been left in the wall, some of them 100 feet wide. The enclosure embraces about a section or square mile.[8]

More detailed is the description by Halbert:

Nanih Waiya is situated on the west side of Nanih Waiya Creek, about 50 yards from it, in the southern part of Winston County, and about four hundred yards from the Neshoba County line. The mound is oblong in shape, lying northwest and southeast, and about forty feet in height. Its base covers about an acre. The mound stands on the southeastern edge of a circular rampart, which is about a mile and a half in circumference. In using the word "circular" reference is made to the original form of the rampart, about one-half of which is utterly obliterated by the plow, leaving only a semicircle. This rampart is not, or rather was not, a continuous circle, so to speak, as it has along at intervals a number of vacant places or gaps, ranging from fifty to one hundred and fifty yards in length. All the sections near the mound have long since been levelled by the plow, and in other places some of the sections have been much reduced. But on the north, where the rampart traverses a primeval forest it is still five feet high and twenty feet broad at the base. The process of obliteration has been very great since 1877, when the writer first saw Nanih Waiya. Some of the sections that could then be clearly traced in the fields on the west have now (1899) utterly disappeared. About two hundred and fifty yards north of Nanih Waiya is a small mound, evidently a burial mound, as can be safely stated from the numerous fragments of human bones that have been exhumed from it by the plow and the hoe. The great number of stone relics, mostly broken, scattered for hundreds of yards around Nanih Waiya, shows that it was the site of prehistoric habitations. In addition to this, the bullets and other relics of European manufacture evidence the continuity of occupancy down within the historic period. The magnitude of these ancient works—the mound and

---

[7] Pubs. Miss. Hist. Soc., VIII, pp. 530, 542, footnotes.
[8] Brown, Calvin S. Archeology of Mississippi, Mississippi Geological Survey. Printed by the University of Mississippi, 1926. Pages 24–26.

the rampart—together with the legendary traditions connected with them, leads one irresistibly to the conviction that this locality was the great center of Choctaw population during the prehistoric period. It should here be stated that the symmetry of the mound has been somewhat marred by a tunnel which was cut into it in the summer of 1896 by some treasure-seekers, who vainly hoped to unearth some wonderful bonanza from out the deep bosom of Nanih Waiya.[9] . . . The ravages of civilization have still spared some traces of two broad, deeply worn roads or highways connected with the mound, in which now stand large oak trees. The remnant of one of these highways, several hundred yards long, can be seen on the east side of the creek, running toward the southeast. The other is on the west side of the creek, the traces nearest the mound being at the northeastern part of the rampart, thence running towards the north. Many years ago this latter road was traced by an old citizen of Winston County full twenty miles to the north until it was lost in Noxubee swamp, in the northeastern part of Winston County.[10]

Correct measurements of the works are contained in Doctor Brown's book.

The famous Nanih Waiya . . . stands in Winston County about ten miles south-east of Noxapater. The name signifies in Choctaw "slanting hill." It is a typical rectangular mound, 218 feet long by 140 feet wide at the base, thus covering seven-tenths of an acre. The axis is north-west by south-east. The dimensions of the flat top are 132 feet by 56 feet, the area being one-sixth of an acre. The height is 22 feet, in some places nearly 25 feet. The slopes of the mound are covered with trees; the top seems to have been cultivated. A heavy rain set in during my survey of the site, July 6, 1917, and prevented a completion of my study.

I visited the site again on August 3, 1923, and located one section of the earth-wall or rampart near the residence, more than half a mile from the great mound. This section of the wall is now 2.5 to 4 feet high and about a hundred yards long. The resident on the farm states that four sections of the earth-wall still exist. The low mound about 250 yards to the north-east of the great mound is now about 7 or 8 feet high, and very much spread by cultivation. Artifacts are scarce.

The great Nanih Waiya retains its original height and is still in a state of excellent preservation, tho the small mounds and the wall have been much reduced. This historic mound should be preserved for all time to come.[11]

The writer examined this interesting spot in May, 1918, and took photographs of the principal mound and the small mound. (Pl. 2.) From a former owner he learned definitely that the top had been cultivated, as Professor Brown supposes. The interest of the site itself and the web of traditions attaching to it should move the State of Mississippi to adopt Professor Brown's recommendation by obtaining permanent possession of it and securing the old structures for all time against the destructive influences to which they are now exposed.

---

[9] Pubs. Miss. Hist. Soc., II, pp. 223–224.
[10] Ibid., p. 227. See also The American Antiquarian, Vol. XIII, pp. 348–349.
[11] Brown, Calvin S., op. cit., p. 24.

To one somewhat familiar with the ethnology of the southeastern tribes this series of mounds is not at all difficult to interpret. The large mound is without doubt that upon which the public buildings were placed. From what Halbert says, the smaller mound is identified as a burial mound, while the engirdling rampart is undoubtedly just what almost every visitor to the spot from Adair down has taken it to be, the remains of a work defending the settlement about the mounds and undoubtedly crowned with a stockade interrupted at intervals by towers. It was in such a good state of repair when Adair wrote that it does not seem likely it had been long abandoned. The first and most natural supposition is that this was a Choctaw town stockaded to protect their northern frontier against the Chickasaw. We know from several of the older writers that the stockaded towns of the Choctaw were on their east against the Creeks and their north against the Chickasaws; indeed, the compiler of the French Relation of 1755 mentions a town called "Ougoulatanap," "Warriors' town," which he describes as "near the Chiquachas on the trail from the Alibamons, and has a fort, because these two nations are very often at war together." This may have been on the site of Nanih Waiya itself, although from Adair's description it is probable that the latter had been abandoned as a permanent native residence shortly before French and English explorers arrived, a fact which would not have prevented the appearance of those "bullets and other relics of European manufacture" to which Halbert refers, since the place no doubt had many temporary occupants long after it had been given up as a permanent residence. The large mound is of a type characteristic of the Creeks, Chickasaw, and lower Mississippi tribes rather than the Choctaw, a possible indication that the group represents two distinct periods and as many distinct tribes.

Several later versions of the migration legend may now be given. The first is from Catlin (1832–1839):

The Choctaws a great many winters ago commenced moving from the country where they then lived, which was a great distance to the west of the great river and the mountains of snow, and they were a great many years on their way. A great medicine man led them the whole way, by going before with a red pole, which he stuck in the ground every night where they encamped. This pole was every morning found leaning to the east, and he told them that they must continue to travel to the east until the pole would stand upright in their encampment, and that there the Great Spirit had directed that they should live. At a place which they named *Nah-ne-wa-ye* (the sloping hill) the pole stood straight up, where they pitched their encampment, which was 1 mile square, with the men encamped on the outside and the women and children in the center, which remains the center of the old Choctaw Nation.[12]

Nanih Waiya is hardly the center of the old Choctaw Nation except in a metaphorical sense. Somewhat older is the version which Gat-

[12] Smithsonian Report for 1885, Part II, p. 213.

schet, and after him Halbert, considered " the most circumstantial." It was communicated to the Missionary Herald by Rev. Alfred Wright, and published in 1828.

They say, that the Creeks, Chickasaws, and Choctaws emigrated together, from a distant country far to the west. The Creeks were in front; the Choctaws in the rear. The Choctaws emigrated under the conduct of a great leader and prophet. While residing at the west, they were led to believe, that there was a good country at a great distance towards the rising of the sun, and they were induced to take a long and perilous journey in search of it. Some of them state, that in consequence of the great distance, their provisions failed, and they stopped during the warm season to plant corn to furnish themselves with food for the remainder of the journey. Their great leader and prophet had the direction of all their movements on their journey. He carried the *hobuna, sacred bag,* containing all their sacred things, and a long white pole as the badge of his authority. When he planted the white pole, it was a signal for their encamping. He was always careful to set this pole perpendicularly, and to suspend upon it the sacred bag. None were allowed to come near it, and no one but himself might touch it. During the time of their encampment, whether for one night or more, the pole was invariably found to alter its position, and incline towards the rising of the sun. This was a signal for them to proceed on their journey. The pole continued to incline towards the east until they reached *Nunih waiya,* and there it remained in its perpendicular position. From this they concluded, that they had found the country of which they were in search. They remained at this place under the direction of their leader, and there adopted their civil policy. This account seems probable. For it is evident that the present inhabitants of this part of the country must, at some former period, have emigrated from the west. The Chickasaws are said generally to retain a traditional knowledge of the emigration of their ancestors from the west. The Choctaws in this part of the nation appear generally to have lost all knowledge of such an event, and refer their origin to *Nunih waiya.* The aged interpreter before mentioned supposes, that when the Choctaws arrived at the country they now inhabit, they killed or drove out by force, the former inhabitants, and having obtained possession of their land by injustice and violence, they wished to erase from their history the memory of such a transaction, and from motives of policy, endeavored to prevent the knowledge of their emigration from being transmitted to posterity, and therefore inculcated the belief that they were created at *Nunih waiya,* where he supposes they adopted their regulations. And in this way he undertakes to account for the prevalence of this belief; and also for the ignorance of the Choctaws with respect to their emigration from the west.[13]

The motive mentioned has certainly operated in some cases, but it is rather more likely that a subterranean origin myth became localized at Nanih Waiya for historical, social, and topographical reasons, some of which have already been given, and the immigration from the west is probably correct as applying to at least a part of the Choctaw people.

But if Wright's narrative is considered " circumstantial," what shall be said of that written by Dr. Gideon Lincecum and published

---

[13] The Missionary Herald, Vol. XXIV, pp. 215–216, Boston, 1828.

by the Mississippi Historical Society? Here we have an elaborate story which purports to detail the various movements of the tribe during that ancient migration, the councils they held, the speeches delivered, and the motives that actuated the various leaders and factions in a manner worthy of a Spanish chronicler, and in fact recalling the Fidalgo of Elvas. However, there can be no question that Lincecum knew the Choctaw thoroughly, and much of the tale is interesting on account of the ethnological information which it contains, whether it be part of the original story or a later amplification. It is put into the mouth of a native informant. We will, therefore, take the liberty to incorporate the entire narrative, which begins abruptly, thus:

The chief halted the advance body of Choctaws on a little river to wait until scouts could be sent forward to explore the region of country round about; and to give time for the aged and feeble and those who were overloaded to come up. Many of the families were loaded with so many of the bones of their deceased relatives that they could carry nothing else, and they got along very slowly. At this stage of their long journey there were a greater number of skeletons being packed along by the people than there were of the living. The smallest families were heaviest loaded; and such were their adoration and affection for these dry bones that before they could consent to leave them on the way, they would, having more bones than they could pack at one load, carry forward a part of them half a day's journey, and returning for the remainder, bring them up the next day. By this double traveling over the route, they were soon left a great distance in the rear. They would have preferred to die and rot with these bones in the wilderness, sooner than leave them behind.

The minko looked upon the notions of the people in regard to the extraordinary and overwhelming burthen of bones as a great evil; and he cast in his mind for some plausible excuse to rid the people of a burthen that was as useless as it was oppressive to them.

And now the scouts had returned and the reports they made of quite an extensive excursion were very favorable and encouraging. They stated that everywhere, and in all directions, they found game of all sorts, fish and fowl and fruits in abundance; tall trees and running brooks; altogether they looked upon it as the most desirable and plentiful region they had found during their pilgrimage. They also stated, that the most convenient place they had found, for a winter encampment, lay in a southeasterly direction at the junction of three large creeks, which coming together at the same point, formed an immense lowland, and a considerable river. In the fork of the first and the middle creeks lay an extensive range of dry, good lands, covered with tall trees of various kinds, grapes, nuts, and acorns; and rivulets (bok ushi) of running water. For the multitude, it was distant eight or ten days' travel, and the route would be less and less difficult to that place.

At the rising of the sun on the ensuing morning, the leader's pole was observed to be inclining to the southeast, and the people were moving off quite early. The nights were becoming cooler, and they desired to have time to prepare shelter before the winter rains should commence. The chief, with the Isht Ahullo, who carried the sacred pole, went in front, and being good walkers, they traveled rapidly until they came to the place which had been designated. Great numbers of the stronger and more athletic people came up the same day.

Early on the next morning the chief went to observe the leader's pole, which, at the moment of sunrise, danced and punched itself deeper into the ground; and after some time settled in a perpendicular position, without having nodded or bowed in any direction. Seeing which the chief said, "It is well. We have arrived at our winter encampment." He gave instructions to the tool carriers to lay off the encampment for the iksas and mark on posts their appropriate symbols. He ordered them to allow sufficient space for the iksas, having particular regard to the watering places.

It was several days before the people had all reached the encampment. Those who were packing the double loads of bones came in several days later, and they complained of being greatly fatigued. They mourned and said, "The bad spirit has killed our kindred; to pack their bones any further will kill us, and we shall have no name amongst the iksas of this great nation. Oh! when will this long journey come to an end?"

There were plenty of pine and cypress trees and palmetto; and in a short time the people had constructed sufficient tents to shelter themselves from the rain. Their hunters with but little labor supplied the camps with plenty of bear meat; and the women and children collected quantities of acorns and oksak kapko, and kapun (large hickory nuts, and scaly barks). It was an extremely plentiful land, and the whole people were rejoicing at the prospects for a pleasant and bountiful winter. Their camps being completed, the chief gave instructions, to have sufficient ground prepared to plant what seed corn might be found in the camps. Search was made by Isi maleli (Running Deer) for the corn. He found a few ears only; they had been preserved by the very old people, who had no teeth. The corn they found was two years old, and they were very much afraid that it was dead. The minko suggested to Isi maleli, that as the tool carriers had iron [!] implements with which to break the ground, it would be best to detail a sufficient number of them to prepare ground to grow it. So the minko called out twenty of the tool carriers for the purpose, and appointed the wise Isi maleli, to direct them, and to select the soil for growing the corn properly, and to preserve it when it matured.

One end or side of the encampment lay along the elevated ground—bordering the low lands on the west side of the middle creek. Just above the uppermost camps, and overhanging the creek, was a steep little hill with a hole in one side. As it leaned towards the creek, the people called it the leaning hill (nunih waya).[13a] From this little hill the encampment took its name, "Nunih Waya," by which name it is known to this day.

The whole people were healthy at Nunih Waya. Full of life and cheerfulness, they danced and played a great deal. Their scouts had made wide excursions around the encampment, and finding no signs of the enemy in any direction, they consoled themselves with the idea, that they had traveled beyond his reach. The scouts and hunters, on returning into camps, from their exploring expeditions, were often heard to say, "The plentiful, fruitful land of tall trees and running waters, spoken of by our great and wise chiefs, who saw it in a vision of the night, is found. We have found the land of plenty, and our great journey is at an end."

They passed through their first winter at Nunih Waya quite pleasantly. Spring opened finely. Their few ears of corn came up well and grew off wonderfully. The creeks were full of fish and the mornings rang with the turkeys and singing birds. The woods everywhere were full of buffalo, bear, deer and elks; everything that could be wished for was there, and easily procured. All were filled with gladness.

[13a] The spelling of Nunih Waiya is not quite accurate.

And when the time for the green corn dance was near, the hunters brought into the camps wonderful quantities of fat meat, and they celebrated this dance five days. They did not eat of their corn, but that it might be properly called the green corn dance, they erected a pine pole in the center of the dance ground, and upon this they suspended a single ear of green corn.

When they had finished this, their forty-third green corn dance in the wilderness, the people began to be concerned as to the probabilities of their having to journey further. Many of them declared that if the sacred pole should indicate a removal, it would be impossible for them to go farther, on account of the great number of bones that had accumulated on their long journey. They could not carry the bones, neither could they think of leaving them behind.

The chief had for some time been considering the great inconvenience the marvelous amount of bones had become to the nation. He knew very well, the feelings of the people on the subject, and how difficult it would be to get them to consent to abandon the useless encumbrance. He could see very plainly, that should they have to go further, a portion of the people, under their present impressions in regard to the dry bones, would be most certainly left behind. On hearing the murmuring suggestions of so many of the people, every day, about the bones of their deceased relatives, and the sacred duty incumbent on the living to preserve and take care of them, he was convinced that the subject must be approached with caution. Yet, the oppressive, progress-checking nature of the burdens was such that they must be disposed of in some way.

He called a council of the leaders of the iksas, and in a very prudent and cautious manner, consulted them in behalf of the suffering people, enquiring of them at the same time, if it was possible to invent any means that would aid them in the transportation of their enormous packs of useless dry bones. It was a subject they had not before thought of, and they required a day or two to make up their minds.

Time was granted to them, and in the meantime the minko convened with many of the people [to consult] about it.

The council met again, and there was some discussion, but nothing conclusive. They were loath to speak of the bones of their deceased friends and relatives. They had packed their bones a great way, and for years; but there had been no conversation, no consultation, on the subject. There were among the young people, many who were carrying heavy packs of bones, who had never heard, and who really did not know, whose bones they were carrying. They had grown up with the bones on their backs, and had packed them faithfully, but never having heard the name of their original owners, they could tell nothing, nor did they know anything about them. That the spirits hovered about their bones to see that they were respectfully cared for, and that they would be offended and punished with bad luck, sickness, or even death for indignities, or neglect of their bones, every one knew. It was a great indignity to the spirits to repeat the names they were known by during their mundane existence. The greater part of the living who were then in the camp, had been born and reared in the wilderness, and were still packing the bones of those who had lived long before and of whom they knew nothing. Yet they worried along with heavy loads of these dry bones on their journey, in good faith, and in a full belief of its necessity as a sacred duty. The leaders of the iksas, who were not in council, were carrying heavy loads of bones themselves which they could not consent to part with; and they esteemed it a subject of too much delicacy to be caviled about in a council. They did not wish to say anything further about it, anyway.

One of the Isht ahullos,[14] who was an old man, and who had long been a secret teacher, among the women and children, on the nature and wants of the spirit world and the causes that made it necessary to pack the bones of the dead, arose from his seat and said:

"Some people can make very light talk about the bones of our deceased friends and relatives. Those sacred relics of our loved ones, who have passed away from our sight are to be irreverently stigmatized by the name of 'oppressive burthen,' 'useless incumbrance,' and the like. Awful! And it was our chief who could dare to apply the uncivil epithet to the precious and far-fetched treasures. From all these things, I am forced, unwillingly, to infer that the next thing the chief has to propose for your consideration will be for you to cast away this 'oppressive burthen.' Shameful! (Hofahya.) This thing must not be. This people must not cast away the precious remains of the fathers and mothers of this nation. They are charged by the spirits, who are hovering thick around us now, to take care of them; and carry them whithersoever the nation moves. And this we must not, we dare not fail to do. Were we to cast away the bones of our fathers, mothers, brothers, sisters, for the wild dogs to gnaw in the wilderness, our hunters could kill no more meat; hunger and disease would follow; then confusion and death would come; and the wild dogs would become fat on the unscaffolded carcasses of this unfeeling nation of forgetful people. The vengeance of the offended spirits would be poured out upon this foolish nation."

The council before which the Isht ahullo made this appeal to the religious sentiment of the tribe was only an assembly of the leaders of the iksas. The people were not present, and did not hear it. The chief, however, was fully apprised of the secret action of these bad men; and to counteract their dark and mischievous influence on the minds of the people, he dismissed the Isht ahullos, and leaders of the iksas, with a severe reprimand, telling them plainly that he had no further business for them to attend to. Then turning to the Isht ahullo, and at the same time pointing at him with an arrow, [he] said:

"When you again get in council with the lazy, bad hearted men to which you belong, tell them that the time has come when you must be cautious how you meddle with the affairs of this nation. Hear my words."

The minko, returning to his tent, sent for Long Arrow, to whom he communicated his designs as to the disposition of the dry bones; after which he directed him to send the tool carriers to the iksas, and instruct them to summon every man, woman and child, except the leaders of the clans and the conjurers of all grades. The minko said:

"Tell the people to assemble at the dance ground early in the day, to-morrow. I wish to consult them on important national business. Let the people, except those I have named, all know it before they sleep."

In accordance with the notice sent by the chief, the entire tribe, male and female, old and young, except the yushpakammi[15] and the leaders, came. These were not found in the great assembly. But the healthy, clean washed, bright, cheerful people were all present, and seated at the time the minko came to his place on the council ground.

The minko looked around on the multitude, and very calmly speaking, addressed them as follows:

"It is to you my brothers, my sisters, my countrymen, that I wish to declare my thoughts this day. I look around upon the bright, cheerful countenances of the multitude and I feel assured that you will hear my words; and that you will hearken to my counsels. You are a great people, a wonderful people, a

---

[14] " Miracle Workers," " Conjurers."   [15] " Wizards."

people of strength, of unparalleled courage and untiring, patient industry. Your goodness of heart has caused you to work and hunt, far beyond the needs of your families, to gain a surplus, to feed a lazy, gluttonous set of hangers on, whose aim it is to misdirect you, whose counsels are all false, and whose greatest desire is confusion and discord amongst this peaceful, happy people. I know the meaning of my words. I speak them boldly and intentionally, I do not catch you in a corner, one at a time, and secretly communicate to you messages from the spirit land; packing you with enormous and insupportable burthens, to gratify wicked and discontented spirits, who are, as you are told, hovering about the camps, threatening mischief. But I call you all in general council and standing up in this bright sunlight, with every eye upon me, and declare in language that cannot be mistaken, words of wisdom and truth. I bring no message from the spirit land. I declare to you the needs and interests of the living. I have no visions of the night; no communications from the discontented spirits, who it is said are hovering around our camps, threatening disaster and death to the living, out of spite for having been rejected from the good hunting ground, to tell you of; but openly, in this bright day, I communicate to you, in deepest solicitude, the long cherished thoughts of a live man; which, when fully carried out, cannot fail to establish peace, harmony, concord and much gladness to this great live nation. I speak not to the dead; for they cannot hear my words. I speak not to please or benefit the dead; there is nought I can do or say, that can by any possibility reach their condition. I speak to the living for the advancement and well being of this great, vigorous, live multitude. Hear my words.

"From new motions and indications made by the sacred pole, which I have never witnessed before, I was led to conclude that our forty-three years' journey in an unknown country had come to its termination. And to avoid hindering and annoying the whole people with what I had on my mind to be considered, I called yesterday (pilashash) a council of the leaders of the iksas, and all the conjurers, for the purpose of examining and deciding on the most prudent course to pursue, in case it should be finally ascertained, that the leader's pole had settled permanently.

"They all came, and after hearing my propositions, they put on wise faces, talked a great deal of the unhappy spirits of our dead friends, of their wants and desires, and of the great dangers that would befall the people, if they failed to obey the unreasonable demands made by the spirits, through the lazy Isht ahullos, conjurers and dreamers, who, according to their own words, are the only men through which the spirits can make manifest to the nation their burthensome and hurtful desires. Finding that they had nothing to say, nor did they even surmise anything on the subject of the affairs and interests of the living, I dismissed them as ignorant of, and enemies to, the rights of the people, and, therefore, improper agents for the transaction of their business. They were dismissed on account of their secret, malicious designs on the people, and their inefficiency in the councils of the nation. I immediately sent out runners to convene the people in general council to-day. You are all here, except the secret mongers, and the leaders of the clans, whose mouths and tongues have been tied up by the Isht ahullo and yushpakammi. The nation is present to hear my words; in them there is no secret or hidden meaning. You will all hear them, and let everyone, who is a man, open his mouth this clear day, and openly and fearlessly pour out his full and undisguised feelings on the topics which will be presented.

"From signs which I have just named, I conclude, and I find it the prevailing impression of this multitude of self-sustaining people, that our long journey of privations and dangers in the pathless wilderness has ended. We are now in the land of tall trees and running waters, of fruit, game of many kinds and fish and fowl, which was spoken of by our good chief, who is missing, in the far off country towards the setting sun. His words have come to pass. Our journey is at an end, and we shall grow to be a nation of happy people in this fruitful land.

" Let us now, like a sensible people, put the nation in a suitable condition for the free enjoyment of the inexahustible bounties that have been so lavishly spread in this vast country for the use and benefit of this multitude. Let us lay aside all useless encumbrance, that we may freely circulate, with our families in this widely extended land, with no burthen to pack, but such as are necessary to sustain life and comfort to our wives and little ones. ˉ Let us call this place; this, Nunih Waya encampment, our home; and it shall be so that when a man, at his hunting camp, in the distant forests, shall be asked for his home place, his answer will be, ' Nunih Waya.' And to establish Nunih Waya more especially as our permanent home, the place to which when we are far away, our thoughts may return with feelings of delight and respectful pleasure, I propose that we shall by general consent and mutual good feelings select an eligible location within the limits of the encampment and there, in the most respectful manner, bring together and pile up in beautiful and tasteful style the vast amount of bones we have packed so far and with which many of the people have been so grievously oppressed. Let each set of bones remain in its sack, and after the sacks are closely and neatly piled up, let them be thickly covered over with cypress bark. After this, to appease and satisfy the spirits of our deceased relatives, our blood kin, let all persons, old and young, great and small, manifest their respect for the dead, by their energy and industry in carrying dirt to cover them up, and let the work of carrying and piling earth upon them be continued until every heart is satisfied. These bones, as we all know, are of the same iksa, the same kindred. They were all the same flesh and blood; and for us to pile their bones all in the same heap and securely cover them up will be more pleasing to the spirits, than it will be to let them remain amongst the people, to be scattered over the plains, when the sacks wear out in the hands of another generation who will know but little and care less about them.

" You have heard my talk. I have delivered to you the true sentiments of my heart. When it comes to my time to depart for the spirit land, I shall be proud to know that my bones had been respectfully deposited in the great mound with those of my kindred. What says the nation? "

Some little time elapsed; and there was no move among them. The multitude seemed to reflect. At length, a good looking man of about sixty winters, arose in a dignified manner, from his seat, and gravely said:

" It was in my boyhood, and on the little river where we had the great fish feast, that my much respected father died. His family remained and mourned a whole moon, and when the cry-poles were pulled down, and the feast and dance had ended, my mother having a young child to carry, it fell to my lot, being the next largest member of the family, to pack on the long journey, the bones of my father. I have carefully carried them over hardships and difficulties, from that little rocky river to the present encampment. Such has been my love and respect for these sacred relics, that I was ready at any time to have sacrificed my life sooner than I would have left them, or given them up to another. I am now growing old; and with my declining years come new thoughts. Not long hence, I too must die. I ask myself, who in the coming generations will remember and respect the bones of my father? Will they not be forgotten and scattered to bleach and moulder on the carelessly trodden plain? I have sought with a heart full of anxious sorrow, for a decent and satisfactory resting place, in which to deposit the bones of my long lost father. I could think of none. And I dare assert, that there are thousands in hearing of my voice, at this very moment, whose faithful hearts have asked the same embarrassing questions. I am happy in the acknowledgment, and I trust with much confidence, that the whole people will view this important matter in the same satisfactory light. The wise propositions of our worthy chief have answered perplexing questions and have fully relieved the unsettled workings of many anxious hearts.

"It is true, as our wise chief has already suggested, that we can now witness the wonderful and never before heard of sight of a live nation packing on their backs an entire dead nation, our dead outnumbering the living. It is a pleasure to me, now that my eyes have been opened by the chief's proposition to the propriety of placing these relics of the dead nation to themselves, that we have power and time to do as he suggests, and most reverently to secure them from being tumbled among our greasy packs, and from the occasional dropping of the precious bones, through the holes in the worn out sacks to be lost forever. Let us, in accordance with the wise and reasonable proposition of our minko, fetch all the sacred relics to one place; pile them up in a comely heap; and construct a mound of earth upon them, that shall protect them from all harm forever."

And the people rose up and with one voice, said, "It is well; we are content."

The minko stood up again and said that in that great multitude there might be some whose feelings in regard to the disposition of the bones of their dead friends would not permit them to pile them with the dead nation. Then they all shouted aloud, "It is good, it is satisfactory."

Men were then appointed to select an appropriate place for the mound to be erected on, and to direct the work while in progress. They selected a level piece of sandy land, not far from the middle creek; laid it off in an oblong square and raised the foundation by piling up earth which they dug up some distance to the north of the foundation. It was raised and made level as high as a man's head and beat down very hard. It was then floored with cypress bark before the work of placing the sacks of bones commenced. The people gladly brought forward and deposited their bones until there were none left. The bones, of themselves, had built up an immense mound. They brought the cypress bark, which was neatly placed on, till the bone sacks were all closely covered in, as dry as a tent. While the tool carriers were working with the bark, women and children and all the men, except the hunters, carried earth continually, until the bark was all covered from sight, constituting a mound half as high as the tallest forest tree.

The minko kindled the council fire, and, calling an assembly of the people, told them that the work on the great monumental grave had been prosecuted with skill and wonderful industry. He said that the respect which they had already manifested for the deceased relatives was very great; that notwithstanding the bones were already deeply and securely covered up, the work was not yet completed. Yet it was sufficiently so to allow them to suspend operations for a season. Winter was drawing near; the acorns and nuts were beginning to fall and were wasting. The people must now scatter into the forests and collect the rich autumnal fruits which were showering down from every tree. That done, the people must return to the encampment; and as the tool carriers had produced seed corn enough for all to have a little field, each family must prepare ground for that purpose. Then, after the corn was grown and the new corn feast and dance celebrated and over, the nation could again prosecute the work on the mound, and so on, from year to year, until the top of the great grave of the dead nation should be as high as the tallest forest tree. And it should be made level on the top as much as sixty steps (habli) in length, and thirty steps in width, all beat down hard, and planted thick with acorns, nuts and pine seeds. "Remember my words," said the chief, "and finish the work accordingly. Now go and prepare for winter."

And the people gladly dispersed into the distant forests. Fruit was found in great quantities and was collected and brought into camp in very large amounts—acorns, hickory nuts, and most and best of all, the otupi (chestnuts), all of which was secured from the worms by the process of drying them by smoke and incasing them in small quantities in airtight mud cells, in the same manner, that the mud daubers (lukchuk chanuskik)[16] preserve their spiders. Their hunters were very successful; and at midwinter, when all the clans had returned to their camps, they found themselves rich in their supplies of so many things that were good for food, they concluded that as the best way of expressing their unfeigned gratitude (yokoke ahni) to the great sun they would celebrate a grand, glad feast, and joyous dance, before they commenced the work of clearing and breaking ground for their cornfields. So they cleaned out the dance ground, and planted the pole with the golden sun in the center of it. The people collected and, with much joy and gladness of heart, feasted and danced five days.

The amount of ground necessary to plant what corn they had was small, and was soon planted. Then having nothing else to be working at, a thoughtful old man, pointing to the great unfinished mound (yokni chishinto) said, "the weather is cool and pleasant, and the grave of your dead kindred is only half as high as a tall tree." Taking the timely suggestion of the man, thousands went to work, carrying dirt to the great mound. Afterwards, it became an honorable thing to carry and deposit earth on the mound at any time they were not engaged at work in their domestic vocations.

The winter over, spring with its green foliage and singing birds and its grand flourish of gobbling turkeys came slowly on. Corn was planted and the companies of hunters went forth. The camps were healthy. Those who were planting soon finished it, and engaged actively forthwith in throwing earth upon the already huge mound. Their corn flourished well, producing enough, after preserving a portion of their fields for seed, to supply a full feast for the green corn dance.

At the Nunih Waya encampment, everything went well and there were no complaints. Their hunters made wide excursions, acquainting themselves with the geography of the country to the extent of many days' journey around. But, as yet, they had discovered no signs of the enemy, or of any other people. In this happy condition of health and plenty—for they had enlarged their fields and were harvesting abundant crops of corn—years rolled round; the work on the mound was regularly prosecuted; and at the eighth green corn dance celebrated at Nunih Waya, the committee who had been appointed at the commencement, reported to the assembled multitude that the work was completed and the mound planted with the seeds of the forest trees in accordance with the plan and direction of the minko, at the beginning of the work.

The minko then instructed the good old Lopina, who had carried it so many years, to take the golden sun to the top of the great mound and plant it in the center of the level top.

---

[16] Lukchuk chanushik. The dance as employed by men is probably wholly imaginary.

When the people beheld the golden emblem of the sun glittering on the top of the great work which, by the united labor of their own hands, had just been accomplished, they were filled with joy and much gladness. And in their songs at the feast, which was then going on, they would sing:

"Behold the wonderful work of our hands; and let us be glad. Look upon the great mound; its top is above the trees, and its black shadow lies on the ground, a bowshot. It is surmounted by the golden emblem of the sun; its glitter (tohpakali) dazzles the eyes of the multitude. It inhumes the bones of fathers and relatives; they died on our sojourn in the wilderness. They died in a far off wild country; they rest at Nunih Waya. Our journey lasted many winters; it ends at Nunih Waya."

The feast and the dance, as was the custom, continued five days. After this, in place of the long feast, the minko directed that, as a mark of respect due to the fathers and mothers and brothers and sisters, for whom they had with so much labor prepared such a beautiful and wonderfully high monumental grave, each iksa should come to the mound and, setting up an ornamental pole for each clan, hold a solemn cry a whole moon. Then, to appease the restless spirits of the deceased nation and satisfy all the men and women with what they had done with the sacred relics of their dead, the Choctaws held a grand and joyous national dance and feast of two days. And returning to their tents, they remembered their grief no more.

All the people said that their great chief was full of wisdom; that his heart was with the people; and that his counsels had led them in the clean and white paths of safety and peace. Each of the iksas selected very tall pine poles, which they peeled and made white and ornamented with festoons of evergreens and flowers. Then in most solemn form, they performed the cry three times every day, during one whole moon. Then at the great national pole pulling, they celebrated a grand feast and dance of two days. The rejoicing of the nation was very great, and they returned to their camps with glad hearts, remembering their sorrows no more.[16a]

Afterward, when a death occurred, and the bones had been properly cleansed, they were deposited in a great cavity which had been constructed for that purpose, as the work of the mound was progressing. It was the national sepulchral vault; and thither the bones of all the people that died at Nunih Waya were carried and neatly stowed away in dressed leather sacks. Thus arose the custom of burying the dead in the great monumental sepulchre. And when a member of a hunting party of more than two men or a family died, too far out in the forest to pack home the bones, which could not be cleaned in the woods—for the bone pickers never went hunting—it was deemed sufficient to appease the wandering spirit to place all his hunting implements close to the dead body, just as death had left it. In such cases it was not lawful to touch the dead, and they were covered with a mound of earth thirty steps in circumference and as high as a man's head. If death occurred at the camp of an individual family in the far off hunt, the survivors would, during the cry moon, carry, in cane baskets and [on] the blade bones of the buffalo, a sufficient amount of earth to construct a mound of the above dimensions. If there should be but two men at a camp, or a lone man and his wife, and one should die, the survivor had to carry the dead body home. Life for life, was the law; and every life had to be accounted for in a satisfactory manner. It would not answer for a man to return home and report that his hunting companion or his wife had been lost or drowned, devoured by wild beasts or died a natural death.

[16a] As will be seen later, the pole-pulling ceremony was of later date than the custom of burying in mounds.

He must show the body. There are occasionally found among the great number of tumuli scattered over the land, mounds of larger dimensions than ordinary ones. These mounds were constructed by females. Upon the death in camp of a man who had an affectionate wife, his mourning tekchi (wife), regardless of the customary time to cry, would throw down her hair and with all her strength and that of her children would carry earth, and build upon the mound as long as they could find food of any kind that would sustain life. They would then return to camp, worn out skeletons.

Now, my white friend, I have explained to you the origin, and who it was that built the great number of mounds that are found scattered over this wide land. The circular, conic mounds are all graves, and mark the spot where the persons, for whom they were built, breathed their last breath. There being no bone pickers at the hunting camps to handle the dead, the body was never touched, or moved from the death posture. Just as it lay, or sat, as the case might be, it was covered up, first with either stones, pebbles, or sand, and finished off with earth. In this way the custom of mound graves originated from the great mound grave, Nunih Waya, and it prevailed with the Choctaw people until the white man came with his destructive, sense-killing " fire water," and made the people all drunk.

After getting in possession of this information, in regard to the origin and make of the mounds, I took pains to excavate quite a number of them, which were found on the " second flat " along the Tombecbee river. They contained invariably a single human skeleton. The bones generally, except the skull, were decomposed. The crania of most of them would bear handling, when first taken out, but when exposed to the air they soon fell to ashes. Along with the ashes of the bones, in most cases, would be found five or six arrow points, a stone ax, and not infrequently a stone skin-dresser. In all cases, the bones would be found enveloped, sometimes lying on the side, feet drawn up ; at other times in a sitting posture, either in sand, pebbles, or small stones. In one or two cases, the coals and the charred ends of the pine knots that lighted up the last sad night of the deceased, lay in front and near the bones, under the sand.

As soon as the national cry was over, the poles pulled down, and the great dance celebrated, the families dispersed into the far off hunting grounds where they enjoyed the game and fruits, until midwinter ; when they returned to their homes to prepare and put their fields in order for the coming planting time. The seasons at Nunih Waya were good every year ; and they had on hand corn in abundance. Their mode of putting it away, in small lots, in air tight earthen cells, preserved it, from year to year, for an indefinite period, as sound and fresh as new corn. To keep it dry and entirely excluded from the air, was all that was necessary, to preserve it for any length of time in the same condition in which it was when put up.

Feeling themselves permanently settled after the mound was completed, they planted larger crops and were beginning to construct good, dry houses in which to dwell. The next year after the mound was finished, having a very large crop of corn, they celebrated the green corn dance, eating nothing besides the corn. On the first day of the feast, and at the time the people had assembled to receive instructions in regard to the manner of conducting the ceremonies, the minko came upon the dance ground, and calling the attention of the multitude said:

" We are a brave and exceedingly prosperous people. We are an industrious people. We till the ground in large fields, thereby producing sustenance for this great nation. We are a faithful and dutiful people. We packed the bones of our ancestors on our backs, in the wilderness, forty-three winters, and at the end of our long journey piled up to their memory a monument that over-shadows the land like a great mountain. We are a strong, hardy, and very shifty [!] people. When we set out from the land of our fathers, the Chata tribe numbered a little less than nineteen thousand. We have traveled over a pathless wilderness, beset with rocks, high mountains, sun-scorched plains, with dried up rivers of bitter waters; timbered land, full of lakes and ferocious wild beasts. Bravely we have battled and triumphed over all. We have not failed, but are safely located in the rich and fruitful land of tall trees and running brooks seen in a vision of the night, and described by our good chief who is missing. And we number now a little more than twenty-one thousand. As-suredly we are a wonderful people. A people of great power. A united, friendly people. We are irresistibly strong (hlampko)."

Then turning and pointing with his hand, he said:

" Behold the sacred pole, the gift of the Great Spirit. To it we are to attribute all our success. When the enemy pursued on our track, its truthful indications gave us timely notice to escape from danger. When we wavered in the trackless desert it leaned and led us onward in the paths of safety. When we reached the swift, wide river, it bowed its ominous head; we crossed to Nunih Waya. Here it danced and made many motions, but did not in-dicate for us to go farther. As a leading light to our feet and as a great power, it has conducted us from the far distant West (hush ai akatula) to the rising sun; to the land of safety and plenty. It is a sacred relic of our pilgrimage in the unknown regions. As such we must preserve it for the coming generations to see and remember the potent leader of their fathers in the wilderness. It is proposed by the wise Isht ahullo, who has faithfully carried the sacred pole ever since the virtuous and ingenious Peni ikbi[17] died, that a circular mound, forty steps in circumference at the base, as high as once and a half the length of the sacred pole, be erected eastward from the great monument, on the high ground towards the middle creek; and that inasmuch as your good, lazy Isht ahullos, yushpakammi, dreamers, spirit talkers and medicine men, did not find it convenient to assist you in the con-struction of the great monument for the dead nation, let them be required to construct with their own hands, this mound for the leader's pole to rest on. They pretend to be always dealing with spirits and sacred things, and no other men should be allowed to work on the mound, that is to constitute a resting place for the sacred pole. The work must be performed and finished by the sacred conjurers, in accordance with the plan and directions of the wise Isht ahullo, who carries the leader's pole, and who is this day appointed to superintend the work."

The pole-bearing Isht ahullo marked off the ground, and placing the sacred pole in the center of it, summoned the whole of the conjurers and sorcerers to commence the work. They came, but they were so extremely awkward and lazy that the work progressed quite slowly. The Isht ahullo, who was superintendent of the work, exerted his whole power to encourage them to facilitate the building of the mound. It was all to no effect. They grumbled from morning till night and moved so slowly at their work, that a child could have done as much work as they accomplished in a day. The superintendent shortened their daily supply of food. They did less work and grumbled more. He made their daily food still less. They, with but few exceptions, ran off into the woods, and scattering themselves among the camps of the hunters, sponged upon them until the hunters, becoming tired of them, drove them

---

[17] " Canoe Maker."

from their camps like dogs. They returned to Nunih Waya, but did not resume their work. The superintendent of the work complained to the chief. The chief called the tool carriers and instructed them to go out, and select a piece of land, that would not interfere with the claims of the iksas. " Lay out a plot of land, twenty steps square for each one of the yushpakammi, who is not found engaged at work on the mound; and set the idle conjurers to work on it, preparing the ground to plant corn. We are settled permanently now, and every member of the nation, who is healthy, must perform sufficient labor to produce, at least, as much food and raiment as he consumes. This people shall not labor and sweat to support a lazy, heartless set of men, whose only duty is falsehood, and whose influence disturbs the quiet of the nation."

The tool carriers laid off the little plats of land, but the conjurers paid no attention to the order for them to work it. The chief then appointed a day for the people to meet in council for the purpose of taking into consideration the bad character of these lazy men and the demoralizing influence they exerted in the nation. The whole number of the conjurers were also summoned to attend the council and defend their right to enjoy all the privileges of the camps, with entire exemption from labor or any visible calling.

On the day appointed for the council, all the people who were out hunting came. But of the spirit talkers and conjurers, there were not exceeding thirty in the assembly, and they were all known to be industrious men. Messengers were sent to warn them to the council. They were not to be found in the camps; and it was discovered that a great number of women were missing. The assembly immediately broke up and parties were sent out to capture and bring home the women at least.

After several days diligent search, the parties all returned and reported that the conjurers must have gone off on the wind; for they could discover no trace nor sign of them in any direction. Nor did they ever know certainly what went with them.

At the time this thing occurred there were so many people absent from the encampment that they were unable to make an estimate of the number that were missing but from the number of children left without mothers in the camp, it was known to be very considerable. As far as could be ascertained, they were the wives of men, without exception, who were out hunting. It was distressing to see the great number of small children who were running to and fro in the camps, and to hear their incessant lament. " Sa ishka muto " (Where is my mother) was heard in all directions. They were mostly small children, and generally of young mothers who had abandoned both them and their absent husbands and run off with the lazy conjuring priests and medicine men.

At midwinter, when the hunting parties had all returned, an effort was made to ascertain the number of women who had left their families to follow the conjurers and priests. From the best computation they could make, the number was nearly 200, and it so much excited the bereaved husbands and the people generally against the Isht ahullo and conjurers of every grade, that it was with much difficulty the minko found himself able to dissuade them from falling upon the few that were left, and who were faithfully at work on the mound. In their rage [they cried] that the whole mass of lazy Isht ahullo, conjurers, spirit talkers, and medicine men were all alike—enemies to the men that fed them, and seducers and prostituters of the women who clothed them. They declared that there was no good in them, and that they ought not to live. This manifestation of the low, gross nature of the priests and conjurers depreciated their standing with the whole people. It sank them to a degree of infamy and suspicion from which they have never recovered. To this day they are pushed aside in decent company and looked upon with scorn and contempt.

The Isht Ahullo, who was so long the bearer of the sacred pole, had always deported himself as a good, industrious man; and it was from his management that the investigation of their conduct, and the flights of the conjuring priests had been brought about. After a time with the small band of Isht ahullos that had been left he completed the mound in good style and, planting the sacred pole permanently on its top, he desired the chief to call the nation to its examination, and if the work met with the approbation of the people, he wished them to receive it and discharge him and his workmen from further duties in regard to the sacred pole.

When the people came, they gave their approbation of the comely proportions of the mound by a long continued shout. And by another uproarious shout congratulated themselves on the certainty that their long journey in the wilderness had most assuredly ended. At this, the sacred pole began jumping up and punching itself deeper and deeper into the ground, until it went down slowly out of sight into the mound. At witnessing the wonderful manifestation of the settling pole, there were no bounds to their rejoicings, and they danced and brought provisions, making a glad celebration that continued three days and nights on the occasion of the departing sacred pole.

Having sufficient ground cleared to produce as much bread as they needed, and a large surplus, the people had time to construct houses to dwell in and to keep their surplus provisions dry and safe. They constructed their houses of earth at Nunih Waya, and that fashion prevailed until the white people came to live in the nation with them.

The larger game was becoming scarcer and the hunters were extending their excursions wider. The people, however, were producing such abundant supplies of corn that they did not require a very great amount of meat and the hunters were extending their explorations more for the purpose of becoming acquainted with a wider range of country and for their own satisfaction than from necessity. Time rolled on, the people were healthy, and had increased at a very great ratio. They had extended their settlements up the Nunih Waya creek, and out in the country between Nunih Waya and Tuli Hikia creeks, to half a day's journey; and they were growing corn over the entire district.

About thirty winters after they had stopped at Nunih Waya, a party of hunters who had progressed a little farther north than usual, fell in with a camp of hunters belonging to the Chickasha tribe. After finding that they spoke the same language with themselves, the Chahtas approached their camp in a friendly manner, and remained several days. The older men amongst them being familiar with the traditional history of the journeyings of their respective tribes, took much pleasure in communicating to each other an account of their travels. From the point where the two tribes separated, the Chickashas diverged widely to the left, found an extremely rough and scarce country for some time, but at length emerging from the mountains on to the wide spread plains, they found the buffalo and other game plentiful. They continued to travel, with only an occasional halt, to rest the women and feeble ones, until they came to the great river, at the place called by them, sakti ahlopulli (bluff crossing)—white people call it now Chickasaw Bluffs, said the old man. They made shift to cross the great river, and traveling onward, the leader's pole came to a stand at a place now called Chickasha Old Town in a high and beautiful country. The leader's pole stood at this place three winters, at the end of which time the pole was found leaning to the northeast. They set out again, and crossed another big river (at little prairie, near Huntsville, Alabama). The pole remained there erect only one winter. At mulberry time the ensuing summer the pole was found leaning almost directly to the south. They packed up, and crossing many bold running rivers, the pole still leading onward, until they came to a large river, near where it emptied into the great okhuta (ocean). At this beautiful country (below where Savannah, Georgia, now stands) the pole stood erect many winters. The fish, opa haksum [opahaksun], oka folush (oysters, clams) and all manner of shell fish and fowl, and small game were plentiful. The people obtained full supplies of provisions with but little labor. In process of time, however, the people became sickly, and they were visited with a very great plague. They called the plague hoita lusa (black vomit) because the people died, vomiting black matter, resembling powdered· fire coals and fish slime. All that took it were sick but a day or two and died so fast that the people became frightened and ran off, leaving great numbers of the dead unburied. They followed the leader's pole back nearly over the same route they went, until finally they returned to the place where the pole made its first stand (Chickasha Old Towns). Here it stood again, and remained erect until it rotted.

After the Chahtas had found where their brother Chickashas had located, they paid occasional visits to their country. But the Chickashas, becoming suspicious that the Chahtas were seeking some advantage, gave them orders not to extend their hunts north of a certain little river. The Chahtas paid no attention to the proclamation sent by the Chickashas, and it turned out that the Chickashas attacked and killed three or four of their hunters who had camped north of the interdicted river.

When the news reached Nunih Waya, the people were grieved; for they had felt proud of finding their Chickasha brethren and were preparing to cultivate their friendship. The minko, thinking it possible that there might be some mistake in the matter, sent an embassy to the chief of the Chickasha nation, to ascertain the cause of the murderous conduct of his hunters. The Chickasha chief ordered the Chahta embassy to be scourged and sent back with no other answer. The Chahtas were very much enraged. They had received an indignity that they could not account for; and they felt mortified in the extreme. The Chahta chief did not feel willing to go to war with them, and made up his mind to give orders to his hunters to abstain from hunting beyond the river named by the Chickashas. But before he had time to carry his peace plans into action, all the hunters north of Nunih Waya had been attacked at their camps on the hunting grounds. Great numbers of the men had been killed, and their women carried off captive. Those hunters who had escaped from the attacked camps reported that the Chickashas were very numerous, and that their warriors were very large and overpowering in battle. The present generation of the Chahta people had never seen any people but their own tribe; and the news of the captured women, murdered hunters and the vast hordes of rushing irresistible warriors that were pouring down into their hunting grounds from the Chickasha country, had frightened the Chahta people into a fearful panic. Some of them had already proposed to evacuate their comfortable homes at Nunih Waya and seek some safer country for their wives and little ones to dwell in. But they did not ponder the matter long. The spies coming in, reported that great numbers of the Chickashas had their camps, and were killing up the game in two days' travel of Nunih Waya.

The Chahta minko kindled the council fire; and calling a national council, submitted for their consideration the whole matter of the Chikasha depredations; and called upon them to investigate the subject and decide on the proper course to pursue in the case. The people promptly assembled and were confessedly very much alarmed. Some of the young warriors moved that the Chahta people should rise at once and kill every Chickasha they could find within the limits of their hunting grounds. Others who were not quite so fiery thought that a precipitate move on the part of the Chahtas would only bring disaster, while there were others who advocated immediate flight as the only chance for safety.

At length, old Long Arrow, who had always been leader of the tool carriers, arose and said:

"I am old now, and cannot, if I desired, make much of a flight. I shall remain at Nunih Waya. My bones shall sleep in the great mound. I am also opposed to precipitate movements. Let us prepare plenty of arms and make systematic movements. Let us organize one hundred companies, with ten active men in each, and a prudent, brave warrior to lead each company. Let these hundred companies be sent forward immediately, with instructions to examine and ascertain the force and position of the enemy; but not to make battle, except when they are attacked. Let them stay a long time, and be seen in many places, as by accident, in the day time; but at night, let them scatter and sleep without fire in dark places. In the meantime, let all those who remain in the encampment go to work and throw up a high circular earth wall that shall include the two mounds and space enough to contain all the women and children, as well as the aged and infirm, in case of a siege. All this completed and all the corn and other provisions that can be had stored away inside of the great wall, we shall be ready to increase our forces; hunt down the enemy and scalp them wherever they may be found."

The multitude breathed easier and looked brighter. The minko then spoke to the people, giving them great encouragement. He said:

"The great war talk of the long tried friend of the people, Long Arrow, is full of wisdom, and his words brace the flagging spirits of the nation. His counsels lead to safety, and his instructions and plans to victory. Let the people not hesitate. Turn out your hundred companies of warriors. Send them out immediately. Appoint wise men to lay off and direct the work on the earth wall and let all that can carry a load of dirt as large as his head be found busily engaged from day to day, until the wall is completed. Be industrious. Let every one do his duty in this great work. Let all people be brave and faithful and danger cannot approach you."

And the people answered and said:

"It is a good talk. Lay off the ground; we are ready for the work; it shall rise up as a cloud in a summer's day."

The companies were organized the same day and took their departure the next day. Men were appointed to lay off and superintend the work on the earthen wall. The people, old and young, stringing themselves around the entire circle, threw up the earth from the outside of the wall to the height of two men, in eight days. And they left two gaps in the wall, of five steps each. One at the east and the other at the west, for the ingress and egress of the people which they did not intend to close until Nunih Waya should be actually invaded by the enemy.

The minko then organized his whole effective force and ordered them to make arrows and war clubs as fast as possible and bring them into the mound of the sacred pole, where he had a house erected, in which to deposit them.[18]

The above is, of course, cut out of the middle of a very much longer narrative, although the volume in which it is contained seems to give

---

[18] Lincecum in Pubs. Miss. Hist. Soc., VIII, pp. 521–542.

us no explanation of the reason for its incomplete state. The core of the narrative is plainly a genuine Choctaw origin myth; the question is how much of the elaboration is native and how much due to Lincecum himself. That there has been a certain amount contributed by both goes without saying, and later influences are discernible here and there, as when " iron " tools are mentioned. At the same time I am inclined to regard it as a fairly elaborate origin myth in which, as in so many of the kind, the initiation of the customs and ceremonies of the tribe is incorporated Thus the explanation of one of the Nanih Waiya mounds is bound up with the explanation of the origin of Choctaw burial customs, the beginning of the " green corn " dance appears to be introduced, and the origin of the almost continuous wars of later times between the Choctaw and Chickasaw, as well as the first use of a stockade. The legend is no doubt absolutely correct in describing the earthen rampart at Nanih Waiya as a defence against Chickasaw incursions, however much it may exaggerate the importance attached to this particular fortification. In his attempts to account for the origin of the two mounds within the enclosure the narrator is not so fortunate. According to him, the larger mound is a burial mound, and the smaller a mound prepared for the sacred pole, while as a matter of fact the small mound was the burial mound, there being no indication that the principal structure was used for that purpose. As I have stated already, it was probably intended as a foundation for the public buildings of the town, which were, it is true, devoted in part to religious purposes. The two gaps are evidently the places where the two " highways " described by Halbert entered, and no doubt they were the old gateways of the fort.

The accounts given by Cushman have been touched up even more by the imagination of the recorder. He says:

Their tradition, in regard to their origin as related by the aged Choctaws to the missionaries in 1820, was in substance as follows: In a remote period of the past their ancestors dwelt in a country far distant toward the setting sun; and being conquered and greatly oppressed by a more powerful people . . . resolved to seek a country far removed from the possibility of their oppression.

A great national council was called, to which the entire nation in one vast concourse quickly responded. After many days spent in grave deliberations upon the question in which so much was involved, a day was finally agreed upon and a place of rendezvous duly appointed whence they should bid a final adieu to their old homes and country and take up their line of march to seek others, they knew not where. When the appointed day arrived it found them at the designated place fully prepared and ready for the exodus under the chosen leadership of two brothers, Chahtah and Chikasah, both equally renowned for their bravery and skill in war and their wisdom and prudence in council; who, as Moses and Aaron led the Jews in their exodus from Egypt, were to lead them from a land of oppression to one of peace, prosperity and happiness. The evening before their departure a "Fabussa" (pole) was firmly set up in the ground at the centre point of their encampment, by direction of their chief medicine man and prophet, whose wisdom in matters pertaining to things supernatural was unquestioned and to whom, after many days fasting and supplication, the Great Spirit had revealed that the Fabussa would indicate on the following morning, the direction they should march by its leaning; and, . . . would indicate the direction they must travel day by day until they reached the sought and desired haven; when, on the following morn, it would there and then remain as erect as it had been placed the evening before. At the early dawn of the following morning many solicitous eyes were turned to the silent but prophetic Fabussa. Lo! it leaned to the east. Enough. Without hesitation or delay the mighty host began its line of march toward the rising sun, and followed each day the morning directions given by the talismanic pole, which was borne by day at the head of the moving multiude, and set up at each returning evening in the centre of the encampment, alternately by the two renowned chiefs and brothers, Chahtah and Chikasah. For weeks and months they journeyed toward the east as directed by the undeviating Fabussa, passing over wide extended plains and through forests vast and abounding with game of many varieties seemingly undisturbed before by the presence of man, from which their skillful hunters bountifully supplied their daily wants. Gladly would they have accepted, as their future asylum, many parts of the country through which they traveled, but were forbidden, as each returning morn the unrelenting pole still gave its silent but comprehended command: "Eastward and onward."

After many months of wearisome travel, suddenly a vast body of flowing water stretched its mighty arm athwart their path. With unfeigned astonishment they gathered in groups upon its banks and gazed upon its turbid waters. Never before had they even heard of, or in all their wanderings stumbled upon aught like this. . . . But what now says their dumb talisman? . . . Silent and motionless, still as ever before, it bows to the east and its mandate "Onward, beyond Misha Sipokni"[19] is accepted without a murmur; and at once they proceed to construct canoes and rafts by which, in a few weeks, all were safely landed upon its eastern banks, whence again was resumed their eastward march, and so continued until they stood upon the western banks of the Yazoo river and once more encamped for the night; and, as had been done for many months before, . . . the Fabussa . . . was set up; but ere the morrow's sun had plainly lit up the eastern horizon, many anxiously watching eyes that early rested upon its straight, slender, silent form, observed it stood erect as when set up the evening before. And then was borne upon that morning breeze throughout the vast sleeping encampment, the joyful acclamation, "Fohah hupishno Yak! Fohah hupishno Yak! ['here is where we rest']."

Now their weary pilgrimage was ended. . . . Then, as commemorative of this great event in their national history, they threw up a large mound embracing three acres of land and rising forty feet in a conical form, with a deep hole about ten feet in diameter excavated on the top, and all enclosed by a ditch encompassing nearly twenty acres. After its completion, it was discovered not to be erect but a little leaning, and they named it Nunih (mountain or mound) Waiyah, leaning. . . .

Several years afterward, according to the tradition of the Choctaws as narrated to the missionaries, the two brothers, still acting in the capacity of

---

[19] Cushman tries to derive the name of the Mississippi River from two Choctaw words, misha, "beyond" (in space or time) and sipokni, "old"; in fact it is from two Algonquian words, missi, "big," and sipi, "river."

chiefs, disagreed in regard to some national question, and, as Abraham suggested to Lot the propriety of separation, so did Chikasah propose to Chahtah; but not with that unselfishness that Abraham manifested to Lot; since Chikasah, instead of giving to Chahtah the choice of directions, proposed that they should leave it to a game of chance, to which Chahtah readily acquiesced. Thus it was played: They stood facing each other, one to the east and the other to the west, holding a straight pole, ten or fifteen feet in length, in an erect position between them with one end resting on the ground; and both were to let go of the pole at the same instant by a pre-arranged signal, and the direction in which it fell was to decide the direction which Chikasah was to take. If it fell to the north, Chikasah and his adherents were to occupy the northern portion of the country, and Chahtah and his adherents, the southern; but if it fell to the south, then Chikasah, with his followers, was to possess the southern portion of the country, and Chahtah with his, the northern. The game was played, and the pole decreed that Chikasah should take the northern part of their then vast and magnificent territory. Thus they were divided and became two separate and distinct tribes, each of whom assumed and ever afterwards retained the name of their respective chiefs, Chahtah and Chikasah." [20]

This writer also believed he discerned traditions of an earlier migration into America by way of Bering Strait, based probably upon references to the crossing of bodies of water in some versions of the old migration story. Farther on he gives us another account taken, he says, from papers of Rev. Israel Folsom, a native Choctaw missionary.

The name Choctaw, or Chahtah, is derived from a prophet warrior who flourished at a time too remote for fixing any date, as it is only handed down by tradition from one generation to another.

Headed by him, tradition informs us, the people in one grand division migrated to the East from a country far toward the setting sun, following the Cherokees and Muscogees, who had moved on, four years previous, in search of a suitable spot for a permanent location. He is said to have been possessed of all the characteristics essential to the carrying out of such an enterprise to a successful termination. His benevolence and many other virtues are still cherished and held in sacred remembrance by his people. The country whence they migrated, or the causes which induced them to seek another place of habitation, are wrapt in mysterious oblivion, as their tradition begins abruptly with the epoch of migration. In moving from place to place, Chahtah is said to have carried a high staff or pole which, on encamping, was immediately placed in front of his wigwam, where it remained until they broke up encampment. His wigwam is represented to have been placed in the van of all the tribe. When the pole inclined forward—a power which it was believed to possess—the people prepared to march. . . . After many years of wanderings, during which they, in common with those who have ever engaged in similar enterprises, suffered many trials and privations, they at length arrived at a certain place, where the staff stood still and, instead of bending forward, inclined backward, which was regarded as a sign they were at their journey's end. To this place where the staff stood still, Chahtah gave the name of Nun-nih Wai-ya. The exact period of the termination of their wanderings is unknown. So soon as they got in some degree settled, Chahtah called the

---

[20] Cushman, Hist. Choc., Chick., and Natchez Inds., pp. 62–66.

warriors together for the purpose of organizing a code of laws for their government. At this place of rest, Nunnih Waiya, they built strong fortifications in order to protect themselves from any foe who might conceive hostile intentions against them. Whether or not they were ever assailed is unknown. The remains of the fortress, however, are still to be seen in Mississippi. A long time did not elapse before their newly acquired territory was found to be too limited to hold their rapidly increasing numbers, and they were in consequence compelled to spread themselves over the adjacent country, and form themselves into villages. It is a well authenticated fact that from this outpouring or scattering, sprang the Indians called Shukchi, Hummas and Yazoos. [21]

The comma between "Shukchi" and "Hummas" is a typographical error, the name of the tribe being Shukchi Hummas. This tribe is indeed known to have been related to the Choctaw and Chickasaw in language, but Adair makes it as old as either of them. The Yazoo proper were in no way related to the Choctaw; Folsom has no doubt confused them with the Choctaw towns called Yashu or Yazoo. Cushman combats the tradition that would bring the Choctaw out of Nanih Waiya hill itself, attributing it to a misunderstanding on the part of some white people who had interrogated Choctaw living at or on the mound and thought that their questioners wished to know from what part of it they themselves had just come. Since Nanih Waiya does not seem to have been occupied permanently after white contact, such a misunderstanding is improbable, though it is more than likely that the application of the term "mother hill" to this mound and the similarity of waiya and waya, as mentioned above, may have had something to do with it. Folsom seems to imply that the term waiya referred to the bending back of the sacred pole when it was planted in the ground at this spot. Frequently a number of folk explanations spring up about a name that has become prominent in the lives of a people. Cushman also adds some remarks regarding ceremonial offerings made here which are of interest. I do not find them noted elsewhere. He says:

As an evidence of their admiration and veneration for this ancestral memento, the Choctaws, when passing, would ascend it and drop into the hole at its top various trinkets, and sometimes a venison ham, or dressed turkey, as a kind of sacrificial offering to the memory of its ancient builders, who only appeared to them through the mists of ages past; and as the highest evidence of their veneration for this relic of their past history, it was sometimes spoken of by the more enthusiastic as their Iholitopa Ishki (Beloved mother). [22]

The following version was recorded about the middle of the nineteenth century by an American traveler, Charles Lanman. He obtained it, he tells us, from "the educated Choctaw Pitchlyn," who can have been none other than the well-known Choctaw chief Peter

[21] Cushman, Hist. Choc., Chick. and Natchez Inds., pp. 361–362.
[22] Ibid., p. 293.

Perkins Pitchlynn, who was born in Noxubee County, Miss., January 30, 1806, and died at Washington, D. C., January 17, 1881, and to whose memory the Choctaw Nation erected a monument in the latter city.

Lanman says that " the sea alluded to in this legend is supposed to be the Gulf of Mexico, and the mighty river the Mississippi." This is the only version known to me which brings the Choctaw from under the ocean.

According to the traditions of the Choctaws, the first of their race came from the bosom of a magnificent sea. Even when they first made their appearance upon the earth they were so numerous as to cover the sloping and sandy shore of the ocean, far as the eye could reach, and for a long time did they follow the margin of the sea before they could find a place suited to their wants. The name of their principal chief has long since been forgotten, but it is well remembered that he was a prophet of great age and wisdom. For many moons did they travel without fatigue, and all the time were their bodies strengthened by pleasant breezes, and their hearts, on the other hand gladdened by the luxuriance of a perpetual summer. In process of time, however, the multitude was visited by sickness, and one after another were left upon the shore the dead bodies of old women and little children. The heart of the Prophet became troubled, and, planting a long staff that he carried in his hand, and which was endowed with the miraculous power of an oracle, he told his people that from the spot designated they must turn their faces towards the unknown wilderness. But before entering upon this portion of their journey he specified a certain day for starting, and told them that they were at liberty, in the meantime, to enjoy themselves, by feasting and dancing, and performing their national rites.

It was now early morning, and the hour appointed for starting. Heavy clouds and mists rested upon the sea, but the beautiful waves melted upon the shore as joyfully as ever before. The staff which the Prophet had planted was found leaning towards the north, and in that direction did the multitude take up their line of march. Their journey lay across streams, over hills and mountains, through tangled forests, and over immense prairies. They were now in an entirely strange country, and as they trusted in their magic staff they planted it every night with the utmost care, and arose in the morning with great eagerness to ascertain the direction towards which it leaned. And thus had they traveled for many days when they found themselves upon the margin of an O-kee-na-chitto [okhina chito], or great highway of water. Here did they pitch their tents, and having planted the staff, retired to repose. When morning came the oracle told them that they must cross the mighty river before them. They built themselves a thousand rafts, and reached the opposite shore in safety. They now found themselves in a country of surpassing loveliness, where the trees were so high as almost to touch the clouds, and where game of every variety and the sweetest of fruits were found in the greatest abundance. The flowers of this land were more brilliant than any they had ever before seen, and so large as often to shield them from the sunlight of noon. With the climate of the land they were delighted, and the air they breathed seemed to fill their bodies with a new vigor. So pleased were they with all that they saw that they built mounds in all the more beautiful valleys they passed through, so that the Master of Life might know that they were not an ungrateful people. In this new country did they conclude to remain, and here did they establish their national government with its benign laws.

Time passed on, and the Choctaw nation became so powerful that its hunting grounds extended even to the sky. Troubles now arose among the younger warriors and hunters of the nation, until it came to pass that they abandoned the cabins of their forefathers, and settled in distant regions of the earth. Thus from the very body of the Choctaw nation have sprung those other nations which are known as the Chickasaws, the Cherokees, the Creeks or Muskogees, the Shawnees and the Delawares. And in process of time the Choctaws founded a great city, wherein their more aged men might spend their days in peace; and, because they loved those of their people who had long before departed into distant regions, they called this city Yazoo, the meaning of which is, home of the people who are gone.[23]

In his history of Mississippi Claiborne has published a version of the legend which had been collected by Mr. H. S. Halbert in 1877. The latter says of it: " It was taken down from the lips of Mr. Jack Henry, an old citizen of Oktibbeha County, he stating that he had received it in early life from an Irishman, who had once lived among the Choctaws, and had heard the legend from an old Choctaw woman." It appears, then, that the legend was transmitted through several memories and mouths before being finally recorded in printer's ink. It did not come directly from Choctaw lips, and no doubt was unconsciously colored, or its details imperfectly remembered in its transmission through the memories of the two white men.[24] It runs as follows:

The Choctaws believed that their ancestors came from the west. They were led by two brothers, Chactas and Chics-a, at the head of their respective Iksas or clans.[25] On their journey they followed a pole which, guided by an invisible hand, moved before them. Shortly after crossing the Mississippi, the pole stood still, firmly planted in the ground, and they construed this as an augury that here they must halt, and make their homes. . . .

The two leaders concluded to reconnoitre the country. Chics-a moved first, and ten days thereafter Chactas followed, but a tremendous snow storm had obliterated his brother's trail, and they were separated. He went southerly to Nanawyya, on the head-waters of Pearl River, about the geographical centre of the State, and the other brother, it was afterwards ascertained, settled near where Pontotoc now stands. At the first meeting of the brothers it was determined that the two clans should constitute separate tribes, each occupying their respective territories, and the hunters of neither band to encroach on the territory of the other. The present Oktibbeha and the Nuslcheah, were indicated as the line of demarkation.

The Choctaws preserve a dim tradition that, after crossing the Mississippi, they met a race of men whom they called Na-hon-lo,[26] tall in stature and of fair complexion, who had emigrated from the sun rise. They had once been a

[23] Extract from Adventures in the Wilds of the United States and British American Provinces (collected 1846–1856), by Charles Lanman. Vol. II, Philadelphia, 1856, pp. 457–459. Pitchlynn derives Yazoo from ya or ia, " to go," and asha, " to sit," " to remain," but it is probably not a Choctaw word.

[24] Halbert in Pub. Miss. Hist. Soc., II, p. 228.

[25] In view of the repeated references to these two brothers it is surprising to read that in 1842 an old Chickasaw chief named Greenwood, while recognizing the fact that his tribe and the Choctaw were once the same people, knew of no tradition regarding it.

[26] Cf. Nahullo, p. 199.

mighty people, but were then few in number and soon disappeared after the incoming of the Choctaws. This race of men were, according to the tradition, tillers of the soil and peaceable. There had likewise been a race of cannibals, who feasted on the bodies of their enemies. They, too, were giants, and utilized the mammoth as their burden bearers. They kept them closely herded, and as they devoured everything and broke down the forests, this was the origin of the prairies.

The cannibal race and the mammoth perished about the same time, by a great epidemic. Only one of the latter escaped, who made his home for several years near the Tombigbee. The Great Spirit struck him several times with lightning, but he presented his head to the bolt and it glanced off. Annoyed, however, by these attempts, he fled to Soc-te-thou-fah [sakti lanfa, " a furrowed bank or bluff "] (the present Memphis), and at one mighty leap cleared the river, and made his way to the Rocky Mountains.[27]

Mr. Halbert gives another version which " came direct from the lips of the Rev. Peter Folsom, a Choctaw from the nation west, who was employed in 1882 by the Baptists of Mississippi to labor as a missionary among the Mississippi Choctaws." " Mr. Folsom stated," adds Halbert, " that soon after finishing his education in Kentucky, one day in 1833, he visited Nanih Waiya with his father, and while at the mound his father related to him the migration legend of his people, as follows:

In ancient days the ancestors of the Choctaws and the Chickasaws lived in a far western country, under the rule of two brothers, named Chahta and Chikasa. In process of time, their population becoming very numerous, they found it difficult to procure subsistence in that land. Their prophets thereupon announced that far to the east was a country of fertile soil and full of game, where they could live in ease and plenty. The entire population resolved to make a journey eastward in search of that happy land. In order more easily to procure subsistence on their route the people marched in several divisions of a day's journey apart. A great prophet marched at their head, bearing a pole, which, on camping at the close of each day, he planted erect in the earth, in front of the camp. Every morning the pole was always seen leaning in the direction they were to travel that day. After the lapse of many moons they arrived one day at Nanih Waiya. The prophet planted his pole at the base of the mound. The next morning the pole was seen standing erect and stationary. This was interpreted as an omen from the Great Spirit that the long sought-for land was at last found. It so happened, the very day that the party camped at Nanih Waiya, that a party under Chikasa crossed the creek and camped on its east side. That night a great rain fell, and it rained several days. In consequence of this all the low lands were inundated and Nanih Waiya Creek and other tributaries of Pearl River were rendered impassable.

After the subsidence of the waters, messengers were sent across the creek to bid Chikasa's party return, as the oracular pole had proclaimed that the long sought-for land was found, and the mound was the center of the land. Chikasa's party, however, regardless of the weather, had proceeded on their journey, and the rain having washed all traces of their march from off the grass the messengers were unable to follow them up, and so returned to camp. Meanwhile, the other divisions in the rear arrived at Nanih Waiya and learned that here

[27] Claiborne, Miss., I, pp. 483–484.

was the center of their new home and that their long pilgrimage was at last finished. Chikasa's party, after their separation from their brethren under Chahta, moved on to the Tombigbee—and eventually became a separate nationality. In this way the Choctaws and the Chickasaws became two separate though kindred nations.[28]

To show what may happen to a myth the following may be quoted from Hitchcock's Diary under date of March 4, 1842. According to an old man who formerly lived on Tombigbee River—

immediately after the revolutionary war of '76 there was a division in the Choctaw Nation under two chiefs, that instead of going into a civil war the parties separated by mutual agreement, one party living in the north west of Mississippi and west Tennessee and the other in east Mississippi and Alabama. That they lived for some short time thus separated having a boundary however established. They afterwards by a regular compact changed the line and the northwest portion took the name of Chickasaws. Jones (the informant) stated also that at about the same time a small portion of Choctaws became dissatisfied with the Chief and went south and lived at the Bay of Boluxy for a time and then moved west upon Pearl river and thence over the Mississippi as far as some villages of Cadoes. Since the emigration of the Choctaws some of those Indians under the name of Boluxy's have been found; their history and almost their language having been for the most part lost.[29]

The Biloxi were a wholly distinct people and the separation between the Chickasaw and Choctaw antedated De Soto's expedition. Probably to this old man the Revolution was as legendary as the Spanish explorer.

Besides the story furnished by Halbert, Claiborne has this version:

They claimed to [have] come, originally from the west. A portion of their people they left behind them. They traveled (*ho-pah-ka*) a long way, encouraged by their *Oon-ka-la*. These priests marched in the centre, bearing a sacred book wrapped in skins. From this book they sung in an unknown tongue, whenever the wanderers became despondent or discontented. They encountered no other people on the route, and passed over a desolate country. A dreadful epidemic broke out among them, and all the priests died but the bearer of the book. They burned their dead, and bore along with them part of the ashes. At a certain point on their journey, near a great river (called by the Indians *Meo-a-she-ba*, by the French, Mississippi,) owing to the frightful mortality, the tribe separated. A portion inclined northward, and took the name of Chickasa, after the great warrior who led them. The main body traveled nearly due south, until they came to the Stooping Hill, *Nane-wy-yah*, now in the county of Winston, Mississippi, on the head waters of Pearl river. There they encamped, and still continued to die. Finally, all perished but the book-bearer. He could not die. The *Nane-wy-yah* opened and he entered it and disappeared. After the lapse of many years, the Great Spirit created four infants, two of each sex, out of the ashes of the dead, at the foot of *Nane-wy-yah*. They were suckled by a panther. When they grew strong and were ready to depart, the book-bearer presented himself, and gave them bows and arrows and an earthen pot,

---

[28] Halbert in Publ. Miss. Hist. Soc., II, pp. 228–229. Also given in Amer. Antiq., vol. XVI, pp. 215–216. In this latter journal Halbert states that Folsom's narrative was obtained through Mr. James Welch, of Neshoba County.

[29] Hitchcock, Diary, in Foreman, Traveler in Ind. Terr., pp. 211–212.

and stretching his arms, said, "I give you these hunting grounds for your homes. When you leave them you die." With these words he stamped his foot—the *Nane-wy-yah* opened, and holding the book above his head, he disappeared forever. The four then separated, two going to the left and two to the right, thus constituting the two Ik-sas or clans, into which the Choctaws are divided. All the very aged Choctaws, on being interrogated as to where they were born, insisted that they came out of *Nane-wy-yah*. One old fellow, who was so dirty it was thought he might be assessed for real estate, swore that he came out of the hill just one thousand years ago, and had never been able to shake the dirt off his back![30]

This story stands quite by itself. The sacred book is of course the result of some post-Columbian rationalization and the source of the version as a whole is a mystery.

That form of the legend which localizes the origin of the Choctaw at Nanih Waiya has outlived the longer form, the migration legend proper, and of this we have some further notes collected by Halbert:

In the very center of the mound, they say, ages ago, the Great Spirit created the first Choctaws, and through a hole or cave, they crawled forth into the light of day. Some say that only one pair was created, but others say that many pairs were created. Old Hopahkitubbee (Hopakitobi), who died several years ago in Neshoba County, was wont to say that after coming forth from the mound, the freshly-made Choctaws were very wet and moist, and that the Great Spirit stacked them along on the rampart, as on a clothes line, so that the sun could dry them.[31]

Like the migration legend, this was worked into a cultural tale including the story of the origin of the dual division in the tribe, and the origin of corn.[32]

Still another version was obtained by Mr. Halbert from Isaac Pistonatubbee, a Choctaw who died in Newton County shortly before 1901 at the age of about 80. Mr. Halbert gives it in both Choctaw and English, the latter being as follows:

A very long time ago the first creation of men was in Nanih Waiya; and there they were made and there they came forth. The Muscogees first came out of Nanih Waiya; and they then sunned themselves on Nanih Waiya's earthen rampart, and when they got dry they went to the east. On this side of the Tombigbee, there they rested and as they were smoking tobacco they dropped some fire.

The Cherokee next came out of Nanih Waiya. And they sunned themselves on the earthen rampart, and when they got dry they went and followed the trail of the elder tribe. And at the place where the Muscogees had stopped and rested, and where they had smoked tobacco, there was fire and the woods were burnt, and the Cherokees could not find the Muscogees' trail, so they got lost and turned aside and went towards the north and there towards the north they settled and made a people.

And the Chickasaws third came out of Nanih Waiya. And then they sunned themselves on the earthen rampart, and when they got dry they went and

[30] Claiborne, Miss., I, pp. 518–519.
[31] H. S. Halbert, in Pubs. Miss. Hist. Soc., II, 229–230.
[32] Ibid., pp. 230–232.

followed the Cherokees' trail; and when they got to where the Cherokees had settled and made a people, they settled and made a people close to the Cherokees.

And the Choctaws fourth and last came out of Nanih Waiya. And they then sunned themselves on the earthen rampart and when they got dry, they did not go anywhere but settled down in this very land and it is the Choctaws' home.[33]

The same writer states that a great Choctaw council was summoned to meet at this mound in 1828 at the instance of Col. Greenwood Leflore in order to make new laws, "so as to place the Choctaws more in harmony with the requirements of modern civilization." He adds that it was "the only known national Indian council held at Nanih Waiya within the historic period." [34]

Similar to the versions given by Halbert is the following which I myself collected from a Mississippi Choctaw, Olmon Comby:

The ancient Choctaw believed that in the beginning of things people came out of the ground at a certain hill and lay about its sides like locusts until they were dried. Several tribes came out in succession. First were the Cherokee. They lay upon the hillside until they were dried and then they went away. Next came the Muskogee. They lay along the hillside, became dry, and went away. After four others had made their appearance successively, the Chickasaw and Choctaw came out together. They derived their names from two brothers who were leaders of the respective bands. They remained together for a long time and became very numerous. Afterwards they started off like the others, still keeping together, but the Chickasaw were in advance. Every night, when the latter camped, they left a mark by which to guide the Choctaw. This went on for a considerable period. One day, however, Chickasaw went out to smoke, and while he was doing so he set the woods on fire, so that the marks were destroyed and the Choctaw lost their way. A long time afterwards they discovered each other again but found that their languages had diverged a little. It is not known which was more like the original tongue.

In this connection consult the version obtained by Alfred Wright (pp. 201–202).

The two following tales were collected by Mr. D. I. Bushnell, jr., from the Choctaw of Bayou Lacomb, La. They show that the sacred hill and its legends had as strong a hold on the beliefs of the southern Choctaw as on those of the northern sections of the tribe.

I

Nané chaha (nané, "hill"; chaha, "high") is the sacred spot in the mountainous country to the northward, always regarded with awe and reverence by the Choctaw.

In very ancient times, before men lived on the earth, the hill was formed, and from the topmost point a passage led down deep into the bosom of the earth. Later, when birds and animals lived, and the surface of the earth was

[33] Halbert in Pubs. Miss. Hist. Soc., IV, pp. 269–270.
[34] Ibid., pp. 233–234.

covered with trees and plants of many sorts, and lakes and rivers had been formed, the Choctaw came forth through the passageway in Nané chaha. And from that point they scattered in all directions but ever afterwards remembered the hill from the summit of which they first beheld the light of the sun.

II

Soon after the earth (yahne) was made, men and grasshoppers came to the surface through a long passageway that led from a large cavern, in the interior of the earth, to the summit of a high hill, Nané chaha. There, deep down in the earth, in the great cavern, man and the grasshoppers had been created by Aba, the Great Spirit, having been formed of the yellow clay.

For a time the men and the grasshoppers continued to reach the surface together, and as they emerged from the long passageway they would scatter in all directions, some going north, others south, east, or west.

But at last the mother of the grasshoppers who had remained in the cavern was killed by the men and as a consequence there were no more grasshoppers to reach the surface, and ever after those that lived on the earth were known to the Choctaw as *eske ilay*, or " mother dead." [35] However, men continued to reach the surface of the earth through the long passageway that led to the summit of Nané chaha, and, as they moved about from place to place, they trampled upon many grasshoppers in the high grass, killing many and hurting others.

The grasshoppers became alarmed as they feared that all would be killed if men became more numerous and continued to come from the cavern in the earth. They spoke to Aba, who heard them and soon after caused the passageway to be closed and no more men were allowed to reach the surface. But as there were many men remaining in the cavern he changed them to ants and ever since that time the small ants have come forth from holes in the ground. [36]

MATERIAL CONDITION

A detailed description of the material culture of the Choctaw is no part of my present purpose, but some notes on this subject, particularly as to the character of their homes and their manner of gaining a livelihood, will furnish a desirable background for the other aspects of their ancient life. A French manuscript of the eighteenth century gives the best early account of the Choctaw house and ménage, from which, with some clarifying emendations, I quote as follows:

The house is merely a cabin made of wooden posts of the size of the leg, buried in the earth [at one end], and fastened together with *lianas*, which make very flexible bands. The rest of the wall is of mud and there are no windows; the door is only from three to four feet in height. The cabins are covered with bark of the cypress or pine. A hole is left at the top of each gable-end to let the smoke out, for they make their fires in the middle of the cabins, which are a gunshot distant from one another. The inside is surrounded with cane beds raised from three to four feet from the ground on account of the fleas which exist there in quantities, because of the dirt. When they are lying down the savages do not get up to make water but let it run through

---

[35] A play upon chishaiyi, the word for " grasshopper;" chiske ilay would be " your mother is dead."

[36] Bushnell in Amer. Anthrop. (N. S.), 12, pp. 526–527.

the canes of their bed. They lie with the skin of a deer or bear under them and the skin of a bison or a blanket above. These beds serve them as table and chair. They have by way of furniture only an earthen pot in which to cook their food, some earthen pans for the same purpose, and some fanners or sieves and hampers for the preparation of their corn, which is their regular nourishment. They pound it in a wooden crusher or mortar, which they make out of the trunk of a tree, hollowed by means of burning embers. The pestle belonging to it is sometimes ten feet long and as small round as the arm. The upper end is an unshaped mass which serves to weight it down and to give force to this pestle in falling back, so that the corn may be crushed more easily. After it is thus crushed they sift it in order to separate the finer part. They boil the coarser in a great skin which holds about three or four buckets of water, and mix it sometimes with pumpkins, or beans, or bean leaves. When this stew is almost done they throw into it the finest of the corn which they had reserved for thickening, and by way of seasoning they have a pot hung aloft in which are the ashes of corn silk, beanpods, or finally oak ashes, and having thrown water upon this they take the lye collected in a vessel underneath, and with it season their stew, which is called *sagamité*. This serves as their principal food, and as well that of the French in the colony who have not the means of living otherwise.

They sometimes make bread without lye, but rarely, because that consumes too much corn, and it is difficult to make, since they reduce it to flour only with the strength of their arms; after which it is kneaded, or they boil it in water, or wrap it in leaves and cook it in the ashes, or finally, having flattened the paste to the thickness of two crowns (ecus), and the diameter of the two hands, they cook it on a piece of a pot on the embers. They also eat it with acorns. Having reduced the acorns to flour they put them in a cane sieve placed near the bank of a stream, and from time to time throw water upon them. By means of this lye they cause it to lose its bitterness, after which they put the paste around a piece of wood which they cook in the fire. When they have meat they boil it in water, without washing it, however dirty it is, saying that [washing] would make it lose its flavor. When it is cooked they sometimes put some of the acorn flour into the broth. They also cook unpounded corn with their meat, and when it is dry they reduce it to bits by pounding. This they boil along with the corn. It has no taste and one must be a savage to eat it.

While the corn is green is the time when they hold the most feasts and they prepare it in different ways. First they roast it in the fire and eat it so; many Frenchmen eat it thus. When it is very tender they pound it and make porridge of it, but the [dish] most esteemed among them is the cold meal. It is corn, considerably mature, which they boil, then roast in order to dry it, and then pound; and this flour has the same effect in cold water as wheat flour put into hot water over the fire and has a fairly agreeable taste; the French eat it with milk. They also have a species of corn which is smaller than the other and comes to maturity in three months. That they dry and then without pounding it boil it with meat. This "little corn," boiled with a turkey or some pieces of fat meat, is a favorite dish with them.[37]

In the "Narrative of a Journey Through Several Parts of the Province of West Florida in the Years 1770 and 1771," by a Mr.

---

[37] Appendix, pp. 246–247; Memoirs of the American Anthropological Association, vol. v, No. 2, 1918, pp. 57–59.

Mease,[38] is the following description of the house of a Choctaw Indian of Imoklasha town named Astolabe:

This house is nearly of a circular figure and built of clay mixed with haulm [straw or grass]. The top is conical and covered with a kind of thatch [the nature of] which I cou'd not make out. The inside roof is divided into four parts and there are cane seats raised about two feet from the ground which go round the building (I mean on the inside), broad enough to lie upon, making the wall serve the purpose of a pillow. Underneath these seats or beds they keep their potatoes and pumpions, cover'd with earth, but their corn is in a building by itself raised at least eight feet from the ground. The fire place is in the middle of the floor, just as in some parts of the Highlands of Scotland only they have no aperture at top to evacuate the smoke.[39] The door is opposite one side (for the house is round without, yet on the inside it approaches near to the figure of an octagon) and is exceeding small both in height and breadth.[40]

One of my own Choctaw informants asserted that entire canes were used for the roof of a house and anciently for the walls as well. He also claimed that, as a rule, they " walled off " only the north side of the house in order to keep the north wind from getting at them. The other winds were thought to be healthful. They also reinforced the north side with pine tops and branches. By the above statement he certainly does not mean that there was but one wall to the house—and at any rate this would be refuted by the descriptions given above—merely that the north wall was the most substantial. Weeds and similar growths were always cleaned out about a house as often as three times a year, and usually by the women. They thought if these were left " it would be a place for the devil to hide in."

Of the Choctaw house and its furniture at the opening of the nineteenth century Cushman says:

They lived in houses made of logs, but very comfortable; not more rude or uncouth, however, than many of the whites even of the present day [1899]. Their houses consisted generally of two rooms, both of which were used for every domestic purpose—cooking, eating, living and sleeping; nor was their furniture disproportionate with that of the dwelling—for the sitting room, a stool or two; for the kitchen, a pot or kettle, two or three tin cups, a large and commodious wooden bowl, and a horn spoon, constituted about the ultimatum [!]—'twas all they needed, all they wanted, and with it they were perfectly contended and supremely happy.[41]

Paths alone, plain and straight, then led the Choctaws where now are broad roads and long high bridges, from village to neighborhood, and from neighborhood to village, though many miles apart; and so open and free of logs, bushes, and all fallen timber, was their country then, rendered thus by

---

38 Copy in Miss. State Archives.
39 The home described by our anonymous Frenchman (p. 37) had two smokeholes and such an arrangement has been described to me.
40 Miss. State Archives, British Dominions.
41 H. B. Cushman: Hist. of the Choc., Chick., and Natchez Inds. Greenville, Tex., 1899. P. 231.

their annual burning off of the woods, it was an easy matter to travel in any direction and any distance, except through the vast cane-brakes that covered all the bottom lands, which alone could be passed by paths.[42]

Other travelers than the author of the Anonymous Memoir complain of Choctaw filthiness, which Bossu hardly excuses sufficiently when he says: " The Chacta men and women are very dirty, since the greater part of them live at a distance from rivers." [43] At any rate few were able to swim, as attested several times by Adair, and again by Romans, who makes an exception, however, in favor of the Chickasawhay and Yowani Indians.[44] It is, therefore, not surprising to learn from one of our earliers French authorities [45] that they used no canoes, but this was determined rather by circumstances than by taste.

For the bottom layer of logs employed in making a raft they are said to have preferred cypress and ash which they fastened together with vines, placing more logs crosswise above.

According to one of my own informants the Choctaw would not swim in running water largely from the great dread they had of snakes, but they scooped out earth close to the river bank and bathed in the water which accumulated there. This may mark an innovation in the ancient Choctaw customs.

The wooden mortars will be described more at length presently and we have no information from early writers regarding their pottery except the mere fact that they had it. The most that we know to-day is the information that has been obtained by Mr. Collins as the result of archeological work on old Choctaw village sites.[46] Their basketry industry, however, has survived to the present time. They collected the canes and made baskets from them in winter because cane is said to be too brittle in summer. The outside skins of the canes which were to be used were split off by means of a knife made especially for the purpose, and usually by the silversmith. Before the whites came it is claimed that they skinned the cane " with a whetstone made of a piece of hickory which had turned to rock." Canes were kept in stacks covered an inch or two with water. After the skins had been removed they were made into rolls of different sizes, selling about fifty years ago for 25 cents to a dollar. A 25-cent roll would make about three baskets, each holding four quarts of meal. A basket of meal packed in this way was formerly sold for 25 cents, but now it brings from 50 cents to a dollar. They had

[42] H. B. Cushman: Hist. of the Choc., Chick., and Natchez Inds. Greenville, Tex., 1899. P. 234.
[43] Appendix, p. 260; Bossu, Nouv. Voy., vol. 2, p. 94.
[44] Adair, Hist. Amer. Inds., pp. 283, 291–292, 304, 404; Romans, Nat. Hist. E. and W. Fla., pp. 72, 86.
[45] Miss. State Archives, French Dominions.
[46] Potsherds from Choctaw village sites in Mississippi. Henry B. Collins, in Journ. Washington Acad. Sci., vol. 17, no. 10, 1927, pp. 259–263.

both single-woven baskets and double-woven baskets. The following names of baskets were given me:

Nanáskáta tapushik, "a scrap basket."

Báshpo apita, "knife basket."

Shapo tapushik, the hamper carrying basket, "load basket."

Hálat nōwa tapushik, dinner basket, "to walk holding basket," hand basket.

Okhinsh apita tapushik, "medicine basket," a basket with a division in it, two lids and two handles.

Okhinsh ahoyo tapushik, "medicine gathering basket."

Ufko tapushik, fanner, a basket for sifting corn, etc.

The word for a plait or weave is pana. A single weave, skipping one, is pana chafa, a double weave, skipping two, is pana tukalo, a triple weave, skipping three, pana tuchina. A double basket is called tapushik pothoma.

A yellowish dye for baskets was obtained from puccoon or "coon" roots, walnut was employed rather rarely to give a brownish color, and maple yielded a dark purple. Roots were gathered in the fall when all the substance was in them. They were boiled until the infusion was thick, when it was strained and put into bottles. According to Simpson bottles of each kind were entrusted to each captain of the five bands which remained in Mississippi after the general removal, and if word was received that certain people were going camping and that the women of the party intended to make baskets, the captain sent them some native dye by pony. Cane was wound into a coil and boiled in a round pot containing the dye. It was turned over once unless the dye had taken hold rapidly. Then it was removed, and hung up after the liquid had been carefully shaken back into the pot. Sometimes they had pots of each of the three dyes in use at the same time.

The butt end of a cane where the outside skin was thick could be used just like a knife. It made a bad wound and cut meat like steel.

Whole canes were also used as a pallet on which to spread hides.

When a hide was to be dressed it was laced to a wooden frame by cords all around the edges. Sometimes a family had two frames, a large one for skins of larger animals like the otter, bear, and deer, and a smaller one for those of smaller animals, such as the mink, opossum, and raccoon. Or the frame might be made so that the size could be altered. It was usually movable but in any case was ordinarily located near the spring. Assuming that the frame was movable, after a skin had been fastened in place it was set in the sunshine and the flesh taken off by means of a large scraper shaped like a knife. Then the skin was worked with a dull hardwood scraper made crescent-shaped so as not to cut the skin. This work must be done a certain length of time after the hide had been removed from the animal, not while it was still green and flabby or after it had hardened. When it had been worked for a time in the sun, it was moved into the shade and worked as long again. This was to make it supple and bring out the grain, and the process required from three to five hours. When they were through and the skin was fairly dry they rolled it up and put it into a shack. If it got too damp they brought it back into the sunshine and sometimes they had to work it again.

Deerhide strings were used to fasten the ends of ball sticks after they had been bent over. The strings forming the basket at the end of the ball stick in which the ball was held were made of raccoon skin because the cords required were shorter. These raccoon skin strings were formerly sold for 15 cents apiece and the deerhide strings for 25 cents apiece. A lot of hide was usually cut up for these purposes at one time.

A large pouch was made of skins of otter, beaver, raccoon, or fox, and in this were carried grease, gun wadding and patching, which was put over a bullet like wadding and had to be of a certain thickness to go down through the gun barrel. Caps were also carried in this pouch if there was no place provided for them in the gun, and a number of small instruments, the time sticks of an officer to remind him of an appointment, and many other things besides. The doctor carried such a pouch all the time for his herbs and powders. The biggest pouch of all was made of the entire hide of a beaver. The head served as the opening and it was bent over between the rest of the pouch and the wearer's body, the tail hanging down at the side.

One could usually tell to which band of Choctaw an Indian belonged by his pouch, though they sometimes wore the same kind. The Bok Chito and Turkey Creek bands used otter skin. The Moklasha band employed skins of fox, wolf, and beaver. This last was never worn by the Bok Chitos.

There was a small pouch for powder and shot slung on the right side during a hunt so that it would be handy. This was generally made of a gourd shaped like a citron on which the skin of an otter, raccoon, or mink had been shrunk and which had afterwards been hardened. Another kind was made by sewing the same kinds of skins over a horn green and allowing them to shrink on. The horn was taken from an adult cow or ox, not so old that the horn would be brittle or so young that it would be too soft. The horn was put into boiling water and boiled until it was soft enough to be worked easily. Then the inside part of the horn would come out readily and they could bend the remainder, straighten it, ornament it, or spread it out by driving a stick into it, handling it like gutta percha

When it was stretched to suit they would make ornamental cuts or notches in it. Holes were pierced at the big end and a notch made around the little end by which to fasten cords for suspension.

To what extent the working of silver was connected with the earlier working of copper is unknown, but the idea of a bellows must have been introduced. Simpson Tubby asserts that they first worked brass taken from guns and resorted to silver later. The bellows was made of a piece of cane narrowed to a small point at one end and fitted at the other with a mouthpiece of tin, horn, or some other suitable material. Through this they were enabled to concentrate the breath on the metal, the latter being laid on one piece of flint and struck with another.

The Choctaw claim that they first obtained beads from the whites at Sugarlock, which received its name shikàlla, "beads," from the circumstance. This, of course, refers to trade beads, the introduction of which enabled the Indians to make a more lavish use of beads in belts, moccasins, and other articles of use or adornment than had before been possible. One person often wore a string of beads of different colors three or four yards in length.

In olden times they made wooden beads as big as acorns. They also strung together bushels of chinquapin nuts which they dyed with the colors used on baskets. The seeds of the red haw were also resorted to, but after they had been used at one or two social gatherings they would disintegrate and it was necessary to collect new ones. For a while they used winter berries (*Ilex verticillata?*) but later stopped the practice lest the cattle or chickens should be poisoned.[46a]

Some people wore $200 worth of silver—bracelets, anklets, ear plugs—besides beaded belts, bead necklaces, and so on. To make ear plugs they merely pierced the lobe of the ear, and Simpson himself used to do this. After the operation a weed which has a red juice was stuck through the perforation and left there until it healed.

Feathers were not merely ornaments but often had special significance. The feather headdresses of the head chief and captains will be described later. It is said that a doctor who could cure rheumatism would put a buzzard feather in his hair. There were certain men who claimed that they could stop the hooting of a common owl (ōpa), considered a sign of bad luck, and these men wore the feather of this same owl. It is said to be easy to stop the noise of a screech owl. The peafowl feather stood for prosperity and happy anticipations, because the peafowl calls out before daybreak, and so most of the men in the tribe wore such feathers. A hawk feather was worn by an active, intelligent man. Crow

---

[46a] An uncertain identification. "Winter berry" is the only common name in Lowe's "Plants of Mississippi" resembling the word "elderberry" used by Simpson. However, Miss Caroline Dorman, an authority on southern flora, thinks it is a berry popularly known as "India berry" and probably not an *Ilex*.

feathers indicated mourning and were the only ones that could be put on when there had been a death in the family. It was principally the chiefs who used them, however, the others confining themselves to black cloth. The turkey feather distinguished a good turkey hunter and also a good hunter of birds in general. When a weather prophet was seen adorned with a feather of the hushi chā'ha, "tall crane," it was a sign of wet weather; if he was seen without it the weather would be dry. A tall, stout man, or one mentally strong or conspicuously honest, donned eagle feathers. These feathers were not worn all of the time, and it is said that only in later times were they used for ornament. All kinds were resorted to except feathers of the ostrich and some other birds introduced by the whites. In later times, however, ostrich feathers seem to have taken the place of crane feathers in the headdresses of the chief and captains.

A deer tail, or, failing that, a horse tail, was mounted on a stick and fastened behind by a man who was a fast runner, particularly by a ball player. The tail of a wild cat or a tiger tail would be worn by a great fighter, and a deer tail indicated a skillful deer hunter.

As a whole their manner of life was similar to that of the Creeks,[47] and this fact is reflected in a certain agreement between the month names used by the two peoples. Regarding their method of counting time, Cushman says:

They had no calendar, but reckoned time thus: The months, by the full or crescent moons; the years by the killing of the vegetation by the wintry frosts. Thus, for two years ago the Choctaw would say: Hushuk (grass) illi (dead) tuklo (twice); literally, grass killed twice, or, more properly, two killings of the grass ago. The sun was called Nittak hushi—the Day-sun; and the moon, Nenak hushi, the Night-sun and sometimes, Tekchi hushi—the Wife of the sun. Their almanac was kept by the flight of the fowls of the air; whose coming and going announced to them the progress of the advancing and departing seasons. Thus the fowls of the air announced to the then blessed and happy Choctaw the progress of the seasons, while the beasts of the field gave to him warning of the gathering and approaching storm, and the sun marked to him the hour of the day; and so the changes of time were noted, not by figures, but by days, sleeps, suns and moons—signs that bespoke the beauty and poetry of nature. If a shorter time than a day was to be indicated an Indian drew two parallel lines on the ground, a certain distance apart, and then pointing to the sun he would say, "It is as long as it would take the sun to move from there to there." The time indicated by the moon was from its full to the next; that of the year, from winter to winter again, or from summer to summer. To keep appointments, a bundle of sticks containing the [same] number of sticks as there were days from the day of appointment to the appointed [day], was kept; and every morning one was taken out and thrown away, the last stick announced the arrival of the appointed [day]. This bundle of sticks was called Fuli (sticks) kauah (broken) broken sticks.[48]

---

[47] See Forty-second Ann. Rept. Bur. Amer. Ethn., pp. 358–470.
[48] Cushman, Hist. Inds., pp. 249–250. But fuli (or fáli) means "to peel off." There is also a reference to the counting of days by means of sticks stuck up in the ground.

In other words the Choctaw methods of reckoning time were essentially the same as those of the Creeks and other southeastern tribes. Cyrus Byington's Dictionary contains a list, or rather three lists, of month names. He says of the months: " But few Choctaws know all the names or know when the months come in or go out." I will quote from my own discussion of these lists and the attempt to reconcile them which I incorporated into Byington's Dictionary as printed in Bulletin 46 of the Bureau of American Ethnology.

At first he (Byington) inserted a list of month names in alphabetical order without stating whether they were obtained from one person or from several. Later he obtained and recorded two others, one October 23, 1854, from Ilapintàbi, and the other December 31, 1856, from Iyapàli. Ilapintàbi told him that the year began in the latter part of September, while, according to Iyapàli, it was in the latter part of March. Both of these statements are reconciled by a subsequent note to the effect that the year was divided into two series of six months each, a summer series and a winter series. From the time when these are said to have begun, September 21 and March 21, it is evident that the autumnal and vernal equinoxes were taken as starting points. The list of months obtained from Iyapàli is in almost complete agreement with the earliest list recorded by Byington, and therefore is probably more nearly correct than that of Ilapintàbi. It is as follows:

March–April	*chafo chito*, from *hohchàfo chito*, " big famine."
April–May	*hàsh koiⁿchush*, " wildcat month."
May–June	*hàsh koichito*, " panther month."
June–July	*hàsh mali* (or *mahali*), " windy month."
July–August	*hàsh watullak* (or *hàsh watonlak*), " crane month."
August–September	*tek iⁿhàshi*, " women's month "?
September–October	*hàsh bihi*, " mulberry month."
October–November	*hàsh bissa*, " blackberry month."
November–December	*hàsk haf*, perhaps *hàsh kàfi*, " sassafras month."
December–January	*hàsh takkon*, " peach month."
January–February	*hàsh hoponi*, " cooking month."
February–March	*chafiskono*, from *hohchàfo iskitini*, " little famine."

No May-June month is given in the earliest list unless it is represented by *luak mosholi*, the specific application of which is not noted, and which appears to have been questioned by Mr. Byington's later informants. Since, however, a year of twelve strictly lunar months must be corrected at intervals to agree with the solar year, the editor suggests that *luak mosholi*, which means " fire extinguished," may have been applied to an intercalary month or period at the beginning of the new year when the fires may have been extinguished and relighted, although we do not know certainly that the Choctaw shared this custom with the Creeks. Ilapintàbi's list differs from that given only in inverting *hàsh koiⁿchush* and *hàsh koichito*, and *hàsh mali* and *hàsh watullak*, the first being made to fall in May-June, the second in April-May, the third in July-August, and the fourth in June-July. This latter inversion would seem to correspond more nearly to the facts, May or early June being more likely to be windy than late June or early July. But in fact the entire series of months as recorded appears to have slipped out of place by at least one month, since there seems no good reason for calling December-January the " peach month." In the list of Creek months given by Swan February is called the " windy month," May the " mulberry month," and June the " blackberry month."

According to my Alabama and Koasati informants February was called "the month when wild peaches are ripe," March "the windy month," and July "the month when mulberries are ripe." These seem much more natural arrangements. Probably Byington's Choctaw informants had kept account of the succession of moons without noticing that the names applied to them were gradually ceasing to be appropriate owing to the difference between the lunar and the solar year. At an earlier period the two would probably have been corrected from time to time.

Cushman thus epitomizes Choctaw agricultural development:

The Choctaws have long been known to excel all the North American Indians in agriculture, subsisting to a considerable extent on the product of their fields.[49]

That this was not a late acquirement is indicated by Romans (1771), who says: "The Choctaws may more properly be called a nation of farmers than any savages I have met with; they are the most considerable people in Florida. . . . Their hunting grounds are in proportion less considerable than any of their neighbors; but as they are very little jealous of their territories, nay with ease part with them, the Chickasaws and they never interrupt each other in their hunting; as I mentioned before."[50] Elsewhere he tells us that the Chickasaw were obliged to apply to them yearly for corn and beans.[51] Their method of cultivation does not seem to have differed appreciably from that in vogue elsewhere in the Southeast. Land was cleared by burning the underbrush and smaller growth, while the trees were girdled and left to die and disintegrate gradually. Before the cornfields were cleared there was a dance. Among the Creeks planting was done in large communal fields and in small private gardens, the former divided, however, into separate plots for the families composing the town. The community field was planted and cultivated by men and women working together but the garden plots were cared for by some of the old women and were private enterprises. Among the Choctaw all memory of the communal plots has been lost and it is possible that they did not exist. The aboriginal agricultural implement was a crude hoe made out of the shoulder blade of a bison, a stone, or on the coast a large shell. A stick was also used to make holes for planting the seed which was put into hills. Small booths were constructed near the community grounds and young people stationed there to drive away the crows.

Something has been said above regarding Choctaw methods of treating corn and preparing it for food, and Romans has the following on their foods in general:

They cultivate for bread all the species and varieties of the *Zea* [maize], likewise two varieties of that species of *Panicum* [probably *Sorghum drummondii*

[49] Hist. Choc., Chick, and Natchez, p. 250.
[50] Romans, Nat. Hist. E. and W. Fla., pp. 71–72.
[51] Ibid., p. 62.

and *Panicum maximum*] vulgarly called guinea corn; a greater number of different *phaseolus* [beans] and *Dolichos* [hyacinth beans] than any I have seen elsewhere; the esculent *Convolvulus* (vulgo) sweet potatoes, and the *Helianthus giganteus* [sunflower]; with the seed of the last made into flour and mixed with flour of the *Zea* they make a very palatable bread; they have carried the spirit of husbandry so far as to cultivate leeks, garlic, cabbage and some other garden plants, of which they make no use, in order to make profit of them to the traders; they also used to carry poultry to market at Mobile, although it lays at the distance of an hundred and twenty miles from the nearest town; dunghill fowls, and a very few ducks, with some hogs, are the only esculent animals raised in the nation.

They make many kinds of bread of the above grains with the help of water, eggs, or hickory milk; they boil corn and beans together, and make many other preparations of their vegetables, but fresh meat they have only at the hunting season, and then they never fail to eat while it lasts; of their fowls and hogs they seldom eat any as they keep them for profit.

In failure of their crops, they make bread of the different kinds of *Fagus* [now including merely the beeches but then in addition the chestnut and chinquapin] of the *Diospyros* [persimmon], of a species of *Convolvulus* with a tuberous root found in the low cane grounds [wild sweet potato], of the root of a species of *Smilax* [Choctaw kantak; Creek kunti], of live oak acorns, and of the young shoots of the *Canna* [imported probably from the West Indies]; in summer many wild plants chiefly of the *Drupi* [plum] and *Bacciferous* [berry] kind supply them.

They raise some tobacco, and even sell some to the traders, but when they use it for smoking they mix it with the leaves of the two species of the *Cariaria* [sumac] or of the *Liquidambar styracistua* [*Liquidambar styraciflua*, sweet gum] dried and rubbed to pieces.[52]

Of Choctaw agriculture at a more recent day Simpson Tubby spoke as follows. The old Indian flint or flour corn had white and blue kernels intermixed. It was not good for much except roasting ears. They also had popcorn. He remembers no town fields such as the Creeks had, all of the corn in his time being planted in small patches near the houses. If the patches were large, several families would sometimes unite and cultivate them in succession, but the fields themselves were entirely separate. The old Choctaw never made the mistake of planting too early. Along with their corn they set out the old cornfield beans which were very prolific. They sometimes planted these in with the corn but more often about poles, four to six beans to a pole, and from these there would be from two to four vines. The beans too high up on the poles to be reached from the ground they left until fall, when they gathered them into hamper baskets and set them aside for seed next spring. They also planted the round melons now called Guinea melons, which can be left in the field until December and keep into the next month. Before the whites came they had pumpkins but no squashes.

---

[52] Romans, Nat. Hist. E. and W. Fla., pp. 84–85. The botanical identifications and corrections were made by Mr. Paul C. Standley and Mr. E. P. Killip. The sorghum, hyacinth beans, sweet potatoes, and, of course, the kitchen garden vegetables represent post-Columbian importations.

Mortars for pounding corn into meal were anciently made by burning hollows in the side of a prone log, a fanner being used to direct the course of the fire, but after axes and chisels were introduced by the whites, they set sections of trees on one end and hollowed out the other end with tools. Corn, hickory nuts, and wild potatoes, as well as meat, were ground up in these mortars. Hickory wood was the kind out of which they were usually made because it conveys the best taste to the food. Failing that, they employed oak, though it gives food a puckery taste. Beech could be used but it was scarce, but some woods were not used because of the bad taste they communicate, in particular maple, which gives a taste "sufficiently bad to ruin one's stomach."

They had corncribs measuring not over 8 by 10 feet, each with a single entrance. They were raised fairly high above the ground so that snakes could not seek refuge there and sting someone before they could be gotten rid of.

Hickory nuts were gathered in summer and the oil extracted from them was added to corn foods as a seasoning, though the meats were sometimes put in whole. To extract the oil they parched the nuts until they cracked to pieces and then beat them up until they were as fine as coffee grounds. They were then put into boiling water and boiled for an hour or an hour and a half, until they cooked down to a kind of soup from which the oil was strained out through a cloth. The rest was thrown away. The oil could be used at once or poured into a vessel where it would keep a long time.

Walnuts were little used for food. Very little use was made of acorns and no oil was extracted from them. Sometimes they cooked pin oak acorns with hominy but these often caused cramps.[53]

Soda or lye was made by burning pea pods. Some day when no wind was stirring to blow the resultant product away they set fire to a pile of pods and allowed the resulting ashes to settle in water. The lye from this was used until it became sour. Lye of different colors was made by the simple expedient of using different colored pods. Meat was sometimes beaten until it was tender, when it was added to hulled corn and the whole boiled for a considerable period, after which the lye was added and the whole boiled again for from 15 to 40 minutes.

My informant did not remember ever having seen bread made out of persimmons, but they had persimmon beer (not, of course, aboriginal) and a kind of persimmon soup in which the fruit was mixed with venison or beef. There were two kinds of wild plum, one of which does not ripen until late in the fall, and there is a wild crabapple. In ancient times they had no peaches.

---

[53] Acorn oil was probably used more extensively in olden times. See p. 38.

The old-time Indians did not like milk and many of them would not take coffee.

An early authority says:

In years of scarcity when the corn crop has failed, all of the savages leave the villages and go with their families to camp in the woods at a distance of 30 or 40 leagues, in places where bison (boeufs sauvages) and deer are to be found, and they live there by hunting and on (wild) potatoes.[54]

Choctaw culture thus partook of the handicap of the culture of the rest of the New World outside of the Andean region of South America in the lack of a domestic animal which could be used as food. The ill effects of this were twofold. The tribe was compelled to scatter at certain seasons of the year in search of game, and in consequence of having no animals upon or near their farms they did not learn the value of fertilizer. This also tended to obstruct the permanent occupation of any one locality and to inhibit advancement toward a higher civilization. As has been pointed out, the Choctaw did, in spite of these obstacles, reach a relatively high position among North American tribes, though this was rather on the economic than the social or ceremonial side. Considerable has been said in previous papers regarding the hunting customs of the southeastern Indians. Those of the Choctaw were essentially the same, though we do not find any reference to the communal hunt which was reported among the Natchez and in some other quarters, nor of bear preserves such as were maintained by the Creeks. It is probable that both institutions were known and occasionally resorted to, but everything connected with the economic life of the people had become centered so completely about the corn complex that hunting occupied a wholly secondary position.

Anciently the bow and arrow were of course the principal hunting implements. In recent times I am told that bows were made of white hickory or "switch hickory," which they cut in the fall, allowed to season all winter and made up in the spring. The string was of rawhide and a piece of dressed hide was used as a wrist guard. White hickory was also used for the arrow shafts because when it seasons it does not warp. As to the points, my informant, Simpson Tubby, remembers that they used the steel from women's corsets. In olden times they were of flint, cane, and perhaps bone, but nothing is now remembered regarding these. It is claimed that a hard yellow or white flint is to be had on Nanih Waiya Creek about 12 miles from Philadelphia, but the principal places of resort for flints were along Tallapoosa River, the name of which is said to refer to them.[54a] Simpson Tubby says the Choctaw used to go in

---

[54] Miss. State Arch., French Dominions.
[54a] It is probably from Alabama or Choctaw táli pushi, "pulverized rock."

crowds to a number of places on that river, including Eclectic, Horseshoe Bend, Talasi, and a place named after Tecumseh.

The present Choctaw apparently assume that the primary arrow release was the one in vogue.

However, Adair says:

'Till they were supplied by the English traders with arms and ammunition, they had very little skill in killing deer; but they improve very fast in that favourite art: no savages are equal to them in killing bears, panthers, wild cats, etc., that resort in thick cane-swamps; which swamps are sometimes two or three miles over, and an hundred in length, without any break either side of the stream.[55]

It seems that the French allowed them only a small number of guns and a limited amount of ammunition.

The French allowed none of them arms and ammunition, except such who went to war against our Chikkasah friends. One of those outstanding companies was composed also of several towns; for, usually one town had not more than from five, to seven guns. When the owners therefore had hunted one moon, they lent them for hire to others, for the like space of time; which was the reason, that their deerskins, by being chiefly killed out of season, were then much lighter than now.[56]

The following quotations from Cushman will give some idea of individual hunting as practiced by the Choctaw.

Seventy years ago,[56a] the Choctaw hunter generally hunted alone and on foot; and when he killed his game, unless small, he left it where it had fallen, and turning his footsteps homeward, traveled in a straight line, here and there breaking a twig leaving its top in the direction he had come, as a guide to his wife whom he intended to send to bring it home. As soon as he arrived, he informed her of his success and merely pointed in the direction in which the game lay. At once she mounted a pony and started in the direction indicated; and guided by the broken twigs, she soon arrived at the spot, picked up and fastened the dead animal to the saddle, mounted and soon went home again; then soon dressed and prepared a portion for her hunter lord's meal, while he sat and smoked his pipe in meditative silence. No animal adapted for food was ever killed in wanton sport by an Indian hunter. . . .

Years ago I had a Choctaw (full-blood) friend as noble and true as ever man possessed. . . . Oft in our frequent hunts together, while silently gliding through the dense forests ten or fifteen rods apart, he would attract my attention by his well known ha ha (give caution) in a low but distinct tone of voice, and point to a certain part of the woods where he had discovered an animal of some kind; and though I looked as closely as possible I could see nothing whatever that resembled a living object of any kind. Being at too great a distance to risk a sure shot, he would signal me to remain quiet, as he endeavored to get closer. To me that was the most exciting and interesting part of the scene; for then began those strategic movements in which the most skillful white hunter that I have ever seen, was a mere bungler. With deepest interest, not unmixed with excitiment, I closely watched his every movement as he slowly and stealthily advanced, with eyes fixed upon his object; now crawling noiselessly upon his hands and knees, then as motionless as a stump; now

---

[55] Adair, Hist. Am. Inds., p. 309.   [56] Ibid., pp. 284–285.   [56a] About 1830.

stretched full length upon the ground, then standing erect and motionless; then dropping suddenly to the ground, and crawling off at an acute angle to the right or left to get behind a certain tree or log, here and there stopping and slowly raising his head just enough to look over the top of the grass; then again hidden until he reached the desired tree; with intense mingled curiosity and excitement, when hidden from my view in the grass, did I seek to follow him in his course with my eyes. Oft I would see a little dark spot not larger than my fist just above the top of the grass, which slowly grew larger and larger until I discovered it was his [seemingly] motionless head; and had I not known he was there somewhere I would not have suspected it was a human head or the head of anything else; and as I kept my eyes upon it, I noticed it slowly getting smaller until it gradually disappeared; and when he reached the tree, he then observed the same caution, slowly rising until he stood erect and close to the body of the tree, then slowly and cautiously peeping around it, first on the right, then on the left; and when, at this juncture, I have turned my eyes from him, but momentarily as I thought, to the point where I thought the game must be, being also eager to satisfy my excited curiosity as to the kind of animal he was endeavoring to shoot, yet, when I looked to the spot where I had just seen him—lo! he was not there; and while wondering to what point of the compass he had so suddenly disappeared unobserved, and vainly looking to find his mysterious whereabouts, I would be startled by the sharp crack of his rifle in a different direction from that in which I was looking for him, and in turning my eye would see him slowly rising out of the grass at a point a hundred yards distant from where I had last seen him.[57]

It was truly wonderful with what ease and certainty the Choctaw hunter and warrior made his way through the dense forests of his country to any point he wished to go, near or distant. But give him the direction, [and that] was all he desired; with an unerring certainty, though never having been in that part of the country before, he would go over hill and valley, through thickets and canebrakes to the desired point, that seemed incredible. I have known the little Choctaw boys, in their juvenile excursions with their bows and arrows and blow-guns to wander miles away from their homes, this way and that through the woods, and return home at night, without a thought or fear of getting lost; nor did their parents have any uneasiness in regard to their wanderings. It is a universal characteristic of the Indian, when traveling in an unknown country, to let nothing pass unnoticed. His watchful eye marks every distinguishing feature of the surroundings—a peculiarly leaning or fallen tree, stump or bush, rock or hill, creek or branch, he will recognize years afterwards, and use them as land marks, in going again through the same country. Thus the Indian hunter was enabled to go into a distant forest, where he never before had been, pitch his camp, leave it and hunt all day—wandering this way and that over hills and through jungles for miles away, and return to his camp at the close of the day with that apparent ease and unerring certainty, that baffled all the ingenuity of the white man and appeared to him as bordering on the miraculous. Ask any Indian for directions to a place, near or distant, and he merely points in the direction you should go, regarding that as sufficient information for any one of common sense.[58]

The Choctaw hunter was famous as a strategist when hunting alone in the woods; and was such an expert in the art of exactly imitating the cries of the various animals of the forests, that he would deceive the ear of the most

---

[57] Cushman, Hist. Choc., Chick. and Natchez Indians, pp. 180–181.

[58] Ibid., p. 182.

experienced. They made a very ingeniously constructed instrument for calling deer to them, in the use of which they were very expert; and in connection with this, they used a decoy made by cutting the skin clear round the neck, about ten inches from the head of a slain buck having huge horns, and then stuffing the skin in one entire section up to the head and cutting off the neck where it joins the head. The skin, thus made hollow from the head back, is kept in its natural position by inserting upright sticks; the skin is then pulled upwards from the nose to the horns and all the flesh and brains removed; then the skin is repulled to its natural place and laid away to dry. In a year it has become dry; hard and inoffensive, and fit for use. All the upright sticks are then taken out except the one next to the head, which is left as a hand-hold. Thus the hunter, with his deer-caller and head decoy, easily enticed his game within the range of his deadly rifle; for, secreting himself in the woods, he commenced to imitate the bleating of a deer; if within hearing distance, one soon responds; but, perhaps, catching the scent of the hunter, stops and begins to look around. The hunter now inserts his arm into the cavity of the decoy and taking hold of the upright stick within, easily held it up to view, and attracted the attention of the doubting deer by rubbing it against the bushes or a tree; seeing which, the then no longer suspicious deer advanced, and only learned its mistake by the sharp crack of the rifle and the deadly bullet.[59]

On hunting excursions, when a party moved their camp to another point in the woods, whether far or near, they invariably left a broken bush with the top leaning in the direction they had gone, readily comprehended by the practiced eye of the Choctaw hunter. They kept on a straight line to where a turn was made, and whatever angle there taken, they travelled it in a straight line, but left the broken bush at the turn indicating the direction they had taken. If a wandering hunter happened to stumble upon the late deserted camp and desired to join its former occupants, the broken but silent bush gave him the information as to the direction they had taken. He took it and traveled in a straight line perhaps for several miles; when suddenly his ever watchful eye saw a broken bush with its top leaning in another direction. He at once interpreted its mystic language—"Here a turn was made." He too made the turn indicated by the bush; and thus traveled through the unbroken forest for miles, directed alone by his silent but undeviating guide, which was sure to lead him to his desired object.[60]

Small game, such as rabbits, squirrels, and birds, were killed by means of the blowgun, but in old times this was handled mostly by boys. Bossu says that the boys " are very skilful in the use of the blowgun. It is made of a cane about seven feet long, into which they put a little arrow provided with thistle-down, and when they see something [which they want to hit] they blow into it, and they often kill small birds." [61]

In our attempts to visualize pre-Columbian hunting among the Choctaw we must, of course, drop horses out of the picture. Later, while they never came to occupy the position which they held among the Plains tribes, their place was an important one. The Indian woman of the Southeast had particular reason to be thankful for

---

[59] Cushman, Hist. Choc., Chick. and Natchez Inds., p. 197.
[60] Ibid., pp. 234–235.
[61] Appendix, p. 263; Bossu, Nouv. Voy., vol. 2, p. 103.

their coming, for the horse relieved her of much of her former labor in bringing game home to camp or to the permanent dwelling after a successful hunting season. Regarding the Choctaw horse and his significance to the family which owned him, as observed in the nineteenth century, Cushman has the following:

The famous little Choctaw pony was a veritable forest camel to the Choctaw hunter, as the genuine animal is to the sons of Ishmael. His unwearied patience, and his seemingly untiring endurance of hardships and fatigue, were truly astonishing—surpassing, according to his inches, every other species of his race—and proving himself to be a worthy descendant of his ancient parent, the old Spanish war-horse, introduced by the early Spanish explorers of the continent. In all the Choctaws' expeditions, except those of war in which they never used horses, the chubby little pony always was considered an indispensable adjunct, therefore always occupied a conspicuous place in the cavalcade. A packsaddle which Choctaw ingenuity had invented expressly for the benefit of the worthy little fellow's back, and finely adapted in every particular for its purpose, was firmly fastened upon his back, ready to receive the burden, which was generally divided into three parts, each weighing from forty to fifty pounds. Two of these were suspended across the saddle by means of a rawhide rope one-fourth of an inch in diameter and of amazing strength, and the third securely fastened upon the top, over all of which a bear or deer skin was spread, which protected it from rain. All things being ready, the hunter, as leader and protector, took his position in front, sometimes on foot and sometimes astride a pony of such diminutive proportions, that justice and mercy would naturally have suggested a reverse in the order of things, and, with his trusty rifle in his hand, without which he never went anywhere, took up the line of march, and directly after whom, in close order, the loaded ponies followed in regular succession one behind the other, while the dutiful wife and children brought up the rear in regular, successive order, often with from three to five children on a single pony—literally hiding the submissive little fellow from view. Upon the neck of each pony a little bell was suspended, whose tinkling chimes of various tones broke the monotony of the desert air, and added cheerfulness to the novel scene.

Long accustomed to their duty, the faithful little pack-ponies seldom gave any trouble, but in a straight line followed on after their master; sometimes, however, one here and there, unable to withstand the temptation of the luxuriant grass that offered itself so freely along the wayside, would make a momentary stop to snatch a bite or two, but the shrill, disapproving voice of the wife in close proximity behind, at once reminded him of his dereliction of order and he would hastly trot up to his position; and thus the little caravan, with the silence broken only by the tinkling pony bells, moved on amid the dense timber of their majestic forests, until the declining sun gave warning of the near approaching night. Then a halt was made, and the faithful little ponies, relieved of their wearisome loads which they had borne through the day with becoming and uncomplaining patience, were set free that they might refresh themselves upon the grass and cane—nature's bounties to the Indian— that grew and covered the forests in wild abundance. Late next morning— (for who ever knew an Indian, in the common affairs of life, to be in a hurry or to value time? Time! He see it not; he feels it not; he regards it not. To him 'tis but a shadowy name—a succession of breathings, measured forth by the change of night and day by a shadow crossing the dial-path of life) the rested and refreshed ponies were gathered in, and, each having received his former load, again the tinkling chimes of the pony bells alone disturbed the quiet of the then far extending wilderness, announcing in monotonous tones the onward march, as the day before, of the contented travelers; and thus was the journey continued, day by day, until the desired point was reached.[62]

Simpson Tubby says that the Choctaw were in the habit of living on squirrels and other small game animals in summer and on large game animals in winter. Dogs were not employed in hunting or for any useful purpose whatever. Deer were stalked at night by means of torches held just back of the head so as not to interfere with their view of the game. The Tombigbee River was a winter hunting ground and they also collected cane there. For pigeons they went to Pigeon Roost, near Macon, Miss. There was a favorite place for squirrels and turkeys called Tashka himmita, "Young Warrior." About 9 miles east of Philadelphia, Miss., and extending for some 20 miles, is another great squirrel section, called Fáni yakni, "squirrel country." Philadelphia itself is named Fáni yakni támaha, "Squirrel-country town." Táshka himmita was not only a famous place for squirrels and turkeys but for beaver, otter, raccoon, opossum, rabbits, and other game, and the Indians formerly congregated there in numbers. They approached game from the lee side so as not to be detected. When game animals came out of the water the hunter would creep up on them, try to intercept them, and shoot them with arrows, but as they often slid back into the water and were lost the chief appointed fast runners to go after the water animals and kill them with clubs. The game was subsequently distributed to the various camps, as was usual on all occasions. If any one of the five Choctaw bands killed a deer it would send to the band nearest it to come over and take a share of the kill home. Indeed, the invitation was extended as widely as the success of the hunt warranted. A similar distribution was made in the case of a surplus catch of fish.

It is claimed that the old native game laws were as strict as those of the present day, the amount of game that might be killed being determined in advance. The various families camped wherever they pleased but the captain of each of the five bands had to find out how much his hunters killed each month and report it to the head chief. During the last of February and March "they would no more kill a rabbit than they would a horse." In the summertime, at least in one place, there were other reasons for refraining from rabbit hunting. The name of a former town, Kastasha, "flea place," was given because there were more rabbits there than anywhere else and all of them were full of fleas. For that reason there was a law against killing any more than they could help in summer, i. e., until after the first heavy frost.

---

[62] Cushman, Hist. Choc., Chick., and Natchez Inds., pp. 235–236.

NANIH WAIYA AS IT APPEARED IN 1918

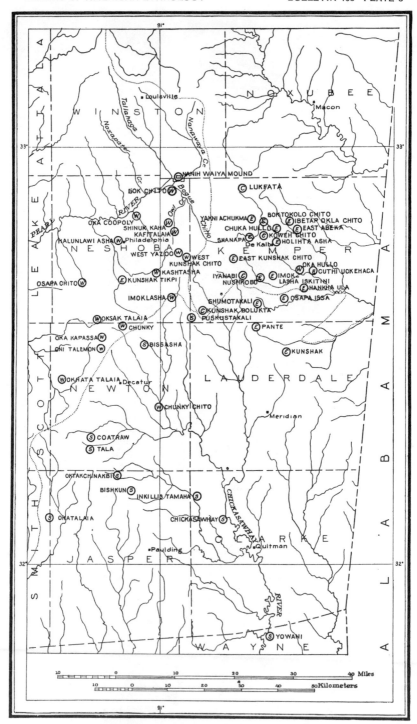

THE OLD CHOCTAW COUNTRY, MISSISSIPPI

C, E, S, W.—Towns belonging to the Central, Eastern, Southern, and Western divisions of the
nation, respectively.   The dotted lines indicate the boundaries between the three latter divisions
in the early part of the nineteenth century.

Simpson speaks of Choctaw woodcraft in much the same terms as does Cushman. When in a strange country the leader of a band of Indians would break twigs to mark the course his followers were to take, or a pole was pointed in that direction and a number of twigs laid at its base to indicate how many miles they were to go.

A fish diet was thought highly of by the ancient Choctaw. Nanih Waiya was the principal fish stream in the Choctaw country but it is claimed that the Indians did not fish in it until the white people brought fishhooks into the country. This was largely because it never goes dry and forms pools that may be poisoned or dragged. When they poisoned a pool with buckeye they cut down trees and bushes and piled them up about it so as to keep the stock away and cautioned their people not to drink from it. For this purpose they also used winter berries and devil's shoestring. The latter is so weak that a great quantity is required, but winter berries (see p. 43) falling into a stream naturally will drive fish away. Ordinarily the Choctaw did not allow anyone to poison the pools but dragged them with a drag made of brush fastened together with creepers. When the water was deep, ponies and oxen were secured to the drag at intervals and men sat upon it to keep it down. The fish caught were trout, jacks, perch, suckers, and sometimes catfish. Regarding the sucker, the claim is made that it can be driven ashore by the simple expedient of throwing objects just behind it one after the other. In poisoning and dragging they were allowed to keep only enough for their families; any surplus must be sent to one of the other bands. If this were not done the credit reposed in the stingy band was destroyed.

They did not allow fish to be shot in the streams but it was permitted in the lakes and rivers at certain seasons.

Big flakes of salt used to appear on the ground at Blue Licks in Noxubee County, and the people resorted to that place in winter to collect them.

SOCIAL ORGANIZATION

GEOGRAPHICAL DIVISIONS AND TOWNS

(See Pl. 3)

When Europeans came to know this tribe intimately, and from that time on, three geographical divisions were recognized, but a careful examination shows that we must treat them as four in order to introduce any order into the several town classifications which have come down to us. It seems pretty clear that the Sixtown Indians (Okla Hannali) and their immediate neighbors, who lived in the southern part of the old Choctaw territory, were early differentiated from the rest, the separation being partly linguistic and partly cultural. Sometimes this division is limited absolutely to the six towns which gave it its name, but more often it is extended to include certain neighboring towns, particularly Chicasawhay and Yowani, which seem to have shared in some measure the peculiarities of the group. Another small body, centrally located, embraced those towns in which, early in the eighteenth century, lived the principal officials of the entire nation, the Kunshak or Cane towns being particularly noteworthy among them. The importance of this group is reflected in the name which Régis du Roullet gives to it, the Big People (Okla Chito). The remaining towns were divided into two parties, one to the west known as the "Long People" (Okla Falaya), and one to the east, the "People of the Opposite Side (or Party)" (Okla tȧnnȧp).

The French officer De Lusser (1730), who was the first to mention any of the above divisions, seems to have heard of but two, corresponding to the ones last mentioned, but two years later Du Roullet adds the central group. The author of the Anonymous Memoir is the first to separate the Sixtowns (Okla Hannali) from the rest, though he commits a curious blunder by calling them the towns "of the east." He also retains the central group, naming it, through an equally curious mis-orientation, the division "of the south." However, the native title he gives as "Taboka," which may be from tabo'koa, "noon"; and hence the position of the sun at noon, i. e., the south. His "western" division seems to include both the eastern and western parties of other writers. The native name for this, as transmitted by him, is "Ougoula tanama." "Ougoula" is, of course, okla, "people." Tanama I at first traced to tanampi, "to fight," but I now think it probable that it is identical with tȧnnȧp, "the other (or opposite) side." This is, as we have seen, Du Roullet's name for the eastern party but it is possible that it was applied reciprocally to the division on the east by those on the west and the division on the west by those on the east. In later lists the central division disappears, its towns being placed partly in the western group, partly in the eastern group, and a few perhaps in the southern group. The western division also appears as the "Big Party" and the eastern as the "Little Party." From an original status as an apparently loose classification of towns the three divisions came finally to have rather clearly marked geographical boundaries, which have been discussed with great care by Halbert.[63]

There were variations of speech not only between the Sixtown Indians and the rest but between the speech of the other parties, but in course of time that of the western group, the Long People, came to be recognized as standard Choctaw.

---

[63] "District Divisions of the Choctaw Nation," in Trans. Ala. Hist. Soc., I, pp. 375–385. See map, Pl. 2.

A late name given to the eastern Choctaw division was Ahepat okla, " Potato-eating People," or Haiyip atokolo, " Second Lake," or " Two Lakes." The first was obtained by Halbert from an old Choctaw. The second was the only one known to my own informants. I am inclined to think that my informants were right, because Haiyip atokolo was also the name of a minor group within the eastern division, and both of the terms Sixtown and Long People were also applied to smaller bands or cantons.

The Sixtown Indians were regarded with some show of contempt by the other Choctaw and their speech was made a subject of ridicule, but they seem to have contributed their full share, if not somewhat more than their full share, to the political and intellectual development of the tribe.   Milfort's unfavorable comments on the southern Choctaw as compared with the northern section of the nation [64] may be attributed in great measure to this internal attitude on the part of the Choctaw themselves and in part to superficial nonconformities with the usages of neighboring tribes, such as a difference in their mode of wearing the hair.   Anciently all Choctaw men, as well as the women, allowed their hair to grow long and hence the tribe were often known as " Long Hairs " (Pan̄s falaya).[65] As late as 1771 Romans tells us that both sexes still wore their hair in this manner " except some young fellows who began to imitate the Chickasaw fashion.[66]   Between twenty and thirty years later, however, Milfort found the northern Choctaw had their hair cut in the Creek manner,[67] which would be practically identical with that of the Chickasaw.   Wholly peculiar to the Sixtowns seems to have been the custom of tattooing blue marks at the corners of the mouth, from which circumstance they acquired the name of " Bluemouth " (or "Blewmouth ") Indians used by some early writers. Certain Choctaw say that the Haiyip atokolo were distinguished by the use of earrings, but others simply state that the eastern and western sections were marked off from the others by the manner in which they wore their ornaments.

These divisions played a great part in the civil war which broke out in the first half of the eighteenth century, instigated by British and French emissaries.   The eastern or Little Party was that principally devoted to the French while the western or Big Party was largely committed to the English, Red Shoes (Shulush Homa), their principal leader, belonging to the western town of Kastasha.   In a letter dated January 12, 1751, Governor Vaudreuil states that the eastern division was the weakest but that, with the help of the

---

[64] Appendix, p. 264; Milfort, Mém., p. 288.
[65] Adair, Hist. Am. Inds., p. 192.
[66] B. Romans, Nat. Hist. E. and W. Fla., p. 82.
[67] Appendix, p. 264; Milfort, op. cit., p. 288.

French and the Indians of Kunshak and Chickasawhay, it had become the strongest and had prevailed. A part of the Sixtown Indians sided with the English, one town in particular committing itself so far in their favor as to be renamed Inkilis Tamaha, or English Town. Tala is also known to have belonged to their party as well as Nuskobo, of which much less is heard, and indeed the ancient Choctaw " capital," Koweh chito, was anglophile.

To date eight authorities for the names of the Choctaw towns are known to us: Iberville (1702), De Lusser (1730), Régis du Roullet (1732), De Crenay (1733), a French Memoir dated conjecturally in 1755, but probably belonging to or representing a still earlier period, a list compiled in 1764 to assist the English in their dealings with the Choctaw, Romans (1771), and a list made in connection with a treaty between Col. Don Estevan Miró, Governor of Louisiana, and Lieut. Col. Don Enrique Gumarest, Military and Civil Governor of Fort Carlota de la Movila, on one side and the Choctaw Nation on the other, July 13–14, 1784.[68] In connection with the Romans list we have the advantage of a careful review and criticism by Henry S. Halbert. It is unfortunate that, when his commentary was published, he did not have access to the other lists mentioned. In the following table all are reproduced, together with Mr. Halbert's identifications and interpretations, and any other interpretations which the writer has been able to supply.

The letters C, E, W, and S placed after the names of towns indicate the division in which the author of that particular list has placed them, whether Central, Eastern, Western, or Sixtown (i. e., Southern). After names given on the authority of Bernard Romans, (M) indicates one taken from his map, (N) one from his narrative, and (WFM) one from a West Florida Map supposed to have been based, at least in part, on his notes.

---

[68] Documents concernant l'histoire des Indiens de la région orientale de la Louisiane, by Le Baron Marc de Villiers (Journal de la Société des Américanistes de Paris, n. s., vol. XIV, 1922, pp. 138–139) ; Ms. Journal in the archives of the Ministry of the Colonies, transcribed for the Library of Congress, Ms. Division ; Notes sur les Chactas d'après les Journaux de Voyage de Régis du Roullet (1729–1732), by Le Baron Marc de Villiers (Journal de la Société des Américanistes de Paris, n. s., vol. XV, pp. 244–248) ; Ms. map in the archives of the Ministry of the Colonies, Paris, copies of which were obtained by Mr. Peter A. Hamilton, of Mobile, who also reproduced portions of it in Colonial Mobile, ed. of 1910, pp. 190, 196, also Pl. 5 in Bull. 73, Bur. Amer. Ethn. ; Ms. French Memoir in the Ayer collection of Americana, Newberry Library, Chicago (see Appendix, p. 257) ; Mississippi Provincial Archives (1763–1766), ed. by Dunbar Rowland, vol. 1, pp. 26–28 ; Bernard Romans, Natural History of East and West Florida, map republished in Vol. 2 of the Publications of the Florida State Historical Society ; copies of Mss. in the Mississippi State Department of Archives and History, Jackson, Miss.

CHOCTAW TOWNS
SOUTHERN OR SIXTOWN DIVISION

Name and meaning	Location	Map of 1733	Iberville (1702)	Ms. of 1755	De Lusser (1730)
1. Nashobawenya, "howling wolf"	S. W. part of Jasper Co	Nachoubaotianja		Nachoubaoüenya (S)	Nacchoubanouanya (W) / Nacchoubanfouny (probably a second form of the same name).
2. Oskelagna, "yellow cane"	Probably in Jasper Co	Tala		Osque alagna (S)	Ouskelagana (W).
3. Tala, "palmetto"	S. part of Newton Co., between Tarlow and Bogue Felamma Creeks.	Tala		Tala (S)	Tala (W).
4. Siniasha, "sycamore place"	Uncertain	Señeacha			Cheniacha (W).
F. Boktoloksi, "little two-streams"	On Boguetuluksi Cr., a S. W. affluent of Chickasawhay R.	Bouktouloukché		Bouktouloutchy (S)	Bouctouloury (W).
6. Coussanna, Cousanna (or Tousanna). (This and the five above were the original six towns.)	Unknown. Probably identical with No. 7.				
7. Inkillis tamaha, "English town" (as the chief of Coussana (No. 6) was a strong partisan of the English, it is probable that this and No. 6 are identical.)	N. E. part of Jasper Co				
8. Chickasawhay (Du Roullet says from the name of a bayou).	On Chickasawhay R., about 3 m. S. of Enterprise, Clarke Co.	Chicachaé		Chicachae (S)	Chicachae (E).
9. Yowani, (Choc. haiyowăni, "June bug").	E. side of Chickasawhay R., in the S. part of Wayne Co.	Youané		Youanny (S)	Ouani (E).
10. Talapokta, "palmetto (where two bayous) unite"—Du Roullet.	Jasper Co	Talapoucta			
11. Chiskilikbacha, "blackjacks in a row".	Probably in Jasper Co				
12. Puskustakali, "child hanging"	S. W. corner of Kemper Co. or the proximate part of Neshoba Co.		Pousconiche tacase	Louscouchetacanlé (W)	Pouscouchelacaie (W).

CHOCTAW TOWNS—Continued

SOUTHERN OR SIXTOWN DIVISION—Continued

Name and meaning	Location	Map of 1733	Iberville (1702)	Ms. of 1755	De Lusser (1730)
13. Bissasha, "blackberry place" (If the forms Beyacha and Beacha could be relied upon Du Roullet's interpretation, "mulberry place" would be correct.)	W. side of Little Rock Cr., in Newton Co., sect. 23, tp. 8, range 12 E.	Bessacha		Bisacha (W)	Bistacha (W).
14. Oktak chito tamaha, "big prairie town."	Unknown				
15. Oktakchinakbi (abbr. Chinakbi), "crooked prairie."	Site of Garlandville, Jasper Co.				
16. Bishkun	N. part of Jasper Co.		Busca (?)		
17. Okatalaia, "spreading (or stagnant) water."	E. part of Smith Co. or W. part of Jasper Co.				
18. Coatraw (a map name evidently misspelled, and probably identical with that of another town of this group, perhaps Tala).	4 m. S. W. of the town of Newton, in sect. 17, tp. 5, range 11 E., Newton Co.				
19. Sakti tamaha, "bluff town"	Unknown				
20. Ikechana, perhaps "notched stick"	do				
21. Shumotakali, "moss (or thistle-down) hanging."	Unknown (there was another town of this name, No. 96).				
22. Tinsealtla (perhaps from tinshkila, "blue jay").	Unknown				
23. Chucafalaya, "long house"	do				
24. Oulacha, perhaps "where there is a brush arbor."	do				
25. Osapa chito, "big field"	Unknown (there was another town of this name, No. 45).				

CENTRAL DIVISION

	Location				
26. Kunshak, "cane (town)," The cane is that from which knives were made.	Lost Horse Cr., 4 m. S. E. of Lazelis, Lauderdale Co.	Conche		Conchats (E)	Conchas (E).
27. Kunshak chito, "big cane (town)"	On or near the upper course of Oktibbeha Cr.			Conchabouloucta (W)	
28. Kunshak bolukta, "round cane brake."	In the S. W. part of Kemper Co., some 2 m. from the Neshoba Co. line, and 1½ from the Lauderdale Co. line.				
29. Okalusa, "black water"	In Romens's time on White's Br., Kemper Co.	Okeloussa	Ougiloussa	Oqué loüsa (E)	Okeloussa (W).
30. Bokfalaia, "long creek" (a village dependent on No. 29) but classed by Du Roullet with the West towns).	Uncertain.	Boukfalaya	Boucfalaya	Boucfalaya (W)	Boucfalaya (E).
31. Iyanábi, "ironwood"	On Yannubbee Cr., about 8 m. S. W. of De Kalb, Kemper Co.	Yanabe	Ayanabé augoula	Yanabé (E)	Yanabé (W),[2]
32. Koweh chito, "a great league" ("because it was a great league in circuit").[1]	N. W. of De Kalb, Kemper Co.	Couentchitou or grand village.	Coincho thoucoua logoule (?).	Coït chitou (E)	Couenchito (E).[3]
33. Boktokolo, "two creeks"	Unknown.	Bouktoukoulou.	Bouctoucoulo	Bouctoucoüiloü (2d) (W)	
34. Boktokolo chito, "big two-creeks"	At the confluence of Running Tiger and Sukenatcha Creeks, about 4 m. N. W. o' De Kalb.		Bouctoucoula	Bouctoucoüiloü (W)	Bouctouconlou (E).
35. Lukfata, "chalk," "white clay"	Headwaters of one of the prongs of Sukenatcha Cr.	Loukfata.		Loucféatá (W)	Loucfeata (E).
36. Skanapa, "the unfortunate ones,"—Du Roullet (fr. ish-kanapa "a disaster").	Probably on Running Tiger Cr., Kemper Co.	Schkanapa.	Iscananba Thousena Togrule.	Scanapa (W)	Scanapa (E).

[1] Du Roullet confounds the word koweh with the word meaning "panther," which is identical in form.

[2] Another Ms. source also places this town in the Western Division.

[3] Another Ms. source places it in the Western Division.

CHOCTAW TOWNS—Continued

WESTERN DIVISION

Name and meaning	Location	Map of 1733	Iberville (1702)	Ms. of 1755	De Lusser (1730)
37. West Kunshak chito (contr. West Congeeto), "west big cane town."	Neshoba Co., near the headwaters of Oktibbeha Cr.				
38. Abissa ("village of the mulberries"—Du Roullet; from bihi, "mulberries," and asha, "are there").	Uncertain	Abissa		Abissa (W)	Abissa (E).
39. Yazoo, or West Yazoo.	Neshoba Co., near the headwaters of Oktibbeha Cr., in sections 13 and 24, tp. 10, range 13 east.	Yazou	Yachou	Yachou (W)	Yazoux (W).
40. Imoklasha, "their people are there" (name of one of the moieties).	On the headwaters of Talasha Cr., Neshoba Co., in sections 4, 9, and 16, tp. 9, range 13 east.	Mongoulacha	Mogoulacha	Mongoulacha (W)	Mongoulacha (W).
41. Kashtasha, "place of fleas" (often the residence of the chief of the Western Division).	S. side of Custusha Cr., about 3 m. a little S. of W. of West Yazoo Town.	Castacha	Cachetacha	Castacha (W)	Kastacha (W).
42. Kafitalaia, "sassafras thicket"	On Owl Cr., in sect. 21, tp. 11, range 13 E., Neshoba Co.	Caffetalaya	Cafeta saya	Caffetalaya (W)	Kafetalaya (W).
43. West Abeka (fr. aiabeka, "unhealthful place").	Unidentified	Abeka	Abiska Thocalogoule	Abeca (W)	Apeca (W).
44. Utapacha, "rows of chestnut trees."	...do	Outapacha		Outapacha (W)	
45. Osapa chito, "big (corn) field"	Site of Dixon P. O., Neshoba Co. (a second town so called; see No. 25).				
46. Okehanea tamaha, perhaps "town in a triangle marked out by streams of water."	Unknown		Ocouhinan		
47. Oksak talaia, "hickory grove."	Near the line between Neshoba and Kemper Counties.				
48. Chunky, perhaps referring to the chunkey game.	On the site of Union, Newton Co.	Tchanké		Etchanqué (W)	Tchanké W.

No. and name	Location				
49. Chunky chito, "big chunkey"	W. bank of Chunky Cr., about half a mile below the confluence of that creek with Talasha Cr. Halbert says this territory was later in the Sixtowns District.				
50. Itichipota, "little trees." Halbert says "each other's children," but is probably wrong.	Between the headwaters of Chickasawhay and the Tombigbee.	Y téchipouta	Y ty thipouta	Stéchipouta (W)	Itéchipouta (E).
51. Bok chito, "big creek."	Probably on Bogue Chitto, Neshoba and Kemper Counties.	Bouktchito			Bouehito (E).
52. Atlantchiton (tchitou, "big").	Unknown	Atlantchitou			Aloné Echito (1729).
53. Hashuk chuka, "grass house"	...do	Achouktchouka			Atchouchouga (W).
54. Bokfoka, "about (or near) the creek." In 1784 it is placed in the Eastern Division.	...do	Boucffouca		Boucfouca (W)	Bouefouka (W).
55. Tiwæle.	...do	Tiotíselé	Tohia sale	Totíaalé (W)	
56. Fani tallemon, said to sig. "land abounding in squirrels" (said by De Lusser to be a dependency of No. 54).	...do			Fílitamon (W)	
57. Oklabalbaha, "people talking unintelligibly," as in a foreign tongue.	Unknown			Ougoulabalbaa (W)	
58. Oka hullo, "sacred (or beloved) water."	Probably on or near the mouth of Sanotœ Cr., which empties into Petickfa Cr., Kemper Co.			Oqué ouïloü (W)	Okeouïlou (W).
59. Otuk falaia (falaia, "long").	Unknown			Otouc falayâ (W)	
60. Hashuk homa, "red grass"	...do			Achouqouma (W)	
61. Okatanap, "war people," so called because on the Chickasaw frontier and fortified.	...do			Ougoulatanap (W)	
62. Oni talemon, "where there are wild onions."—Du Roullet.	S. of Pinckney Mill, Newton Co. (possibly in the S. Division).				
63. Oka kapassa, "cold water."	About Pinckney Mill, in section 23, tp. 8, range 11 E., Newton Co. (possibly in S. Division).				
64. Shinuk kaha, "lying in the sand".	About 7 m. a little N. of E. of Philadelphia, Neshoba Co.				

CHOCTAW TOWNS—Continued
WESTERN DIVISION—Continued

Name and meaning	Location	Map of 1733	Iberville (1702)	Ms. of 1755	De Lusser (1730)
65. Oka coopoly, perhaps "water where the biting is" (oka akobli).	On Ocobly Cr., Neshoba Co.				
66. Halunlawi asha, "bullfrog place".	On the site of Philadelphia, Neshoba Co				
67. Lushapa, perhaps intended for Lusalaka, "swamp edge (or border)."	Perhaps on Lussalaka Cr., a tributary of Kentarcky Cr., Neshoba Co.				
68. Oka chippo, perhaps from Oka shippa, "water run down" from a scant supply of water.	Unknown				
69. Konshak osapa, "canebrake field".	Somewhere W. of West Imoklasha		Onsacousba (?)		
70. Tonicahaw, perhaps Tonik hikia, "standing post."	Unknown				
71. Cabea hoola.	do				
72. Okapoola.	do				
73. Wiatakali, "hanging loft" (or arbor), so named from a brush arbor under which these people were accustomed to meet.	About 1 m. S. of the De Kalb and Jackson road, Neshoba Co.	Ayoutakale (?)			
74. Fani yakni, "squirrel country".	Unknown				Faniakné (W).
75. Shinuk chukillissa, "the deserted sand."	do				
76. Nita asha, "bears' home" (already abandoned in 1702).	do				
77. Balupak, probably "where there are slippery elms" (balup).	do				
78. Ite ousano, "hard wood"—Du Roullet.	do				
79. Kinte oké, "water where there are beaver," or "beaver there."	do				
80. Nusi kon chitto, "big acorns".	do				
81. Okhata talaia, "spreading pond".	In the Conehatta District of Newton Co., SW. corner sect. 11, tp. 7, range 10 east.				

EASTERN DIVISION

82. Holihta asha, "fort place"	Site of De Kalb, Kemper Co	Oulectacha	Tolistache Boulistaché (perhaps repeated).	Oulitacha (W).	Oulictacha (W).
83. Chichatalya (talya=talaia, "to stand").	Unknown				
84. East Abeka (Abeka—from aiabeka, "unhealthful place").	At the junction of Straight Creek with the Sukanatcha, Kemper Co.	Abeka	Abiska	Abeca (W).	Apeca (W).
85. Ibetap okla iskitini, "little source people."	At the head of the main prong of Yazoo Cr., Kemper Co.	Bitoupougoula le petit.	Bitabogoula	Ebitoupougoula (W).	Bitoupgoula (E).
86. Kunshak tikpi, "canebrake knob."	On Coonshark Cr., a tributary of Kentarcky Cr., Neshoba Co.	Yteoutchako	Itouichacou	Iteókchaqüo (or Iteópchaqüo) (W). Osapaissa (W).	Iteotchako (W).
87. Itokchako, "green wood"	Near East Abeka, Kemper Co				
88. Osapa issa "field abandoned"	N. side o: Blackwater Cr., Kemper Co.				
89. Yazoo iskitini, "little Yazoo"	Both sides of Yazoo Cr., between its mouth and the fork, 1 m. above.	Yazou	Yacho	Yachoï or Achoualoüá (W).	Yasoux (E) (and Alibamons chougalougole).
90. Ibetap okla chito, "big source people."	Perhaps on Straight Cr., Kemper Co.	Bitoupougoula le grand.	Bita bogoula	Ebitoupougoula (W).	Bitoupgoula (W).
91. Imoklasha iskitini, "little band of relations." (See No. 40.)	On Flat Cr., the E. prong of Yazoo Cr., Kemper Co.	Mongoulacha	Mongoulacha	Mongoulacha (W).	Mongoulacha (W).
92. Pachanucha, "where the pigeons sleep."—Du Roullet.	Unknown	Patchanoucha			
93. Athlepole, probably from alipilla, "at or toward the end."	...do	Athlépelé			Attepelé (W).
94. Chuka lusa, "black house"	...do	Tchuké lussa			Chonkelissa (E).
95. Hankha ula, "wild goose crying."	On a flat-topped ridge between the Pettickfa and Blackwater Creeks, in Kemper Co.				
96. East Kunshak chito (contr. East Congeeto), "east big cane town."	Near Moscow, Kemper Co.				
97. Shumotakali, "moss hanging" (a second town so called; see No. 21).	Kemper Co., between the two head prongs of Blackwater Cr.				
98. Watonlula, "whooping crane"	Uncertain	Ouantonloula	Suabonloula	Ouatonaoüá (W).	Ouantoroullon (E).

CHOCTAW TOWNS—Continued

EASTERN DIVISION—Continued

Name and meaning	Location	Map of 1733	Iberville (1702)	Ms. of 1755	De Lusser (1730)
99. Pante, Du Roullet says from pinti, "mouse," referring to "white rats found in the prairies."	At head of Ponta Cr., Lauderdale Co.	Pante		Pinté (W)	Panty (E).
100. Cutha simethaw	Unknown				
101. Oka altakala, probably "between the waters."	Probably at the confluence of Petickfa and Yannubbee Creeks, Kemper Co.				
102. Nushkobo, "head" 1	Perhaps on or near Petickfa Cr., Kemper Co.				
103. Yakni achukma, "good land"	Perhaps on Indian branch of Running Tiger Cr.				
104. Chuka hullo, "sacred (or beloved) house."	On the N. side of Sukenatcha Cr., somewhere between the mouths of Running Tiger and Straight Creeks, Kemper Co.				
105. Cuthi uckehaca	Probably on or near the mouth of Parker's Cr., which empties into Petickfa Cr., in sect. 30, tp. 10, range 17 E.				
106. Yanatoe	Probably in S. W. Kemper Co.				
107. Alamucha	10 m. from Sukenatcha Cr., Kemper Co.				

TOWNS OF UNCERTAIN POSITION

108. Thicacho oulasta, perhaps Chicacha oulasita, from "Chickasaw," olasi, "near" and some verbal ending (possibly intended for No. 60).	Unknown		Thicacho oulasta		

109. Ahipata bita Brugoula, perhaps contains ibitáp and okla, and was a 3d town of the name. It may have been an independent tribe at one time, as there was a tribe of the name on Yazoo R. Ahipata may mean "potatoes spread about," indicating a place where they were common.[2]	do	Ahipata bita Brugoula	
110. Tabogoula, may be from the same root as the above or the same as Taboka, one name applied to a band of Choctaw.	do	Tabogoula	
111. Thata tascanan gouchy, probably Cha'ta tascanan gouchy, from the name of the Choctaw and táshka nangushi, the title of an official.	do	Thata tascanan gouchy	
112. Choutoua togoule, the latter part perhaps from okla, "people," and toklo, "two," or takali, "hanging."	do	Choutoua togoule	

TOWNS OUTSIDE OF THE ORIGINAL TOWN CLUSTER

113. Teeakhaily ekutapa, the first word sig. "standing pine."	On the lower Tombigbee R.
114. Chisha foka, "among the post-oaks."	On the site of Jackson, Miss
115. Shukhata, "opossum".	On the site of Columbus, Ala

[1] This was abandoned, whether permanently or not is uncertain, in 1748.

[2] The name ahipaṭ okla is said to have been one of those applied to the Eastern Division of the Nation. See p. 57.

CHOCTAW TOWNS—Continued

SOUTHERN OR SIXTOWN DIVISION

Name and meaning	Location	Doc. of 1764	Romans's Map & Narr. 1771	Journal of Régis du Roullet (1732)	Spanish List of 1784
1. Nashobawenya, "howling wolf".	S. W. part of Jasper Co.	Natchoubaouenia (S).	Nashoopawaya.	Nachou baouania (W).	Nachuba huanya (S).
2. Oskelagna, "yellow cane".	Probably in Jasper Co.	Oskelagana (S).	Oskelagna.	Oske laguna (W).	Usque lagana (S).
3. Tala, "palmetto".	S. part of Newton Co., between Tarlow and Bogue Felamma Creeks.	Tala (S).	Tallaw.	Tala (W).	Tala (S).
4. Siniasha, "sycamore place".	Uncertain.	Séneachaes (S).	Shanhaw (W FM).	Seneacha (W).	Seniacha (S).
5. Boktoloksi, "little two-streams".	On Boguetuluksi Cr., a S. W. affluent of Chickasawhay R.	Bouktouoonlouxy (S).	Bootolooee.		
6. Coussana, Cousanna (or Tousanna). (This and the five above were the original six towns).	Unknown. Probably identical with No. 7.				
7. Inkillis tamaha, "English town" (as the chief of Coussana (No. 6) was a strong partisan of the English, it is probable that this and No. 6 are identical).	N. E. part of Jasper Co.				Yngles tamaha (S).
8. Chickasawhay (Du Roullet says from the name of a bayou).	On Chickasawhay R., about 3 m. S. of Enterprise, Clarke Co.	Tchikachahé (S).	(Chicasawhay R.).	Chikachoé (W).	Chicachae (S).
9. Yowani (Choc. haiyowáni, "June bug").	E. side of Chickasawhay R., in the S. part of Wayne Co.	Eouanné (S).	Ewany.	Youannes (W).	Yoanni (S).
10. Talapokta, "palmetto (where two bayous) unite"—Du Roullet.	Jasper Co.	Talpa Etoka (S).	Talpahoka.	Tala poukta (W).	Taulepa (S).
11. Chiskililkbacha, "blackjacks in a row."	Probably in Jasper Co.	Thellbatcha (S).	Chiskelikbatcha.		Escalibacha (S).
12. Puskustakali, "child hanging".	S. W. corner of Kemper Co. or the proximate part of Neshoba Co.	Pouscouoh Jacale (S).	Pooscoos te Kalé (N).	Poucecoutte Fakalé (W).	Puscus tacale (S).

	Location				
13. Bissasha, "blackberry place." (If the forms Beyacha and Beacha could be relied upon Du Roullet's interpretation, "mulberry place," would be correct.)	W. side of Little Rock Cr., in Newton Co., sect. 23, tp. 8, range 12 E.	Beyacha (S)	Bishapa	Bisacha (W)	Beacha (S).
14. Oktak chito tamaha, "big prairie town."	Unknown	Oktakchitotamaha (S)			Octacchito (S).
15. Oktakchinakbi (abbr. Chinakbi), "crooked prairie."	Site of Garlandville, Jasper Co.		Otakshanabe (W F M)		
16. Bishkun	N. part of Jasper Co.				Bisconne (S).
17. Okatalaia, "spreading (or stagnant) water."	E. part of Smith Co. or W. part of Jasper Co.				
18. Coatraw (a map name evidently misspelled, and probably identical with that of another town of this group, perhaps Tala).	4 m. S. W. of the town of Newton, in sect. 17, tp. 5, range 11 E., Newton Co.		Coatraw		
19. Sakti tamaha, "bluff town".	Unknown				Sacte tamahá (S).
20. Itechana, perhaps "notched stick."	do.				Itechana (S).
21. Shumotakali, "moss (or thistle-down) hanging."	Unknown (there was another town of this name, No. 96).				Chemon tacanté (S).
22. Tinscaitla (perhaps from ti°shkila "blue jay").	Unknown				Tinsca itla (S).
23. Chucafalaya, "long house".	do.				Chuca falaya (S).
24. Ouiacha, perhaps "where there is a brush arbor."	do.				Ouiacha (S).
25. Osapa chito, "big field".	Unknown (there was another town of this name, No. 45).				Ozapachito (S).

CHOCTAW TOWNS—Continued

CENTRAL DIVISION

Name and meaning	Location	Doc. of 1764	Romans's Map & Narr. 1771	Journal of Régis du Roullet (1732)	Spanish List of 1784
26. Kunshak, "cane (town)." The cane is that from which knives were made.	Lost Horse Cr., 4 m. S. E. of Lazelia, Lauderdale Co.	Conchaes (W)	Coosa	Concha (C)	
27. Kunshak chito, "big cane (town),"	On or near the upper course of Oktibbeha Cr.				
28. Kunshak bolukta, "round cane brake."	In the S. W. part of Kemper Co., some 2 m. from the Neshoba Co. line, and 1½ from the Lauderdale Co. line.	Conchaboulonkta (W)	Coosak Baloagtaw (N)		Concha bulucta (S).
29. Okalusa, "black water"	In Romans's time on White's Br., Kemper Co.	Okéloussaes (W)	Oaka Loosa (M), Oka Loosa (N).	Okéloussa (C)	Oqueluza (E).
30. Bokfalaia, "long creek" (a village dependent on No. 29) but classed by Du Roullet with the West towns).	Uncertain.	Bouksalaya (W)		Bouk falaya (W)	Buflaya (E).
31. Iyanábi, "ironwood"	On Yannubbee Cr., about 8 m. S. W. of De Kalb, Kemper Co.	Ayanabé (W)	Ayanabi	Ayanabé (C)	Yanabe (E).
32. Koweh chito, "a great league" ("because it was a great league in circuit").[1]	N. W. of De Kalb, Kemper Co.			Coué tchitou (C)	
33. Boktokolo, "two creeks"	Unknown.				
34. Boktokolo chito, "big two creeks."	At the confluence of Running Tiger and Sukenatcha Creeks, about 4 m. N. W. of De Kalb.	Bouktouclouchito (E)	Bogue Toocolo chitto.	Bouk toucoulou (C)	Buctueuiu (E).
35. Lukfata, "chalk," "white clay"	Headwaters of one of the prongs of Sukenatcha Cr.	Loukseata (E)	Lukfa	Loukfeata (C)	Lucfeata (E).
36. Skanapa, "the unfortunate ones"—Du Roullet (fr. ishkanapa "a disaster").	Probably on Running Tiger Cr., Kemper Co.		Skunnepaw	Schkanuapa (C)	

WESTERN DIVISION

37. West Kunshak chito (contr. West Congeeto), "west big cane town."	Neshoba Co, near the headwaters of Oktibbeha Cr.		West Congeeto or Cooncheto.		
38. Abissa ("village of the mulberries."—Du Roullet; from bihi, "mulberries," and asha, "are there").	Uncertain	Abissa (W)		Abisa (W)	Bezahacha (W).
39. Yazoo, or West Yazoo	Neshoba Co., near the headwaters of Oktibteha Cr., in sections 13 and 24, tp. 10, range 13 east.	Yaroux de L'ouest (W)	West Yaso	Jachou (W)	Yasu (W).
40. Imoklasha, "their people are there" (name of one of the moieties).	On the headwaters of Talasha Cr., Neshoba Co., in sections 4, 9, and 16, tp. 9, range 13 east.	Immongoulacha (W)	West Imongalasha	Mongoulacha (W)	Mongulacha (W).
41. Kashtasha, "place of fleas" (often the residence of the chief of the Western Division).	S. side of Custusha Cr., about 3 m. a little S. of W. of West Yazoo Town.	Casstaches (W)	Cuctachas	Castacha (W)	
42. Kaftalaia, "sassafras thicket"	On Owl C-., in sect. 21, tp. 11, range 13 E., Neshoba Co.	Kasatalaya (W)	Kaffetalya	Caffé taloya (W)	Cafe talaya (W).
43. West Abeka (fr. aiabeka, "unhealthful place").	Unidentified¹	Abekaes (W)	West Abeika	Abeka (W)	
44. Utapacha, "rows of chestnut trees."	...do			Outtapoucha (W)	
45. Ossapa chito, "big (corn) field"	Site of Dixon P. O., Neshoba Co. (a second town so called; see No. 25).	Ossapatchito (W)	Sapa Chitto		Ozapachito (W).
46. Okehanea tamaha, perhaps "town in a triangle marked out by streams of water."	Unknown	Okehaneatamaha (W)			
47. Oksak talaia, "hickory grove"	Near the line between Neshoba and Kemper Counties.	Oksaktalaya (W)	Osuktalaya		Ochactalaya (W).
48. Chunky, perhaps referring to the chunkey game.	On the site of Union, Newton Co.	Thanke (W)	Chankl		
49. Chunky chito, "big chunkey"	W. bank of Chunky Cr., about half a mile below the confluence of that creek with Talasha Cr. Halbert says this territory was later in the Sixtowns District.				Chanké (W).

¹ Du Roullet confounds the word koucha with the word meaning "panther," which is identical in form.

CHOCTAW TOWNS—Continued

WESTERN DIVISION—Continued

Name and meaning	Location	Doc. of 1764	Romans's Map & Narr. 1771	Journal of Régis du Roullet (1732)	Spanish List of 1784
50. Itichipota, "little trees." Halbert says "each other's children," but is probably wrong).	Between the headwaters of Chickasawhay and the Tombigbee.	Itétchipouta (W)		Ite chipunta (W)	Etuc Cambulé (W) (?).
51. Bok chito, "big creek"	Probably on Bogue Chitto, Neshoba and Kemper Counties.			Bouk tchitou (W)	
52. Atlantchitou (tchitou, "big")	Unknown				
53. Hashuk chuka, "grass house"	..do..			Achouk tchuka (W)	Achonchuba (?) (E).
54. Bokfoka, "about (or near) the creek." In 1784 it is placed in the Eastern Division.	..do..			Bouk fouca (W)	Bucplea (E) (or Bucjuca).
55. Tiwæle	..do..				
56. Fani tallemon, said to sig. "land abounding in squirrels" (said by De Lusser to be a dependency of No. 54).	..do..			Fany tallemon (W)	
57. Oklabalbaha, "people talking unintelligibly," as in a foreign tongue.	Unknown				
58. Oka hullo, "sacred (or beloved) water."	Probably on or near the mouth of Sanotee Cr., which empties into Petickfa Cr., Kemper Co.	Okeoullou (W)	Oka-hoolah	Oke oullou (W)	
59. Otuk falaia (falaia, "long")	Unknown				
60. Hashuk homa, "red grass"	..do..				
61. Oklatanap, "war people," so called because on the Chickasaw frontier and fortified.	..do..				
62. Oni talemon, "where there are wild onions,"—Du Roullet.	S. of Pinckney Mill, Newton Co. (possibly in the S. Division).	Onny (W)	Oony	Ouni talemon (W)	Uni (W).
63. Oka kapassa, "cold water"	About Pinckney Mill, in section 23, tp. 8, range 11 E., Newton Co. (possibly in S. Division).		Oka Kapassa		

Name and meaning	Location		
64. Shinuk kaha, "'lying in the sand'"	About 7 m. a little N. of E. of Philadelphia, Neshoba Co.	Schekaha	Chenucaha (W).
65. Oka coopoly, perhaps "water where the biting is" (oka akobli).	On Ocobly Cr., Neshoba Co.	Oka Coopoly	Oguecuple (W).
66. Halunlawi asha, "bullfrog place"	On the site of Philadelphia, Neshoba Co.	Alloon Looanshaw	Olonlauacha (W).
67. Lushapa, perhaps intended for Lu⁼salaka, "swamp edge (or border)."	Perhaps on Lussalaka Cr., a tributary of Kentarcky Cr., Neshoba Co.	Lushapa	
68. Oka chippo, perhaps from Oka shippa, "water run down," from a scant supply of water.	Unknown	Oka Chippo	
69. Konshak osapa, "canebrake field."	Somewhere W. of West Imoklasha	Consha Consapa	
70. Tonicahaw, perhaps Tonik hikia, "standing post."	Unknown	Tonicahaw	
71. Cabea hoola	do	Cabea Hoola	
72. Okapoola	do	Okapoola	
73. Wiatakali, "hanging loft" (or arbor), so named from a brush arbor under which these people were accustomed to meet.	About 1 m. s. of the De Kalb and Jackson road, Neshoba Co.		Ayoutaka (C) (possibly only an alternative name for Ayanabe).
74. Fani yakni, "squirrel country"	Unknown		Fany jakena (W)
75. Shinuk chukilllissa, "the deserted sand."	do		Chenouk Tchankelisa (W)
76. Nita asha, "bears' home" (already abandoned in 1702).	do		Nitacha (W)
77. Balupak, probably "where there are slippery elms" (balup).	do		Baloupouk (W)
78. Ite ousano, "hard wood"—Du Roullet.	do		Ite ousano (W)
79. Kinte oké, "water where there are beaver," or "beaver there."	do		Kinta oké (W)
80. Nusi kon chitto, "big acorns".	do		Nouec kou tchitou (W)
81. Okhatalaia, "spreading pond".	In the Conehatta District of Newton Co. SW. corner sect. 11, tp. 7, range 10 east.		

CHOCTAW TOWNS—Continued
EASTERN DIVISION

Name and meaning	Location	Doc. of 1764	Romans's Map & Narr. 1771	Journal of Régis du Roullet (1732)	Spanish List of 1784
82. Holihta asha, "fort place"	Site of De Kalb, Kemper Co.	Oilktachaes (E)	Olitassa (M)	Oulitacha (E)	Olonlauacha (W).
83. Chichatalya (talya=talaia, "to stand").	Unknown	Chichatalya (E)			
84. East Abeka (Abeka—from aiabeka, "unhealthful place").	At the junction of Straight Creek with the Sukenatcha, Kemper Co.	Abekaes de La Est (E)	East Abeika, East Abeeka, East Abecka.	Abeka (E)	Abeca (E).
85. Ibetap okla iskitini, "little source people."	At the head of the main prong of Yazoo Cr., Kemper Co.	Ebitipougoulaskatamié (E).	Ebita poocola skatane	Ebitipougoula (E)	Ebitabuguluchi (E).
86. Kunshak tikpi, "canebrake knob."	On Coonshark Cr., a tributary of Kentarcky Cr., Neshoba Co.	Conchaktekpé (E)	Conchatikpi.		
87. Itokchako, "green wood"	Near East Abeka, Kemper Co.	Itéochakko (E)	Etuck Chukke	Ite ouktchako (E)	Ite Ochacó (E).
88. Osapa issa, "field abandoned".	N. side of Blackwater Cr., Kemper Co.	Ossapaissa (E)	Sapeesa (M), Sapa-Pessh (N).		
89. Yazoo iskitini, "little Yazoo"	Both sides of Yazoo Cr., between its mouth and the fork, 1 m. above.	Yaroux de L'Est (E)	East Yazo Skatane.	Jachou (E)	Yasu (E).
90. Ibetap okla chito, "big source people."	Perhaps on Straight Cr., Kemper Co.	Ebitipougoulachito (E)	Ebita Poocola Chitto (M), Ebeetap-oooolo-cho (N).	Ebitoupougoula (E)	Ebitábugula (E).
91. Imoklasha iskitini, "little band of relations." (See No. 40.)	On Flat Cr., the E. prong of Yazoo Cr., Kemper Co.	Immongoulachaskatanne (E).	Imongolasha Skatane (M), East Moka-Lassa (N).	Mongoulacha (E)	Mongulacha Esquetani (E).
92. Pachanucha, "where the pigeons sleep."—Du Roullet.	Unknown			Pattcha nouce (E)	
93. Athlepele, probably from alipilla, "at or toward the end."	do				
94. Chuka lusa, "black house"	do				
95. Hankha ula, "wild goose crying."	On a flat-topped ridge between the Petickfa and Blackwater Creeks, in Kemper Co.		Haankah Ullah		Ankkaula (E).
96. East Kunshak chito (contr. East Coongeeto), "East big cane town."	Near Moscow, Kemper Co.		East Coongeeto		Coucha (E).

Name	Location				
97. Shumotakali, "moss hanging" (a second town so called; see No. 21).	Kemper Co., between the two head prongs of Blackwater Cr.	Choumontakale (W)	Chomontakali		Chomontaeaie (E).
98. Watonlula, "whooping crane".	Uncertain.	Onatonloula (W)		Onatonioula (E).	
99. Pante, Du Roullet says from pinti, "mouse," referring to "white rats found in the prairies."	At head of Ponta Cr., Lauderdale Co.	Panthés (W)	Panthe (M), Paonte (N).	Panté (E).	Panté (E).
100. Cutha aimethaw	Unknown.		Cutha Aimethaw		
101. Oka altakala, probably "between the waters."	Probably at the confluence of Petickfa and Yannubbee Creeks, Kemper Co.		Oka Altakala (M), Oka attakkala (N).		
102. Nushkobo, "head" [1]	Perhaps on or near Petickfa Cr., Kemper Co.		Escooba		Nascobó (E).
103. Yakni achukma, "good land"	Perhaps on Indian branch of Running Tiger Cr.		Yagna Shoogawa		Yagane achucuma (S).
104. Chuka hullo, "sacred (or beloved) house."	On the N. side of Sukenatcha Cr., somewhere between the mouths of Running Tiger and Straight Creeks, Kemper Co.		Chooea-hoola		
105. Cuthi uckehaca	Probably on or near the mouth of Parker's Cr., which empties into Petickfa Cr., in sect. 30, tp. 10, range 17 E.		Cuthl Uckehaca.		
106. Yanatoe	Probably in S. W. Kemper Co.		Yanatoe.		
107. Alamucha	10 m. from Sukenatcha Cr., Kemper Co.				
TOWNS OUTSIDE OF THE ORIGINAL TOWN CLUSTER					
113. Teeakhally ekutapa, the first word sig. "standing pine."	On the lower Tombigbee R.		Teeakhaily Ekutapa		Town of Tombecbé (E).
114. Chisha foka, "among the post oaks."	On the site of Jackson, Miss.				
115. Shukhata, "opossum"	On the site of Columbus, Ala.				

[1] This was abandoned, whether permanently or not is uncertain, in 1748.

We are helped to visualize the appearance presented by some of these towns in the early part of the eighteenth century by passages in the journal of Du Roullet, who was among them from April to August, 1732.

I will say that the village of Boukfouka is one of those of the Choctaw Nation whose Huts are the most separated one from the other; this village is divided into three hamlets, each hamlet at a quarter of a league from the others, and all three surrounded by Bayous: lastly this village is at least twenty leagues [68a] in circumference. . . .

The village of Castachas is one of the finest of the nation; it is situated in a large plain, in the middle of which there is a small hill from the top of which one can see all the Indian huts placed on the plain and the (blank in ms.) around the Huts of each savage. . . .

The village of Jachou [Yazoo] is situated in a great plain which lies on a neight; the savages have their fields in this plain and a large part of their huts are around the plain. The plain of Jachou is not so vast as that of Castachas, but it is of about two leagues circumference at the least. . . .

The village of Jachene atchoukima [Yakni achukma] is situated on a little elevation or height. The huts are well separated from one another.

The village of Crouetchitou [Kowi chito] or the Great Village is situated on a small plain surrounded by very high hills, where nearly all the huts of the savages are built and their fields are in the plain. . . .

Sapatchitou [Sapa chito] . . . is a small hamlet of the village of Boukfouka, which lies in a small plain where the savages have built a little stockaded fort, into which they retreat with their families every night on account of the frequent incursions of the Chikachas [Chickasaws] who cross the river near this hamlet when they come in a band upon the Choctaws.[69]

MOIETIES

Like the Chickasaw, the Choctaw were divided into two great moieties, but in contradistinction to them these were strictly exogamous and there was greater constancy in the terms applied to them. All of the four authorities on which we have to depend give the same name to one of these divisions, i^nhulahta. Morgan, who derived his information from Byington, gives the form "Wă-tăk-i-Hŭlä'-tä," but "Wă-tăk" is evidently a misspelling of Hă-tăk, "man," "person." Similarly "Ukla," in the "Ukla i^nhulá'hta" of Alfred Wright, is "people." I- is the objective pronominal prefix of the third person, used in singular or plural, and ^n- is the sign of the indirect object. These are used with either substantives or verbs. Hulahta or hula'ta resembles holihta, "fence," "yard," or "fort," with which Cushman does, in fact, identify it,[70] or it may be related to holitopa, "beloved," "dear,"

[68a] A figure which includes all the town lands, but even so, must be regarded as excessive.

[69] See "Notes sur les Chactas d'après les Journaux de Voyage de Régis du Roullet (1729–1732)," by Le Baron Marc de Villiers, in the Journal de la Société des Américanistes de Paris (n. s.), Vol. xv, 1923, pp. 239–241.

[70] Cushman, Hist. Inds., p. 73.

" esteemed," a meaning apparently attached to hulahta by the informants of Byington and Wright. However, I have little doubt that it is the Timucua and Apalachee word for " chief," or " leading man," which is practically identical in form and was widely employed by the Creeks as a ceremonial title. For the other moiety we find two names. That earliest mentioned is imoklasha, which appears in the speech of a Choctaw chief in 1751. It consists of im- (equivalent to i^n- of i^nhulahta), okla, " people " (see úkla above), and asha, " to sit," or " to dwell," the whole meaning " their people are there," or " their people who are there." In a general way it signifies " friends." However, the name obtained by Byington, Wright, and Cushman is Kashapa okla or Kashap okla, " Divided people," referring probably to the dual division itself. Possibly the first name was given by one of the same moiety and the second by one of the opposing moiety, but in that case there seems to be no good reason why the name of the i^nhulahta should not also have changed. As we shall presently see, these names appear again as those of subdivisions within this moiety, and it may have derived its collective designation from them. We shall find a similar extension of the names of local groups.

The following regarding Choctaw moieties, furnished by Alfred Wright, was published in the Missionary Herald in 1828:

They state, that when the Creator had provided the means of their subsistence, he proceeded to give them their civil regulations. By his direction the Choctaws, before their dispersion from *Nunih waiya*, were divided into two great families, or clans, embracing the whole tribe, or nation. Intermarriages between those of the same clan were forbidden. The husband and wife must always be of different clans. The children are reckoned with the clan to which the wife belongs. Of course there is a division in every family, the father on one side, the mother and children on the other. And at their funeral solemnities and other public meetings, where they are arranged according to this order, the father is seen sitting at one fire, and the mother and children at another. As the mother takes her children into her own clan, the father has no control over them, but the woman's brothers are considered the natural guardians of the children. Each of these great clans is again divided into three subdivisions, or smaller clans, making *six* in all. All these clans intermix and live together in the same town and neighborhood, yet they preserve a knowledge of the clan, and of the particular subdivision to which they belong.

These two great clans are considered as having a kind of precedency over the others in point of authority. In ancient times if a person had been guilty of a crime which required the interference of public authority, the people were assembled in council, and seated according to their respective clans. The subdivision to which the criminal belonged appeared as his counsel and advocates, and the opposite subdivision as his accusers. The case was then taken up. If the principal men of these divisions succeeded in adjusting the case, satisfactorily to all concerned, the business was terminated there; but if not, the principal men of the next larger division took it up, and if they also failed, the case then came before the *itimoklushas* and the *shakchuklas*, whose decision was final. But this practice, like some other of their ancient customs, has gone into disuse.[71]

Halbert repeats and supplements this:

Soon after the creation, the Great Spirit divided the Choctaws into "iksa," the "Kashapa Okla," and the "Okla in Holahta," or "Hattak in Holahta." Stationing one iksa on the north and the other on the west side of the sacred mound [of Nanih Waiya], the Great Spirit then gave them the law of marriage, which they were forever to keep inviolate. This law was that children were to belong to the iksa of their mother, and that one must marry into the opposite iksa. By this law a man belonging to the Kashapa Okla must marry a woman of the Okla in Holahta. The children of this marriage belong, of course, to the iksa of their mother, and whenever they marry it must be into the opposite iksa. In like manner a man belonging to the Okla in Holahta must marry a woman of the Kashapa Okla, and the children of this marriage from being Kashapa Okla must marry into the Okla in Holahta. Such was the Choctaw law of marriage, given, they say, by Divine authority at Nanih Waiya just after the creation of their race. The iksa lived promiscuously throughout the nation, but as every one knew to which iksa he belonged, no matrimonial mistake could possibly occur.[72]

Elsewhere he tells us that—

In the ancient days the iksa system was regarded so strictly that a man was treated with contempt if he should marry into his own iska. Prior to 1820, a woman thus offending was severely whipped by her uncles and brothers and taken away from her husband. But with the gradual progress of civilization, the law was first broken by the half-breeds, who thus set a precedent which began to be followed by the full bloods, so that at the present day among the Choctaws west, the iksa division is now practically extinct.[73]

It will be noted that Halbert applies the term iksa only to the moieties, but, while this may have been its original usage, it was later employed for all of the minor subdivisions, and even extended to include Christian sects.

The trivial note of a British official in 1772 to the effect that a Choctaw chief named "Concha Oumanstabe" was "of the Immongoulasha or Peace Family of the Town of Chickasawhays," casts a flood of light upon the nature of the moieties.[74] Evidently the Imoklasha corresponded to the White or peace party among the Creeks and we are quite safe in assuming that the Inholahta had to do with war. Each moiety also discharged the burial offices for members of the opposite moiety.

In recent times a kind of town or band moiety system existed which made itself evident in the ball games. This is described on

[71] The Missionary Herald, June, 1828, vol. XXIV, No. 6, p. 215.
[72] Pubs. Miss. Hist. Sov., II, p. 230; cf. Claiborne, Miss., I, p. 521. This information is based on the communication to the Missionary Herald, above quoted, and "conversations in 1884 with the aged Hemonubbee of Neshoba County, Miss., who clearly remembered the tradition of the iksa system instituted at Nanih Waiya."
[73] The facts in this paragraph were abstracted from the records of the "Court of Claims," p. 927.
[74] Miss. State Archives, English Dominions, vol. 1.

page 153. It may have been formed under Creek influence or may have been a late sporadic growth, yet it is possible that it perpetuates something more ancient.

CLANS AND LOCAL GROUPS

There are only the faintest traces of groups with truly totemic designations, the animal and plant names which occur seeming not to have had a totemic connotation. The most important apparent exception is furnished by Adam Hodgson, who traversed the territory of most of the large southeastern tribes on a missionary journey in the year 1820. On the banks of the Yalobusha River " he reached the dwelling of a half-breed Choctaw, whose wife was a Chickasaw, and whose hut was on the frontier of the two nations." This man, who " spoke English very well," told him among other matters " that there were tribes or families among the Indians, somewhat similar to the Scottish clans; such as, the Panther family, the Bird family, the Raccoon family, the Wolf family: he belonged to the Raccoon family, but his children to the family of his wife." All of these totemic groups except the Wolf are known with certainty to have been present among the Chickasaw, and the Wolf occurs in Morgan's list. It is possible, therefore, that this Choctaw, on marrying into the Chickasaw tribe, had been assigned a totemic group, or that some northern Choctaw had adopted the Chickasaw system. Claiborne states that six clans, Wind, Bear, Deer, Wolf, Panther, and Holly Leaf, extended throughout the Choctaw, Cherokee, and Creek tribes, but his information was evidently derived from the Creeks, it is only partially true of the Cherokee, and otherwise not to be relied upon.[75] Aside from these questionable statements there seems to be nothing to warrant the assumption that totemic groups existed among the Choctaw. There is every reason to believe that the Crawfish people, the only division of any size bearing an animal name, were descended from the originally independent tribe of that name (the Chokchiuma) living between the Choctaw and Chickasaw.

But even though there were no totemic iksa, it is quite possible that there were nontotemic divisions corresponding to the Chickasaw totemic clans and differentiated in some manner from the smaller geographical bands. If there were such, the eight " gentes " enumerated by Morgan on the authority of Cyrus Byington and the six mentioned by the Rev. Alfred Wright would fall into this category. The former are, in the moiety of the Beloved People, the Chu-fan-ik'-sä, Is-kŭ-la'-ni, Chi'-to, and Shak-chuk'-la, and, in the moiety of the Divided People, the Kush-ik'sä,[76] Law-ok'lä, Lu-lak Ik'-sä,

[75] Claiborne, Miss., I, p. 493.
[76] Cushman says that the full form of this is " Kunsha-a-he " (kuⁿshak ahe), " reed-potato." P. 297. He states that Apushmataha belonged to it.

and Lin-ok-lŭ'-sha. The first of these names is translated " Beloved
People " like the name of the moiety itself, though the Choctaw
equivalents are totally distinct, and in this case I have no way of
accounting for the interpretation. Bushnell's Bayou Lacomb informants translated the name "Bunches of flies people," deriving
chufan (or chufa, as he has it) from chukani, " fly," but this origin
is hardly probable. The only Choctaw word which seems to hold
out a promising suggestion is chàfa, " exile," " banishḙd person,"
which recalls the Creek word " seminole " and brings to mind one
origin for distinct clans of which we have abundant examples. Is-
kŭ-la'-ni is a misprint of Is-kŭ-ta'-ni, but a better spelling would be
Iskitini. This is mentioned by Cushman, who calls it " Okla Isski-
tini." [77] As stated above, the Shak-chuk'-la (or in full Shakchi
humma okla, " red crawfish people ") undoubtedly represented the
formerly independent tribe of that name incorporated among the
Choctaw. Kush-ik'-sä is shortened from Ku^{n}shak iksa, " Reed iksa,"
while Law-ok'-lä contains okla, people, and perhaps laue, " equal,"
or " able," the name connoting people who are equal to anything or
able to do anything. Lu-lak Ik'-sä is probably a misprint of Tu-lak
Ik'-sä, the Tula'îksa' ogla, or " Fall-in-bunches people " of Bushnell,
also remembered by two of my own informants.

" Tula " was evidently derived by Bushnell's Indians, whether
rightly or not it would be impossible to say, from tulli, to jump, to
frisk. The last name, Lin-ok-lŭ'-sha, is again undoubtedly a misprint, intended for Itim-ok-lŭ'-sha, or better Itimo^{n}klasha, " their
own people," or " friends," being, as we have seen, one of the names
given to a moiety. The two first and the two last were known to the
Rev. Alfred Wright, whose account of them leads one to suspect that
the eight clans just mentioned are actually to be differentiated from
the other local groups next to be considered, although all of the
living Choctaw confound them hopelessly. Mr. Bushnell's informants at Bayou Lacomb treat the names of the moieties, clans, and
local groups as if they were all the same thing, and it is apparent
that the names of the larger bodies were from time to time identified
with local groups. At any rate the Kashapa okla and I^{n}holahta okla
are given as names of Choctaw bands at certain definite spots in
Louisiana, two of the others belong in the class of primary iksa or
clans just considered, while three would fall into the miscellaneous
class of local groups. My own experience has been like that of Mr.
Bushnell. The Choctaw whom I have interviewed have drawn no
distinction between the three sorts of divisions, although in fact
none of them seemed to have heard about the i^{n}holahta okla, and the
kashapa okla were barely remembered.

---

[77] Cushman, Hist. Choc., Chick., and Natchez Ind., p. 90.

Cushman mentions two original moieties, "subsequently divided into six clans," thus confirming Wright, but the names which he gives to the latter are wholly different, including those of the three great geographical divisions, and three of the smaller local groups. They are the Okla falaya, Haiyip atokola, Okla hannali, Konshak, Chickasawhay, and Apela ("a help"), all but the last of which are well known.[78]

The remaining divisions apparently correspond to the local groups, or "house names," of the Chickasaw. Perhaps Dr. Gideon Lincecum, an old resident among the Choctaw before they removed from Mississippi, best expresses the internal organization of the nation when he says, speaking of the three major territorial divisions of the Choctaw Nation, "each district was subdivided, with but little system, into Iksas, or kindred clans, and each of these Iksas had its leader." My own informant, Simpson Tubby, said much the same thing. "The same iksa was spread through a number of towns, and there might be several in each." He attributed exogamy to the iksa instead of to the moieties, of which he remembered nothing, saying, "If it was found that two people of the same iksa had married, they were separated even though they belonged to different towns. Sometimes a man pretended that he belonged to an iksa different from that of a woman whom he wished to marry, when in fact it was the same, and did marry her, but as soon as the truth was known they were separated." In the breakdown of an old exogamic system, however, among tribes having clans and moieties, it commonly happens that clan exogamy is maintained for a time after moiety exogamy has been abandoned.

In fact these local groups seem to have been of all sizes and grades of importance, and were probably frequently increased by subdivision or the incorporation of foreign elements and decreased by the dying out of older iksas. At the present day it is impossible to make anything like a complete list of iksas, and I do not feel sure that the names which I give are all properly used in this connection. They are the following: Bok Chito, "Big Stream," on the stream so called (Bogue Chitto), which flows into Pearl River near its head, the only iksa to remain aloof from missionary teachings; Biasha, "Mulberry place," still living a few miles west of Philadelphia, Miss.; Okla hannali, "Sixtowns," in and about Jasper County, Miss.; Okla untuklo, "Seven towns," near Hays, about 23 miles southwest of Philadelphia; Yàkan-okàni, "Land Creek," just west of Carthage, in Leake County, Miss.; Haiyip atokola, "Second lake," or "Two lakes," in the northeastern part of the old Mississippi territory;[79]

[78] C. B. Cushman, Hist. Choc., Chick., and Natchez Inds., p. 73. Possibly Apela is intended for Athlepele (see pp. 65, 74).
[79] Cushman speaks of a Choctaw named Apakfolichipubih, a contemporary of Apushmataha, belonging to this iksa. (Cushman, p. 336.)

Chikashahe, " Chickasaw potato(?)," said by one informant to have been east of Mashulaville, but anciently, at all events, on the headwaters of the Chickasawhay River; Kunshak, " reedbrake people" (though by one informant affirmed to have been the name of a bird found in the reedbrakes), said to have been north of Mashulaville, but anciently much farther south; Okla falaia, " long people," according to some Mississippi Choctaw about 16 miles north of Philadelphia, according to others near Harperville in Scott County; [80] Spani okla, " Spanish people," 25 to 40 miles east of Jackson, Miss.; Obâla chaha iksa, along Turkey Creek, in the northeastern part of Scott County and the southeastern part of Neshoba; Koe chito, " Panther," not located; Bok falaia, " Long Creek," not located; and Yanabe, Yashu, Abeka, Lukfata, and Haiyowani, which were also names of well-known Choctaw towns and may easily be located. Mr. Bushnell adds the Shunkwane ogla (Shunkâni okla), "Ant people," and Cushman, as we have seen, speaks of one known as Apela, " to help," " to assist." Gatschet mentions a few groups besides which may belong in this category, Cofetaláya, " quail are there," Pineshuk Indians, " on a branch of Pearl River, in Winston County," the name perhaps transposed from " pishânnuk," the bass or linden tree; Sukinatchi or " Factory Indians," in Kemper County; the Cobb Indians, called after their leader, Colonel Cobb, but also known as Hopahka Indians; and the Shuqualak, in Noxubee County. Simpson Tubby spoke of a band in the Sixtown country called Tâshka himmita. Some of these may have been temporary or town groups instead of true iksa, and it is difficult to find out where the application of the term iksa begins or ends. Sometimes it seems to have been identical with a town, sometimes it appears to have embraced several towns, but more often I believe that each town was composed of several iksa.

Later local applications have been given to the names of the dual divisions and clans, as follows. A band called Kashapa okla lived at Bayou Lacomb, La., in a village called Butchu'wa, another known as Inholahta okla was considered the largest in southeastern Louisiana, their principal settlement being on Hatcha, or Pearl River. The Shakchi homa okla lived " near Chinchuba, some 12 miles west of Bayou Lacomb," and also west of Louisville, Miss. Imonklasha continue to live to this day about seven miles south of Philadelphia, Miss., where they have been missionized by the Catholic Church; some Chufan iksa lived in Noxubee County, Miss., and there was a body of Tula iksa okla in Louisiana.

---

[80] " It is said the name of this clan had its origin in a Choctaw family who, both parents and children, were uncommonly tall."—Cushman, Hist. Choc., Chic., and Natchez, p. 336. This is, of course, a folk etymology. Cushman mentions a chief of this iksa named Amoshollhubih, who was connected with the family of the old head chiefs.

Since these names possess few peculiarities by which they may be distinguished from the names of towns or other divisions it will always be impossible in the present decadent condition of the old organization to distinguish the true local groups. So far as we can now observe, the functions of these divisions closely approached those of the corresponding groups among the Chickasaw. As stated above, marriage was regulated by the two moieties, each man or woman ordinarily taking a spouse from any group of the opposite moiety, but Halbert notes as an exception that marriage between the Chufan iksa and Kush iksa was prohibited. Probably there were various additional modifications the nature of which is now forgotten. Each moiety also piled up the bones and buried the dead of the other,[81] but every local group had its own bone house. Lincecum says that each local group had its own chief, corresponding probably to the " oldest uncle " of the Creek clans. We know that each household was so organized because Israel Folsom affirms that " in the domestic government the oldest brother or uncle was the head; the parents being required merely to assist in the exercise of this duty by their advice and example." [82] The duty of extending hospitality to strangers belonging to the same moiety, or indeed toward strangers of any sort not recognized as enemies, was rigidly inculcated. A man called the people of his own iksa or band imokla, "his own people," and all others imoksinla.

Only one origin myth dealing with a clan or local group has come down to us, Pitchlynn's story of the Crawfish People, or properly Red Crawfish People, as related to Catlin.

They formerly, but at a very remote period, lived under ground, and used to come up out of the mud—they were a species of crawfish; and they went on their hands and feet, and lived in a large cave deep under ground, where there was no light for several miles. They spoke no language at all, nor could they understand any. The entrance to their cave was through the mud—and they used to run down through that, and into their cave; and thus, the Choctaws were for a long time unable to molest them. The Choctaws used to lay and wait for them to come out into the sun, where they would try to talk to them and cultivate an acquaintance.

One day a parcel of them were run upon so suddenly by the Choctaws, that they had no time to go through the mud into their cave, but were driven into it by another entrance, which they had through the rocks. The Choctaws then tried a long time to smoke them out, and at last succeeded—they treated them kindly—taught them the Choctaw language—taught them to walk on two legs—made them cut off their toe nails, and pluck the hair from their bodies, after which they adopted them into their nation—and the remainder of them are living under ground to this day.[83]

---

[81] Cushman, Hist. Choc., Chick., and Natchez Inds., p. 367.
[82] Ibid., p. 362.
[83] Catlin, the North American Indians, vol. II, p. 146.

Without doubt this is a folk-explanation of an already existing name. While it has totemic suggestions, it is applied to a non-totemic group.

As we shall see when we consider Choctaw government, the men of every town were ranged in four classes, the first consisting of the chiefs, the second of the Hatak holitopa, " beloved men," or leading warriors, the third of the Tashka or common warriors, and the fourth of " those who have not struck blows or who have killed only a woman or a child." We may suspect that, as was the case among the Creeks and apparently among the Chickasaw, the path to advancement was to a certain extent smoothed by circumstances of birth. But this is a vicious disturbance of the survival of the best which is not confined to Indian society.

TERMS OF RELATIONSHIP

The principal terms of relationship are given in the following table, constructed in part from data collected by myself and in part from data obtained from the lists of Morgan and the entries in Byington's dictionary.

CHOCTAW TERMS OF RELATIONSHIP
(SELF MALE)

paternal grandfather (imafo) = paternal grandmother (ippokni)

maternal grandfather (imafo) = maternal grandmother (ippokni)

father's sister's husband (imafo)

father's sister (inhukni)

father's brother's wife (ishki)

father's brother (i^nki) (i^nki toba) (i^nkusi)

father (i^nki)

mother (ishki)

mother's sister (ishki) (ishki toba) (ishkusi)

mother's sister's husband (i^nki)

mother's brother (immoshi)

mother's brother's wife (ihaiya)

father's sister's son (i^nki)

father's sister's daughter (inhukni, or ishki)

father's sister's daughter's husband (imafo or i^nki)

father's sister's daughter's son (inakfish) (tibapishlili)

father's sister's daughter (intek)

elder brother (imanni)

younger brother (inakfish)

sister (intek)

self

mother's brother's son (iso)

mother's brother's son's wife (ipok)

mother's = mother's brother's brother's daughter daughter's husband (iso tek) (iyup)

father's sister's son's daughter (intek)

father's sister's son's son (i^nki)

brother's son (iso, imalla)

brother's daughter (iso tek, imálla tek)

son (iso, imálla)

daughter (iso tek, imálla tek)

sister's son (imbaiyi)

sister's daughter (imbitek)

grandson (ipok nakni)

granddaughter (ipok)

father-in-law (ipochi) = mother-in-law (ipochi ohoyo)

wife (iutekchi)

wife's sister = wife's sister's husband (imalakosi ohoyo)

sister's daughter = sister's daughter's husband (iyup)

wife's brother (imalakosi)

wife's brother's wife (iyup)

son = son's wife (ipok)

daughter = daughter's husband (iyup)

brother = brother's wife (ihaiya)

sister = sister's husband (imalak)

self

sister's son = sister's son's wife (ipok)

brother's = brother's daughter daughter's husband (iyup)

brother's = brother's son son's wife (ipok)

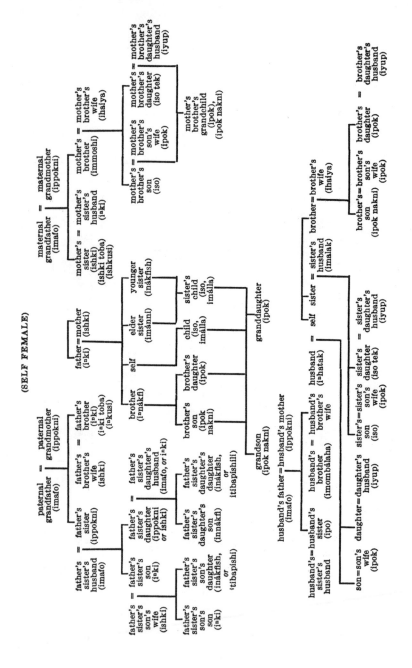

(SELF FEMALE)

NOTES

In my diagrams illustrative of Chickasaw relationship terms [83a] I gave the term pok nakni (or ipok nakni) as that applied by a woman to the husband of the mother's brother's daughter. This may have been stated by an informant but it is evident that it should be iyup, as in Choctaw and as Morgan has it. In my Chickasaw and Creek lists I have used the stem of each term of relationship, omitting the pronominal prefixes, but in the present lists I have decided to include them, all the more since it develops that the kind of prefix used varies with the term. Incidentally the stem of i^nki, father, should evidently have been given as ^{n}ki instead of ki. I assumed the ^{n} was the sign of the indirect object but the Creek form lki shows that it belongs to the stem because there is a shift from l to n in Choctaw. The oldest brother was called itichapa, "the father's mate" (see p. 196), and would seem to be equivalent to the term "ancestor" in the loosest sense in which we employ it. Imafo was also employed for the father's sister's husband and sometimes for the father's sister's daughter's husband. In Chickasaw ippokni is given to the father's sister herself and to her female descendants indefinitely, in which particular it is unlike Choctaw. It is true that a Choctaw woman does employ this term for her father's sister and sometimes for her father's sister's daughter, but a new term i^nhukni is used by males and it sometimes extends to the father's sister's daughter. The next generation in either case becomes brothers and sisters. The words for father and mother were similarly extended to the brothers of the former and the sisters of the latter and we know from Morgan's tables that they extended to the father's father's brother's sons, the father's father's father's brother's son's sons, the mother's mother's sister's daughter, and the mother's mother's mother's sister's daughter's daughter. It is probable that they took in all of the men and women of the band, of the corresponding generation, and perhaps those of the moiety of the father and mother respectively. Moreover, the term for father had, as we have just seen, a still wider extension. It was applied to the mother's sister's husband, the father's sister's son, and sometimes to the husband of the father's sister's daughter, while the term for mother was given to the wives of these men. It is evident, however, that these other terms are derived from the usage of i^nki and ishki for own father and mother, because the other uses are often qualified by the diminutive, as i^nkosi, ishkosi, or the word toba, " to make," " to become," and sometimes the postposition pila, " toward."

[83a] Forty-fourth Ann. Rept. Bur. Amer. Ethnol., p. 186.

The terms for brother and sister, whether elder, younger, or indifferent, are similarly extended to the children of the father's brother, the mother's sister, the father's father's brother's son's children, the mother's mother's sister's daughter's children, and an indefinite number of collaterals beside. A collective term itibapishili, "those who nursed together," is employed by a man or a woman to indicate brothers and sisters collectively. Although our records of its usage indicate considerable irregularity, it was probably employed particularly when a man wanted to refer to all of his brothers without differentiating them as elder or younger, and similarly when a woman wished to speak of all of her sisters. However, one of Morgan's informants stated that in such situations a woman could employ intek, which is commonly used by a man.

There were similarly extensions of the terms for uncle to the older men on the mother's side or belonging to her band, and of the word child by a man to the children of those called brother, and also uncle, and by a woman to those called sister and uncle, except, as I have already said, certain descendants of the father's sisters whose designation is in doubt. The terms for nephew and niece were applied by a man to his mother's mother's sister's daughter's daughter's children and corresponding collaterals. A woman, however, called her brother's children grandchildren. The terms used for relations brought about through marriage were also extended. A particularly close relation existed between a man and his father-in-law and mother-in-law, but especially the former. A woman called her father-in-law and mother-in-law merely "grandfather" and "grandmother," but a man had special terms ipotci and ipotci ohoyo. The use of ohoyo, "woman," "female," shows pretty clearly that the father-in-law was the more important of the two, and this is confirmed by Byington who tells us that father-in-law and son-in-law called each other by the word halloka which also means "sacred," "beloved," "dear." Sometimes the father-in-law was called ipochi halloka. It is said by Byington to have been given to the niece's husband and the wife's uncle. We shall see presently that the father-in-law was distinguished in another way. Impusnaki is given by Byington as a name applied to a woman by her husband's brothers, uncles, and nephews. It is to be noted that the son's wife and all of the women married into the family belonging to her generation are called "grandchildren," while there is usually a special term, iyup, for the men.

A man and a woman call their sister's husband by the same term, and their brother's wife by the same term, and the terms which a man applies to his wife's brother and wife's sister are variants of the term used by them both for the sister's husband. A woman had distinct terms for her husband's brother and her husband's sister. While the use of these terms was probably somewhat extended, I find few cases. The mother's brother's wife was, however, called by the same term as the brother's wife. The term most restricted in its use seems to have been that applied by a woman to her husband's sister.

There are traces of a reciprocal use of terms. Thus ipok is ordinarily used in the sense of "his granddaughter," while if one wants to say "his grandson," nakni, the word for male, is added, and ippokni, grandmother, seems to be based upon this.

In the tables given above a few points are still somewhat obscure, but it is not unlikely that usage also differed, because more than one term of relationship was often applicable to the same person. Thus one authority calls the father's sister's daughter ippokni (woman speaking) or i^{n}hukni (man speaking), the term used for the father's sister, and her husband imafo, "grandfather," which is also the term for the father's sister's husband; but a second authority uses the terms ishki, "mother," and i^{n}ki, "father," respectively. If we had satisfactory examples of two more generations of the father's sister's descendants we should probably find that the children of the father's sister's son's daughter and the father's sister's daughter's son and daughter would be called iso and iso tek and that their children would be numbered with the ipok and ipok nakni. On the other hand the descendants of the father's sister's son in the male line all appear to have been called i^{n}ki, "fathers." In both of these cases we find the terms running straight across iksa and moiety lines.

Most of these terms had a more extended application. Those for grandfather and grandmother covered all ancestors and all individuals of the same generation as the grandfather and grandmother, at least those closely related to them. Unless limited in some way of which we now have no knowledge, it would extend to the boundaries of the tribe. In such cases it is usual to find that the unmodified word is original. As noted above, ippokni, "grandmother," resembles ipok rather closely, but imafo, "grandfather," does not, and so it seems possible that ipok and ippokni were differentiated from the same original word. As has been suggested, i^{n}hukni may also be derived from it.

However, the Choctaw have evolved a new device for indicating reciprocal relationships. This does not define them minutely but merely sets off the older from the younger speaker, or rather the one entitled to the term belonging to the elder generation from the one who must use a term belonging to the younger generation. This device is the employment of the pronominal prefix indicating the indirect object in the former terms and the employment of the pronominal prefix indicating the direct object in the latter. The following comparative table will illustrate:

Taking the indirect pronominal prefix	Taking the direct pronominal prefix
imafo, grandfather____ ⎫ ippokni, grandmother__ ⎭ -------------------	{ ipok, granddaughter. { ipok nakni, grandson.
iⁿki, father____ ⎫ ishki, mother__ ⎭ --------------------------	iso, iso tek, child (also imálla).
imánni, elder brother or sister_____	inákfish, younger brother or sister.
immoshi, uncle_____ ⎫ ippokni, aunt (w. sp.) __ ⎬ ------------------- iⁿhukni, aunt (m. sp.). ⎭	{ ibaiyi, nephew. { ibi tek, niece.
iⁿhatak, husband_____	itekchi, wife.
imombalaha, husband's brother_____	ihaiya, brother's wife.

In the last two cases there is no apparent difference in the generation to which the two belonged. Also, in the case of a woman speaking, ipo, husband's sister, and ihaiya, brother's wife, would be reciprocals, yet both take the direct object. Imalák, sister's husband, and imalakosi, wife's brother, are also reciprocals but they take the indirect object, being in fact the same word with the diminutive suffix placed after one of them. Aside from imálla, one term used for " child," the only flat contradiction we meet is in the father-in-law–son-in-law relation in which ipochi and iyup both take the direct object, but there may be some special ceremonial cause here. I have spoken above of the endearing term in use between a father-in-law and son-in-law. My belief is that the indirect object carried a note of deference, such as other languages express in using the third person for the second. Chickasaw usage is practically identical with Choctaw, but in Muskogee the direct object is the one commonly employed. The principal exceptions are the terms for " grandchild," nephew, niece, daughter's husband, sister's husband (m. sp.), wife's brother, father-in-law, and mother-in-law. Here are certain relations considered very close in Choctaw and Chickasaw. As the background of the relationship system, and much of the foreground, is now lost, it will probably be impossible to determine the cause of this custom in any other way than inferentially.

GOVERNMENT

Some information on this subject has already been introduced. The greatest illumination on the ancient form of government is given in the following paragraph from the Anonymous French Memoir: [83b]

This nation is governed by a head chief whose power is absolute only so far as he knows how to make use of his authority, but as disobedience is

---

[83b] Appendix, pp. 243–244; Mem. Amer. Anthrop. Assn., v, No. 2, pp. 54–55.

not punished among them, and they do not usually do what is requested of them, except when they want to, it may be said that it is an ill-disciplined government. In each village, besides the chief and the war chief, there are two Tascamingoutchy ["made a war chief"] who are like lieutenants of the war chief, and a Tichou-mingo ["assistant chief"] who is like a major. It is he who arranges for all of the ceremonies, the feasts, and the dances. He acts as speaker for the chief, and oversees the warriors and strangers when they smoke. These Tichou-mingo usually become village chiefs. They (the people) are divided into four orders, as follows. [The first are] the head chiefs, village chiefs, and war chief; the second are the Atacoulitoupa [Hatak-holitopa] or beloved men (hommes de valleur); the third is composed of those whom they call simply tasca or warriors; the fourth and last is atac emittla [hatak imatahâli?]. They are those who have not struck blows or who have killed only a woman or a child.

As already stated, a considerable number of the leaders of the Choctaw Nation resided in 1732 in the central group of towns. Thus, at the time when the memoir just quoted was written, or in the period to which it refers, the head chief of the nation lived in Koweh chito, the name of which is said to signify "a big league," because it was a league in circuit. Later the word koweh (koi) came to mean "a mile." Its aboriginal connotation has been lost, but it is identical in form with the word for "panther," and Du Roullet, writing in 1732, confounds the two. D'Anville's map, of about the same date, labels this town "the village of the head (grand) chief," and on other maps it is called the "Choctaw capital." The author of the Anonymous Memoir informs us that "in this village, besides the head chief of the nation, there are three leading national chiefs, two of whom are head war chiefs and the other a chief who assigns duties." He also says that the heir apparent of the Choctaw head chiefship was always chief of Boktokolo and adds that "the head chief also lives there, very often."

The authority which we have been following calls Skanapa "the village of the chief." He places it in the western division but, as Du Roullet informs us that the chief of Kashtasha was leader of the western towns, Skanapa may actually have been the headquarters of the chief of the eastern district, with which it is classed by De Lusser.

None of these writers indicates which Sixtown chief was recognized as the head of that group, but since the author of the Memoir says that the prerogatives of the chief of the Sixtowns were "the same as those of the head chief [of the nation]," we know that there was such a divisional chief and that he had considerable independence.

The above represents Choctaw conditions about the third decade of the eighteenth century, but the reader must be warned against the assumption that it was a hard-and-fast system. Aside from Father Baudouin's assertion that the head chieftainship was a new institution, we learn of various shifts in the location of both head

and divisional chiefs. Thus, in 1748, the chief of the eastern town
of Holihta asha is called head chief of the Choctaw, while Franchimastabe, who occupied that position in 1787, belonged to West Yazoo.
At one time during the French régime the chief of the eastern division lived at Ibetap okla, probably the larger town of the name, but
in a council held in 1787 the spokesman for this group was the chief
of Okalusa. During the early period of French intercourse the
leadership of the Sixtown section seems to have rested with the chief
of Chickasawhay, and upon his town the six towns proper are said
to have depended, but at another time the headship seems to have
been with Nashobawenya, while in 1784 it was in Oskelagna.

While some of our informants may have been mistaken, it is evident that the head chiefships were not definitely located in any one
town. Evidently merit and popularity determined leadership.

In spite of what has been said regarding the limited authority
of the national leader, it was not entirely negligible because, in 1731,
the "Consideré" or Honored Man of Okalusa awaited his consent
before going out to fight the Chickasaw.[84]

The institution of a second or vice chief seems to have been usual,
and this is said to be preserved in Mississippi down to the present
day. Head and second chiefs are often mentioned in the documents.

In a Spanish letter written in 1792 the statement is made that the
head chief of the Choctaw, at that time Franchimastabe, had the
right " according to their laws to leave his position to the Indian who
pleased him best (quien segun sus leyes tiene el arritrio de dejar
su empleo al Indio que guste)," but undoubtedly this power could
be exercised only within certain limits set by public sentiment.

There were probably other officials and no doubt, as in the case of
the Creeks, usage varied between town and town. This lends interest to the following list of chiefs to whom presents were made by
the French officer, Du Roullet, in 1729:

Village of Koweh Chito:
    Mingo tchito (Mi^{n}ko chito), head chief [of the nation], capitané.
    Oulatimataha (Holahta imataha).
    Soulouche oumastabé (Shulush hummastabe).
    Atakabe mingo (Hatak abe mi^{n}ko).
    Pakanaoulacta (Pakna holahta).
    Mingo tcito ouchi (Mi^{n}ko chito ushi).
    Eyachoumataha (Iyasha imataha, or Yashu imataha).
Village of Bouktoukoulou:
    Ataché mingo (Atashi mi^{n}ko), the town chief.
    Chikacha oulakta (Chikasha holahta).
    Tascanangouchi (Táshka nanukachi).

[84] Du Roullet Ms. in the French archives.

Soulouche mastabé (Shulush imastábi).
Sonakabé tachka (Asonakabe táshka).
Pacana sulacta (or Pacana oulacta) (Pakna holahta).
Village of Ayanabé:
     Astchichaa (Ashachi chaha?).
     Tachikcaoulakta (Táshka holahta).
Village of Okeloussa:
     Mingo pousecouche (Mi^{n}ko puskus ushi).
     Oulatouktalé (Holahta oktáni?).
     Taskanangouchi (Täshka nanukachi).
Village of Concha (or Coucha):
     Asatchioullou (Ashachi hollo).
     Alibamon mingo (Alabama mi^{n}ko).
     Taskanangouchi (Táshka nanukachi).
     Tichou mingo (Tishu mi^{n}ko).
Village of Yté tchipota:
     Opatchi mingo (Hopakachi mi^{n}ko).
     Tachka mingo (Táshka mi^{n}ko).
Village of Chkanppa:
     Mingo emitta (Mi^{n}ko imataha).
     Tachka mingo nakfich (Táshka mi^{n}ko nakfish).
     Tachka oumma (Táshka homma).
     Taskanangouchi (Táshka nanukachi).
Village of Nachoubaouanya:
     Oultetachéo (ulhti táshioha ?).
Village of Oskelagana:
     Fani mingo tchaa (Fáni mi^{n}ko chaha).
     Oulabessenya (Okla bisanli ?).
     Mingo pouscouche (Mi^{n}ko puskus ushi).
     Moungoulacha mingo (Moklasha mi^{n}ko).
Village of Tala:
     Tchikacha oulakta (Chikasha holahta).
     Oulakta benéya (Holahta biniya ?).
Village of Youané:
     Opaé mingo (Hopaii mi^{n}ko).
     Mongouchi rhtaboka (Mi^{n}ko ushi ishtabokoa).
     Tchoukaoua ala (Chuka wahkála ?).
Village of Tchikachaé:
     Patlako (from patála, "flat" ?), capitané.
     Mingo émitta (Mi^{n}ko imataha).
     Taskanangouchi taboka (Táshka nanukachi tabokoa).
     Ogoulabissénya (Okla bisanli ?).
     Taskanangouchi (Táshka nanukachi).
     Sonak abé (Asonak abe).
     Mingo taskanangouchi (Mi^{n}ko táshka nanukachi).
     Mongoulacha mingo (Moklasha mi^{n}ko).
Village of Kastacha:
     Atakabé oulakta (Hatak abe holahta), capitané.
     Ounatekélo (Ona tikeli ?).
Village of Kaffétalaya:
     Taskanangouchi taboka (Táshka nanukachi tabokoa).
     Tchitou mingo (Chito mi^{n}ko).

Village of Boukfouka:
    Opaemikko (Hopaii mi^{n}ko).
    Atakabé oulakta (Hatak abe holahta).
    Taskanangouchi (Táshka nanukachi).[85]

" Capitané " is, of course, borrowed from the Spaniards, and was perhaps assumed as a title by some chiefs who had received honors at Pensacola or St. Augustine. In another place Du Roullet speaks of the chief and the "tascanagouchi " of the village, from which it is clear that "tascanagouchi " or " tascanangouchi " was an official title. It is possible that where this word appears in the above list it belongs with the name just preceding, having been inserted simply as his title, but there is nothing in the punctuation of the original to confirm this. In Hopaii mi^{n}ko we recognize the equivalent of a name often applied to great war leaders among the Creeks and the Chickasaw. Elsewhere Fani mingo, probably the Fani mingo tchaa of the above list, is called " calumet chief of this nation," but just what these words are intended to imply is not clear. They may signify merely that he had once carried a calumet to some other tribe when peace was being arranged. In later documents, as for instance the treaty of July, 13–14, 1787, between representatives of Spain and the Choctaw, the Indians who subscribed their names to it are classed as " great medal chiefs," "little medal chiefs," and " capitanes," the last term being used for the least important class of leaders.

The head chief is again mentioned in a much later note from the manuscript of Israel Folsom:

> The tribal or national government was vested in the royal family. . . . They were under the government of custom or common law of the Nation. All their matters of dispute or difficulty were settled in open council. They had no such officers as constables or sheriffs, but the chief had power at any time to order out any number of warriors to bring offenders to justice. The chief's office was one merely of supremacy or leadership and consequently there was no pay attached to it as at the present [1899].[86]

The relative functions of the major local groups or clans within this larger body—perhaps also within each town—is outlined by

---

[85] Of the above words mi^{n}ko is " chief "; chito " big "; holahta a name used in war titles and signifying " chief " in the Timucua and Apalachee languages; imataha, probably " a supporter "; shulush hummastabe, " he took red shoes and killed "; hatak, " man " or " person "; abe, " to kill "; p kna, " on the top "; ushi, " little "; iyasha, " kettle "; Yashu, name of a town; atáshi, " a war club " or possibly the Creek town of Atasi; Chikasha, the Chickasaw tribe; táshka, " warrior "; nanukachi, " one who advises "; shulush im stabi, " shoes he took and killed "?; asonak, " a brass kettle "; ashachi, " to lay something down "; chaha, " up high "; puskus, " little " or " an infant "; oktáni, " to appear at a distance "; hollo, " sacred "; Alabama, the tribe; tishu, " assistant " (to a chief); hopakáchi, " to wander far off "; nakfish, " younger brother "; ulhti, " council fire "; táshioha, " several things with corners, sharp edges, or ridges "; fáni. " squirrel "; okla, " people "; bisanli, " to sprout "; moklasha, " one's own people "; biniya, " seated "; hopaii, " a prophet " or " a military leader "; ishtabokoa, " he took something when it was noon "; chuka, " house "; wakála, " cracked "; tabokoa, " noon "; ona, " to reach going "; tikeli, " to touch " or " to press against."

[86] Cushman, Hist. of Inds., p. 362.

Wright in a communication to the Missionary Herald. This has already been quoted but deserves repetition at this place.

In ancient times if a person had been guilty of a crime which required the interference of public authority, the people were assembled in council, and seated according to their respective clans. The subdivision to which the criminal belonged appeared as his counsel and advocates, and the opposite subdivision as his accusers. The case was then taken up. If the principal men of these divisions succeeded in adjusting the case, satisfactorily to all concerned, the business was terminated there; but if not, the principal men of the next larger division took it up, and if they also failed, the case then came before the *itimoklushas* and the *shakchuklas*, whose decision was final. But this practice, like some other of their ancient customs, has gone into disuse.[87]

In 1751 a Choctaw chief in a speech asking pardon for some French deserters who had been condemned to death exclaims to the officer whom he is addressing: "I beg you to write to Mr. de Vaudreuil [the governor], my father, that when the two first (or original) races, Inoulactas and Imougoulachas, venture to ask for the life of a man, they are never refused, even though the man were already bound to the frame [at which they were to be burned]."[88]

My list of towns contains 115 entries, but the places designated were probably not all occupied at the same time and there is reason to suspect that, on moving to a new site, a Choctaw community sometimes changed its name. Moreover, certain of these names no doubt belonged to villages never permanently detached from some larger town. Making all due allowances, however, there were probably at one time from 40 to 50 communities constituting small States, each with its chief, war chief, two lieutenants of the war chief, or Taskaminkochi, and an assistant to or speaker for the town chief, the Tishu minko. These offices were probably held by the local groups which happened to contain such and such towns, but the relation between the town and the local group remains obscure and probably always will.

Cushman says that " in the domestic government the oldest brother or uncle was the head; the parents being required merely to assist in the exercise of this duty by their advice and example."[89]

In other words the domestic government was identical with that existing among the Creeks.

In the nineteenth century the head chieftainship appears to have been abolished, the head chief's power being shared by the three regional chiefs. Thus Wright says:

---

[87] The Missionary Herald, June, 1828, vol. XXIV, No. 6, p. 215.

[88] Je te prie d'acrire à M. de Vaudreuil, mon pere que quand les deux premieres Races Inoulactas, et Imougoulachas font tant que de demander la vie d'un homme quelle ne leur est jamais refusée, quand même l'homme seroit desja amaré au cadre.—Miss. State Archives. French Dominion. Correspondence générale.

[89] Cushman, Hist. Inds., p. 362.

The Choctaw nation is divided into three *districts*, each of which has a *principal chief* elected by the people; and . . . each of these districts is divided into many smaller portions, over each of which a *headman* or *captain* presides, who is elected by the people of his clan.[90]

Claiborne gives a more detailed description of Choctaw government in which the three coordinate chiefs appear again:

The Choctaws, from time immemorial, were divided into three beats or districts, each under charge of a head chief, who never exercised their authority, in important junctures, without the counsel and consent of the sages and warriors. . . .

The names of the chiefs in the three Choctaw districts, at the removal west, were Ne-ta-ca-che, for the lower district; Ma-shu-la-tubbee, for the central, and Greenwood Le Fleur [Le Flore], for the northern.

They were independent of each other, and with the co-operation of the head men, were supreme in authority in their respective districts. They consulted and acted in concert only in external matters, when the whole nation assembled to decide on peace or war. In later times the whole nation assembled to receive their annuity, the goods, on the occasion, being delivered to the chiefs or captains, and by them impartially apportioned to the people. These captains were taken from the respective villages in which they lived.

In each of the districts, there were sub-chiefs or captains, called in the Choctaw tongue, mingos, who were the leaders in their respective towns or beats. Their jurisdiction and authority embraced all matters of local concern.

In the event of war, the sub-chief or mingo leads the warriors of his village or town. The Choctaws, for a long period, had no regular wars, until Pushmataha joined Gen. Claiborne against the Creeks or Mus-cogees. But their hunting parties often went west of Red river and into Arkansas, and had many bloody forages there. . . .

Occasionally, a general council of the nation, or of the district, was called. The head chief of the district, or if it be a national council, the three chiefs, send out runners to the subordinate chiefs, giving to each runner a bundle of sticks, corresponding to the number of days to intervene between the time of despatching and the day of meeting. The runner, every morning, throws away a stick, until he reaches the chief to whom he has been sent. He then delivers the bundle, with the remainder of the sticks, and the sub-chief throws away one every morning, which brings him to the place appointed when the last stick has been thrown away. This was the primitive method of transmission between the Indians, and was long adhered to, after they had become more civilized, out of respect to the ancient custom.

On the day appointed, the Chiefs and Mingos assembled in the square or open space of the town, and the common people made it a holiday and engaged in ball playing or dancing.

The council square was generally central, and about 60 feet long and 40 wide. On each side were two rows of posts, the outer one filled in with mud, about six feet high, and the whole roofed over with straw or boards. There were two rows of wooden benches covered with matting of woven cane, or white bark; on these benches the Chiefs and Captains take their seats and smoke their pipes, slowly passing them from one to another. The Indians are very deliberate, and are slow in reaching conclusions. The Speaker or Orator of the district or nation (as the case may be) usually opens with a speech. explaining why the assembly has been called, and discloses the views of the

---

[90] Missionary Herald, April, 1829, vol. xxv, No. 4, p. 121.

Chiefs. If the Speaker be absent, the Chief himself opens the assembly, and sometimes does so whether the Speaker be present or not. The Speaker is a salaried officer, and his share of the annuity is only inferior to [that of] the head chief. Any sub-chief or Mingo is then at liberty to give his opinion. Ample time is allowed. After the debate has ceased, and the pipe has been passed all around, the Head Chief, or the Speaker, by his orders gives the *Big Talk*, collecting the decision of the council from the opinions that have been expressed, and giving his views as to how the conclusion arrived at is to be realized. He speaks very deliberately, and at the end of each sentence, if what he says be approved, the Mingos exclaim *Ma!* (yes) in a loud voice. There is seldom any collision between the Chief and the subordinates. If the superior be a man wise in council and bold in war, the counsellors usually decide in consonance with his recommendations, and if he be a man of tact he generally recommends what he finds, from their debates, is most agreeable to them.[91]

After removal west of the Mississippi, the head chieftainship was reestablished and lasted until the end of autonomous government. The three districts were preserved and for a time a fourth district was constituted out of the Chickasaw, but in 1855 they were formed into a distinct republic.

Régis du Roullet gives us some additional information regarding the conduct of Choctaw councils. When he went to see the head chief of the tribe in 1729 accompanied by two Chickasaw chiefs the visitors found mats spread out for them in the shade of four great trees. Presently the chief himself came thither " singing the calumet," and one of the principal honored men (considerés) approached the Frenchman with a white or peace pipe in his left hand and a burning torch in his right. He offered the pipe to his visitor and after he had smoked presented it in turn to the two Chickasaw. Then three of the honored men raised Du Roullet on their shoulders and carried him to the council ground where an elaborate feast had been prepared.

We learn that, before the Natchez outbreak, one of the chiefs of the latter tribe had presented a Choctaw chief with a red calumet " which is the token of a promise when one accepts it," urging him to attack the French.[91a]

When De Lusser visited the Choctaw in 1730 to induce them to take up arms against the Natchez he held a council at Kaffetalaya in the western part of their territory, of which he gives us some details. After speeches had been exchanged " a great feast consisting of potatoes and bear's oil was held and then the dance followed. . . . The dance of the men having come to an end, that of the women began. They [the men] were all armed and daubed with paint, with headdresses of eagle feathers. They danced the dance of the Amediches [Nabedache, a Caddo tribe] who are Indians in the direc-

[91] Claiborne, Miss., I, pp. 490–491.
[91a] Journal of De Lusser in French Archives.

tion of Mexico, which a slave of that nation who is at the house of the great chief taught this nation. This is the finest of all the Indian dances. They performed it very well. Moreover, they are the best dressed and the neatest of all the Choctaw women I have seen."

On his way home De Lusser passed through the village of the Yellow Canes (Oskelagna), where he witnessed a similar ceremony. The latter part "consisted of a dance which the women executed around the scalps, but it was pitiful in comparison with that of Kaffetalaya." The speech of the chief of this town De Lusser has attempted to report entire and it may be appended as an example of Choctaw forensics in the third decade of the eighteenth century, though the sentiments expressed are not on a very high plane. The chief's devotion to the French and past deficiencies of the latter are enlarged upon with hope that compensations for the same will be proportionately ample.

Warriors, I am very glad to have brought you back to your wives and your children. I am a witness that it was not in your power to die for the French. As soon as I learned that the Great Chief of the French had sent a letter to the feet of the Great Chief of the Choctaws to tell him that the French had died at Natchez and that he had to send his warriors as soon as possible to avenge their death he did not hesitate one moment to obey this word which he had always had engraved in his heart and to march at once on the promise that had been made to pay for the death of his warriors; that nevertheless they had given nothing. That on the contrary Mr. De Louboey had robbed them by having gone away with the slaves both French and Negroes whom they had taken from the Natchez without giving them goods or notes; that they had attacked the Natchez and had killed many of them; that they had waited for the French a very long time and that after the latter had arrived they had said that they were going to make a breach in the fort with their cannon and that the Choctaws had only to put themselves in the places by which the Natchez might flee that not a single one might escape; but that the cannon of the French had made much noise but had had little effect; that it was as if one spat on the ground; that nevertheless they kept telling them at every moment, pointing at the sun meanwhile, that at such and such an hour the fort would be laid low; but that the ball did not even touch the palisade; that when the Natchez put a calumet of peace at the end of a stick the French had been very glad and had made peace on the terms that they should return the French and the Negroes to them; that the French had no hearts, that they had seen the corpses of their people as well as those that had been recently burnt, but that that had not touched them at all; that for his part he could not think of it without saddening of the heart; that the Tunicas and other small nations had not wished to fight because the French had put some of them in chains and treated the red men like slaves; that also they had the French everywhere; that they stole the skins of the Indians, being ungrateful for their goods; that for their part very far from killing the French they were avenging their death, and that for his part he would always listen to the word of the French, and would never abandon them.

Something will also be said about Choctaw councils in connection with the ceremonies connected with war and the restoration of peace. The following excerpts have been taken from Cushman:

In their ancient councils and great national assemblies, the Choctaws always observed the utmost order and decorum, which, however, is universally characteristic of the Indians . . . In those grave and imposing deliberations of years ago convened at night, all sat on the ground [?] in a circle around a blazing fire called The Council Fire. The aged, who from decrepitude had long retired from the scenes of active life, the war-path and the chase, formed the inner circle; the middle age warriors, the next; and the young warriors, the outer circle. The women and children were always excluded from their national assemblies. The old men, beginning with the oldest patriarch, would then in regular succession state to the attentive audience all that had been told them by their fathers, and what they themselves had learned in the experience of an eventful life—the past history of their nation; their vicissitudes and changes; what difficulties they had encountered, and how overcome; their various successes in war and their defeats; the character and kind of enemies whom they had defeated and by whom they had been defeated, the mighty deeds of their renowned chiefs and famous warriors in days past, together with their own achievements both in war and the chase; their nation's days of prosperity and adversity; in short, all of their traditions and legends handed down to them through the successive generations of ages past; and when those old seers and patriarchs, oracles of the past, had in their turn gone to dwell with their fathers in the Spirit Land, and their voices were no longer heard in wise counsel, the oldest occupied the chairs of state, and in turn rehearsed to their young braves the traditions of the past, as related to them by the former sages of their tribes, together with their own knowledge.[92]

Whether the Choctaws assembled for social conversation or debate in council, only one spoke at a time, and under no circumstances was he interrupted. This noble characteristic belongs to all the North American Indians, as far as I have been able to ascertain. In the public councils of the Choctaws, as well as in social gatherings and religious meetings, the utmost decorum always prevailed, and he who was talking in the social circle or addressing the council or lecturing in the religious meeting, always had as silent and attentive hearers as ever delighted and blessed a speaker. A noble characteristic. And when a question had been discussed, before putting it to a vote, a few minutes were always given for silent meditation, during which the most profound silence was observed; at the expiration of the allotted time, the vote of the assembly was taken; and which, I have been informed, is still kept up to this day [1899], For many years after they had arrived from their ancient homes at their present place of abode [in Oklahoma], no candidate for an office of any kind ever went around among the people soliciting votes; the candidate merely gave notice by public announcement, and that was all; and had a candidate asked a man for his support, it would have been the death knell to his election.

On the day of the election, the names of all the candidates were written in regular order upon a long strip of paper, with the office to which each aspired written upon it, was handed to the voter when he presented himself at the polls to vote, who commenced at the top of the list and called out the name of the candidate he wished to support for the different offices; if the voter could not read, then one of the officers in charge of the election, who

---

[92] Cushman, Hist. Inds., pp. 205–206.

could read, took the paper and slowly read the names and the office each aspirant desired; and the voter called out the name of each candidate for whom he wished to vote as he read; and no candidate ever manifested any hard feelings toward those who voted against him. Here was exhibited true liberty and free suffrage.[93]

The latter part of the quotation of course refers to the method of conducting an election after the removal west of the Mississippi under the constitution then adopted. Cushman thus speaks of the native orators:

There were many natural orators among the ancient Choctaws when living in undisturbed prosperity and happiness east of the Mississippi river. Their orations were very concise, animating and abounding in many beautiful metaphors.[94]

Cushman gives the following as the ancient formula for beginning a speech: " O-mish-ke!   A numpa tillofasih ish hakloh," "Attention! Listen you to my brief remarks." [95]

Before concluding this section I will append some notes given me by Simpson Tubby. This must represent that form of government maintained by the eastern Choctaw after the bulk of the tribe had moved west. I am uncertain how far this represents a functioning government and how far an ideal. My informant, like many of the best native assistants in other tribes, has a tendency to give a logical completeness to his story of former governmental and religious conditions which very probably goes beyond the actual realization. Whether objectively or subjectively realized, his narrative shows the increasingly important part played by the mounds at Nanih Waiya in the thought of the Mississippi Choctaw. This must be taken in connection with Halbert's statement that he knew of but one national council of the tribe held at the great mound. Simpson's account is, in substance, as follows:

Nanih Waiya was the center of the Choctaw Nation and the Choctaw came together there in council from as far west as Yazoo City and as far east as the Tombigbee. Close to it five streams meet to form Pearl River, the " river " (Hahtca) of the Choctaw. One of these is Nanih Waiya itself. Two others, Owl Creek (Opa Bok) and Bogue Chitto (Big Creek) come in from the south, uniting a short distance before they empty into Pearl River, and the two others, Talla Haga (Táli hikia, " Standing Stone "), and Noxapater (Naki chiponta, " Small Shot " for a shotgun), come in in succession from the north. At the small mound of Nanih Waiya the five captains of the five bands living on these streams met to make laws for them which they afterwards carried to the chief on the big mound for approval or veto, but the laws for the nation as a whole were made at the big mound. The Choctaw originally spread out from this place in all directions and so the region of the five river cantons was called " my mother earth " (cháshki yakni), but it was not known how they came to be at that place. [Simpson apparently knew nothing of a sub-

---

[93] Cushman, Hist. Inds., pp. 174–175.   [94] Ibid., p. 253.   [95] Ibid., p. 315.

terranean origin there. He had heard, however, that the first national assembly was held at the Blue Hole Cave and that after that they put up the big mound and had their later national assemblies by it.] Both the national and cantonal laws were executed by the head chief. He and each of the band captains had vice-chiefs. After the death of a head chief the vice-chief took his place until the people had a chance to assemble and elect a new one, and the vice-chief was not necessarily the one chosen. It is said that if the women wanted a certain chief he was almost certain of election.

At the small mound laws were made like those governing the amount of game that might be killed by each family on the five rivers and how much by the whole band or okla. When the small mound could not settle any difficulty it was referred for final adjudication to the big mound.

If the head chief or a captain died suddenly and the vice-chief could not be present at an assembly which had already been summoned, the wife of the deceased took his place and spoke for him, she having been kept informed by him of any business in hand. She wore a blue veil as a symbol of truth (red was a symbol of war or anything hostile) and when she rose to speak with this on, all kept quiet and listened attentively. If the woman had to speak with reference to some death, she wore black.

Before the head chief called a meeting, six bundles of sticks were prepared, one for each of the five bands and one for the head chief himself. Before the latter were sent out, they were all brought to the head chief, laid out before him, and the number of sticks "certified." If one of the captains who had charge of a bundle lost a stick, he had to come to the head chief to get a new one. Sometimes one forgot to remove it at the proper time and afterwards, at the council, each had to state how many mistakes he had made. The one who was most accurate in this respect was apt to be made head chief after the death of the incumbent. There are said to have been two sets of sticks, twelve for the months and thirty for the days. One of the latter had to be removed every day before noon. It might be on the evening of the night before, at midnight, or in the morning. When thirty had been removed, one of the month sticks was taken away and the process gone over with the second month, and so on. This means that the sticks were not actually destroyed, and, in fact, they were generally kept in the large pouch and removed to another compartment in the same. Apparently month sticks were not used in all cases, but it is said that appointments were seldom made more than ninety days in advance and this kept the number of day sticks within reason.

The chief was a quiet man who indicated his wishes largely by signs. Whether he was to hold a general council or merely summoned one particular captain for a special purpose, he chose a day when he knew it would be calm. Before opening the council he lighted a fire on top of the big mound and when the smoke went upward in a straight line he bent over it and the people said he was communing with some unseen being. Or he looked upward with his arms folded for perhaps half an hour. Then he would let his arms fall to his sides and turn successively to the east, north, west, and south in silence. If he wished to address some particular band he would point in the direction in which it lived. If he was speaking to all, he would point to each creek in succession before beginning his speech. If he happened to have four points to consider, he would hold up four fingers in sight of the assembly without uttering a word. After that he opened the assembly with a speech.

Then he would vanish into his house and the captains and their subcaptains would meet on the small mound and decide which of the bands would hold its meeting first. All of the captains met there so that they might make no mistake in delivering the message to their village exactly as their chief had uttered it. They went through with this formula every time so that there would be no argument. The old speeches of this character were in a set form and were uttered in a low voice so that they could not be heard very far off. Special speakers, other than chiefs or captains, were chosen to address great audiences on moral matters. Instruction was given wholly in this way. These men were usually prophets, men who foretold the weather [at all seasons], and sometimes wizards.

A headdress of a special pattern was worn by the head chief, and one somewhat similar by each of the captains. The chief's hat was high and had a narrow brim. It could be made of any kind of skin. The base of the captain's headdress could be of any material except deer, bear, and opossum skin, but it must be different from that of the head chief. Two silver bands tied at the ends with red tape encircled the chief's headdress, one at the top and one halfway up. Around the top were ranged six ostrich feathers, and at the outer ends of each of these were hung twelve beads. Each feather was slipped into one or two silver pieces at the butt end to hold it in place. At an earlier period crane feathers seem to have been used instead of ostrich feathers and the captains had but four of these. The headdresses of the captains were otherwise similar except that they had less silver. When one of these headdresses was worn, the beads fastened to the feathers moved continually, glittering like stars, no matter how still the wearer stood. The head chief also wore bearskin moccasins. His costume was prescribed by the captains, not by himself, and his wife's clothing was made by the captains' wives. The chief's headdress was made by the captains with the help of some women. At times the captains as well as the chief wore moccasins and all might have fur caps.

The chief also had a pipe. It was given by Simpson Tubby's great-grandfather, Mashulatubbi, to his grandfather, Aliktàbbi, and then passed to his son, Lewis Tubby, who was to have given it to a man named Yitombi but the latter died before the owner of the pipe. It was offered to Little Leader but he said that Greenwood Leflore was to have it and Lewis Tubby gave it to him. However, Leflore betrayed his people to the whites and fled to Leflore County and Greenwood City, leaving the pipe behind him, and it again fell into the hands of Lewis Tubby, who left it in trust for Simpson when he should reach the age of forty. However, most of the custodians having died, it was presented to him a little before that time. Later Simpson loaned it to a local college and it is said to have been stolen from the collection there along with some other objects. Simpson says that the stone of which it was made was brownish or yellowish in color.

PROPERTY

Although when attacked the Choctaw defended themselves with great bravery, it appears that they were not particularly jealous of their hunting rights. This was evidently because they depended less upon the products of the chase than any other of the southeastern tribes. Roman says:

Their hunting grounds are in proportion less considerable than any of their neighbours; but as they are very little jealous of their territories, nay with ease part with them, the Chicasaws and they never interrupt each other in their hunting; as I mentioned before.[96]

Yet Halbert reports bitter contests between the two tribes over certain preserves. Romans states elsewhere that his party saw little game in their country.[97]

Certainly their territories were not as extensive as those of the Chickasaw, Creeks, or Cherokee, being closely shut in on the north and east by the Chickasaw and Creeks, and to the westward not reaching even to the Mississippi River where the Natchez and a number of smaller tribes dwelt. The part of this territory continuously occupied was divided up among the local groups treated of above, each controlled in about the same manner as by the separate tálwa among the Creeks. Romans says: "Although they have a strict notion of distinction in property, and even divide their lands, we never hear them quarrel about boundaries." [98]

So far as the Choctaw are concerned the following paragraph from Cushman appears to be in line with all other information on the subject of property. It applies, as will be seen, to the claims of individual families as well as to those of larger bodies:

When a Choctaw erected a house upon a spot of ground, and prepared a few acres for his corn, beans, potatoes, etc., so long as he resided upon it as his home, it was exclusively his, and his rights were strictly respected by all; but if he left it and moved to another place, then his claim to his forsaken home was forfeited; and whoever saw proper could go and take possession; nor was the second occupant expected to remunerate the first for the labor he had done. However, if No. 1 afterward should desire to return to his previous home he could do so, provided no one had taken possession. [At] the present time [1899], if one improves a place and leaves it, no one has the right to take possession of the deserted place without permission of the one who improved it.[99]

Claiborne, who derived much of his information from Cushman, is naturally confirmatory:

The land is common to the nation—chiefs and people; particular lands being unknown among them but by reservations in the treaties. Their title to their houses and fields of corn is entirely by occupancy. As soon as the house is abandoned, any other person may take it. Their right, however, while in possession or use of the property, is scrupulously respected. When the husband and wife die leaving no children, the relations of the wife generally take their house. But if the house was built entirely by the husband, without the assistance of the wife, in such case, his relations usually take possession. If the house be an old house and built by neither, it goes to the blood of him who built it. But these rights mean nothing unless acted upon at the time of the house being left vacant, for if another be permitted to enter, occupancy, as above stated, becomes the sole title.[1]

[96] Romans, E. and W. Fla., p. 72.
[97] Ibid., p. 86.
[98] Romans, E. and W. Fla., pp. 87–88.
[99] Cushman, Hist. Inds., p. 235.
[1] Claiborne, Miss., I, p. 494.

Certainly the instinct in opposition to absentee landlordism was a true one, however little it may have reflected a deep-seated, abstract desire for justice.

Regarding the disposition of movable property or chattels the same writer says:

The law of distribution of their personal effects is the same in the three nations. What came by the husband or by the wife, upon their death without issue, goes to their respective relations. When the wife dies leaving children, her property goes to her children—her relations taking care of it for them and of them. The woman having to make the crop and raise the hogs does not miss her husband so much when he is killed, except on account of the game, because with the exception of the game she had the support of the family on her hands previous to his death.[2]

Adopted children shared equally with the others (see p. 118).

Many chattels were, however, scaffolded or buried with the deceased and hence placed beyond the consideration of possible heirs.

CRIME AND PUNISHMENT

Murder, i. e., intratribal man-killing, could be atoned for ordinarily only by the death of the murderer himself or some substitute acceptable to the injured family. The anonymous author of the Memoir of 1755 says: "They cherish a desire for revenge for a generation. The grandson will avenge an insult made to his great-grandfather by killing one of the descendants of the one who gave the blow. They bring up their children in this spirit of revenge."[3]

Ordinarily the substitute was from the family or clan of the murderer but Gregg tells us that "any one might take the place of the murderer, and in the death of the substitute the law was satisfied, and the true criminal remained exempt." The case he cites was, however, within the family. "An intelligent and [reliable] Choctaw related to me an affecting incident, for the truth of which he vouched. An Indian had remained responsible for the appearance, on a certain day, of his brother, who had killed a man. When the day arrived, the murderer exhibited some reluctance to fulfill the pledge, when the other said to him: 'My brother, you are no brave—you are afraid to die—stay here and take care of my family—I will die in your place': whereupon he immediately attended the appointed spot, and was executed accordingly."[4]

We learn from Romans that such retribution was sometimes resorted to inside the domestic group itself.

There are no laws or regulations observable among these people, except the *Lex Talionis*, . . .; the above law is so strictly followed, that I am furnished

---

[2] Claiborne, op. cit., p. 494; see also p. 134.
[3] Appendix, p. 247; Mem. Amer. Anthrop. Assn., v, p. 59.
[4] Gregg, Commerce of the Prairies, in Early Western Travels, ed. R. G. Thwaites, vol. 20, pp. 311–312.

with the following anecdote: It happened that a young Choctaw having done something deserving reproof, he was therefore chid by his mother; this he took so ill as in the fury of his shame to resolve his own death, which he effected with a gun; his sister as his nearest relation thought herself bound to avenge his death, and knowing the circumstances told her mother she had caused her brother's death and must pay for his life; the old woman resigned herself to her fate, and died by the hands of her daughter, who shot her with a gun which she had provided for the catastrophe.[5]

This law of retaliation bulks large in reports sent in by the early white emissaries and agents. In a letter to Henry Dearborn, Secretary of War, dated March 4, 1803, Claiborne says:

Some Indian depredations have been committed on the road leading to Nashville, but they are by no means as great as has been represented. In the course of four months past one person has been killed and two wounded. The deceased (a Mr. White) was shot by some Creeks, as satisfaction for a Creek Indian who was murdered not long since in Kentucky. A Mr. Patterson was shot and wounded by Lewis Vaun, a Choctaw, with a view to avenge the loss of his brother, who was supposed to have been killed in this territory about two years ago; and a Mr. Hogan was lately wounded by a party of Choctaws, who had set out to take a life as compensation for an Indian who was killed in Natchez about two months ago. No other mischief has been done by the Indians in the Wilderness (unless it be the stealing of some horses) for some years, and this has proceeded from the rigid execution of the " Lex talionis."

Several other letters were written by Claiborne regarding these cases.[6]

A curious account of a murder, apparently grounded in jealousy, is thus related in detailing the proceedings of a congress of Chickasaw and Choctaw Nations opened at Mobile by John Stuart, the British agent, on December 31, 1771:

A party of hunters from Toussanna [or Coussana] had in [the] winter last met a white man in the woods who had lost his way and was at the point of death for want of nourishment, that they the Indians had fed and taken great care of him, by which means he had recovered entirely. That after some days he joined another party of Choctaws, in order to return to the nation, at which the person who had taken such care of him being offended, pursued and killed him. The agent insisted that the Indian who had done the deed be himself killed, and after a conference among themselves the Choctaw chiefs agreed to it.[7]

Claiborne attempted to encourage the substitution of monetary compensation for blood revenge, the usual route by which this custom was modified and brought to an end. In a letter to Dearborn, written August 16, 1804, he says:

Hooshe Hoomah, or the Red Bird, a Choctaw chief, regrets the loss of a relation killed some years ago in Kentucky. Some of the connections of the deceased speak of revenge but the Red [Bird] is much opposed to the shedding

[5] Romans, E. and W. Fla., pp. 87–88.
[6] MS. vol. of " The Proceedings of the Governor of the Mississippi Territory as Superintendent of Indian Affairs." Miss. State Dept. of Archives. For the religious motive behind man-killing see p. 220.
[7] Miss. State Archives, English Dominions.

of innocent blood and supposes that the resentment of the family might be appeased by suitable presents in goods or money.

Later he adds:

Mr. Dinsmore (agent to the Choctaw) has been requested to make the Red Bird and his connections presents to the amount of 50 or 80 dollars, but I fear a sum less than 300 dollars will not be deemed adequate compensation.

The following rather verbose and emotional account by Cushman embodies some important illustrations of the ancient attitude on the subject of this cardinal crime:

Their severest law was that of blood revenge. "Whosoever sheddeth man's blood, by man shall his blood be shed" was a statute rigidly enforced among all North American Indians. It was acknowledged among all, not only to be the right, but also the imperative duty of the nearest relative on the male side of the slain, to kill the slayer wherever and whenever a favorable opportunity was presented. Under many existing circumstances the law might, perhaps, have been just and salutary; but unfortunately it went too far, as any male member of the murderer's family, though innocent and even ignorant of the crime, might become the victim of the avenger of blood, if the guilty had fled; but such seldom occurred, as the murderer rarely ever made any effort whatever to escape, but passively submitted to his fate. Still, this law, revolting as it may appear to many, exercised a good influence among the Choctaws, as it had a salutary effect in restraining them in the heat of passion, by rendering them cautious in their disputes and quarrels, lest blood should be shed; knowing the absolute certainty of murder being avenged sooner or later upon the murderer himself, or some one of his nearest male relatives; hence no man, or family, would with impunity commit or permit, if he could avoid or prevent it, an act that would be sure to be avenged, no one could tell when or where. Days, weeks, and even months perhaps, might pass, yet the avenger sleepeth not nor has he forgotten; and, at an hour least expected and from a source least apprehended, the blow at last falls, and there the matter ends. Nor did the slayer find any protection from any source whatever, not even from his nearest relatives. Yet calmly and with stoical indifference [he] awaited his certain doom; nor was the avenger, though known, interrupted in any manner whatever, either before or after he had accomplished his revenge. The avenger of blood never took the life of a female of the slayer's family, but satisfied himself in the death of the slayer himself or in the person of someone of his nearest male relatives.[8] If the murderer had fled, and the life of one of his male relatives had been sacrificed in lieu of his own, he then could return without fear of molestation; but the name of coward was given to him—an appellation more dreaded and less endurable than a hundred deaths to all North American Indians.

A few instances have been known among the Choctaws, where a relative proposed to die for the slayer, and was accepted on the part of the relatives of the slain; but such instances were very rare.[9]

Cushman, however, describes one such case, that of a woman who offered to take the place of her son and was accepted by the family of the murdered man. Cushman says:

---

[8] Claiborne states that the husband of a slain woman who should venture to avenge her death would himself be killed by the proper avenger of blood. He affirms this of the Creeks and Cherokee also.

[9] Cushman, Hist. Choc., Chick., and Natchez Inds., pp. 263–264.

It is natural to suppose that Hohtak Lahba [10] would have refused the offer of his devoted mother. But custom denied him the privilege of any action whatever in the matter. If the offer was made and accepted by the relatives of the slain, he no longer stood condemned before the violated law, or in the eyes of the avenger, and he or she, who had voluntarily assumed the position, could alone make the atonement. The mother, in this case, had offered her life, a voluntary sacrifice for that of her son's; it had been accepted as a sufficiency by the avenger, and, even as the law of the Medes and Persians that "changeth not," so Tohto Pehah [11] could not reverse her accepted proposal, even if she had relented, nor the son refuse, she must die, and Hohtak Lahba must live; and the Amen was the response of the law.[12]

Nevertheless, Hohtak Lahba was not relieved from accusations of cowardice and, stung by the constant taunts of his associates, he finally murdered the son of his first victim and then shot himself over a grave which he had already prepared.[13]

During the civil war between the English and French parties a body of Choctaw on the English side attacked Holihta asha, the village of the head chief, but were repulsed and their leader, the chief of Bokfoka, was " killed, disemboweled, and his intestines cast at his feet, an insult unknown to the Choctaw before that." [13a] Indeed, this is the only case of mutilation of the body of a fellow tribesman that has come to the author's notice.

In later years considerable modifications were introduced into the criminal system of the Choctaw. To quote Cushman further:

Soon after the missionaries were established among them, a company of armed and mounted police, called "Light Horse Men," were organized for each district, in whom was vested the power of arresting and trying all violators of the law.[14] They were continually riding over the country settling all difficulties that arose among parties or individuals, and arresting all violators of the law. The custom of leaving the murderer to be disposed of as the relatives of the deceased saw proper, was then set aside, and the right of trial by the Light Horse who acted in the three-fold capacity—sheriff, judge, and jury—was awarded to all offenders. The Light Horse were composed of a brave and vigilant set of fellows, and nothing escaped their eagle eyes; and they soon became a terror to white whiskey peddlers who invaded the Choctaw territories at that time. When caught, the whiskey was poured upon the ground and the vendor informed that his room was preferable to his company.

When a murder was committed, the Light Horse at once took the matter into consideration, and after hearing all the testimony pro and con, pronounced the verdict in accordance thereto. If the person accused was found to be guilty, there and then, the time and place of his execution was designated,

---

[10] " Warm Pond."
[11] " Red Elm Seed."
[12] Cushman, op. cit., p. 265.
[13] Ibid., pp. 265-267.
[13a] Miss. State Archives.
[14] Claiborne says they were originally organized by the chiefs Greenwood Le Flore and David Folsom.—Miss., I, p. 505.

and the doomed man was informed that his presence would accordingly be expected. He never failed to make his appearance at the appointed place and hour, and all things being ready, a small red spot was painted directly over his heart as a target for the executioner; and being placed in position, [he] calmly received the fatal bullet, soon the grave closed over him and thus the matter ended. Sometimes the condemned would request a short respite, a few days extension of time, assigning as a reason for the desired delay, that a grand ball-play, dance or hunt, was soon to take place, in which he desired to participate, and as it did not take place until after the appointed day of his execution, he requested the favor of postponing his little affair until afterward. The request was seldom refused. The doomed man then designated the day and hour on which he would return and attend to the matter under consideration. He went to the ball-play, the dance, or the hunt, engaged in and enjoyed his anticipated fun, then returned true to his promised word and paid the penalty of the violated law, by calmly receiving the fatal shot. The rifle was invariably used as the instrument of execution, for the soul of the Choctaw who had been executed by hanging was regarded as accursed—never being permitted to join his people in the happy hunting grounds, but his spirit must forever haunt the place where he was hung. Hence their horror of death by hanging, and the gallows has ever been unknown among them.[15] If the condemned should fail to appear, which was never known to be, at the time and place of his execution, or should [he] manifest any emotion of fear during his execution, it was regarded as a disgrace to himself, his relatives and his nation as a Choctaw warrior, which no length of time could ever efface; hence their honor, resting upon their firmness in the hour of death, was watched with jealous care. Never was a full-blood Choctaw known to evade the death penalty, passed upon him by the violated law, by flight. If he violated the law he calmly abided the consequences, hence all places of imprisonment were unknown.[16]

As noted elsewhere, suicide was looked upon as a contemptible act, yet a kind of duel existed among these Indians which involved the mutual suicide of the parties to it, when suicide was not only honorable but practically enforced by popular opinion. The following account of this custom is quoted by Cushman from a manuscript left by the native missionary, Rev. Israel Folsom:

They had duels too; but they were quite different from any that has been practiced by any of the [other] Indians of the continent or the whites; and which most commonly proved fatal to both parties. When a quarrel or difficulty occurred between two warriors, a challenge was sent by one to the other; not to meet and take a pop at each other with pistols, as is the case in civilized and refined Nations, but in reality, it was a challenge for both to die. It was understood in no other way; this was the mode of trying the man's bravery, for they believe that a brave man, who possesses an honest and sincere heart, would never be afraid to die: It was usual for each one to select his own friend to dispatch him. If one should back out from the challenge, they considered it as a great mark of cowardice and dishonesty in him, and he would be despised by his relations and friends, and by the whole tribe. If a challenge was given and accepted, it was certain to end in the death of both parties;

---

[15] But cf. p. 110.
[16] Cushman, Hist. Inds., pp. 217–218; Claiborne, Miss., I, p. 488.

this mode of deciding difficulties had a strong tendency to restrain men from quarreling and fighting among themselves, for fear of being challenged and conseqeuntly compelled to die, or be forever branded with dishonesty and cowardice, and afterwards live a life of degradation and disgrace. Hence, it was a common saying among them, that a man should never quarrel, unless he was willing to be challenged and to die. On one occasion a sister seeing her brother about to back out from a challenge stepped forward and boldly offered herself to die in his stead, but her offer was not accepted, and she was so mortified at her brother's want of courage that she burst into tears.[17]

Cushman adds:

When one Choctaw challenged another the challenge was given verbally, face to face, the time and place then and there designated. If accepted (and it was almost certain to be) the two went to the place each with his second. The two combatants then took their places unarmed about twenty feet apart, each with a second at his right side with a rifle in hand. At a given signal each second shot the combatant standing before him. That closed the scene. Each had proved himself a Tush-ka Siah (warrior I am) and that was satisfactory to all.[18]

Bushnell contributes some additional information on this subject from the Louisiana Choctaw. He says:

Murder was the one great crime recognized by the Choctaw, and the life of the murderer was invariably claimed by the friends or relatives of the victim. It is said that murderers seldom attempted to escape, holding it a duty to their families to receive the punishment of death. To attempt to escape was regarded as a cowardly act, which reflected on every member of the family. If, however, a murderer did succeed in escaping, another member of the family usually was required to die in his stead.

The following account of a native execution, the last to occur according to tribal custom, was related by the two women at Bayou Lacomb. This event occurred some thirty years ago [about 1880] at a place not far from Abita Springs:

One night two men who were really friends, not enemies, were dancing and drinking with many others, when they suddenly began quarreling and fighting; finally one was killed by the other. The following day, after the murderer had recovered from the effects of the whisky, he realized what he had done, and knowing he would have to die, he went to the relatives of the murdered man and told them he was ready to meet his doom, but asked that he be allowed to remain with them about two weeks longer, as he did not want to miss a dance to be held within that time. To this they consented, and during the following days he was given many small presents, as pieces of ribbon, beads, and tobacco. He was treated by everyone, by old and young alike, with the greatest respect and kindness; all endeavored to make his last days enjoyable. At last came the event on account of which his life had been prolonged and for three days and nights all sang and danced. The next day, just at noon, when the sun was directly overhead, was the time fixed for the execution. Shortly before that time his friends and relatives gathered at his house, where he joined them. All then proceeded to the cemetery, for the execution was to take place on the edge of the grave that he himself had helped to dig, in a spot he had selected. The murderer stood erect at one end

---

[17] Cushman, Hist. Inds., pp. 200–201.   [18] Ibid., p. 201.

of the grave, and with his own hands parted his shirt over his heart. Four of his male friends stood near with their hands on his shoulders and legs, to keep his body erect after death. His female relatives were on each side, and all were singing loudly. Soon he announced that he was ready. A relative of the murdered man advanced and, pressing the muzzle of a rifle against the murderer's chest, fired.

As provided for, the body was held in an upright position and immediately a piece of cloth was inserted into the wound to stop the flow of blood. Late that afternoon the remains were placed in the grave, which was filled with earth without ceremony.[19]

The few notes which I myself obtained on this subject simply confirm the main points in the foregoing narratives. I was told that a man might sometimes obtain a sufficient suspension of his sentence to raise a crop. Simpson Tubby thought that the death sentence was carried out by about 12 men of the murderer's own family, but ordinarily it was a relative of the man he had killed who acted as executioner.

Romans tells us that one who had committed suicide was classed as an enemy, the bodies of both being buried in the earth as quickly as possible, but this attitude can not have been invariable. Besides the cases just mentioned, we are told by the French officer Du Roullet of several in which no such onus seems to have been placed upon the dead. He expresses the opinion that in these instances the idea of suicide had been derived from Negroes at New Orleans, but the case of the last Mobile warrior to survive in the battle between his people and De Soto's men in 1540 proves that the custom was native. That aboriginal American hero hung himself by means of his bowstring. Romans himself says that it was not uncommon for an unsuccessful gambler to end his life with a gun.[20]

Witchcraft was punished with death no less than murder, but the two seem to have been closely associated in the native mind, the former being regarded with even more horror on account of the uncanny nature of the offense and the underground methods employed in connection with it.

The general attitude of the Choctaw toward sexual offenses is best given by Romans in the following words:

Fornication is among them thought to be a natural accident, therefore a girl is not worse looked on for ten or a dozen slips;[21] but although they are not over jealous of their wives, they punish adultery in the woman, unless she happens to belong to a stronger or more noted and numerous family than the husband; in which case he scarce ventures even to put her away; but if she is doomed to suffer, her punishment is to be at a publick place (for that purpose set apart at every town) carnally known by all who choose

---

[19] Bull. 48, Bur. Amer. Ethn., p. 25.

[20] See p. 155 (under games).

[21] Claiborne says that seduction was less common than adultery, but he is probably incorrect (Hist. of Miss., I, p. 521).

to be present, young and old; thus the poor wretch after defending herself and struggling hard with the first three or four, at last suffers motionless the brutality of perhaps an hundred or a hundred and fifty of these barbarians; the same treatment is undergone by a girl or woman who belonging to another town or quarter of the nation comes to a place where she is a stranger and can not give a very good account of herself and her business, or the reason of her coming there; this they call running through the meadow, and if a white man happens to be in the town, they send him an offer of invitation to take the first heat; they plead in excuse for so barbarous a custom, that the only way to disgust lewd women is to give them at once what they so constantly and eagerly pursue.[22]

This method of punishing unfaithful wives is also described in the Anonymous Relation de La Louisiane (see pp. 248–249 and Mem. Amer. Anthrop. Assn., v, pp. 60–61), by Bossu (p. 264 and Nouv. Voy., vol. 2, p. 106, Paris, 1768), and by Milfort (pp. 269–270, and Milfort's Mémoire, pp. 304–308).

Milfort adds in a footnote that this is the only case in which children, if the woman happened to have any, are assigned to the father's family in preference to that of the mother. If this means an absolute transfer from one moiety to the other, it is the only suggestion of such a thing in all of our material and must be viewed with suspicion. The custom naturally fell into disuse very soon after the coming of the whites, and is mentioned by no writer later than those quoted. Flagellation and a summary divorce marked the limits of the later usage.

Incest, in the Indian sense of the word, including marriage within certain degrees of consanguinity and within the same moiety or similar social division, was anciently a major crime, but we have no record of the punishments inflicted on account of it. One of my informants had heard that a brother and sister among the Bok Chito Indians once married. They were separated but the woman was pregnant and so they were driven away. Some of her people followed her, however, and together they became the nucleus of the Natchez tribe. This last statement shows, of course, that the event was purely imaginary.

Bossu says that "the majority" of the Choctaw "are addicted to sodomy. These corrupt men (the male concubines) wear their hair long and a short skirt like the women, by whom they are in return held in supreme contempt."[23] The statement is echoed by Romans, but he maintains that this nation was less addicted to the crime than either the Chickasaw or Creeks.[24]

Turning to offenses against property we find considerable difference of opinion. Romans, always favorable to the Choctaw, says:

---

[22] Romans, Nat. Hist. of E. and W. Fla., pp. 86–87.
[23] Appendix, pp. 261–262; Bossu, Nouv. Voy., vol. 2, p. 100.
[24] Romans, Nat. Hist. E. and W. Fla., pp. 82–83.

" They are given to pilfering, but not so much as the Chickasaws," and in another place, "Although they have a strict notion of distinction in property, and even divide their lands, we never hear them quarrel about boundaries." [25]   On the other hand, Adair, who resided among their bitter enemies, the Chickasaws, declares:

They are such proficients in the art of stealing, that in our store-houses, they often thieve while they are speaking to and looking the owner in the face. It is reckoned a shame to be detected in the act of theft; but, it is the reward they receive, which makes it shameful: for, in such a case, the trader bastinadoes the covetous sinner, almost as long as he seems sensible of pain. A few years ago one of the Chikkasah warriors told me, he heard a middle-aged Choktah warrior, boast in his own country, at a public ball-play, of having artfully stolen several things from one and another trader, to a considerable amount, while he was cheapening goods of us, and we were blind in our own houses.[26]

Speaking of the Choctaw of Bayou Lacomb, Louisiana, Bushnell reports that " thieves apprehended with the stolen property in their possession were forced to return it. If they could not produce the property, either they or their families were compelled to return goods of equal value." [27]

Whipping appears to have been the usual punishment for this offense in later times, and is thus referred to by Cushman:

For minor offenses, whipping was the punishment; fifty lashes for the first offense, one hundred for the second, and death by the rifle for the third offense in case of theft, and so it is to-day (1899).

He who had been condemned to receive this punishment never attempted to evade it; but promptly presented himself, or herself, at the designated place of punishment. This punishment was inflicted several times at the mission of Hebron, to which I was an eye witness. Before the hour appointed, the neighborhood assembled around the church which stood about forty rods distant from the mission-house, where they indulged in social conversation and smoking; never, however, mentioning, or even hinting the subject which had brought them together. The culprit was as gay and cheerful as any of them, walking with an air of perfect indifference, chatting and smoking with the various groups sitting around on blankets spread upon the ground. Precisely at the moment designated, the Light-Horse, who constituted a sort of ambulatory jury, to arrest, try and punish all violators of the law, would appear. The crowd then went into the church, closed the door and commenced singing a religious hymn, taught them by the missionaries, which they continued until the tragedy outside was over. At the same time the culprit shouted " Sa mintih!" (I have come!) then ejaculated " Sa kullo!" (I am strong!) He then elevated his arms and turned his back to the executioner and said: "Fummih!" (whip!). When he had received fifteen or twenty blows, he calmly turned the other side to the Fum-mi (one who whips); and then again his back, uttering not a word nor manifesting the least sign of pain. As soon as the whipping was over, the church door was opened and the whole assembly

[25] Romans, E. and W. Fla., pp. 76, 87–88.
[26] Adair, Hist. Am. Inds., p. 283.
[27] Bushnell, Bull. 48, Bur. Amer. Ethn., p. 26.

came out and shook hands with the " Fumah " (whipped), thus reinstating him to his former position in society, and the subject was then and there dropped, never to be mentioned again, and it never was.[28]

The punishment varied in proportion to the value of the articles stolen and the previous record of the culprit. I was told that for stealing a horse the punishment for a first offense was one hundred lashes and for the second offense hanging, while " only " thirty-nine lashes were given for stealing a chicken.

Israel Folsom mentions fines among the punishments for minor offenses.[29]

Our appreciation of the native attitude toward theft is rendered difficult owing to the fact that the estimates of most of our earlier authorities have reference to thefts of property belonging to white men, or at most Indians of other tribes, who were in a different category, to the Indian manner of thinking, from individuals of one's own group. On the other hand the later penalties have distinct traces of white influence. It should be said that almost all early writers speak of the freedom from violation of the native granaries and caches which was characteristic of almost all the tribes of North America.

Failure to understand the Indians' point of view is also responsible for many accusations of treachery and untruthfulness, which we find on the pages of various early writers. Thus Adair gives an exceedingly biased view of the capacities of the Choctaw in this direction in the following words:

Those who know the Choktah, will firmly agree in opinion with the French, concerning them, that they are in the highest degree, of a base, ungrateful, and thievish disposition—fickle, and treacherous—ready-witted, and endued with a surprising show of smooth artful language on every subject, within the reach of their ideas; in each of these qualities, they far exceed any society of people I ever saw.[30]

He seems to have been highly impressed with the persuasive powers of speech possessed by the members of this tribe, for he says a little farther on:

The Choktah are the craftiest, and most ready-witted, of any of the red nations I am acquainted with. It is surprising to hear the wily turns they use, in persuading a person to grant them the favour they have in view. Other nations generally behave with modesty and civility, without ever lessening themselves by asking any mean favours. But the Choktah, at every season, are on the begging lay. I several times told their leading men, they were greater beggars, and of a much meaner spirit, than the white-haired Chikkasah women, who often were real objects of pity. I was once fully

[28] Cushman, Hist. Inds., pp. 218–219 ; cf. Claiborne, Miss., I, p. 493.
[29] Cushman, Hist. Inds., p. 362.
[30] Adair, Hist. Am. Inds., p. 283.

convinced that none was so fit to baffle them in those low attempts without giving offence, as their own country-men. One, in my presence, expatiated on his late disappointment and losses, with the several unexpected causes, and pressingly solicited his auditor as a benevolent kinsman, to assist him in his distress: but the other kept his ear deaf to his importunity, and entirely evaded the artful aim of the petitioner, by carrying on a discourse he had begun, before his relation accosted him as a suppliant. Each alternately began where the other left off, the one to inforce the compliance of his prayer, and the other, like the deaf adder, to elude the power of its charming him. Nature has in a very surprising manner, indued the Indian Americans, with a strong comprehensive memory, and great flow of language. I listened with close attention to their speeches, for a considerable time; at last the peti-tioner despairing of impressing the other with sentiments in his favour, was forced to drop his false and tragical tale, and become seemingly, a patient hearer of the conclusion of the other's long narrative, which was given him with a great deal of outward composure, and cool good-nature.

In the years 1746 and 1747, I was frequently perplexed by the Choktah mendicants; which policy directed me to bear, and conceal as well as I could, because I was then transacting public business with them. In 1747, one of their warriors and a Chokchooma came to me for presents; which according to my usual custom in those times, I gave, though much less than they pre-sumed to expect. The former, strongly declaimed against the penurious spirit of the French, and then highly applauded the open generous tempers of the English traders: for a considerable time, he contrasted them with each other, not forgetting, in every point of comparison, to give us the preference in a high degree. He was endued with so much eloquence and skill as to move the passions, and obtain his point. A considerable number of Chikkasah war-riors who were present, told me soon after that his skilful method of address-ing me for a bottle of spirituous liquors, seemed to them astonishing: an old beloved man replied, that the worst sort of snakes were endued with the greatest skill to insnare and suck their prey, whereas, the harmless have no such power.[31]

But Romans remarks:

I believe they are a nation whose word may be depended on when they give in to the interest of any person, and that their faith is to be better relied on than that of the Chicasaws or Creeks, which two last are really versed in all the gallic tricks of deceit.[32]

And he adds farther on:

I have a great opinion of a Chactaw's faithfully performing his promises. I have seen several little instances thereof; they detest a liar, and shew grati-tude to a man that keeps his word; my guide whose name was Pooskoos Mingo gave me an instance of this; when I left him he said I had satisfied him for every thing like a true man, but if I would give him a speaking paper to the great white man at Mobile (meaning John Stuart Esq.) then he would still better know it; I gave him a note recommending him to that gentleman, and because he had been of extraordinary service on the journey, begged he would allow him something more than common; it had the desired effect, he got a good many things extraordinary; when I was afterwards missing, and it was thought the Creeks had destroyed us in coming from the Chicasaw nation, this savage armed to avenge my death, and was actually taking the

---

[31] Adair, Hist. Am. Inds., p. 305.
[32] Romans, Nat. Hist. of E. and W. Fla., pp. 73–74.

war physick as they term it, when news was brought to the nation of my arrival at Mobile.[33]

Bossu says that "although they are barbarous and fierce, it is necessary in order to keep their confidence to keep one's word scrupulously when one has made them any promises.   Otherwise they will treat you with the greatest scorn, telling you haughtily that you are a liar, an epithet which these savages have bestowed on the present governor whom they call *Oulabé-Mingo* [Holabi minko], that is to say, the Liar Chief." [34]

Of the few Choctaw surviving near Bayou Lacomb in 1908–9 Bushnell says that they "bear a good reputation among the people of the surrounding country for honesty and truthfulness.   They regard lying as a crime and they have no respect for a person whom then can not believe." [35]

Claiborne, when acting as United States Commissioner to the Choctaw, encountered one Indian who professed to have no beliefs in regard to a good or bad spirit or a future state of existence.   "Of course," says the historian, "this claimant was not sworn, but we received his declaration of his case.   On being interrogated, he declared that the statement was true in all particulars.   'A man,' said he, 'who will lie is not fit to associate with warriors, but should be compelled to keep company with squaws.'"

And Claiborne adds: "Several witnesses confirmed his statement, and moreover, swore that he was a singularly upright man, and had never been known to tell a lie." [36]

There are several references in the literature of the Southeast which indicate that oaths were known to them, in which the sun was called to witness to the truth of their professions.   Claiborne says that a Choctaw named Lewis Vaun "solemnly promised in my presence and in the face of the Sun, not to do mischief until we had another talk." [37]

REGULATIONS FOR WOMEN AND CHILDBIRTH

The Choctaw, in agreement with all of the neighboring tribes, imposed upon their women complete separation from the family at every menstrual period.   The author of the French Relation says regarding this:

When a woman finds herself inconvenienced in the accustomed manner she immediately leaves the house, and goes a certain distance from it to a retired

---

[33] Romans, Nat. Hist. E. and W. Fla., pp. 81–82.

[34] Appendix, p. 263 ; Bossu, Nouv. Voy., vol. 2, p. 104.

[35] Bushnell, Bull. 48, Bur. Amer. Ethn., p. 26.

[36] Claiborne, Miss., I, p. 523.

[37] The Proceedings of the Governor. of the Mississippi Territory as Superintendent of Indian Affairs.   MS. in Miss. State Archives.   Letter of Claiborne, dated June 18, 1804.

place. She lights a fire there with flint and steel (briquet). They say that they must use new fire, and if they took some of that of the house, the house would be polluted, and the woman would die from the strength of the sickness which would be increased. The men do not live with their wives while they are in this condition. They [the women] hide themselves from the sight of the men; the husbands then get their own food or go to the homes of their neighbors.

One day I found myself at the house of a savage who had gone hunting for me the evening before. On awakening next morning, not finding the woman of the house, and seeing a fire at a distance I went to find her. I was then ignorant of this ceremony and having begged her to make me some porridge of little corn, it was only by means of entreaties that I obtained my request. As I was beginning to eat her husband arrived. I asked him if he wanted some, and having assured me that he did, he began to eat with me, but, when the plate was half emptied it occurred to him to ask me who had prepared it; it is to be remarked that he had recognized the cause of his wife's absence through some articles which were missing from the house; when I replied that it was his wife who had been my cook, he was at once seized with sickness and went to the door to vomit. Then, reëntering and looking into the dish, he noticed some red things in the porridge, which were nothing else than the skin of the corn, some grains of which are red. He said to me: "How have you the courage to eat of this? Do you not see the blood in it?" Then he began vomiting again and continued until he had vomited up all that he had eaten; and his imagination was so strongly affected that he was sick on account of it for some days afterward. It is a thing which they take such great care to observe as to absent themselves during that time, and to bathe well before reëntering the house.[38]

The same authority says:

When a man's wife is pregnant and near the time of delivery, so long as she is in travail the husband eats only in the evening after sunset, and if the child is a girl he observes this fast eight days longer.[39]

Romans remarks:

The women suffer no more by child birth than any other savage women; they retire into a place of solitude at the time, and after delivery return to their daily labour; however while I staid at *Oka Altakkala* in this nation one died in labour within about eighty yards of the house I resided in.[40]

Bossu's statements are somewhat more ample:

When the women are pregnant, their husbands abstain from salt and eat no pork, with the false notion that these foods would harm their children. The women never bring forth their children in the cabin; they do this in the woods without assistance from anyone.

Immediately after they are delivered, they wash their infants themselves. The mothers also apply to their foreheads a mass of earth in order to flatten the head and as fast as they can bear it they increase the load. It is considered beautiful by these people to have a flat head. They do not swathe their children nor tie them down in clothing with bands.

---

[38] Appendix, pp. 247–248; Mem. Am. Anth. Ass'n, v, pp. 59–60.
[39] Appendix, p. 248; Mem. Am. Anth. Ass'n, v, p. 60.
[40] Romans, Nat. Hist. E. and W. Fla., p. 87.

They do not wean them until they are tired of the maternal breast. I have heard very strong children say to their mothers " Sit down so that I may nurse," and the mother immediately sat down. Their cradle is made of canes. The mothers lay their children in these so that their heads are three or four finger-widths lower than their bodies. That is why one never sees crooked or hunch-backed children among the savages.[41]

There are no other early statements of consequence bearing upon the customs of childbirth. The following is extracted from Cushman and applies to the latter half of the nineteenth century:

With the Choctaw wife, as with all Indians, parturition was [a] matter that gave no uneasiness whatever; nor did it interfere with her domestic affairs, but for a few hours. Unlike her civilized sister, she neither required nor desired, nor accepted any assistance whatever. I have known them to give birth to a child during the night, and the next morning would find them at the cowpen attending to the affairs of the dairy. To have a man physician, on such occasions, was as abhorrent to her sense of modesty and revolting to her feelings, as it was wholly unnecessary. And the old custom is still [1899] adhered to by the present Choctaw wife and mother. After a child was born, after undergoing the usual necessary preliminaries, it was placed in a curiously constructed receptacle called Ullosi afohka, (infant receptacle) where it spent principally the first year of its life, only when taken out for the purpose of washing and dressing. This curiously made little cradle (for such it may truly be called) was often highly ornamented with all the paraphernalia that a mother's love and care could suggest or obtain. The little fellow's face, which was always exposed to view, was carefully protected by a piece of wood bent a few inches above and over it. Contented as Diogenes in his tub, the babe would remain in its little prison for hours without a whimper; part of the time asleep, and part of the time awake looking around in its innocence with calm and tranquil resignation. According to her convenience, the mother suspended her thus cradled child on her back, when walking, or the saddle when riding; or stood it up against a neighboring tree, if a pleasant day, that it might enjoy the fresh and pure air, and exhilarating sunshine; or suspended it on the projecting limb of a tree there to be rocked to sleep and pleasant dreams by the forest breeze. As soon as it was old enough to begin to crawl, it bade an informal adieu to its former prison, but to be found perched upon its mother's back, where it seemed well contented in all its journeys—long or short. It was truly astonishing with what apparent ease the Choctaw mother carried her child upon her back. The child was placed high up between the shoulders of the mother, and over it was thrown a large blanket, which was drawn tightly at the front of the mother's neck, forming a fold behind; in this the child was placed and safely carried, with seemingly little inconvenience to either mother or child. When the little chap had grown to such proportions as to be no longer easily thus transported, he was fastened to the saddle upon the back of a docile pony, which followed the company at pleasure; though here and there stopping momentarily to bite the tempting grass that grew along the pathway, then briskly trotting up until it had again reached its proper place in rank and file, indifferent to the jolting experienced by the youthful rider tied upon its back, who, however, seemed to regard it with stoical indifference. When arrived at the age of four or five years, he was considered as having passed through his fourth and last chrysalis stage, and was then untied from

---

[41] Appendix, p. 263; Bossu, Nouv. Voy., vol. 2, pp. 104–105.

the saddle and bid ride for himself; and soon did the young horseman prove himself a true scion of the parent tree, as a fearless and skillful rider.[42]

From Simpson Tubby I obtained the following interesting notes regarding customs within his own remembrance:

They would not let a pregnant woman drive a wagon or cross a running stream. In the latter case it was because they thought she would leave the spirit of the child upon the other side and his life would be short. They would not allow her to get off of the ground and thought that it was well for her to walk a great deal. They were terribly afraid to have her cough for they believed that the straining on her stomach would displace the child and make the birth hard. Before the child was born the father had to abstain from work and keep quiet. The prospective mother was tended by an old woman skilled in midwifery. They used to send everybody away at such a time except the midwife and the woman's husband.

They believed that if a child was not tempered like a piece of metal it was likely to die and so they plunged infants into water just after their birth. Then they took them back to the house, put them in out of the wind, and let their clothing dry on them.

An eelskin was tied around an infant at the level of the navel to prevent the stomach from protruding too much, and to make it high chested, supple in the back and straight.

Claiborne is the only writer to speak specifically of adoption, which was probably confined in ancient times to individuals of the same iksa as the deceased mother. He says:

The custom of adopting relatives or orphan children is very common. Even married people, who have children, occasionally adopt one or more. They take an equal part with the other heirs, and are sometimes even allotted the best share.[43]

The custom of head deformation, alluded to by Bossu, is mentioned by several other writers, and on account of it the traders sometimes spoke of the Choctaw as "flat heads." Adair speaks as follows regarding it:

The Choktah Indians flatten their fore-heads, from the top of the head to the eyebrows with a small bag of sand; which gives them a hideous appearance; as the forehead naturally shoots upward, according as it is flattened: thus, the rising of the nose, instead of being equidistant from the beginning of the chin, to that of the hair, is, by their wild mechanism, placed a great deal nearer to the one, and farther from the other. The Indian nations, round South-Carolina, and all the way to New Mexico, ... to effect this, fix the tender infant on a kind of cradle, where his feet are tilted, above a foot higher than a horizontal position,—his head bends back into a hole, made on purpose to receive it, where he bears the chief part of his weight on the crown of the head, upon a small bag of sand, without being in the least able to move himself. The skull resembling a fine cartilaginous substance, in its infant state, is capable of taking any impression. By this pressure, and their thus flattening the crown of the head, they consequently make their heads thick, and their

42 Cushman, Hist. Inds., pp. 232–233.   43 Claiborne, Miss., I, p. 523.

faces broad: for, when the smooth channel of nature is stopped in one place, if a destruction of the whole system does not thereby ensue, it breaks out in a proportional redundancy in another.[44]

He is somewhat too comprehensive in mapping the distribution of the custom. The only other good description is Bartram's, which runs thus:

The Choctaws are called by the traders flats, or flat-heads, all the males having the fore and hind part of their skulls artificially flattened, or compressed; which is effected after the following manner. As soon as the child is born, the nurse provides a cradle or wooden case, hollowed and fashioned, to receive the infant, lying prostrate on its back, that part of the case where the head reposes, being fashioned like a brick mould. In this portable machine the little boy is fixed, a bag of sand being laid on his forehead, which by continual gentle compression, gives the head somewhat the form of a brick from the temples upwards; and by these means they have high and lofty foreheads, sloping off backwards.[45]

PERSONAL NAMES

None of our authorities treats this subject adequately; we merely know that, as in the case of the Creeks and Chickasaw, there were two kinds of names, those bestowed in infancy and the war titles given in later life in commemoration of military exploits or events. Cushman suggests a totemistic significance in the names of the first class:

The names of the ancient Choctaws, as well as their entire race, as far as I have been enabled to learn, were nearly always connative referring generally to some animal, and often predicating some attribute of that animal. Such names were easily expressed in sign language; as the objectiveness of the Indian proper names with the result, is that they could all be signified by gesture, whereas the best sign talker among deaf mutes, it is said, is unable to translate the proper names in his speech, [and] therefore resorts to the dactylic alphabet.[46]

Claiborne's remark that children were "never named after their parents, but take their names from some incident at the moment of their birth," [47] seems, however, more in harmony with what we know of the neighboring peoples.

From the French manuscript so often quoted we learn that there were gradations among the warriors and it is probable that, as with the Creeks, the war titles were connected with the grades. Such a gradation seems to be indicated by Byington when he says in his dictionary, under the heading "humma," that it is "an addition to a man's name which gives him some distinction, calling on him for courage and honor. The ' na humma ' may not run or

---

[44] Adair, Hist. Am. Inds., pp. 8–9.   [46] Cushman, Hist. Inds., p. 98.
[45] Wm. Bartram, Travels, p. 515.   [47] Claiborne, Hist. Miss., I, p. 517 ; see also p. 520.

turn the back on the field of battle." [48]　A great many war names ended in ábi, signifying "killer," an appropriate termination of course for titles of this character.　A little light is thrown upon the manner of giving names by Cushman:

> The Indian, unlike the white man, often received a new name from some trivial incident or some extraordinary adventure, which frequently occurred, especially in their wars.　Anciently the Choctaws and Muscogees were uncompromising enemies, ever making raids into each others territories.　At one time a Muscogee party invaded the Choctaw country, and made a sudden and unexpected attack upon a band of Choctaw warriors.　The Choctaws, though surprised, made a brave resistance, and, after a short but furious fight, defeated and put their assailants to flight.　A vigorous pursuit at once ensued in which a fleet young Choctaw warrior named Ahaikahno (The Careless) had far in advance of his comrades, killed a Muscogee, and was in the act of scalping him, when two Muscogee warriors turned and rushed toward him with their utmost speed.　The Choctaws in the rear, seeing the danger of Ahaikahno, who was ignorant of his two fast approaching foes, shouted to him with all the strength of their voices—Chikke-bulilih chia!　Chikke bulilih chia! (pro. Chik-ke (Quickly) bul-elih (run) che-ah (you!).　Ahaikahno, hearing the shout and seeing his danger, was not slow in heeding the advice.　Ever afterwards Ahaikahno bore the additional name Chikke Bulilih Chia.[49]

The French Governor of Louisiana, De Kerlérec, informs us that at a great assembly at which he was present the Choctaw gave him the name " Tchakta youlakty mataha tchito, anké achoukema, which in our language signifies the king of the Choctaw and the greatest of the race of the youlakta which is ' the finest and the oldest,' the whole terminating in anké achoukema which means a very good father."　We would write this Chahta holahta imataha chito, aⁿki achukma, " big supporting holahta of the Choctaw, [and] my good father."　It is added that speeches and various ceremonials usually accompanied the bestowal of such a title.

As in the case of the Creeks, a Choctaw was averse to telling anyone his name.　Cushman says: " It was impossible to get it unless he had an acquaintance present, whom he requested to tell it for him." [50]　William Cobb, an intelligent half-breed, told Claiborne that " he never knew the name of his mother, though living under the same roof with her, till two years ago." [51]　They also avoided mentioning the names of the dead.[52]　Claiborne throws considerable light upon this last custom in the following passage:

> A singular fact was established before the commissioners: the Choctaws will not speak of the dead.　Our instructions required us to exact proof of the number of children each claimant under the 14th article, had at the date of the treaty, because each was entitled to a certain portion of land.　Upon being

[48] Byington, A Dictionary of the Choctaw Language, in Bull. 46, Bur. Amer. Ethn., p. 170.
[49] Cushman, Hist. Inds., pp. 236–237.
[50] Cushman, Hist. Inds., p. 202.　See also Gregg, as quoted on p. 129.
[51] Claiborne, Miss., I, p. 520.
[52] Cushman, op. cit., p. 246.

Interrogated the claimants uniformly omitted in the enumeration those that were dead, although well aware that by this omission they would lose a portion of land. Very old claimants would even deny that they ever had more children than they presented to the commissioners, and the facts had to be proved by kindred or neighbors. To arrive at the truth in these cases, we required them to arrange their families in a line according to their ages. They uniformly left a vacancy in the line to denote where the deceased would have stood; and this established, not only the number but the age. Thus, if the second child be dead an interval of some three feet was left between the first and the third child. Sometimes they planted stakes along the line to represent the dead, but could not be induced to mention their names.[53]

The Choctaw have always been a tribe of such importance that multitudes of names borne by individual Choctaw are preserved. Cushman mentions Shulush humma (Red Shoes), who was prominent in the eighteenth century as leader of the English faction in his tribe; Ibanowa (" one who walks with "—Cushman) ; "A-push-a-ma-ta-hah-ub-i (a messenger of death; literally, one whose rifle, tomahawk, or bow is alike fatal in war or hunting) ; A-pak-foh-li-chih-ub-ih (to encircle and kill, corrupted by the whites to A-puck-she-nubee, and so used by the Choctaw of the present day) ; A-to-ni Yim-in-tah (a watchman infatuated [!] with excitement) ; Olubih (to take by force) ; . . . Nit-tak-a chih-ub-ih (to suggest the day and kill).[54] He also mentions " Tunapoh Humma (Red Gum)," probably one of the " humma " class of which mention has been made above.[55]

The following war names were remembered by Simpson Tubby:

Istàbi, (to) take and kill.

Mishimishtàbi, (to) take away and kill.

Mashtàbi, (to) go (to war) and kill.

Imishtàbi, (to) kill for him.

Onatàbi, when you get there, kill him !

Màsholitàbi, (to) do away with everything except peace. [Probably in reality " when it was clear weather, he killed."]

Tàbi, said to mean " royalty " or " peace," but probably the common ending of a war title, signifying " to kill."

The following women's names are from the same source. They are said to have been given to women used as official messengers.

Maⁿtema or Mantema, " to go and carry or deliver something sacred or particular."

Onatima, " when you get there give it (to him)."

Wakayatima, " get up and hand it or deliver it."

Nompashtika, and Nompatisholi, both signifying " speaker," are said to have been official names given to the wives of the head chief and the band captains.

---

[53] Claiborne, Miss., I, pp. 519–520   [54] Cushman, Hist. Inds., p. 297.   [55] Ibid., p. 348.

The following names have been collected by the writer from various sources, but principally from early documents:

Anchaha humma, Painted-one Red.

Apushi imataha, Sprout Imataha.

Aseta humma, Stringer Red.

Achowa humma, Quarreler Red.

Atoni hopaii, Watchful War-chief (*or* War-prophet).

Chahta humma, Choctaw Red.

Chisha humma, Postoak Red.

Chikasha humma, Chickasaw Red.

Chilita humma, Brave Red.

Chuka holahta, House Holahta (see holahta hacho below).

Chuka ishtàbi, (In-a)-house-he-took and-killed.

Chula humma, Fox Red.

Chulosa imast bi, Quietly-he-took-and-killed.

Espana humma, Spaniard Red.

Fàni mi^{n}ko imastàbi, Squirrel-chief-he-took-and-killed.

Foe bila, Honey.

Frantci imastabi, He-took-a-Frenchman-and-killed-him (or perhaps rather French Imastàbi).

Hoshi^{n}sh humma, Red Feather.

Holahta hacho (holahta was a ceremonial name and originally a term applied to a chief in some dialects; hacho is adopted from a Creek war term).

Holahta hopaii, Holahta War-leader (*or* War-prophet).

Holahta humma, Holahta Red.

Hopaii humana, War-leader (*or* War-prophet) Red.

Hopaii iskitini, Little War-leader (*or* War-prophet).

Hushi humma, Bird Red.

Imaàbi, Give-and-kill.

Istipatapo, He-takes-and-spreads-out.

Istonna humma, Red-who-came-with.

Itilakna, Yellow Tree.

Itipatapo, Floor (*or* Bridge).

Itoti humma, War Red.

Iyasha humma, Kettle Red.

Kanalichabi, He-caused-to-remove-and-killed.

Ku^{n}shak humma, Cane Red.

Mi^{n}ko holisso, Book Chief (*or* Marked Chief).

Mi^{n}ko humma, Chief Red.

Mi^{n}ko imastàbi, Chief-who-took-and-killed.

Mi^{n}ko puskus, Child Chief.

Naholo imastàbi, He-seized-a-white-man-and-killed-him (*or* Whiteman imastàbi).

Nahotàbi, He-separated-with-the-hand-and-killed.

Nàshoba miⁿko chito, Great Wolf Chief.

Nàshoba nowa, Walking Wolf.

Nacholi imastàbi, Stripping-off-he-seized-and-killed.

Nukpala humma, One-who-is-excited Red (*or* One-who-lusts-for-(war) Red).

Okchalintàbi, He-saved-and-killed.

Paⁿshi imastàbi, He-took-by-the-hair-and-killed.

Pusha humma, Meal Red (*or* One-who-pulverizes Red).

Pushi imastàbi, (Having)-meal-he-takes-and-kills (see above).

Pushi imataha, Meal Imataha (?). (Unless it is a contraction of Apushi imataha.)

Pushi istonnàbi, He-came-with-meal-and-killed.

Shakchi humma, Crawfish Red.

Shikoba humma, Feather Red.

Taⁿshi hacho, Corn Hatco (the last word being from Creek hadjo).

Taⁿshi imastàbi, (In or with)-corn-he-took-and-killed.

Tàshka hopaii, Warrior Prophet (*or* Warrior Leader).

Tàshka imataha, Warrior Imataha.

Tàshka miⁿkushi humma, Little-chief-warrior Red.

Tàshka nanukachi, Warrior Counsellor.

Tàshka pilla hacho, Warrior-in-a-distant-place Hatco.

Tàmaha imastàbi, (In-the-)town-he-took-him-and-killed-him.

Tànàp humma, Enemy Red.

Tanitàbi, Rise-and-kill.

Tapena humma chito, Warclub Big Red.

Tiak humma, Pine Red.

Tish holahta, Waiter Holahta (see above).

Tishu miⁿko, Waiter Chief.

Tupa humma chito, Bed Big Red.

Ushissish humma, Bloody-child Red.

Uskula humma, Flute Red.

Wishakchi humma, Top Red.[56]

While the above translations are as close as it is possible to give at the present time, it must be remembered that these names are highly abbreviated mnemonics and sometimes a knowledge of the circumstances under which the name was originally given is necessary in order to determine the actual meaning. It is also evident that in many of the names composed of two words the words are to be understood separately as is the case with the corresponding Creek terms. Thus the words humma, holahta, imastàbi, imataha,

---

[56] Other names will be found in Claiborne's History of Mississippi, pp. 524–526, and Chickasaw names, which are similar, in the Forty-fourth Ann. Rept. Bur. Amer. Ethn., pp. 201–204.

hacho, and others, when in second position, really indicate certain classes of warriors, not perhaps classes that were very clearly defined, but still forming rough categories. So far as humma is concerned, it is indicated by what has been quoted from Byington regarding the na humma. Thus Tiak humma is not really a Red Pine but a Pine Red, Red being the classifier. And so we have a Flute Red, a Postoak Red, a Choctaw Red, a House Holahta, a Corn Hacho, a White-man Imastàbi, a Warrior Leader, a Warrior Imataha.

EDUCATION

This differed but slightly from education among the Creeks and Chickasaw. Our earliest authority gives very little on the subject specifically except to remark that "they never whip their children." [57] Bossu declares that—

Although the savages count descent only on the female side, the women are not permitted to correct the boys; they have authority only over the girls. If a mother ventured to strike a boy, she would receive sharp reprimands and would be struck in her turn, but when her little boy errs she takes him to an old man who gives him a lecture and then throws cold water over his body.[58]

Romans confirms this in the following paragraph which, however, concerns only male children:

Their exercises agree pretty much with what I have seen among other nations: from their infancy they learn the use of bows and arrows; they are never beaten or otherwise rudely chastised, and very seldom chid; this education renders them very wilful and wayward, yet I think it preferable to the cruel and barbarous treatment indiscriminately used by some European parents, who might with slight punishments by the excellency of wholesome christian Admonitions, work in a very different manner on the tender inclinations of pliable infancy. . . . [With the blowgun] they often plague dogs and other animals according to the innate disposition to cruelty of all savages, being encouraged to take a delight in torturing any poor animal that has the misfortune to fall into their hands; thinking best of him, who can longest keep the victim in pain, and invent the greatest variety of torture. When growing up, they use wrestling, running, heaving and lifting great weights, the playing with the ball two different ways, and their favourite game of *chunké*, all very violent exercises.[59]

Bossu says that the boys contended against each other with bow and arrows, "the one who shoots best being awarded the prize of praise from the lips of an old man, who names him an apprentice warrior." [59a]

---

[57] Appendix, p. 249; Mem. Am. Anth. Assn., v. p. 61.
[58] Appendix, pp. 263–269; Bossu, Nouv. Voy., vol. 2, pp. 105–106.
[59] Romans, E. and W. Fla., pp. 76–77.
[59a] Appendix, p. 263; Bossu, Nouv. Voy., vol. 2, p. 101.

A half-breed Choctaw, married to a Chickasaw, encountered by the missionary Hodgson in 1820, told him—

That great changes had taken place among Indians, even in his time—that in many tribes, when he was young, the children, as soon as they rose, were made to plunge in the water, and swim, in the coldest weather; and were then collected on the bank of the river, to learn the manners and customs of their ancestors, and hear the old men recite the traditions of their forefathers. They were assembled again, at sunset, for the same purpose; and were taught to regard as a sacred duty, the transmission to their posterity of the lessons thus acquired. . . . He said, that this custom is now abandoned by all the tribes with which he is acquainted, except, to use his own words, "where there is, here and there, an old ancient fellow, who upholds the old way"—that many have talked of resuming their old customs, which the whites have gradually undermined; but are unable, from the loss of their traditions.[60]

From other matters communicated to Hodgson by this Indian and from the statement, reiterated by several of our best authorities, that most of the Choctaw were unable to swim, it is evident that this man's testimony applied rather to the Creeks or Chickasaw than to the Choctaw, and it is therefore of but slight assistance, nor do our later authorities mention the subject in other than an incidental way. Claiborne but confirms the testimony of all other writers on the southeastern Indians when he says: "In all that concerns the child, the oldest maternal uncle, or if he is dead, the nearest male relative in that line is consulted. Instances frequently came before the Commissioners," he adds, "where a wife, though living happily with her husband, was induced by the maternal uncle to take her children and go west after 'leaving him,' as one of them expressed it, 'without cook, child, or comrade.' . . .

"It is the right of the wife, when a separation takes place, to take all the children to aid her to live, and even after her death her relatives have a claim to them paramount to the father."[61]

Cushman says:

But little restraint, parental or otherwise, was placed upon their children, hence they indulged in any and all amusements their fancy might suggest. The boys in little bands roamed from village to village at their own pleasure, or strolled through the woods with their blow-guns and bow and arrows, trying their skill upon all birds and squirrels that were so unfortunate as to come in their way. They were but little acquainted with the principles of right and wrong, having only as their models the daring deeds of their fathers in war and in the chase, they only yearned for the time when they might emulate them in heroic achievements; and one would very naturally infer that these boys, ignorant of all restraint from youth to manhood, would have been, when arrived at manhood, a set of desperadoes, indulging in every vice and committing every crime. But not so. No race of young people ever grew up to manhood in any nation who were of a more quiet nature and peaceful

---

⁶⁰ Hodgson, Travels, pp. 278–279.   ⁶¹ Claiborne, Miss., I, p. 517, also p. 521.

disposition than the youths of the old Mississippi Choctaws. They seldom quarreled among themselves even in boyhood, and less, when arrived at the state of manhood. To them in youth as well as in advanced years, as to all of their race, the dearest of all their earthly possessions from childhood to manhood, from manhood to old age, and from old age to the grave, was their entire and unrestrained freedom; and though untrammeled by moral restraint, yet there seemed to exist in their own breasts a restraining influence, a counteracting power, that checked the ungoverned passions of their uncultivated natures through life, and kept them more within the bounds of prudence and reason, than any race of uneducated people I ever knew.[62]

He tells us also of tests of endurance which they imposed upon themselves:

Even the little Choctaw boys took delight in testing the degrees of their manhood by various ways of inflicting pain. I have often seen the little fellows stir up the nests of yellow jackets, bumble-bees, hornets and wasps, and then stand over the nests of the enraged insects which soon literally covered them, and fight them with a switch in each hand; and he who stood and fought longest without flinching—foreshadowed the future man—was worthy the appellation of Mighty Warrior. But the business ends of the hornets, bees and wasps, noted for their dispatch in all matters of this kind, universally effected a hasty retreat of the intruder upon their domiciles, sooner or later— much to the delight of his youthful companions and acknowledged by an explosion of yells and roars of laughter. But the discomfited embryo warrior consoled himself by daring any one of his merrymaking companions to "brave the lion in his den," as he had and endure longer than he did the combined attacks of the valiant little enemy. The challenge was most sure to be accepted, but invariably with the same result, a retreat at the expense of a hearty laugh. From one to three minutes was the average length of a battle, the insects holding the field invariably. I have also seen them place a hot coal of fire on the back of the hand, wrist and arm, and let it burn for many seconds—bearing it with calm composure and without the least manifestation of pain, or experience the deepest sorrow without the slightest emotion.[63]

Simpson Tubby says that the old-time Choctaw would not take a child to a strange country while it was asleep, but he did not explain why. He added that they would not let children sleep on their sides or on a pillow or doubled up. They must sleep on their backs, and he has seen them straighten out sleeping children. "An eel is a straight fish, yet it can double up in any way; man should lie straight when he sleeps for the same reason." Nor would they let a child sleep with its head to the west. The pallet was raised under the head in order to keep the blood from flowing thither. Indeed, if a person complained of a dead feeling in the legs and thighs, the doctor would reduce the height of the head end of his pallet so that the blood would not flow so much toward his feet.

When girls were growing up they were not allowed to carry anything heavy, and a boy would be given nothing weightier than

---

[62] Cushman, Hist. Inds., pp. 215–216.   [63] Ibid., p. 214.

a gun or a fishing rod, when a family was moving. To cure children of laziness they made them play ball and run races. Sometimes they scratched them with a nettle to improve their circulation and cure them of laziness by forcing them to scratch themselves. But some became infected in that way and died, and the doctors told them to stop it.

The captain of Simpson's band recommended him to Mashulatubbi, last great chief of the Choctaw, to be made chief when he was 40 years old. When he was 10 months old they bathed him in a pond of cold water in the month of January, and Mashulatubbi said that he was to eat only "wild food." This was about a year before the chief died. For a year Simpson was fed on the flesh of small game animals, and after that, on big game animals, but when he was 18 he joined the white men's church.

MARRIAGE

Our anonymous French authority says regarding this:

When a youth wishes to marry, he goes to find the father and the mother of the girl whom he desires. After having made his request he throws before the mother some strings of glass beads, and before the father a breechclout. If they take the presents it is a sign of their consent, and then the youth leads the girl away to his home without other ceremony. From this moment the mother can no longer appear before her son-in-law; if they are obliged to remain in the same room they make a little partition between them for fear lest they see each other. . . . They may abandon their wives whenever they wish, and take many of them at a time. I saw one who had three sisters. When they marry a second time they take the sister of the dead wife, if she had one, otherwise a woman of the family.[64]

Romans merely remarks:

They take wives without much ceremony, and live together during pleasure, and after separation, which is not very frequent, they often leave the second to retake the first wife.[65]

The Rev. Israel Folsom, a native Choctaw missionary, is thus quoted by Cushman on this subject:

When the young Choctaw beau went the first time to see his "Fair One," after having resolved upon matrimony, he tested his own standing in the estimation of his anticipated bride by walking indifferently into the room where she was seated with the rest of the family, and, during the general conversation, he sought and soon found an opportunity to shoot, slyly and unobserved, little sticks or small pebbles at her. She soon ascertained the source whence they came, and fully comprehended the signification of those little messengers of love. If approved, she returned them as slyly and silently as they came. If not, she suddenly sprang from her seat, turned a frowning face of disapproval upon him and silently left the room. That ended the matter, though not a word had been spoken between them.

[64] Appendix, pp. 248–249; Mem. Am. Anth. Association, v. pp. 60–61.
[65] Romans, E. and W. Fla., p. 86.

But when the little tell-tales skipped back to him from her fingers, followed by a pair of black eyes peeping out from under their long, silken eye-lashes, he joyfully comprehended the import and, in a few minutes, arose and, as he started toward the door, he repeated his informal "Ea li" (I go), upon which a response of assent was given by the father or mother in the equally informal "Omih" (very well).

He returned in two or three days, however, with a few presents for the parents, and to secure their approval. Which, being obtained, a day was appointed for the marriage—a feast prepared and friends invited. When all had assembled, the groom was placed in one room and the bride in another and the doors closed. A distance of two or three hundred yards was then measured off, and at the farther end a little pole, neat and straight, was set up. Then, at a given signal, the door of the bride's room was thrown open, and at once she springs out and starts for the pole with the lightness and swiftness of an antelope. As soon as she has gotten a few rods the start, enough for her to keep him from overtaking her if she was so inclined, the door of his room was thrown open, and away he runs with seemingly superhuman speed, much to the amusement of the spectators. Often, as if to try the sincerity of his affection, she did not let him overtake her until within a few feet of the pole; and sometimes, when she had changed her mind in regard to marrying him, she did not let him overtake her, which was public acknowledgement of the fact, and the groom made the race but to be grievously disappointed—but such a result seldom happened. As soon as he caught her, after an exchange of a word or two, he gently led her back by the hand, and [they] were met about half way by the lady friends of the bride, who took her from the hands of the groom yielding to their demands with seeming reluctance, and led her back into the yard to a place in front of the house previously prepared for her, and seated her upon a blanket spread upon the ground. A circle of women immediately formed around her, each holding in her hands the various kinds of presents she intended to bestow upon her as a bridal gift. Then one after another in short intervals began to cast her presents on the head of the seated bride, at which moment a first-class grab-game was introduced. For the moment a present fell upon her waiting head it was snatched therefrom by some one of the party—a dozen or more making a grab for it at the same instant—regardless of the suffering bride, who was often pulled hither and thither by the snatchers' eager fingers becoming entangled in her long, black ringlets. When the presents had all been thus disposed of, the bride not receiving a single article, the twain were pronounced one—man and wife; then the feast was served, after which all returned to their respective homes with merry and happy hearts.

Cushman adds:

As the land was free to all, the happy groom, a few days after his nuptials, erected with the assistance of his friends, a neat little cabin in some picturesque grove by the side of some bubbling spring or on the banks of some rippling brook. A small iron kettle in which to boil their venison, and a wooden bowl in which to put it when cooked, were sufficient culinary utensils for the young house-keepers.[66]

The same writer thus refers to the taboos between son-in-law and mother-in-law already mentioned, and also those between husband and wife:

[66] Cushman, Hist. Inds., pp. 369–370.

There was a peculiar custom among the ancient Choctaws, prior to 1818, which, according to tradition, was as follows: For many years after the marriage of her daughter, the mother-in-law was forbidden to look upon her son-in-law. Though they might converse together, they must be hidden the one from the other by some kind of screen, and when nothing else offered, by covering their eyes. Thus the mother-in-law was put to infinite trouble and vexation lest she should make an infraction upon the strange custom; since, when travelling or in camp often without tents, they were necessarily afraid to raise their heads, or open their eyes through fear of seeing the interdicted object.

Another peculiarity, which, however, they possessed in common with other tribes, was, the Choctaw wife never called her husband by name. But addressed him as " my son or daughter's father "; or more commonly using the child's name, when if Shah-bi-chih, (meaning, to make empty, the real name of a Choctaw whom I know) for instance, she calls her husband " Shah-bi-chih's father."[67]

Gregg parallels this bit of information closely enough to indicate that he obtained his knowledge from the same source.

There is [says he] a post-nuptial custom peculiar to the full-blood Indians of the Choctaws, which deserves particular notice. For years, and perhaps for life, after the marriage of her daughter, the mother is forbidden to look upon her son-in-law. Though they converse together, he must be hidden from her by a wall, a tent, a curtain, or, when nothing else offers, by covering the eyes. During their emigration, it is said these poor superstitious matrons were put to infinite trouble so as not to infract this custom. While travelling, or in camp often without tents, the mother-in-law was afraid to raise her head or open her eyes, lest they should meet the interdicted object.

It is another peculiarity, which they have in common with some of the more northern tribes, that the Choctaw wife, of the " old school," can never call her husband by name. But if they have offspring—she calls him " my son's father "; or, more commonly using the child's name, when, if " Ok-le-no-wa," for instance, she calls the husband " Ok-le-no-wa's father." And yet another oddity regarding names: the ignorant Choctaw seems to have a superstitious aversion to telling his own name: indeed it appears impossible to get it from him, unless he have an acquaintance present, whom he will request to tell it for him.[68]

In this connection a bit of folklore might be added as reported by Cushman relative to the traditional first marriage between the Choctaw and the whites:

A white man at an early day, came into their country, and in course of time married a Choctaw girl and as a natural result, a child was born. Soon after the arrival of the little stranger, (the first of its type among them), a council was called to consider the propriety of permitting white men to marry the women of the Choctaws. If it was permitted, they argued, the whites would become more numerous and eventually destroy their national characteristics. Therefore it was determined to stop all future marriages between the Choctaws and the White Race, and at once [they] ordered the white man to leave their

---

[67] Cushman, Hist. Inds., pp. 201–202.
[68] Gregg, Commerce of the Praries in Early Western Travels, ed. R. G. Thwaites, vol. 20, pp. 313–314. See also p. 120.

country, and the child [to be] killed. A committee was appointed to carry the decision into execution, yet felt reluctant to kill the child. In the meantime, the mother, hearing of the resolution passed by the council, hid the child, and when the committee arrived they failed to find it, and willingly reported that the Great Spirit had taken it away. The mother kept it concealed for several weeks, and then secretly brought it back one night, and told her friends the next morning that the Great Spirit had returned during the night with her child and placed it by her side as she slept. The committee had previously decided, however, that if ever the child returned it might live; but if it never came back, they then would know that the Great Spirit had taken it. The boy was ever afterwards regarded as being under the special care of the Great Spirit, and became a chief of their Nation. The law was repealed; the father re-called and adopted as one of the tribe; and thus the custom of adopting the white man originated and has so continued from that day to this—so affirms one of their ancient traditions, those Indian caskets filled with documents from the remote past, but which have long since passed into the region of accepted fables.[69]

Interesting divergencies are shown in Claiborne's description of Choctaw courtship and marriage. I am not sure that his understanding of the ceremony is to be relied upon in all particulars:

Bah na-tubbe, an intelligent fellow, in the course of his examination, stated that it was usual for the woman, especially widows, to give "the first banter," viz: first advances. This is usually done at night, in the dance, by squeezing the hand or treading gently on the foot of the favored warrior. Perhaps this may be rather a necessity than a freedom; because if a man should take these liberties with a squaw she would immediately resent it by attacking him with a stick, and every squaw present would assist her. Witness had seen twenty squaws thus beating a too ardent lover. These "banters" are often given by old women, invariably to very young men. Old women usually select a lazy fellow, who takes her for her house and her ponies. Witness had, when only eighteen, been taken by a woman of fifty, but he soon left her for a very young girl. When the "banter" is mutually agreeable the parties quietly slip out of the crowd, and when they re-appear are considered man and wife.

Courtship and marriage, however, are sometimes more formal. A young warrior who is in love applies to the maternal uncle—never to father or mother—and they agree on the price, which is paid to the uncle. On a certain day the groom and his relatives appear at an appointed place, dressed in their best, where they loiter till noon. The bride then leaves the lodge of her parents, and the friends on both sides gather about her. She watches an opportunity and flies to the adjacent woods, her attendants hovering around to cover her retreat. She is pursued by the female relatives of the groom. If she is anxious for the match, it is not difficult to overtake her. But if she dislikes it, she runs until she falls exhausted, and sometimes escapes, and wanders away to a remote village, where she is adopted and cannot be reclaimed. If the fugitive is overtaken, she is brought back among the groomsman's friends, but he has disappeared. She sits down, and the friends on both sides throw some little presents in her lap. Each female relative ties a ribbon or some beads in her hair, and then the provisions brought by friends are divided among the company to be taken to their respective homes. The bride is then conducted to a little lodge adjoining her parents, and late at night her

[69] Cushman, Hist. Inds., pp. 373–374.

lover finds his way to her arms. In the morning they have disappeared, and the fawn of the woods must be sought in the camp of her husband.

The marriage endures only during the affection or inclination of the parties, and either may dissolve it at pleasure. This, of course, very often occurs, in which case the children follow the mother; the father has no control over them whatever.[70]

His reference to polygamy is most illuminating. He says:

This was tolerated by the Choctaws, but not universal. When a man had two wives, and died, each wife claimed to be the head of a separate family. They always occupied separate cabins, and generally ten or more miles apart. No instance came before us where a man had two wives in the same house, or even in the same yard or enclosure, unless they were sisters, and then they sometimes lived in the same yard, but in different houses.

An amusing instance came before the commissioners, I-og-la [Imokla or Yukla?] presented her claim. The witness, Hi-a-ka [Haiaka] deposed that at the time of the treaty claimant was one of the wives of Tusk-a ma-ha [Táshka imataha], who had emigrated west. He had many wives. He made the circuit among them regularly, and thus passed his time. He neither hunted nor worked. He had ten wives, scattered round the country, fifteen or twenty miles apart, and he had his regular stands, going from one to the other, being well fed, and a favorite with all of them. He was a fellow of medium height, about five feet seven, well built, very muscular and active, lazy and fond of eating and drinking. He provided his own clothing—nothing more. He made his home at the house of Ho-pia-ske-tena [Hopaii iskitini], (Little Leader,) at the old town of Yocka-no-chick-ama [perhaps Yakni achukma, see p. 75]. Two years before the treaty he married claimant, but only visited her about two days in every month; her house was one of the stands on his circuit; he never worked for her or contributed to her support; it was his custom to spend some time with every woman when he first took her, but the novelty soon wore off, and he went his usual round. Claimant had a house before she married this man; he finished it for her; he had several wives before he met her, and took several afterwards. He threw none of them away. Witness never heard any complaint on the part of his wives of neglect on his part. But when he emigrated, he left them all.[71]

The next description of a wedding ceremony is from Halbert:

When a young Choctaw, of Kemper or Neshoba county, sees a maiden who pleases his fancy, he watches his opportunity until he finds her alone. He then approaches within a few yards of her and gently casts a pebble towards her, so that it may fall at her feet. He may have to do this two or three times before he attracts the maiden's attention. If this pebble throwing is agreeable, she soon makes it manifest; if otherwise, a scornful look and a decided " ekwah " indicate that his suit is in vain. Sometimes instead of throwing pebbles the suitor enters the woman's cabin and lays his hat or handkerchief on her bed. This action is interpreted as a desire on his part that she should be the sharer of his couch. If the man's suit is acceptable the woman permits the hat to remain; but if she is unwilling to become his bride, it is removed instantly. The rejected suitor, in either method employed, knows that it is useless to press his suit and beats as graceful a retreat as possible.

When a marriage is agreed upon, the lovers appoint a time and place for the ceremony. On the marriage day the friends and relatives of the prospective

---

[70] Claibourne, Miss., I, pp. 516–517.   [71] Claiborne, Miss., I, p. 520.

couple meet at their respective houses or villages, and thence march towards each other. When they arrive near the marriage ground—generally an intermediate space between the two villages—they halt within about a hundred yards of each other. The brothers of the woman then go across to the opposite party and bring forward the man and seat him on a blanket spread upon the marriage ground. The man's sisters then do likewise by going over and bringing forward the woman and seating her by the side of the man. Sometimes, to furnish a little merriment for the occasion, the woman is expected to break loose and run. Of course she is pursued, captured and brought back. All parties now assemble around the expectant couple. A bag of bread is brought forward by the woman's relatives and deposited near her. In like manner the man's relatives bring forward a bag of meat and deposit it near him. These bags of provisions are lingering symbols of the primitive days when the man was the hunter to provide the household with game, and the woman was to raise corn for the bread and hominy. The man's friends and relatives now begin to throw presents upon the head and shoulders of the woman. These presents are of any kind that the donors choose to give, as articles of clothing, money, trinkets, ribbons, etc. As soon as thrown they are quickly snatched off by the woman's relatives and distributed among themselves. During all this time the couple sit very quietly and demurely, not a word spoken by either. When all the presents have been thrown and distributed, the couple, now man and wife, arise, the provisions from the bags are spread, and, just as in civilized life, the ceremony is rounded off with a festival. The festival over, the company disperse, and the gallant groom conducts his bride to his home, where they enter upon the toils and responsibilities of the future.[72]

The above account is based largely upon the following specific description of a wedding found among Mr. Halbert's notes:

The following account of a marriage in Jasper County, Mississippi, in August, 1891, of two Six Towns Indians, Oliver Chubbee and Susan Simpson, may be considered as describing a typical Choctaw marriage in the closing years of the nineteenth century.

" The Indians in large numbers arrived on the ground the evening before the wedding day, and spent the night in their camps. The next morning, extensive preparations were made in the way of cooking the big dinner which was to follow immediately after the marriage ceremoney. The place was a kind of glade in the woods. Pots, kettles and pans were there in profusion and a number of Indian women were soon immersed in the culinary operations, preparing beef, bread, coffee, pudding and pie for the marriage feast. About eleven o'clock the long table was set, and it was announced that the marriage would now take place. Miss Susan then modestly made her appearance on the spot selected for the ceremony. A shawl was spread upon the ground, upon which she seated herself, and four men then took another shawl, and held it, one at each corner, over her head. ' Hálbina, hálbina ' (presents, presents) was the cry that now resounded on every side. Forthwith many came forward and threw their presents on the shawl upheld by the four men. These presents consisted of bundles of calico, ribbons and other female paraphernalia, and even some little money—whatever in fact the donors chose to give. The presents, however, were not for the bride, but for the female relatives. They were intended as a kind of remuneration to these relatives for their assistance in cooking the

---

[72] H. S. Halbert, " Courtship and Marriage among the Choctaws of Mississippi," in the American Naturalist, vol. XVI, pp. 222–224. Philadelphia, 1882.

marriage dinner. When all the presents had been deposited on the shawl, Miss Susan arose, walked off about fifty yards, where some of her female friends were assembled, and again seated herself. Here the presents were brought, taken possession of by some of the women and distributed among Miss Susan's female kinsfolk. At the same time that Miss Susan had seated herself on the shawl, and while the men were holding the other shawl over her head, Mr. Chubbee came within about twenty feet of her, spread a blanket on the ground and seated himself upon it, and quietly waited for the passive part he was to perform in giving a finality to the marriage ceremony. When Miss Susan rose from the ground, some half a dozen men, relatives of Chubbee, came forward and seated themselves in a line on his left. The male relatives [of the bride] now in succession, approached the patient bridegroom, addressing him by the title of relationship created by the marriage, and then delivered a short complimentary or congratulatory address.

" When each had finished his talk to Chubbee, he then moved along the line, and shook hands with each one of Chubbee's seated kinsmen, calling him by the term of relationship created by the marriage, to which the kinsman responded simply by the assenting term *Ma*. For instance, A shook hands with B, and simply said Amoshi ma, (my uncle) to which B responded with Ma. The Choctaw terms of relationship and their application are very intricate and perplexing to a white man. The following is the very short congratulatory address of one of the old Indians, George Washington, to Oliver Chubbee, ' Nittak chashpo hokno sabaiyi chi ahanchi li beka tok akinli kia himak a^n annumpa holitopa chi anochi lishke. Sayup chi ahanchi li hoke.' *In former days I called you sabaiyi* [my sister's son], *but now I put a sacred name on you,—I call you sayup* [my son-in-law]. Only two or three women came forward and spoke to the bridegroom and to him alone, for they paid no attention to the other men on the ground. To a subsequent inquiry made to George Washington as to the cause of so few women coming to give the bridegroom the term of relationship, the response was ' Ohoyo at takshi fehna,' *Women are very modest*. When the men had finished their little congratulatory talks to Chubbee, the marriage was complete, and bride and bridegroom were now one. Without any further ceremony dinner was now announced to which all hands forthwith repaired and did it full justice. As a general thing, after the feast comes the big dance which was omitted on this occasion. Generally too an old-fashioned Choctaw wedding takes place about sunset, after which comes the big feast and the night-long big dance. In another feature Chubbee's wedding differed from the usual old style, for commonly the couple sit side by side, and the wedding gifts are placed upon the head of the bride and are instantly snatched off by her kin. With the usual Indian impassiveness Chubbee did not go near or even look at his bride until all got ready to go home, which was about the middle of the afternoon."

Following is Bushnell's account of the ceremonies known to the Choctaw of Bayou Lacomb:

The marriage ceremony as performed until a few years ago, at a time when there were many Choctaw living in the region, was thus described by the women at Bayou Lacomb.

When a man decided he wanted to marry a certain girl he confided in his mother, or if she was not living, in his nearest female relative. It was then necessary for her to talk with the mother or the nearest living relative of the girl, and if the two women agreed, they in turn visited the chiefs or heads of the two *ogla*, or families, to get their consent to the union. As a man was not

allowed to marry a girl who belonged to his *ogla*, often the women were
obliged to make a long journey before seeing the two chiefs, whose villages
were frequently a considerable distance apart.

After all necessary arrangements had been made, a day was fixed for the
ceremony. Many of the man's friends and relatives accompanied him to the
girl's village, where they seem to have had what may be termed "headquarters"
of their own. As the time for the ceremony drew near, the woman with her
friends was seen some distance away. The man and his party approached and
he endeavored to catch the girl. Then ensued much sham fighting and wrestling between the two parties, and the girl ran about apparently endeavoring
to escape, but she was finally caught by the man and his relatives and friends.

Then all proceeded to the place where the feast had been prepared, to which
both parties had contributed. Off to one side, four seats had been arranged in
a row; usually a log covered with skins served the purpose. The man and
girl then took the middle seats and on the ends sat the two male heads or
chiefs of their respective *ogla*. Certain questions were then asked by the
chiefs, and if all answers were satisfactory, the man and girl agreed to live
together as man and wife and were permitted to do so. This closed the ceremony and then the feasting and dancing began.

The man continued to live in his wife's village, and their children belonged
to her *ogla*.

By mutual agreement the two parties could separate and, in the event of so
doing, were at liberty to marry again. The man usually returned to his own
village, taking all his property with him.

If a man died in his wife's village, even though he left children, his brothers
or other members of his *ogla* immediately took possession of all his property
and carried it back to his native village. His children, being looked on as
members of another *ogla*, since they belonged to their mother's family, were
not considered as entitled to any of this property.[73]

The following descriptions of the marriage ceremony were given
me by two of the best-informed men of the Mississippi Choctaw.

Olmon Comby stated that courting among the young people took
place principally during the dances, such dances being held when
the community happened to be together and there was plenty of food.
If a youth's advances were accepted, he carried the product of his
next hunt to the girl's mother and by that they knew that he wanted
to marry her. Very soon his father would question him on the subject, and, having learned the girl's identity, his mother was dispatched to the mother of the girl to obtain her consent. The latter
would inquire whether her visitor's son was a good hunter, and,
if she could truthfully say, "Yes, he is a great hunter," the reply
was sure to be favorable and the wedding day was fixed.

The youth then bought a piece of cloth, 75 or 80 feet long, which
he gave to the girl's mother, and she cut it into smaller parts to
distribute among her female relatives, indicating to each of them as
she did so that she wished her to provide a certain kind of food for a
feast to be given to her future son-in-law's kindred.

---

[73] Bushnell in Bull. 48, Bur. Amer. Ethn., pp. 26–27.

Before either party sat down to eat, the girl, at a given signal, started away on the run and the youth pursued her, she being assisted by her relatives and he by his. After she had been caught and brought back to the scene of the festivities, she was seated beside her intended husband, and his relatives brought quantities of cloth, ribbons, and similar things, as also various kinds of food, such as bread, beef, and pork, which was allowed to rest upon the girl's head for a minute and then gathered up by her uncle, who tied the cloth up in bundles. These presents cost perhaps $60 to $75, and by them the girl was " bound."

Then each family feasted the other, the relatives of the girl eating first. That made them kindred and they shook hands.

The girl's people now brought baskets, sacks, and other similar receptacles and her uncle distributed to them in succession the articles provided by the groom. These had been placed in a pile and the distribution was made indifferently, beginning at the top, so that it was a matter of chance who received the best pieces.

Finally the chief delivered a long address, directed mainly to the newly married couple, telling them that they must be faithful until death and take good care of each other when either was sick. The chief also extended his remarks to the other young people, warning them not to run away to marry, and, so that the world might stand a great deal longer, not to marry near relatives. If they married persons already connected by blood, they would not know how to name their relatives. Thus the same man would be called father-in-law and uncle, and they wanted the names to be applied to different individuals.

From Simpson Tubby I gathered the following information.

The old people used to watch their children carefully, especially during the dances, to discover what attachments were springing up between them and prevent any taking root between those who were too closely related or whose associations were too distant or too diverse. That was the way in which they kept their children pure.

Mention has been made already of the taboos against marriage within the iksa and the still older taboo against marriage within the moiety. It is also said that they would not allow those related within four degrees to marry, no matter to what iksa they belonged, and that fifth cousins might marry only if they could prove there was nobody more distantly related who would make a suitable partner. (Claiborne mentions the case of a Choctaw named Pahlubbee who married his step-daughter but was widely censured in consequence.[74])

---

[74] Claiborne, Miss., I, p. 521.

Simpson affirmed that the girl must be between 20 and 25 years of age and the youth between 25 and 30. When they began to marry younger the offspring were "runts," the tribe got smaller and weaker and ultimately became reduced to its present fragmentary condition. They also did not like to have their children marry into a band opposed to their own in the ball games. (See p. 153.) Opposition to marriage in other tribes had a practical consideration anciently because, should war break out between the two peoples, intermarried foreigners of the hostile tribe were generally killed.

A youth showed his fondness for a girl by calling often upon her brother, making him an especial companion, and so on. These various signs having been observed by the old people, a courtship dance was held in the neighborhood and by watching the behavior of the young people, their parents satisfied themselves of the state of affairs. Sometimes attachments between three or four couples would be discovered on the same occasion. Then the father of one of the two parties would call upon the father of the other to talk the matter over. The mothers would also confer, after which all four had a meeting and came to an understanding. Then either the boy or the girl spent three days in the family into which he or she was to marry to see whether they would fit in there, because it was intended that they should spend the first few years of their married life in that particular household. If one of the parties was very young, such a disposition of them might be ordered by the chief.

While two young people were engaged, even though they were near neighbors, they did not see each other all the time. The old people meanwhile would visit back and forth, exchange salutations, and then bid good-by as if they had come from great distances and lived far apart.

The preliminaries having been satisfactory, the parents of the couple met and fixed upon a date for the wedding. Usually this was some time in the fall, because it was claimed that the nation would be weakened if people had sexual relations in the summer, a belief that was equally impressed on all married persons.

If a death took place the wedding would be postponed, the period of postponement being longer in proportion to the age of the deceased.

A great quantity of food was now procured—by the girl's family apparently, though Simpson omitted this point—and they began cooking for the marriage feast about midnight, keeping it up until morning. On the other hand the youth's parents made a considerable present of clothing and merchandise to the parents of the girl, consisting of some such articles as the following: One pair of shoes for each, a dress for the mother, a hat for the father, a barrel of flour, one side of meat, and $2 worth of coffee. If the young people eloped before such presents had been made, the marriage was not recognized as legal, and they legalized it by calling them in and going over the proper ceremony. At that time the head chief and captains made a final inquiry as to whether there was any possible blood connection between the two parties. Sometimes this took an entire day.

All obstacles having now been removed, the girl was placed some 25 paces in advance of the crowd and the youth set out in pursuit of her. They followed a circular course, each being assisted by the members of his or her respective family. The harder the race the stronger it was believed would be their love for each other, but if the girl were soon caught, it was considered a sign that her love was weak. There was great excitement and much shouting. Sometimes the youth would fall and so enable his intended bride to get a long lead; sometimes she would fall and be caught almost immediately. It is claimed that the object of this race was to determine whether either party was indifferent to the match, as would be shown by running in a half-hearted manner. It is said that Little Leader (Hopaii iskitini), captain of the Sukanatcha band, put an end to the marriage race at the time when Sukanatcha was settled. The other marriage laws held on longer.

The girl having at last been caught, the two were brought back to the place where the feast was to be held and seated side by side, the boy being placed in his seat by the girl's people and she in her seat by the boy's. The chief or captain now made a speech in which he stated upon whom the obligation fell of decorating the girl, and upon whom the obligation of decorating the boy, the boy's people in the former case and the girl's in the latter. Those not related were directed to decorate both unless unable, for any reason, to do so, when they must remain quiet. Each party brought several yards of ribbon—perhaps from 5 to 7—or 10 to 40 yards of cloth, or dresses, which they laid upon the heads of the two until they were completely covered. This was to indicate their consent, and it was made the occasion of a property contest between the families, each striving to " outdress " the other. Afterwards each family took the property which had been acquired in this way and distributed it to the nearest blood relations. Then they sat down to eat, a long speech was made by the chief or captain, and the dance followed, in which, if all was harmonious, all of the connections of both participated. If all of the relatives were not present the wedding was outlawed, and this was one of the ways in which trouble was created, usually by some outsiders, and perhaps by some one who had wanted to marry one of the parties to the match.

When a married woman came back to visit her parents, her husband did not usually accompany her. Whether or not she were present, he would not speak to her sisters and only to her father or mother if he were spoken to. Mother-in-law avoidance was common in old times, but it is said that the husband spoke more freely to his wife's mother than to her father, because when his wife had a message to send to her parents it went more often to her mother than to her father, and so the husband had more occasion to meet the former.[74a]

Some white men who have witnessed native ceremonies furnished confirmation of details of the above, though with minor variations. They said that on the morning of the wedding day the youth, accompanied by a number of his male relatives, started toward the home of his intended bride and she at the same time, with a party of girl companions, set out to meet him. When the two parties had come within a short distance of each other, the girl and her company began running, and the young man, followed by his own company, gave chase until he caught her. Very often the girl carried a pack basket on her back filled with corn or with biscuits and as she ran the contents were scattered along the way and those who were present scrambled for them. After having overtaken his intended the groom brought her back to an open space where the ceremony was to be completed. They sat down side by side, and the headman usually made a speech. A feast, followed by a dance, concluded the day's program, but on the next day there was usually a ball game. Some of these ceremonies are also remembered by the Choctaw in Oklahoma.

Nowadays it is said that the Choctaw of Bok Chito, the only band in Mississippi which is not formally Christianized, simply have a meeting between the two parties, a speech, and a feast.

Regarding widowhood and remarriage Claiborne says:

When a Choctaw husband dies the wife lays aside her jewelry or ornaments, and suffers her hair to fall dishevelled over her shoulders. Some six months after the cry for the dead is over the husband's mother (or if she be dead, his nearest female relative) ties up and dresses the widow's hair, and she is then at liberty to marry again. If she marries prior to this ceremony, or dances or flirts, she is discarded by the family of the deceased.[75]

What I myself learned was practically the same. It was that the widow or widower had to wait until the mortuary ceremonies were completed, when the people of the iksa to which the deceased be longed dressed the bereaved in good clothing and said, " You are now free." However, if there were little children, they usually preferred that the widower should espouse his wife's sister, and similarly, a woman was more apt to marry her husband's brother.

[74a] This must represent a later custom, for we have many references to mother-in-law avoidance in early times.

[75] Claiborne, Miss., I, p. 516.

DIVISION OF LABOR BETWEEN THE SEXES

Our earliest source, the anonymous French writer, says:

Their women . . . are like slaves to their husbands. They do everything in the house, work the ground, sow, and harvest the crop. The men sometimes aid them at a distance from the town, but never go for water or fire after they are made warriors, considering that that would dishonor them. They occupy themselves only with hunting.[76]

To the male occupations must of course be added war and all governmental duties, besides the manufacture of certain wooden and stone implements, and houses.

In contradistinction to the above informant, Romans, writing a few years later, says of the men:

They help their wives in the labour of the fields and many other works; near one half of the men have never killed a deer or turkey during their lives. Game is so scarce, that during my circuit through the nation we never saw any, and we had but two or three opportunities of eating venison in as many months.[77]

The following item may be added from Cushman:

He [the Choctaw man] struggled for what was immediate, the war path, the chase and council life; but when not engaged therein, the life of the national games, under the head of social amusements, filled up the measure of his days— the ball play, horse-race, foot-race, jumping and wrestling—to them as honorable as the gymnastic exercises of the eastern nations of antiquity; enduring heat and cold, suffering the pangs of hunger and thirst, fatigue and sleeplessness.[78]

Says Claiborne:

Generally the wife is very submissive. We met with but one case of a henpecked husband. In that case, it was shown that the wife packed up all the movables, took all the horses, and moved away some sixty miles. He followed after a while. "She was," said the same witness, "master of the camp, and he was the squaw."[79]

Simpson Tubby affirmed that "about 65 years ago" it was a rule among the Choctaw for the women to carry all of the burdens, the men being barehanded except for a gun, a fishing pole, or something similar. He claimed that the custom of requiring women to carry hampers of corn on their backs was abolished by Little Leader (Hopaii iskitini), captain of the Sukanatcha band, at the very last Green Corn dance. "Before that they not only carried hampers of corn on their backs but babies, and other burdens in their arms at the same time."

---

[76] Appendix, p. 247; Mem. Am. Anth. Ass'n, v, p. 59.
[77] Romans, E. and W. Fla., p. 86.
[78] Cushman, Hist. Inds., p. 252; see also Claiborne, Miss., i, p. 487.
[79] Claiborne, Miss., i, p. 517.

GAMES

As was the case with all of the other tribes of the Southeast, the 2-stick racket game [80] was the most important, and we probably have more descriptions of this game from the Choctaw than from any other in the region. The earliest of these is in the French memoir of which we have made such constant use. These people were, the author says:

... very great gamblers in a ball game which is like the long racket [game]. They place about twenty of one village against as many of another, and put up wagers against each other to very considerable amounts for them. They wager a new gun against an old one which is not worth anything, as readily as if it were good, and they give as a reason that if they are going to win they will win as well against a bad article as against a good one, and that they would rather bet against something than not bet at all. ... When they are very much excited they wager all that they have, and, when they have lost all, they wager their wives for a certain time, and after that wager themselves for a limited time.

They count by nights, and when they wish to play with another village, they send a deputy, who carries the word, and who delivers to the chief a number of little sticks. Every day one is thrown away, and the last which remains shows that the next day is the day chosen.[81]

Bossu's account is nearly as old as this. He says:

The *Chactas* are very active and very nimble. They have a game similar to our long racket game at which they are very skilful. Neighboring villages invite one another, inciting their opponents with a thousand words of defiance. Men and women gather in their finest costumes and pass the day singing and dancing; indeed they dance all night to the sound of the drum and rattle. Each village has its own fire lighted in the middle of a wide prairie. The day following is that on which the match is to come off. They agree upon a goal 60 paces distant and indicated by two large poles between which the ball must pass. Usually they play for 16 points. There are forty players on a side, each holding in his hand a racket two and a half feet long, of almost the same shape as ours, made of walnut [hickory] or chestnut wood and covered with deer skin.

In the middle of the ball ground an old man throws up a ball made by rolling deer skin together. At once each player runs to try to catch the ball in his racket. It is a fine sight to observe the players with their bodies bare, painted in all sorts of colors, with a tiger tail fastened behind and feathers on their arms and heads which flutter as they run, giving a remarkable effect. They push. They tumble over one another. He who is skillful enough to catch the ball sends it to the players on his side. Those on the opposite side run at the one who has seized it and return it to their own party, and they fight over it, party against party, with so much vigor that shoulders are sometimes dislocated. The players never become angry. The old men present at these games constitute themselves mediators and consider that the game is only a recreation and not something over which to fight. The wagers are considerable; the women bet against one another.

---

[80] Usually called Toli, but that word is applicable to any kind of ball game and the specific term for the game under discussion is ishtaboli.

[81] Appendix, p. 254; Mem. Am. Anth. Assn., v, p. 68.

After the players have finished, the women whose husbands have lost assemble to avenge them. The racket which the women use differs from that of the men in being bent. They play with much skill. They run against one another very swiftly, and shove one another like the men, being equally naked except for the parts which modesty dictates they shall cover. They merely redden their cheeks, and use vermilion on their hair instead of powder.[82]

Bossu's proof seems to have suffered from the wrong kind of editorial handling, so that we get the impression that each of the players in this game was provided with but a single racket and that there was but a single goal. Mention here and by Romans that women played this game is important because most of the other tribes of the Southeast do not seem to have permitted it. Slightly later than the last is the account preserved by Romans, who introduces us to two games or two types of the same:

Their play at ball is either with a small ball of deer skin or a larger one of woolen rags; the first is thrown with battledores, the second with the hand only; this is a trial of skill between village and village; after having appointed the day and field for meeting, they assemble at the time and place, fix two poles across each other at about a hundred and fifty feet apart, they then attempt to throw the ball through the lower part of them, and the opposite party, trying to prevent it, throw it back among themselves, which the first party again try to prevent; thus they attempt to beat it about from one to the other with amazing violence, and not seldom broken limbs or dislocated joints are the consequence; their being almost naked, painted and ornamented with feathers has a good effect on the eye of the bystander during this violent diversion; a number is agreed on for the score, and the party who first gets this number wins.

The women play among themselves (after the men have done), disputing with as much eagerness as the men; the stakes or bets are generally high. There is no difference in the other game with the large ball, only the men and women play promiscuously, and they use no battledores.[83]

Speaking of the men's game Hodgson says: "All violence on these occasions is forgiven; and I was informed that it is the only case in which life is not generally required for life." [84]

Other evidence indicates that this was true in the main, but we know that at times a ball game was an occasion which allowed old feuds to come to the surface and that, on the other hand, it sometimes gave rise to feuds.

The most celebrated description of the game is by Catlin, who illustrates his text with three sketches. Two of these sketches I am not reproducing, partly because it has been done frequently and partly because they do not represent a typical game. There happened to be a much larger number of participants present than usual.

---

[82] Appendix, p. 262; Bossu, Nouveaux Voyages aux Indes occidentales. 2 vols. Paris, 1768. Vol. 2, pp. 100–103.
[83] Romans, Nat. Hist. E. and W. Fla., p. 79.
[84] Hodgson, Travels, p. 271.

It is no uncommon occurrence for six or eight hundred or a thousand [!] of
these young men to engage in a game of ball, with five or six times that
number of spectators, of men, women, and children, surrounding the ground,
and looking on. . . .

While at the Choctaw agency it was announced, that there was to be a
great play on a certain day, within a few miles, on which occasion I attended,
and made the three sketches which are hereto annexed; and also the following
entry in my note-book, which I literally copy out:

"Monday afternoon at three o'clock, I rode out with Lieutenants S. and
M., to a very pretty prairie, about six miles distant, to the ball-playground
of the Choctaws, where we found several thousand Indians encamped. There
were two points of timber about half a mile apart, in which the two parties
for the play, with their respective families and friends, were encamped; and
lying between them, the prairie on which the game was to be played. My
companions and myself, although we had been apprised, that to see the whole
of a ball-play, we must remain on the ground all the night previous, had
brought nothing to sleep upon, resolving to keep our eyes open, and see what
transpired through the night. During the afternoon, we loitered about amongst
the different tents and shantees of the two encampments, and afterwards, at
sundown, witnessed the ceremony of measuring out the ground, and erecting
'byes' or goals which were to guide the play. Each party had their goal
made with two upright posts, about 25 feet high and six feet apart, set firm
in the ground, with a pole across at the top. These goals were about forty
or fifty rods apart; and at a point just half way between, was another small
stake, driven down, where the ball was to be thrown up at the firing of a gun,
to be struggled for by the players. All this preparation was made by some
old men, who were, it seems, selected to be the judges of the play, who drew
a line from one bye to the other; to which directly came from the woods, on
both sides, a great concourse of women and old men, boys and girls, and
dogs and horses, where bets were to be made on the play. The betting was
all done across this line, and seemed to be chiefly left to the women, who
seem to have martialled out a little of everything that their houses and their
fields possessed, goods and chattels—knives—dresses—blankets—pots and kettles—dogs and horses, and guns; and all were placed in the possession of the
stake-holders, who sat by them, and watched them on the ground all night,
preparatory to the play.

"The sticks with which this tribe play, are bent into an oblong hoop at
the end, with a sort of slight web of small thongs tied across, to prevent the
ball from passing through. The players hold one of these in each hand, and by
leaping into the air, they catch the ball between the two nettings and throw
it, without being allowed to strike it, or catch it in their hands.

"The mode in which these sticks are constructed and used, will be seen in
the portrait of *Tullock-chish-ko* (he who drinks the juice of the stone), the
most distinguished ball-player of the Choctaw nation (Pl. 4), represented
in his ball-play dress, with his ball-sticks in his hands. In every ball-
play of these people, it is a rule of the play, that no man shall wear
moccasins on his feet, or any other dress than his breech-cloth around his
waist, with a beautiful bead belt, and a 'tail' made of white horsehair or
quills, and a '*mane*' on the neck, of horsehair dyed of various colours.

"This game has been arranged and 'made up,' three or four months before
the parties met to play it, and in the following manner:—The two cham-
pions who led the two parties, and had the alternate choosing of the players
through the whole tribe, sent runners, with the ball-sticks most fantastically

A CHOCTAW BALL PLAYER (AFTER CATLIN)

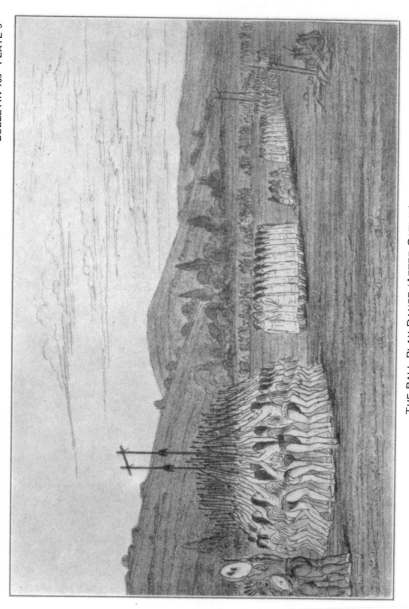

THE BALL PLAY DANCE (AFTER CATLIN)

ornamented with ribbons and red paint, to be touched by each one of the chosen players; who thereby agreed to be on the spot at the appointed time and ready for the play. The ground having been all prepared and preliminaries of the game all settled, and the bettings all made, and goods all 'staked,' night came on without the appearance of any players on the ground. But soon after dark, a procession of lighted flambeaux was seen coming from each encampment, to the ground where the players assembled around their respective byes; and at the beat of the drums and chants of the women, each party of players commenced the 'ball-play dance.' Each party danced for a quarter of an hour around their respective byes, in their ball-play dress; rattling their ball-sticks together in the most violent manner, and all singing as loud as they could raise their voices; whilst the women of each party, who had their goods at stake, formed into two rows on the line between the two parties of players, and danced also, in a uniform step, and all their voices joined in chants to the Great Spirit; in which they were soliciting his favour in deciding the game to their advantage; and also encouraging the players to exert every power they possessed, in the struggle that was to ensue. In the meantime, four old *medicine-men*, who were to have the starting of the ball, and who were to be judges of the play, were seated at the point where the ball was to be started; and busily smoking to the Great Spirit for their success in judging rightly, and impartially, between the parties in so important an affair. (Pl. 5.)

" This dance was one of the most picturesque scenes imaginable, and was repeated at intervals of every half hour during the night, and exactly in the same manner; so that the players were certainly awake all the night, and arranged in their appropriate dress, prepared for the play which was to commence at nine o'clock the next morning. In the morning, at the hour, the two parties and all their friends, were drawn out and over the ground; when at length the game commenced, by the judges throwing up the ball at the firing of a gun; when an instant struggle ensued between the players, who were some six or seven hundred in numbers, and were mutually endeavouring to catch the ball in their sticks, and throw it home and between their respective stakes; which, whenever successfully done, counts one for game. In this game every player was dressed alike, that is *divested* of all dress, except the girdle and the tail, which I have before described; and in these desperate struggles for the ball, when it is *up* (where hundreds are running together and leaping, actually over each other's heads, and darting between their adversaries' legs, tripping and throwing, and foiling each other in every possible manner, and every voice raised to the highest key, in shrill yelps and barks)! there are rapid successions of feats, and of incidents, that astonish and amuse far beyond the conception of any one who has not had the singular good luck to witness them. In these struggles, every mode is used that can be devised, to oppose the progress of the foremost, who is likely to get the ball; and these obstructions often meet desperate individual resistance, which terminates in a violent scuffle, and sometimes in fisticuffs; when their sticks are dropped, and the parties are unmolested, whilst they are settling it between themselves; unless it be by a general *stampedo*, to which they are subject who are down, if the ball happens to pass in their direction. Every weapon, by a rule of all ballplays, is laid by in their respective encampments, and no man allowed to go for one; so that the sudden broils that take place on the ground, are presumed to be as suddenly settled without any probability of much personal injury; and no one is allowed to interfere in any way with the contentious individuals.

"There are times when the ball gets to the ground, and such a confused mass rushing together around it, and knocking their sticks together, without the possibility of anyone getting or seeing it, for the dust that they raise, that the spectator loses his strength, and everything else but his senses; when the condensed mass of ball-sticks, and shins, and bloody noses, is carried around the different parts of the ground, for a quarter of an hour at a time, without any one of the mass being able to see the ball; and which they are often thus scuffling for, several minutes after it has been thrown off, and played over another part of the ground.

"For each time that the ball was passed between the stakes of either party, one was counted for their game, and a halt of about one minute; when it was again started by the judges of the play, and a similar struggle ensued; and so on until the successful party arrived at 100, which was the limit of the game, and accomplished at an hour's sun, when they took the stakes; and then, by a previous agreement, produced a number of jugs of whiskey, which gave all a wholesome drink, and sent them all off merry and in good humour, but not drunk." [85]

The numbers taking part in this particular match do not seem to have been approached in later times. Among the more recent writers Cushman gives a very vivid description, though, as usual, he is verbose. He says:

When the warriors of a village, wearied by the monotony of everyday life, desired a change that was truly from one extreme to . . . another, they sent a challenge to those of another village of their own tribe, and, not infrequently, to those of a neighboring tribe, to engage in a grand ball-play. If the challenge was accepted, and it was rarely ever declined, a suitable place was selected and prepared by the challengers, and a day agreed upon. The Hetoka (ball ground) was selected in some beautiful level plain easily found in their then beautiful and romantic country. Upon the ground, from three hundred to four hundred yards apart, two straight pieces of timber were firmly planted close together in the ground, each about fifteen feet in height, and from four to six inches in width, presenting a front of a foot or more. These were called Aiulbi (Ball posts). During the intervening time between the day of the challenge and that of the play, great preparations were made on both sides by those who intended to engage therein. With much care and unaffected solemnity they went through with their preparatory ceremonies.

The night preceding the day of the play was spent in painting with the same care as when preparing for the war-path, dancing with frequent rubbing of both the upper and lower limbs, and taking their "sacred medicine."

In the mean time, tidings of the approaching play spread on wings of the wind from village to village and from neighborhood to neighborhood for miles away; and during the first two or three days preceding the play, hundreds of Indians—the old, the young, the gay, the grave of both sexes, in immense concourse, were seen wending their way through the vast forests from every point of the compass, toward the ball-ground; with their ponies loaded with skins, furs, trinkets, and every other imaginable thing that was part and parcel of Indian wealth, to stake upon the result on one or the other side.

On the morning of the appointed day, the players, from seventy-five to a hundred on each side, strong and athletic men, straight as arrows and fleet as antelopes, entirely in a nude state, excepting a broad piece of cloth around

---

[85] George Catlin, North American Indians, 2 vols., Phila., 1913. Vol. 2, pp. 140–144.

the hips, were heard in the distance advancing toward the plain from opposite sides, making the heretofore silent forests ring with their exulting songs and defiant hump-he! [or humpah] (banter) as intimations of the great feats of strength and endurance, fleetness and activity they would display before the eyes of their admiring friends. The curiosity, anxiety and excitement now manifested by the vast throng of assembled spectators were manifested on every countenance. Soon the players were dimly seen in the distance through their majestic forests, flitting here and there as specters among the trees. Anon they are all in full view advancing from opposite sides in a steady, uniform trot, and in perfect order, as if to engage in deadly hand to hand conflict; now they meet and intermingle in one confused and disorderly mass interchanging friendly salutations, dancing and jumping in the wildest manner, while intermingling with all [was an] artillery of wild Shakuplichihi [shakablichi, "to cause a noise"] that echoed far back from the solitudes of the surrounding woods.

Then came a sudden hush—a silence deep, as if all Nature had made a pause—the prophetic calm before the bursting storm. During this brief interval, the betting was going on and the stakes being put up; the articles bet were all placed promiscuously in one place, often forming a vast conglomeration of things too numerous to mention, and the winning side took the pile. This being completed, the players took their places, each furnished with two kapucha (ball-sticks), three feet long, and made of tough hickory wood thoroughly seasoned. At one end of each ka-puch-a, a very ingenious device, in shape and size, very similar to that of the hand half closed, was constructed of sinews of wild animals, in which they caught and threw the ball. It was truly astonishing with what ease and certainty they would catch the flying ball in the cups of the sticks and the amazing distance and accuracy they would hurl it through the air. In taking their places at the opening of the play, ten or twenty, according to the number of players engaged, of each side were stationed at each pole. To illustrate, I will say, ten of the A. party and ten of the B. party were placed at pole C.; and ten of the B. party and ten of the A. party at pole D. The ten of the B. party who were stationed at the pole C. were called Fa-la-mo-li-chi (Throw-backs); and the ten of the A. party also stationed at pole C. were called Hat-tak fa-bus-sa (Pole men), and the ten of the A. party stationed at the pole D. were called Falamolichi, and the ten of the B. party stationed at the pole D., Hattak fabussa. The business of the Falamolichi at each pole was to prevent, if possible, the ball thrown by the opposite party, from striking the pole C.; and throw it back towards the pole D. to their own party; while that of the Hattak fabussa at pole C. was to prevent this, catch the ball themselves, if possible, and hurl it against the pole C., and the business of the Falamolichi and Hattak fabussa at the pole D. was the same as that at the pole C. In the centre, between the two poles, were also stationed the same number of each party as were stationed at the poles, called Middle Men, with whom was a chief "Medicine man," whose business was to throw the ball straight up into the air, as the signal for the play to commence. The remaining players were scattered promiscuously along the line between the poles and over different portions of the play-ground.

All things being ready, the ball suddenly shot up into the air from the vigorous arm of the Medicine Man, and the wash-o-ha (playing) began. The moment the ball was seen in the air, the players of both sides, except the Falamolichi and Hattak fabussa, who remained at their posts, rushed to the spot, where the ball would likely fall, with a fearful shock. Now began to be exhibited a scene of wild grandeur that beggared all description. As there were no rules and regulations governing the manner of playing nor any act considered unfair, each of course, acted under the impulse of the moment regardless of consequences.

They threw back and ran over each other in the wild excitement and reckless chase after the ball, stopping not nor heeding the broken limbs and bruised heads or even broken neck of a fallen player. Like a herd of stampeded buffaloes upon the western plains, they ran against and over each other, or anything else, man or beast, that stood in their way; and thus in wild confusion and crazed excitement they scrambled and tumbled, each player straining every nerve and muscle to its utmost tension, to get the ball or prevent his opponent, who held it firmly grasped between the cups of his trusty kapucha, from making a successful throw; while up and down the lines [were heard] the shouts of the players—"Falamochi! Falamochi!" (Throw it back! Throw it back!) as others shouted Hokli! Hoklio! (Catch! Catch!) The object of each party was to throw the ball against the two upright pieces of timber that stood in the direction of the village to which it belonged; and, as it came whizzing through the air, with the velocity comparatively of a bullet shot from a gun, a player running at an angle to intercept the flying ball, and when near enough, would spring several feet into the air and catch it in the hands of his sticks, but ere he could throw it, though running at full speed, an opponent would hurl him to the ground, with a force seemingly sufficient to break every bone in his body—and even to destroy life, and as No. 2 would wrest the ball from the fallen No. 1 and throw it, ere it had flown fifty feet, No. 3 would catch it with his unerring kapucha, and not seeing, perhaps, an opportunity of making an advantageous throw, would start off with the speed of a deer, still holding the ball in the cups of his kapucha—pursued by every player.

Again was presented to the spectators another of those exciting scenes, that seldom fall to the lot of one short lifetime to behold, which language fails to depict, or imagination to conceive. He now runs off, perhaps, at an acute angle with that of the line of the poles, with seemingly super-human speed; now and then elevating above his head his kapucha in which safely rests the ball, and in defiant exultation shouts, "hump-he! hump-he!" (I dare you) which was acknowledged by his own party with a wild response of approval, but responded to by a bold cry of defiance from the opposite side. Then again all is hushed and the breathless silence is only disturbed by the heavy thud of their running feet. For a short time he continues his straight course, as if to test the speed of his pursuing opponents; then begins to circle toward his pole. Instantly comprehending his object, his running friends circle with him, with eyes fixed upon him, to secure all advantage given to them by any strategic throw he may make for them, while his opponents are mingled among them to defeat his object; again he runs in a straight line; then dodges this way and that; suddenly he hears the cry from someone in his party in the rear of the parallel running throng, who sees an advantage to be gained if the ball was thrown to him, "Falamolichi"! "Falamolichi"! He now turns and dashes back to the line and in response to the continued cry—"Falamolichi"! he hurls the ball with all his strength; with fearful velocity it flies through the air and falls near the caller; and in the confusion made by the suddenly turning throng, the latter picks it up at full speed with his kapucha, and starts toward his pole. Then is heard the cry of his hattak fabussa, and he hurls the ball toward them and, as it falls, they and the throw-backs stationed at that pole, rush to secure it; and then again, though on a smaller scale, a scene of wild confusion was seen—scuffling, pulling, pushing, butting—unsurpassed in any game ever engaged in by man. Perhaps, a throw-back secures the ball and starts upon the wing, in the direction of his pole, meeting the advancing throng, but with his own throw-backs and the pole-men of his opponents at his heels; the latter to prevent him from making a successful throw and the former to prevent any interference, while the shouts of " Falamolichi! " " Falamolichi! " arose from his own men in the advancing runners. Again the ball flies through the air, and is about to fall directly among them, but ere it reaches the ground many spring into the air to catch it, but are tripped and they fall headlong to the earth. Then, as the ball reaches the ground, again is brought into full requisition the propensities of each one to butt, pull, and push, though not a sound is heard, except the wild rattling of the kapucha, that reminded one of the noise made by the collision of the horns of a drove of stampeding Texas steers. Oft amid the play women were seen giving water to the thirsty and offering words of encouragement; while others, armed with long switches stood ready to give their expressions of encouragement to the supposed tardy, by a severe rap over the naked shoulders, as a gentle reminder of their dereliction of duty; all of which was received in good faith, yet invariably elicited the response— " Wah!" as an acknowledgment of the favor.

From ten to twenty was generally the game. Whenever the ball was thrown against the upright fabussa (poles), it counted one, and the successful thrower shouted; " Illi tok," (dead) meaning one number less; oft accompanying the shout by gobbling vociferously like the wild turkey, which elicited a shout of laughter from his party, and a yell of defiance from the other. Thus the exciting, and truly wild and romantic, scene was continued, with unabated efforts on the part of the players until the game was won. But woe to the inconsiderate white man, whose thoughtless curiosity had led him too far upon the hetoka, (ball ground) and at whose feet the ball should chance to fall; if the path to that ball was not clear of all obstructions, the 200 players, now approaching with the rush of a mighty whirlwind would soon make it so. And right then and there, though it might be the first time in life, he became a really active man, if the desire of immediate safety could be any inducement, cheerfully inaugurating proceedings by turning a few double somersets, regardless as to the scientific manner [in which] he executed them, or the laugh of ridicule that might be offered at his expense; and if he escaped only with a broken limb or two, and a first-class scare, he might justly consider himself most fortunate. But the Choctaws have long since lost that interest in the ball-play that they formerly cherished in their old homes east of the Mississippi River. 'Tis true, now and then, even at the present day [1899], they indulge in the time honored game, but the game of the present day is a Lilliputian—a veritable pygmy—in comparison with the grand old game of three quarters of a century ago; nor will it be many years ere it will be said of the Choctaw tolih, as of ancient Troy—" Ilium fuit."

To any one of the present day, an ancient Choctaw ballplay would be an exhibition far more interesting, strange, wild and romantic, in all its features, than anything ever exhibited in a circus from first to last—excelling it in every particular of daring feats and wild recklessness. In the ancient ball-play, the activity, fleetness, strength and endurance of the Mississippi Choctaw warrior and hunter, were more fully exemplified than anywhere else; for there he brought into the most severe action every power of soul and body. In those ancient ball-plays, I have known villages to lose all their earthly possessions upon the issue of a single play. Yet, they bore their misfortune with becoming grace and philosophic indifference and appeared as gay and cheerful as if nothing of importance had occurred. The education of the ancient Choctaw warrior and hunter consisted mainly in the frequency of these muscular exercises which enabled him to endure hunger, thirst and fatigue; hence they often indulged in protracted fastings, frequent foot-races, trials of bodily strength, introductions to the war-path, the chase and their favorite tolih.[86]

Cushman also quotes from Halbert stories of two famous ball games between the Choctaw and Creeks, the first about 1790 for the possession of a beaver pond on Noxubee River, and the second over the ownership of the territory between the Tombigbee and Black Warrior Rivers, the winner's title to be recognized as valid. It may be added that each ended in a battle so that, in these particular instances, the " moral equivalent for war " seems to have been a failure.[87]

Halbert's own manuscript notes contain the following account of this game:

The ball play was and still is the great Choctaw game. It is always arranged by the chiefs or captains of the opposing parties. They confer with each other, select the players of their respective sides, appoint their prophets, agree upon the day and place of the play, and then see that all this is duly announced to their people. The day appointed is always sufficiently distant to give ample time to the players for drilling themselves in playing and to the women for preparing a bountiful supply of food for the great occasion.

The day preceding the ball play, the two opposing parties, men, women and children, assemble on the ball-ground, which is prepared for the play by removing all obstructions. Each party erect their respective ball posts, which are about two hundred and fifty or three hundred yards apart. The ball posts are about twenty feet high, and are the split halves of a log planted in the earth, side by side, the split sides of the posts of one party facing the split sides of the posts of the other party. The exact center between the ball posts of the two parties is ascertained by a careful measurement and the spot marked. On the border of the ball ground and opposite the central spot noted, a scaffold about ten feet high is erected. The two parties make their camps near their respective posts. As night approaches both sides for an hour or more go through a repetition of ceremonies. As each party goes through the same ceremonies one description will suffice for both. A mingo seats himself on the ground in the rear of his ball post with his back to it. By rear is meant the farther side from the post of the opposite party. A number of girls and young women now come forward and arrange themselves in two parallel lines facing each other, extending outward from where the mingo sits. The painted ball-players with their ball sticks in hand then come forward, dance and shout around their post, then form a circle at the outer end of the line of women where they clash their ball sticks overhead, then hold them poised erect for a few moments. While they are thus standing in silence, the women, prompted by the mingo, dance and chant a song in a low tone, keeping time with their feet. The song generally is:

" Onnakma, àbi hoke." *To-morrow we will win it.*

---

[86] Cushman, Hist. Inds., pp. 184–190; also cf. Claiborne, Miss., I, pp. 485–486.
[87] Cushman, Hist. Inds., pp. 190–193.

When this has been chanted several times, the players break up their circle, again dance around the post, then again form their circle at the end of the outer line of the women, perform the same action with their ball sticks, while the women dance and chant the same song. These ceremonies by the players and dancers are performed twelve times, after which they disperse to participate in the revelries and amusements which are kept up during the entire night. There is nor can be much sleep on such a noisy camp ground. The prophets with their blackened faces are busy all night with their magic performances, each claiming the ability to propitiate and secure for his own side every mysterious influence in nature. In the morning the same ceremonies are performed by the players and the women, only with different songs, of which the following are specimens: " Himak nitak achukma àbi hoke." *To-day is good we will win it.* " Towa itonla achukma àbi hoke." *The ball lies so handy, we will win it.*

After breakfast for several hours all hands are busy in making their bets. The parties betting articles with each other tie the articles together and deposit them on the scaffold. The women are as great betters as the men. One woman, for instance, bets a dress against a blanket. The articles at once are tied together and placed on the scaffold. Two men may bet guns against each other, and they are likewise placed on the scaffold tied together. Nothing was considered too sacred for a bet. Parties even would bet their ponies and it was not unusual to find two ponies tied near the scaffold. About midday, preparations are made for the play. Each mingo stations his players, the most expert being placed near the posts of the opposite party as here the struggle is generally the most violent. The rest of the players assembled at the marked spot in the center and some time is spent in betting. This over, a prophet throws up the ball and the play begins. Twelve is the number of rounds usually played. The party that wins a round has the privilege of throwing up the ball, which is done by one of their prophets. The posts of the two parties have lines extending out on each side. The rule is that the posts must be struck on the inside, that is on the split sides, and the ball must fall on the inside of the drawn line; if otherwise, it is not counted. During the play, no outsider is expected to interfere in the play in any manner whatever. Should he do this, the party to which the offender belongs is expected to forfeit one round or otherwise make some reparation. Before and during the play, the prophets on each side in the midst of the players, continue their usual performances. Each carries a small looking-glass. He turns to the sun, holds his glass towards it with a gyratory motion then turns and throws the rays upon the bodies of the players of his side. This action of the prophet is a survival of the sun worship of the olden time. As all life and power comes from the sun, the prophet flatters himself that he can infuse a portion into his own party; and if he can utilize more of it than the prophet of the opposite side, his side will win the day. The ball play was generally finished in one day. Sometimes, however, the play was protracted during two days. When it was finished, the vanquished always cheerfully accepted their defeat. The victors repaired to the scaffold where they received (the wagers) and then all separated and returned to their homes. It sometimes happened that some of the vanquished party went home half naked, having bet even their clothes on the result of the play.

The only games or plays of the Choctaw women, was the ball play, which they played exactly like the men; and a play resembling the game of battle-dore, played with sticks and balls.

Another excellent description was furnished Mr. Stewart Culin by Mr. George E. Starr and incorporated into Culin's work on Games of the North American Indians.

The game was between Tobucksey and Sugarloaf counties of the Choctaw Nation. On the night before, the players went into camp near the place agreed upon. The season was the traditional one of the full moon of one of the summer months, and the company slept, without shelter, upon the ground. On their arrival, the new players, who had never been allowed to play before on the county teams, dressed themselves in ball costume, and while their elders were arranging rules, ran around making themselves conspicuous to their own side in the hope they would be chosen the next day. Before retiring, the managers on each side and the principal players assembled to make regulations to govern the play. They sat in a circle, and, no matter how heated the argument became, a speaker was never interrupted by one of the opposite side. There were about 250 Indians present, about evenly divided on each side, being chiefly men, with a few women and children. Each side brought with them a conjurer, or medicine man. At about 7 o'clock on the following morning the managers assembled for some purpose, after which they collected their sides, and took their places, a little apart, to prepare for the play. They stripped for the game, putting on nothing but a breech clout. Their heads were bare, with the hair cut short, without feathers. Their only ornament was a coon tail stuck up straight along the spine, or a horse tail falling on the breech clout behind. This was attached to the belt, a leather strap or revolver belt. The men carry their weapons to the ball game, but are not allowed to wear them in the field. The majority of the players were of splendid physique, spare and wiry. Several were, in part, of negro blood, and many showed the result of intermixture with the whites. The sides each numbered 30, of ages varying from 18 to 35. Among them were some that were crippled, the result, it may be, of former play.

The goal posts, which the ball must touch, were about 200 to 225 yards apart. They consisted of two trees, lashed together with ropes. They were about 8 inches in diameter, and were cut flat on one side, and were set at an angle so that they presented a face of about 12 inches to the ball. This must hit the post, to which it may be carried between a player's sticks, but it must bounce [back] over a line in front of the posts, otherwise it does not count and is still in play.

The conjurers were conspicuous throughout the game. At the commencement, after the sides were chosen, all went to their goal posts. When within about 10 feet of the posts they broke their formation, and, uttering a cry, ran up to the posts, battering them with their ball sticks. They did this to scare the spirit of bad luck away.

Then they lined up in a kind of alley between the goals. Near the middle of the field, however, there were about eight men of each side ranged opposite to each other in a line running horizontally across the goal line. When all the others were ready, the men who were to take these places crossed the field. A medicine man put the ball in play, tossing it into the air. One of them had his face painted half red and half black, and carried in his hand a small branch of a tree resembling hickory. They both stood near their respective goals and sung and clapped their hands. The game lasted from 10 to 5, with an intermission for luncheon. The score is 12 goals, but if this number is not completed on either side, the one having the highest number is adjudged the winner. Butting with the head is prohibited, under a penalty of 5 goals.

The Indians bet everything they possess upon the game, even to their clothes and boots. The bets are made through stakeholders—four or five Indians—who constantly ride about on horseback. Whatever is bet is put with what is bet against it. If handkerchiefs, they are knotted together and thrown over the stakeholder's shoulder; if money, the sums are put together in his pocketbook. His memory is remarkable, and he never fails to turn over the stakes correctly. Much skill is shown during the game. In a scrimmage the ball is tossed backward through the bent legs of the players, and when the player secures it he utters a signal cry—hogle á! [or hokli á]. This is repeated by those along the line, and each grabs the opponent nearest to him and holds him. While they are wrestling the player with the ball tries to run with it, so that he can throw it and make a goal.

The ball, it should be observed, is about the size of a golf ball, made of rags and covered with white buckskin. Several are provided, as they are frequently lost in the tall grass. The players on the side with the wind sometimes substitute a ball with a long tail and a loose cover that comes off during the play. The tail then impedes their opponents in throwing it against the wind. The women are extremely active in aiding their side. They are not permitted to touch the ball sticks, but they are constantly running about and giving hot coffee to the men. In one hand they carry a cup of coffee and in the other a quirt with which they whip the players when they think they are not playing hard enough. At times a player will get a woman to give him a pin, with which he will scarify his leg, making from three to five scratches from near the ankle to the middle of the calf, until the blood comes. This, they say, prevents cramps.

When the players return to the game after lunch hour they place their ball sticks in rows opposite each other in the middle of the field, where they are counted by the umpire or the leaders on each side. This is done to see that no more are playing than started in the game. The spectators cry out and encourage the sides. When a goal is made there is a shout. The most exciting point in a close game is when the last goal is neared. Then the play becomes very fast and the rules are not strictly observed. A goal may be made in a few moments or the contest may last for an hour. In wrestling, the players seize each other by the belts, dropping the ball sticks. With the exception of the prohibited butting almost everything is permitted. At the present game five men were crippled, of whom two died. The injuries inflicted upon a man during a game are frequently avenged by his relatives. The result of the game described was a victory for Tobucksey county. The conjurer on the Sugarloaf side was said to have sent his men to the creek to bathe in the morning, which weakened them. They were penalized five goals for butting at the end, and so lost the game. There was no celebration afterwards. All were tired out and went home quietly to their mud-chinked log cabins at the close of the day.[88]

The hand ball game mentioned by Romans evidently survived into modern times among the Louisiana Choctaw. Under the heading " Tole," Bushnell has the following regarding it:

The players were divided into two equal groups, or sides, which may be designated A and B. Two stakes, each about 10 feet in height and only a few inches in diameter, served as goals; these were about 200 feet apart. One-third of the A players were on the B side of the field and one-third of the B

---

[88] Twenty-fourth Ann. Rept. Bur. Amer. Ethn., Washington, 1907, pp. 602–604.

players were near their opponents' goal. One player belonging to each- side remained in the middle of the field. The ball was put in play by being thrown from one end of the field to the two players in the middle. No rackets were used, the ball being caught in the hands and thrown or held while the player endeavored to reach his opponents' goal. To score a point a player was required to touch the goal post with the ball, or if the ball was thrown and hit the post, the play likewise counted. The first side to score a chosen number of points won the game. This game is seldom played, and the older game, formerly played with rackets (kapocha), has not been played for several years.[89]

Mr. T. J. Scott, the farmer connected with the Eastern Choctaw Agency at Philadelphia, Miss., who has grown up in this country, gave me the following information regarding the ceremonies preliminary to a game:

To initiate a regular game, the chief of one settlement visited the chief of another and the two made all of the provisional arrangements. Then each of them sent out a little bundle of sticks (what the Creeks call " the broken days ") to the families in his settlement. One stick is thrown away each day, and when but one is left they meet at a place appointed. In the afternoon there are practice games. After supper the chief sets up two posts and places himself between them facing the east. In front of him are ranged two lines of women extending toward the east and beyond them are the ball players, who form a circle. Then the chief sings, using words which mean, " We are going to win a game," the words being repeated over and over, and the women begin to dance. They dance for four or five minutes when they stop and the players begin dancing, singing such words as these: " Play ball right and we will win the game," " Handle the sticks right and we will win the game," " If the witch doctor conjures right we will win the game." The women and men danced and sang alternately in this manner up to 12 times, because the game is to be for 12 points. The chief had to sing right through, with both parties, and the whole lasted from one and a half to two hours. Afterwards the chief distributed " the broken days " determining the date of the game, and then all went home. Both sides had to agree who was to be first to throw up the ball. The doctors were the score keepers. The parties sometimes agreed to call in help from other bands, but it now seems impossible to determine whether there was any definite arrangement of allied towns such as existed among the Creeks. Of the local bands known to Mr. Scott—Bok Chito, Biasha, Moklasha, Red Water, Sixtowns, Turkey Creek, and Konhutta—he does not know of any two which did not play against each other except Moklasha and Turkey Creek, and that exception may have been accidental.

[89] Bushnell: The Choctaw of Bayou Lacomb, Louisiana, Bull. 48, Bur. Amer. Ethn., p. 20.

There may be some question, however, whether Mr. Scott has distinguished between regular games and practice games. Simpson Tubby asserted that the bands were arranged into what we should call town moieties, the Bok Chito, Turkey Creek, and Biasha bands playing on one side and the Moklasha, Chankey, Sixtowns, and Seventowns playing on the other. Noxapater and Talla Hikia were branches of Bok Chito. The first moiety used the colors blue and white; the latter the colors yellow and green. Practice games were held between the bands on each side in order to pick out the best players for the regular games, in which 40 men were usually entered on a side. In such games each side usually bore the name of some one band, but players from the other bands were drawn in to help them out. Later Simpson modified his original statement regarding the moieties by saying that the Bok Chito and Biasha bands played on one side, the Moklasha, Sixtowns, and Seventowns on the other, while the Turkey Creek and Red Water bands played sometimes on one side and sometimes on the other. Some of this confusion was no doubt due to intermarriage, which Simpson says occasioned much trouble in selecting the players. He added that the band captains made up the parties but the head chief might interfere if he disliked their arrangements. The matter is still further confused by Simpson's statement that they did not play games band against band before the coming of the whites but made up squads drawn from any source. This was called the " peace game." He claimed that the first Choctaw to manufacture ballsticks was named Musholeika (" to go out " or " to put out " like a light). By 1893, he said, most of the Choctaw had left the country, and then the whites got the Indians into the habit of betting, dishonesty crept in, and when trouble arose between the players, the spectators took up for their respective sides until free fights resulted. So far as gambling is concerned, we know it to have been an inseparable feature of native ball games from primitive times, but it is true that games are now more apt to end in a riot than was formerly the case.

Each captain had to indorse the players of his band as bona fide members of it, and they must satisfy him that they had observed the regulations. They were obliged to remain away from their wives for 30 days preceding. They must not eat hog meat or any kind of grease, but were given barbecued beef cooked in quarters. The night before the game they were allowed scarcely anything, and only a little water at any one time. The play was very rough and lasted as a rule from about 9 to 4.30.

The date for a game might be fixed from 15 to 100 days ahead but usually between 30 and 90. A set of counting sticks with the number of sticks equal to the days intervening was given to each side after having been counted over twice. Every morning one of these sticks was taken away and put in a safe place.

Olmon Comby said that from two to six sticks went into the construction of a goal post. Foul lines were drawn through each post perpendicular to a line between them, and a goal was made by striking the post in such a manner that the ball came to the earth inside of the foul line. Otherwise it was still in play. A goal could also be made by touching the post with the ball. The players of each side were divided into three parties, as shown in Figure 1.

Two to four men of each side were placed at each goal, the rest distributed in the middle. Anciently one or more doctors were employed by each party, and these made all kinds of motions and blew into the air. They must not advance farther beyond their own goal than to the middle line.

Practice games in which less than 12 men participated were played about a single goal post, each party striving to hit one side of it. In games where betting took place there were always two goal posts.

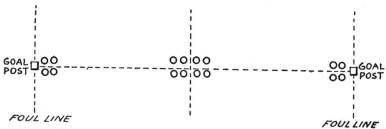

FIGURE 1.—Arrangement of players preparatory to ball game

From another Choctaw informant I obtained the following notes, mainly confirmatory of what has gone before.

Each goal post consisted of a slab of wood a foot wide or of two pieces of wood fastened together to make up this width. "Regular games" were played between two distinct local groups.[90]

In regular games great quantities of property were wagered and there was intense excitement. The night before both teams danced, and in the morning, just before the game, a woman on each side danced and sang around the goal post belonging to her party. Each side also had a medicine man who carried on his ceremonies during the whole of the preceding night and on the following day until the end of the encounter. He attempted to "witch" the post belonging to his own people so that the ball would come to it, and in the course of his conjurations he would beckon to the ball continually. As

---

[90] Mention has been made of a game between the Tobucksey and Sugarloaf districts, and Henry C. Benson, in Life Among the Choctaws, Cincinnati, 1860, p. 154, tells us that the Puckchenubbee and Moshulatubbee districts were also opposed.

must have been noted already, the object of the players was not to score against the enemy's goal but to bring the ball home to one's own.

The players were divided into five squads, each composed of equal numbers of players from the opposite sides. One was at the center of the ground, one at each goal, and the two others midway between the goals and the center.[91] The ball was thrown into the air at the halfway point and each side tried to bring it home to the post belonging to his side. They usually played for 12 points, each side keeping the tally by making marks on its goal post near the bottom. After one side had secured 11 points it was privileged to have the ball thrown up at its own goal. Sometimes the score was marked, as seems to have been the usual custom among the Creeks, by sticking bits of wood into the ground and pulling them out again. That is, if the game were 12, six sticks would be stuck into the ground in succession and then removed in the same manner.

A form of this game was adopted by the French Creoles of Louisiana and the Louisiana negroes, and a game between two negro teams played in the summer of 1901 was witnessed and described by Mr. Culin.[92]

The chunkey game, called by the Choctaw àɫchàpi, alhchahpi, or achahpi, now long discontinued, seems formerly to have been resorted to to satisfy the demands of gamblers when intertown ball games were not in prospect. Romans says:

Their favourite game of *chunké* is a plain proof of the evil consequences of a violent passion for gaming upon all kinds, classes and orders of men; at this they play from morning till night, with an unwearied application, and they bet high; here you may see a savage come and bring all his skins, stake them and lose them; next his pipe, his beads, trinkets and ornaments; at last his blankets and other garments, and even all their arms, and after all it is not uncommon for them to go home, borrow a gun and shoot themselves; an instance of this happened in 1771 at East Yasoo a short time before my arrival. . . .

The manner of playing this game is thus: They make an alley of about two hundred feet in length, where a very smooth clay ground is laid, which when dry is very hard; they play two together having each a streight pole of about fifteen feet long: one holds a stone, which is in shape of a truck, which he throws before him over this alley, and the instant of its departure, they set off and run; in running they cast their poles after the stone, he that did not throw it endeavors to hit it, and the other strives to strike the pole of his antagonist in its flight so as to prevent its hitting the stone; if the first should strike the stone he counts one for it, and if the other by the dexterity of his cast should prevent the pole of his opponent hitting the stone, he counts one, but should both miss their aim the throw is renewed; and in case a score is

---

[91] This is the Creek style. I may have misunderstood my informant.
[92] Twenty-fourth Ann. Rept. Bur. Amer. Ethn., pp. 604–605.

won the winner casts the stone and eleven is up; they hurl this stone and pole with wonderful dexterity and violence, and fatigue themselves much at it."

Cushman also has something regarding this game:

They also indulged in another game in which they took great delight, called Ulth Chuppih, in which but two players could engage at the same time; but upon the result of which, as in the Tolih, they frequently bet their little all. An alley, with a hard smooth surface and about two hundred feet long, was made upon the ground. The two players took a position at the upper end at which they were to commence the game, each having in his hand a smooth, tapering pole eight or ten feet long flattened at the ends. A smooth round stone of several inches in circumference was then brought into the arena; as soon as both were ready, No. 1 took the stone and rolled it with all his strength down the narrow inclined plane of the smooth alley; and after which both instantly started with their utmost speed. Soon No. 2, threw his pole at the rolling stone; instantly No. 1, threw his at the flying pole of No. 2, aiming to hit it, and, by so doing, change its course from the rolling stone. If No. 2 hits the stone, he counts one; but if No. 1 prevents it by hitting the pole of No. 2, he then counts one; and he, who hits his object the greater number of times in eleven rollings of the stone was the winner. It was a more difficult matter to hit either the narrow edge of the rolling stone, or the flying pole than would be at first imagined. However, the ancient Chahtah Ulth Chuppih may come in at least as a worthy competitor with the pale-face Ten-pin-alley, for the disputed right of being the more dignified amusement."

Halbert says that this game "became practically obsolete in the early years of the nineteenth century, though it was occasionally played by the Six Towns Indians as late at 1842." He continues:

The achahpi game, called chungkee by eighteenth century writers, was played with poles and a circular stone about six inches in diameter (called *tali chanaha*, "stone wheel" (or ring)). It was a game common to all the Southern Indian nations. To play the game an oblong piece of ground was well cleaned and sprinkled over with fine sand. The two players took their stand about eighteen feet from one end of the achahpi ground. One held the stone. Their poles were about eight feet long, smooth and tapering at each end with a flat point. They were anointed with bear's oil. When the players were ready, they started from their stand, and as they reached the edge of the achahpi ground, the one with the stone hurled it towards the middle of the yard, and as it rolled along the ground, the two men, after running a short distance darted their poles at it. When the throw was completed, the player the head of whose pole lay nearest to the stone, counted one for himself; and otherwise, one was counted for the pole lying nearest to the stone. The Indians were very much given to this play, the players often engaged in it the greater part of the day, and staking upon the issue their silver ornaments, and even all their clothing, except their flaps."

In another place he has left us a more extended description, varying in some details from the one just given.

Some ten years ago there lived in Neshoba County an aged Choctaw named Mehubbee, who had often seen the achahpih game played in his youth, and who

" Romans, Nat. Hist. E. and W. Fla., pp. 79–80.   " H. S. Halbert, Ms. notes.
" Cushman, Hist. Inds., p. 190.

still had an achahpih stone in his possession.   One day in the summer of 1876, this aged Indian prepared an achahpih yard, in an old field on Talasha Creek, and instructed some young Choctaws how to play this almost forgotten game of their forefathers.   This was, undoubtedly, the last time this ancient Indian game was ever played in the State of Mississippi.   From a recent conversation with one of the players on that occasion, the following facts about the achahpih are here given:

A level piece of ground is selected, and an achahpih yard (ai achahpih) is laid off, being about one hundred feet long and twelve feet wide.   The yard is cleared off, tramped hard and made as smooth and level as possible.   The achahpih poles were made of small, slender swamp hickory saplings, from which the bark was stripped, and the poles scraped down perfectly smooth and then seasoned over a fire.   They were about ten feet long and the size of an ordinary hoe handle.   The head or striking end of the pole (noshkobo) was made rounded.   Near the head were cut around the pole four parallel notches or grooves.   One-fourth of the way down were cut two more notches, and then a single notch around the center of the pole, making seven notches in all.   Twelve was the number of the achahpih game, and the play alternated from one end of the yard to the other.   Two men played the game.   Taking their stand at one end of the yard, a third man stood between them, whose duty it was to roll the stone towards the other end.   The two players, whom we will name Hoentubbee and Tonubbee, held their poles, so to speak, in a pitching position; that is, with one end of the pole resting against the palm and on the upturned fingers of the right hand, which was thrust to the rearward, while the body of the pole rested loosely in the left hand.   As soon as the thrower had launched the stone, and it began to roll along the ground towards the other end of the yard, both players darted their poles at it, each endeavoring to strike it with the head.   Their object in hitting the stone was, that in so doing, there was a greater probability than otherwise, of the pole of the striker and the stone stopping and lying near each other.   As soon as the throw was completed, the distance of the nearest notch or notches on the respective poles was then measured.   If, for instance, the four notches on Hoentubbee's pole should lie nearest to the stone, and nearer than any of the notches on Tonubbee's pole, then Hoentubbee counted four for himself.   If, however, the single notch around Hoentubbee's pole should be the nearest of all the notches on either of the poles, then Hoentubbee counted one for himself.   And if Hoentubbee's two notches should lie nearest of all to the pole, then Hoentubbee counted two of the game for himself.   But if the nearest notch or notches on each pole should be exactly the same distance from the stone, then it was a tied game, and both parties tried it over.   Sometimes, by extraordinary good fortune, the achahpih player could make the game in three throws, making four each time.   If two achahpih players should happen to have no one to throw the stone for them, they then threw it, alternately, for each other.   The achahpih play was not unfrequently kept up during the entire day.   As usual in all Indian games, there was much betting on the ground, both by players and spectators.   My informant considered the achahpih as a very tedious game, and expressed some surprise that his ancestors should have taken any pleasure in such a dull, uninteresting pastime.

An immense amount of labor was unquestionably used by the ancient Choctaws in making their achahpih stones, which were handed down as precious heirlooms from one generation to another.[96]

---

[96] H. S. Halbert, The Choctaw Achahpih (Chungkee) Game, in the American Antiquarian, vol. x, pp. 283–284.

From these accounts, and others that have come to us from early visitors among other tribes, it would appear that the method of play varied considerably.

Halbert also mentions the so-called moccasin game, which was called by the Choctaw Naki Lohmi, " the hidden bullet," but Bushnell is the only writer to describe the manner in which it was played in that tribe. He says:

Twelve men were required in playing this game. They knelt or sat on the ground in two rows, or sides, facing each other, six players in each row. Seven hats were placed on the ground in a line between the two rows of players.

The player who was to start the game and who was always at one end of his row held in one hand a small stone or shot. With his other hand he raised all the hats in order, placing under one of these the stone or shot; during the entire performance he sang a particular song. After the stone or shot had been placed, the player sitting opposite him guessed under which it lay. If he did not succeed in three guesses, the leader removed the object and again hid it under either the same or another hat. Then the second player on the opposite side had three guesses. If a player guessed under which hat the object was hidden, he in turn became the leader.

Unfortunately, those who described the game could not now recall how the points were counted. They agreed, however, that the side having the greater number of points made by the six players combined, won.[97]

The missing information regarding this game was supplied to me by Olmon Comby, a Mississippi Choctaw. He stated that two or more could play so long as the number was even, for there must be two opposing sides. Fifty sticks are used as counters, and at the beginning of the game he who is to guess first takes 48 of these and gives his opponent 2. Between the players are 4 socks or handkerchiefs under which the one who has the bullet passes his hands successively. He leaves it under one, striving to deceive his opponent as to the identity of that one. The latter guesses in one of two ways. If he wants to remove a sock but does not believe that the bullet is under it, he lifts it gently; if he believes it to be there he pulls it back to his breast with a sudden jerk. The count is as follows:

If he jerks off the first and finds the bullet he wins_____ 4
If he lifts first and jerks second and finds it he wins_____ 2
If he lifts first and second and jerks third and finds it he wins_____ 2
If he jerks off first and it is not there he loses_____ 4
If he lifts first and jerks second and it is not there he loses_____ 2
If he lifts first and second and jerks off third and it is not there he loses___ 2
If he lifts off first and it is there he loses_____ 4
If he lifts off first and then second and it is there he loses_____ 2
If he lifts off first and second he is not allowed to lift the third but must jerk it.

It is curious that if the opponent has 2 sticks and the guesser makes 4 the latter does not win; instead, they swap sticks, the guesser

[97] Bushnell, Bull. 48, Bur. Amer. Ethn., p. 19.

taking 4 and the opponent 46. If the opponent of the guesser has 2 and the guesser makes 2, the latter takes all of the sticks, but the other has a chance to guess.

Romans is our only authority for the following diversion which recalls our use of jackstones:

The women also have a game where they take a small stick, or something else off the ground after having thrown up a small ball which they are to catch again, having picked up the other; they are fond of it, but ashamed to be seen at it.[98]

Our earliest authority tells us that they " have a game with four pieces of cane " which we may surmise to have resembled the games played with kernels of corn, about which Culin and Bushnell both have something to say. Culin, who witnessed this as it was played near Mandeville, La., says that eight grains of white corn were used, charred on one side.

These are used as dice in the corn game, baskatanje [bàska taⁿ chi, " corn game "]. Two or more men play, throwing the corn with the hand upon the ground. The throws are either white, tobeh, or black, losah, up. The game is twenty-five, and the counts are as follows: All black up, untachaina, counts 8; all white up, 8; seven white up, untokalo, 7; six white up, hanali, 6; five white up, tutslata, 5; four white up, oshta, 4; three white up, tuchaina, 3; two white up, takalok, 2; one white up, chofa, 1.[99]

Bushnell describes it as follows, incorporating a comparison with the description given by Culin:

Tanje boska, or corn game.—This was played, the writer was informed, with either five or seven kernels of corn blackened on one side. Holding all the grains in one hand, the players tossed them on the ground, each player having three throws. The one making the greatest number of points in the aggregate, won. Each " black " turned up counted 1 point; *all* " white " turned up counted either 5 or 7 points, according to the number of kernels used. Any number of persons could play at the same time, but usually there were only two. Culin, who witnessed this game at Mandeville, some ten miles from Bayou Lacomb, in 1901, described it as played with eight grains of corn; hence it seems evident that no regular number was employed. The count, as described by Culin, is also somewhat different from that now followed at Bayou Lacomb.[1]

The same writer adds some notes on a few comparatively trivial games played in Louisiana:

During the hot months of the year a favorite pastime of the boys and men consisted in trying to swim blindfolded a wide stream to a certain point on the opposite bank. The first to reach the goal was declared the winner.

A somewhat similar amusement participated in by the boys and young men consisted in rolling down hills while wrapped and tied in blankets or skins, the first to reach a certain line being the winner. As there are few hills in

---

[98] Romans, Nat. Hist. E. and W. Fla., p. 81.
[99] Twenty-fourth Ann. Rept. Bur. Amer. Ethn., p. 146.
[1] Bull. 48, Bur. Amer. Ethn., p. 19.

the vicinity of Bayou Lacomb, they resorted to the sloping banks of streams or bayous, but avoided the water.

At the present time both men and children play marbles, drawing rings on the ground and following the child's game.

The children play also " tag " after the manner of white children.[2]

Bossu mentions archery contests.[3]

TRAVEL AND GREETINGS

There is very little to be said under this heading. We know that the Choctaw towns were linked to one another and to the surrounding peoples by numerous trails of the usual Indian one-man pattern, but the Choctaw seem to have strayed from home less than most Indians, and trade with the French, English, and Spanish posts so rapidly displaced the much less prominent aboriginal intertribal trade that very little may be gathered regarding the latter. That these Indians had little difficulty in making their way about, even in unfamiliar parts of the country, when they had occasion to do so is evident from everything related by the travelers who came in contact with them. Cushman says on this point:

It was truly wonderful with what ease and certainty the Choctaw hunter and warrior made his way through the dense forests of his country to any point he wished to go, near or distant. But give him the direction, was all he desired; with an unerring certainty, though never having been in that part of the country before, he would go over hill and valley, through thickets and canebrakes to the desired point, that seemed incredible. I have known the little Choctaw boys, in their juvenile excursions with their bows and arrows and blow-guns to wander miles away from their homes, this way and that through the woods, and return home at night, without a thought or fear of getting lost; nor did their parents have any uneasiness in regard to their wanderings. It is a universal characteristic of the Indian, when traveling in an unknown country, to let nothing pass unnoticed. His watchful eye marks every distinguishing feature of the surroundings—a peculiarly leaning or fallen tree, stump or bush, rock or hill, creek or branch, he will recognize years afterwards, and use them as landmarks, in going again through the same country. Thus the Indian hunter was enabled to go into a distant forest, where he never before had been, pitch his camp, leave it and hunt all day—wandering this way and that over hills and through jungles for miles away, and return to his camp at the close of the day with that apparent ease and unerring certainty, that baffled all the ingenuity of the white man and appeared to him as bordering on the miraculous. Ask any Indian for the directions to a place, near or distant, and he merely points in the direction you should go regarding that as sufficient information for any one of common sense.[4]

The skill of the forest Indian, as we now know, arose from the conditions of his life. Under similar circumstances white men have developed equal sagacity.

---

[2] Bushnell, Bull. 48, Bur. Amer. Ethn., p. 20.
[3] Appendix p. 263; Nouv. Voy., vol. 2, p. 101.
[4] Cushman, Hist. Inds., p. 182.

On account of the lack of large rivers dugouts were little used by the Choctaw until after they began to leave their old homes.[5]

Cushman gives the following form of greeting:

If a Choctaw of the long ago met a white man with whom he was acquainted and on terms of social friendship, he took his proffered hand, then with a gentle pressure and forward inclination of the head, said, in a mild and sweet tone of voice: "Chishno pisah yukpah siah it tikana su," I am glad to see you my friend, and if he had nothing of importance to communicate, or anything [of which he desired] to obtain information, he passed on without further remarks; no better proof of good sense can be manifested, and well worthy of imitation.[6]

A Mr. Mease, who traveled through the Choctaw country in 1770 and 1771, says of the reception of his party at Coosa:

At this place the inhabitants were very hospitable. On alighting they spread bear skins for us to sit upon and soon after brought large jars of homony which tho' unseasoned even with salt I then thought delicious eating.

The Choctaw were noted for their gypsylike fondness for camping about in one place after another. Dr. John Sibley says, writing in the period 1803–21, "they . . . are always wandering about in families among the white settlements. Many of them don't see their towns for two or three years."[7] In this connection one is reminded of the "vagrant people" alluded to in the anonymous Relation.[8]

Simpson Tubby said that about 65 years ago it was customary for the Choctaw to scatter out annually into camps from forty to a hundred miles from home. They set out early in the fall and returned to their reserved lands at the opening of spring to prepare their gardens. They usually took along their Indian ponies, short, dumpy animals, which would, however, carry as much as any horse they have to-day. Every night they had a dance and were lectured by their chief, being particularly charged not to disturb the white man. The men made bows and arrows and blowguns and killed all of the game they were allowed to, because the native game laws were made to apply to foreign places as well as to their own country. The older women cut and dried canes and made baskets every night, while the young people danced. At that time they visited the whites at Columbus, Miss., Macon, Brookesville, and Crawfordville, and the region where Yazoo City now is. The Yalobusha (Yaloba asha, "tadpole place"), and Yaganogani (Yakni, "land," noñka, "low"?) were favorite places for gathering canes. Táshka himmita is said to have been the name of a Sixtowns Band, and their country, which was full of lakes, could hardly be beaten for beaver, otter, raccoon, opossum, squirrels, rabbits, and other game. The Indians formerly congregated there in

---

[5] See p. 40.
[6] Cushman, Hist. Inds., p. 173.
[7] Letters of Dr. John Sibley of Louisiana to His Son Samuel Hopkins Sibley, 1803–1821 (in The Louisiana Historical Quarterly, vol. 10, no. 4 (Oct., 1927), pp. 499–500.
[8] See p. 258.

great numbers and many resort to that region still. Fåni yakni, about 9 miles east of Philadelphia, was a great place for squirrels. The whites used to give them sacks of flour and other provisions, which were relied upon to carry them through until their own crops came in.

When the Choctaw first obtained money, a few learned how to trade in advance of the rest and the others intrusted their money to them. Simpson traded for many of his people in this way up to 10 or 15 years ago.

WAR CUSTOMS

The anonymous Relation tells us that—

When any of their enemies has declared war on them, they take counsel together over the affront which they have received, and after having resolved to make war on the nation by which they have been insulted, they begin the war dance. This commonly lasts eight days, and serves to encourage each one of the warriors who scarcely eat at all during this time, and who make libations of the juice of herbs which the medicine-man gives them, and with which they rub themselves, which has the virtue they say of giving them strength and courage, an invaluable herb if it were known in Europe. After this they set out to war. On the way, when they have to light a fire in order to cook food, they usually light it in a little valley for fear of being discovered by some party, for in that case the party will follow them until it has found a good opportunity to rush upon them. They never attack their enemies when they are awake; but in the evening, when they have discovered the place where they intend to pass the night, they try to get as close to them as they can, and, as the ground in the woods is covered with dry leaves which make a noise in walking, they have patience enough to remove them, one by one, with their toes, of which they make use as of the hand, and if unfortunately they break some small branches, they immediately mimic the cry of certain birds which they imitate very well, in order to have it thought that it is this bird which has made the noise;[9] if they perceive their enemy asleep, especially just at day-break, they utter the death cry, and on the instant all shoot at once, each on his man, and they spring upon them war club in hand in order to finish those who are only wounded, from whom they carry away the scalps. If they have time they strip them and return to their village, within sight of which they utter the cry of warriors who have struck a blow, and who bring scalps. Each one [in the village] comes before them ceremoniously and they are led into the square in the same manner. They engage in dances as a sign of rejoicing over their victory and if any of the party has a child or nephew who has not yet taken part in such a triumph, he shares half of the scalp he has taken with him and has him received as a warrior. The ceremony is that the one who undergoes it suffers two hundred blows of a neck-band, which is a piece of hide five or six fathoms long, of the breadth of a finger, doubled many times, with which the warriors strike him full arm blows in turn on his back and on his belly, in order to make him understand that a warrior must endure everything patiently, even when he is taken by the enemy, and sing while they make him suffer and die. He must suffer these blows while singing, for if he should

---

[9] Du Roullet says that the cry of an owl is "what the savages make when they approach an enemy." (Journ. Soc. Amér. de Paris, vol. xv, pp. 242–243.)

weep he will never be received and would pass as a woman, and unworthy of being admitted into the body of warriors. When they hold these ceremonial dances, each wears on his head a crown made of a piece of otter skin to which are fastened as many broken white feathers as they have killed men in their lives. Each family has its quarterings tattooed on the stomach and on the arms [of its warrior members]. They also put them on the handles of their war clubs, and when they wish to meet in the woods they make a mark on the trees, where they put their arms, by which the one who has made the mark is known; the trail he has taken, and where he has gone.

When they capture any young people—girls, women, or young boys—alive, they carry them to their villages and make slaves of them. There are nations which adopt them as their dogs; then they make them perform all the functions of a dog, guard the doors, growl when anyone enters or goes out, eat the leavings of the dishes, and gnaw the bones. When they are able to bring home prisoners, they have them burned at their villages, and it is a great joy to them when that happens.[10]

Bossu's account is nearly as old:

The Chactas love war and have some good methods of making it. They never fight standing fixedly in one place; they flit about; they heap contempt upon their enemies without at the same time being braggarts, for when they come to grips they fight with much coolness. Some women are so fond of their husbands that they follow them to war. They keep by their sides in combat holding a quiver of arrows and encourage them by crying out continually that they must not fear their enemies but die like true men.

The Chactas are extremely superstitious. When they are about to go to war they consult their Manitou, which is carried by the chief. They always exhibit it on that side where they are going to march toward the enemy, the warriors standing guard about. They have so much veneration for it that they never eat until the chief has given it the first portion.

As long as the war lasts the chief is scrupulously obeyed, but after they have returned they have consideration for him only proportionate to his liberality with his possessions.

It is an established usage among them that, when the chief of a war party has taken booty from the enemy, he must divide it among the warriors, and the relatives of those who have been killed in combat, in order, say they, *to wipe away their tears*. The chief retains nothing for himself except the honor of being the restorer of the nation. . . .

If the chief of a Chacta party does not succeed in the war he loses all his credit; no one has confidence in his leadership any longer, and he must descend to the rank of a common warrior. However, consider the varying views of different nations! Among these warlike peoples it is no shame to desert. They attribute the desertion to a bad dream. If the chief of a big party himself, having dreamed the night before that he would lose some of his people, assures his warriors that he has had a bad dream, they turn back immediately to their village. After they have returned, they make medicine, for they use it on all kinds of occasions. Then they return toward the enemies. If they encounter any of them on their way, they kill five or six and then go home as well pleased as if they had subjugated a great empire.

A general who should win a victory with the loss of many people would be very badly received by his nation, because these people consider a victory of

---

[10] Appendix, pp. 252–253; Mem. Am. Anth. Ass'n, v, No. 2, pp. 65–67. The compulsion to imitate dogs may safely be set down as folklore.

no account when it is won at the price of the blood of their relatives and their friends. So the war chiefs take great pains to save their warriors and to attack the enemy only when they are sure to win, either on account of their numbers or natural topographical advantages, but as their adversaries have the same skill and know as well as they how to avoid the snares which are laid for them, the most cunning is the one who conquers. For that reason they hide themselves in the woods during the day and travel only at night, and if they are not discovered, they attack at daybreak. As they are usually in wooded country, the one who goes in advance sometimes holds a very thick bush in front of him, and, as all follow in a line, the last effaces the marks of those who have gone ahead, so arranging the leaves, or the earth over which they have passed, that there remains no trace that might betray them.

The principal things which serve to reveal them to their enemies are the smoke of their fires, which they scent at a great distance and their tracks which are recognized in an almost incredible manner. One day a savage showed me, in a place where I perceived nothing, the footprints of Frenchmen, savages, and Negroes who had passed that way, and told me how long before they had been by. I confess that this knowledge appeared to me miraculous. One must admit that when the savages apply themselves to a single thing they excel at it.

The art of war, among them, as you see, consists in watchfulness, care to avoid ambuscades and in taking the enemy unawares, patience and endurance to withstand hunger, thirst, the inclemency of the seasons, the labors and the fatigues inseparable from war.

He who has struck a blow in war, carries off the dead man's scalp as a trophy, and has a record pricked or outlined on his body. Then he goes into mourning, and during that time, continuing for a month, he must not comb his hair, so that if his head itches, he is permitted to scratch himself only with a little stick fastened to his wrist for that particular purpose.[11]

Romans, writing at a little later period, has this to say regarding the warlike character and war customs of the tribe:

They are in their warlike temper far from being such cowards as people in general will pretend, but it is true they are not so fond of wandering abroad to do mischief as the other savages are; few of such expeditions are undertaken by them, and they give for a reason, that in going abroad they may chance to be obliged to content themselves with a woman's or child's scalp, but in staying at home and waiting the attack of the enemy, they by pursuing them, are sure to take men, which is a greater mark of valour: be this as it will, it is certain they are carefully, cunningly, and bravely watchfull at home, and on several occasions they have, after many insults, boldly offered to meet their enemies in equal numbers on a plain, which has always been by the other savages treated with scorn, as cowardice; however when it has happened by chance that they meet so, we have seen them brave and victorious. Even in the very town of Mobile, an action of this kind happened deserving a record, when they drove their enemies (the Creeks) through the river, and but for their inability to swim, they would have totally destroyed them; the Captain *Hooma* or red Captain fighting with forty men against three hundred Creeks, and with his own hand destroying thirteen of their Chiefs, even when fighting on his knees, and when he fell, bravely telling who he was, and his being flead alive for his

---

[11] Appendix, pp. 258–260; M. Bossu, Nouveaux Voyages aux Indes occidentales, 2 vols., Paris, 1768. Vol. 2, pp. 89–94.

heroism, is so fresh in every one's memory (being not above six years ago) that many living evidences can testify it; I thought the action worthy of this attempt, to save it from oblivion. They have deserted many of their eastern frontier towns since their present war with the Creeks, but during my stay in their nation, I saw four or five instances of their not suffering their enemy to escape unpunished, when he dared to commit depredations, and they valued themselves on the vent of the present war, when in 1771, news coming among the Traders, that the Creeks computed their loss at near three hundred persons, and they having guessed the number of their's, lost much the same; they said, we have lost many women and children and even of them some Scalps have been retaken, but we like men, have killed men only, and got all the marks thereof; this war began in August 1765; the readers may judge at the greatness of their exploits, when I assure them, that that number was the total loss during all that time. . . .[12]

. . . I take them to be a brave people, who can upon occasion defend themselves very coolly, for during my stay in the nation, a woman of that tribe made a bargain with me to give her ammunition for some provisions I bought of her; and when I expressed my surprise thereat, she informed me that she kept a gun to defend herself as well as her husband did; and I have several times seen armed women in motion with the parties going in pursuit of the invading enemy, who having completed their intended murder, were flying off.

They never exercised so much cruelty upon their captive enemies as the other savages; they almost always brought them home to shew them, and then dispatched them with a bullet or hatchet; after which, the body being cut into many parts, and all the hairy pieces of skin converted into scalps, the remainder is buried and the above trophies carried home, where the women dance with them till tired; then they are exposed on the tops of the hot houses till they are annihilated. The same treatment is exercised on those who are killed near the nation, but he that falls in battle at a distance is barely scalped.

Their addictedness to pretended witchcraft leads them into a very superstitious behaviour when on an expedition which is remarkable, they carry with them a certain thing which they look on as the genius of the party; it is most commonly the stuffed skin of an owl of a large kind; they are very careful of him, keep a guard over him, and offer him a part of their meat; should he fall, or any other ways be disordered in position, the expedition is frustrated; they always set him with his head toward the place of destination, and if he should prove to be turned directly contrary, they consider this as portending some very bad omen, and an absolute order to return; should therefore any one's heart fail him, he needs only watch his opportunity to do this to save his character of a brave or true man. There is also a species of *Motacilla* (which I often endeavored to catch, in vain) whose chirping near the camp, will occasion their immediate return. . . .[13]

. . . a Chactaw war camp is circular, with a fire in the center, and each man has a crutched branch at his head to hang his powder and shot upon, and to set his gun against, and the feet of all to the fire. . . .[14]

They are given to pilfering, but not so much as the Chicasaws.

They are the swiftest of foot of any savages in America, and very expert in tracking a flying enemy, who very seldom escapes.

Their leader can not pretend to *command* on an expedition, the most he can do, is to endeavor to *persuade*, or at the extent, he can only pretend to a

---

[12] Romans, Nat. Hist. E. and W. Fla., pp. 72–73.   [14] Ibid., p. 65.
[13] Ibid., pp. 75–76.

greater experience in order to enforce his counsel; should be pretend to order, desertion would at least be his punishment, if not death.[15]

When they prepare for war, and when they return they use exorcisms, they call them all physic though only bare words or actions; and if they prove unsuccessful, they say the physic was not strong enough; it is no small diversion to see a Chactaw during this preparation act all his strange gestures, and the day before his departure painted scarlet and black almost naked and with swan wings to his arms run like a bacchant up and down through the place of his abode; not drunk either as rum is by them avoided like poison during this preparation.[16]

Adair knew of the Choctaw only as bitter enemies of the English and allied Chickasaw and estimates their character very differently from Romans. Nevertheless the few items which he furnishes confirm in many particulars what the latter writer tells us. Thus, regarding the effect of their wars with the Chickasaw and Creeks on the massing of the Choctaw population, he says:

The barrier towns, which are next to the Muskohge and Chikkasah countries, are compactly settled for social defence, according to the general method of other savage nations; but the rest, both in the center, and toward the Mississippi, are only scattered plantations, as best suits a separate easy way of living. A stranger might be in the middle of one of their populous extensive towns, without seeing half a dozen of their houses, in the direct course of his path.[17]

He gives the following information regarding their war customs, which for the most part evidently closely resembled those of the Chickasaw and Creeks. Incidentally it will be noticed that he confirms what Romans tells us regarding their disinclination to offensive warfare but bravery when attacked at home.

The Choktah being employed by the French, together with their other red confederates, against the English Chikkasah, they had no opportunity of inuring themselves to the long-winded chace, among a great chain of steep craggy mountains. They are amazingly artful however in deceiving an enemy; they will fasten the paws and trotters of panthers, bears, and buffaloes, to their feet and hands, and wind about like the circlings of such animals, in the lands they usually frequent. They also will mimick the different notes of wild fowl, and thus often outwit the savages they have disputes with. Their enemies say, that when at war, it is impossible to discover their tracks, unless they should be so lucky as to see their persons. They act very timorously against the enemy abroad, but behave as desperate veterans when attacked in their own country. . . ."[18]

Scalps taken in war were painted red,[19] and were treated with considerable ceremony, as the following account derived from Adair's own personal experience shows:

I proceeded, and met several parties of the same main company, several miles distant from each other, carrying small pieces of a scalp, singing the triumphal song, and sounding the shrill death-whoop, as if they had killed hundreds. On

[15] Romans, Nat. Hist. E. and W. Fla., p. 76.
[16] Ibid., p. 78.
[17] Adair, Hist. Am. Inds., p. 282.
[18] Ibid., p. 309.
[19] Ibid., p. 302.

my resting and smoking with the last party, they informed me, that their camp consisted of two hundred and fifty warriors, under great leaders, who were then returning from war against a town of the Koo-saahte Indians, who had settled twenty-five miles above Mobille, on the eastern side of the river; that they had killed and wounded several of them, suspecting them of abetting the Muskohge, and fortunately got one of their scalps, which the warriors of separate towns divided, and were carrying home, with joyful hearts.

A stranger would be much surprised to see the boasting parade these savages made with one scalp of a reputed enemy. To appearance, more than a thousand men, women, lusty boys, and girls, went loaded with provisions to meet them; and to dance, sing, and rejoice at this camp, for their success in war, and safe return. Their camps were made with the green bark and boughs of trees, and gave a striking picture of the easy and simple modes of early ages. Their chieftains and great warriors sat in state, with the assuming greatness of the ancient senators of imperial Rome. I had the honor to sit awhile with them, and was diverted with the old circling and wheeling dances of the young men and women. I smoked with them, and then took my leave of this last camp of rejoicing heroes.[20]

In 1730 De Lusser observed the following treatment of the scalps of enemies and the head of one of their own people by the Choctaw of Oskelagna:

Those who had killed were carrying the scalps that they had taken and all were daubed with white earth from head to foot. There was one who brought the head of one of their people who had been killed. He threw it at my feet telling me that he was a warrior who had lost his life for the French and that it was well to weep for his death. In a minute all the men assembled around this head and set themselves to howling for half a quarter of an hour. To give evidence of the regret that I felt for his death I did not fail to make grimaces as they did. After this it was taken up again to be carried to the women who did the same.

When he reached the town of Chicachaé he witnessed the name-giving ceremony.

The warriors of this village who slept near the bayou of the Chicachaé arrived this morning at about nine o'clock. They were all bedaubed with paint like those of the Yellow Canes and passed howling in front of the cabin to which I went. I found all the warriors who had taken part in the fighting sitting on the ground forming a semi-circle. The captains and the honored men were sitting on a bed of canes on which I took my seat with Reverend Father Beaudouin. After this they made several warriors . . . This ceremony consists only of changing the names.

We learn from the same officer that a red calumet was presented to a tribe when their alliance was desired against a third, and the acceptance of it was equivalent to promise of assistance.

In a letter sent by M. de Vaudreuil, Governor of Louisiana, to the French minister and dated March 3, 1749, dealing with conflicts between the French and English parties in the Choctaw Nation, we find it stated that the chief of Yowani was able to identify a body of the

---

[20] Adair, Hist. Am. Inds., pp. 298–299.

enemy as belonging to the village of Oka hullo by means of a war club which they had left behind. It is uncertain whether this means that each town had its individual mark or whether the object identified was unique.

It is only natural that war customs should have been among the first to recede from the memories of the later Choctaw, and in fact Cushman is practically the only relatively modern writer who mentions them—as usual in an emotional setting.

The Choctaw warrior was equally as expert in deceiving his enemy as . . . the wild denizens of his native forests. When upon the war-path the Choctaws always went in small bands, which was the universal custom of their entire race, traveling one behind the other in a straight line; and, if in the enemy's territory, each one stepped exactly in the tracks of the one who walked before him, while the one in the extreme rear defaced, as much as possible, their tracks, that no evidence of their number, or whereabouts might be made known to the enemy. In these war excursions, the most profound silence was observed; their communications being carried on by preconcerted and well understood signs made by the hand or head; if necessary to be audible, then by a low imitative cry of some particular wild animal.

The dignity of chieftainship was bestowed upon him who had proved himself worthy by his skill and daring deeds in war; and to preserve the valiant character of their chief, it was considered a disgrace for him to be surpassed in daring deeds by any of his warriors; at the same time, it was also regarded as dishonorable for the warriors to be surpassed by their chief. Thus there were great motives for both to perform desperate deeds of valor—which they did; nor did they wait for opportunities for the display of heroism, but sought perils and toils by which they might distinguish themselves. These war parties, gliding noiselessly like spectres through the dense forests, painted in the most fantastic manner conceivable, presented a wild and fearful appearance, more calculated to strike terror to the heart of the beholder than admiration. Though they advanced in small bodies and detached parties, yet in their retreats they scattered like frightened partridges, each for himself, but to unite again at a pre-arranged place miles to the rear. No gaudy display was ever made in their war excursions to their enemy's country. They meant business, not display, depending on the success of their expedition in their silent and unexpected approach, patient watching, and artful stratagems. To fight a pitched battle in an open field giving the enemy an equal chance, was to the Choctaws the best evidence of a want of military skill. Not unlike most of their race, they seldom invaded an enemy's territory from choice; but woe to the enemy, who, attributing this to cowardice, should have the presumption to invade their country; like enraged bears robbed of their young, they would find the Choctaw warriors, to a man, ready to repel them with the most desperate and fearless bravery ever exhibited by any race of men. Yet, to them, no less than to the whites, strategy was commendable, and to outwit an enemy and thus gain an advantage over him, was evidence of great and praiseworthy skill.[21]

As with all their race, so war was, in the estimation of the ancient Choctaws, the most patriotic avocation in which a man could engage; they seldom began a war with another tribe, but rather waited for an attack; then no braver or

---

[21] Cushman, Hist. Choc., Chick., and Natchez Inds., pp. 198–199.

more resolute warriors ever went upon the war-path. The opening of hostilities was always preceded by the famous Hoyopa-hihla, War-dance. Night was the chosen time for engaging in that time-honored ceremony; and as soon as evening began to spread her dark mantle o'er their forests, a huge pile of dry logs and brush previously prepared was set on fire, whose glaring and crackling flames intermingling with their hoyopa-taloah (war-songs) and soul-stirring hoyopa-tassuhah [hoyopa tasaha] (war-hoops) presented a scene as wild and romantic as can possibly be imagined.

The manly forms of the dusky warriors with their painted faces illuminated with the wildest excitement; the huge fire blazing and crackling in the centre of the wide extended circle of excited dancers, [of] which, now and then, a kick from a dancing warrior, caused to send the flames and sparks high up among the wide extended branches of the mighty forest trees that stood around; the stern visages of the old warriors, whom age and decrepitude had long since placed upon the retired list from further duty upon the war-path or in the chase, sitting around in little groups where the light of the burning log-heap disputed precedency with the gloom of night, calm and silent spectators of the weird scene in which they could no longer participate, but which awakened thrilling memories of the past; the Goddess Minerva's favorite birds, allured from their dark abodes in the forest by the glaring light, flitted here and there overhead through the extended branches of the overshadowing oaks, and anon joined in with their voices, to which in wild response, the distant howl of a pack of roving wolves filled up the measure of the awe inspiring scene. . . .

On the return of a successful war-party, the village at once became the scene of festivity and triumph. The varied trophies—scalps, painted shields, etc., were hung on poles near the houses. Then followed war-feasts, scalp-dances, accompanied with war-songs and shouts of victory, while the old men went from house to house rehearsing in a loud tone of voice the events of the battle and the various daring exploits of the warriors. But, amid all this, sounds of another kind were also heard mingling in discordant tones with those of joy; they were the pious wailings of the women borne upon the air from the surrounding hills, where they had retired to mourn in darkness and solitude for their slain in battle. There the mother, wife and sister gave full sway to the anguish of their hearts.[28]

Simpson Tubby asserts that enemies used to poison springs or the meat hung up about a spring and for that reason springs were sometimes abandoned, and the Indians preferred to use running water which could not be poisoned, rather than wells.

The earliest of all our authorities is the only one who attempts to describe the peace making ritual of the Choctaw in anything like detail. He says:

When they have promised to conclude a peace five or six leading men of the nation come, bearing a calumet or pipe made of a stone, red like coral, which is found in rocks in the Illinois country. This calumet has a stem about two or three feet in length surrounded by red feathers artistically worked, and from which hangs eight or ten black and white feathers. This serves them as a war standard, as a seal in alliances, as a mark of the continuation of faithfulness among friends, and as a sign of war with those with whom they wish to break. It is true that there is one which is the calumet of peace and another that of

---

[28] Cushman, Hist. Choc., Chick., and Natchez Inds., pp. 253–254.

war. They are both made similarly. When they have concluded the peace the master of ceremonies lights this calumet and has all those who are in the assembly smoke two or three whiffs. Then the treaty is concluded and inviolable. They deliver this calumet to the chief with whom they make the contract which is as a hostage of their good faith and the fidelity with which they wish to observe the articles on which they have agreed.[23]

BURIAL CUSTOMS

This feature of ancient Choctaw culture was developed so strikingly that more attention is devoted to it by writers on the tribe than to any other native custom. In his History of Alabama [24] Pickett furnishes a lengthy account of the burial ceremonies based upon earlier materials, but by all odds the best is that by the late Henry S. Halbert, which not only draws upon all earlier sources available to him at the time but incorporates a mass of material from the personal observations of the author and the memories of the best informed Choctaw with whom he was acquainted.[25] In fact this single paper contains a sufficiently full account for all practical purposes and leaves little to be added. However, it being the plan of the present writer to incorporate all of the material contained in original sources and a few of these not having been available to Mr. Halbert, the entire ground will be reviewed again, Halbert's narrative being placed at the end.

Two descriptions have been left by French writers, and these are put first, since at least one of them is undoubtedly the earliest of all, while the second is practically contemporary with the account given by Adair. The anonymous French narrator says:

When a sick person is near death the doctor leaves him and informs his relatives of it, assuring them that he cannot recover. Then the women come to wash his body, paint him, daub his face, dress him in all of the finest clothes which he had, and lay him on the ground in the open space in front of his door. His wife lies on his stomach weeping, with his nearest relatives who also lie upon him and stifle him. They ask him why it is that he hungers to die, if he has lacked anything, if his wife did not love him enough, if he was not well respected in his village; in fact this unfortunate patient is obliged to die in spite of himself. Those who have lain down on him cry at the top of their lungs, imagining that he does not hear, since he does not reply. Besides these, there are the hired criers who during this time come to weep or rather howl to music beside the body, before and after his death. As soon as he is dead his relatives erect a kind of cabin in the shape of a coffin, directly opposite his door six feet from the ground on six stakes, surrounded by a mud wall, and roofed with bark, in which they enclose this body all dressed, covering it with a blanket. They place food and drink beside him, giving him a change of shoes, his gun, powder, and balls. They say that it is because he is going into another

---

[23] Appendix, pp. 253–254; Mem. Am. Anth. Assn., v, p. 67.
[24] Pickett, Hist. of Alabama, Sheffield, Ala., 1896, pp. 129–131.
[25] Pubs. Miss. Hist. Soc., III, pp. 353–366.

country, and it is right that he have everything he needs in his journey. They believe that the warriors go to war in the other world, and that everyone there performs the same acts that he did in this. The body rests in this five or six months, until they think that it is rotted, which makes a terrible stench (*infection*) in the house. After some time all the relatives assemble ceremoniously and the honored woman (*femme de valleur*) of the village who has for her function (*distrique*) to strip off the flesh from the bones of the dead, comes to take off the flesh from this body, scrapes the bones well, and places them in a very clean cane hamper, which they enclose in linen or cloth. They throw the flesh into some field, and this same flesh stripper, without washing her hands, comes to serve food to the assembly. This woman is very much honored in the village. After the repast, singing and howling, they proceed to carry the bones into the charnel-house of the canton, a cabin with only one covering in which these hampers are placed in a row on poles. The same ceremony is performed over chiefs except that instead of putting the bones in hampers they are placed in chests locked with keys in the charnel-house of the chiefs.²⁶

Female "bone-pickers" are mentioned by no other writer, but there is no occasion to doubt their existence. Such offices were usually held by men.

The second French informant is the traveler Bossu.

They have [he says] great regard for the bodies of their dead which they never bury.²⁷ After a Chacta has died, his body is put into a bier made of cypress bark expressly for the purpose and placed on four forked sticks about fifteen feet high. After the worms have consumed the flesh, the entire family assembles. The bone-picker comes and dismembers the skeleton. He tears off the muscles, nerves, and tendons which may be left. Then they bury the latter and deposit the bones in a chest after having painted the head with vermilion. During this entire ceremony the relatives weep and it is followed by a feast to the friends who have come to pay the compliment of their condolence, after which the remains of the deceased are carried to the common cemetery, to the place where are deposited those of his ancestors. While these mournful ceremonies are taking place a gloomy silence is observed. There is no singing or dancing; each one retires weeping.

Early in November, they hold a great ceremony which they call the ceremonial of the dead or of the souls. Each family then comes to the common cemetery and visits, weeping all the while, the mortuary chests of its relations, and when they have returned they have a great feast terminating the ceremony.²⁸

We now turn to English writers, of whom the earliest is Adair. He touches upon the subject in two different places, the first a brief note introduced in the description of Choctaw medical practice, the second a fairly full narration. These accounts are as follows:

The Choktah are so exceedingly infatuated in favour of the infallible judgment of their pretended prophets, as to allow them without the least regret, to dislocate the necks of any of their sick who are in a weak state of body,

---

²⁶ Appendix, pp. 251–252; Mem. Am. Anth. Assn., vol. v, No. 2, pp. 64–65, 1918.

²⁷ Bossu seems to have failed to learn of the periodical burials in mounds.

²⁸ Appendix, p. 260; Bossu, Nouv. Voy., vol. 2, pp. 95–96.

to put them out of their pain, when they presume to reveal the determined will of the Deity to shorten his days, which is asserted to be communicated in a dream; by the time that this theo-physical operation is performed on a patient, they have a scaffold prepared opposite to the door, whereon he is to lie till they remove the bones in the fourth moon after, to the remote bone-house of that family: they immediately carry out the corpse, mourn over it, and place it in that dormitory, which is strongly pallisadoed around, lest the children should become polluted even by passing over the dead. Formerly when the owner of the house died, they set fire to it, and to all the provisions of every kind; or sold the whole at a cheap rate to the trading people, without paying the least regard to the scarcity of the times. . . .[29]

Having placed the dead on a high scaffold stockaded round, at the distance of twelve yards from his house opposite to the door, the whole family convene there at the beginning of the fourth moon after the interment, to lament and feast together; after wailing a while on the mourning benches, which stand on the east side of the quadrangular tomb, they raise and bring out the corpse, and while the feast is getting ready, a person whose office it is, and properly called the *bone-picker*, dissects it, as if it was intended for the shambles in the time of a great famine, with his sharp-pointed, bloody knife [?]. He continues busily employed in his reputed sacred office, till he has finished the task, and scraped all the flesh off the bones; which may justly be called the Choktah method of embalming their dead. Then, they carefully place the bones in a kind of small chest, in their natural order, that they may with ease and certainty be sometime afterward reunited, and proceed to strike up a song of lamentation, with various wailing tunes and notes: afterwards, they join as cheerfully in the funeral feast, as if their kinsman was only taking his usual sleep. Having regaled themselves with a plentiful variety, they go along with those beloved relicks of their dead, in solemn procession, lamenting with doleful notes, till they arrive at the bone-house, which stands in a solitary place, apart from the town: then they proceed around it, much after the manner of those who performed the obsequies of the Chikkasah chieftain, already described, and there deposit their kinsman's bones to lie alongside of his kindred-bones, till in due time they are revived by *Ishtohoollo Aba*, that he may repossess his favourite place.

Those bone-houses are scaffolds raised on durable pitch-pine forked posts, in the form of a house covered a-top, but open at both ends. I saw three of them in one of their towns, pretty near each other—the place seemed to be unfrequented; each house contained the bones of one tribe, separately, with the hieroglyphical figures of the family on each of the odd-shaped arks: they reckon it irreligious to mix the bones of a relation with those of a stranger, as bone of bone, and flesh of the same flesh, should be always joined together; and much less will they thrust the body of their beloved kinsman into the abominable tomb of a hateful enemy. I observed a ladder fixed in the ground, opposite to the middle of the broadside of each of those dormitories of the dead, which was made out of a broad board, and stood considerably bent over the sacred repository, with the steps on the inside. On the top was the carved image of a dove, with its wings stretched out and its head inclining down, as if earnestly viewing or watching over the bones of the dead: and from the top of the ladder to almost the surface of the earth, there hung a chain of grape-vines twisted together, in circular links, and the same likewise at their domestic tombs. . . .[30]

---

[29] Adair, Hist. Am. Inds., p. 129.   [30] Ibid., pp. 183–184.

The custom of wailing over the dead is mentioned by nearly all early writers. Chiefs assembled to mourn at the tomb of one of their number, as is noted in some of the early documents. The following account is by William Bartram:

The Choctaws pay their last duties and respect to the deceased in a very different manner [from the Creeks]. As soon as a person is dead, they erect a scaffold eighteen or twenty feet high, in a grove adjacent to the town, where they lay the corpse, lightly covered with a mantle: here it is suffered to remain, visited and protected by the friends and relations, until the flesh becomes putrid, so as easily to part; then undertakers, who make it their business, carefully strip the flesh from the bones, wash and cleanse them, and when dry and purified by the air, having provided a curiously wrought chest or coffin, fabricated of bones and splints, they place all the bones therein; it is then deposited in the bone-house, a building erected for that purpose in every town. And when this house is full, a general solemn funeral takes place; the nearest kindred or friends of the deceased, on a day appointed, repair to the bone-house, take up the respective coffins, and following one another in order of superiority, the nearest relations and connexions attending their respective corpse, and the multitude following after them, all as one family, with united voice of alternate Allelujah and lamentation, slowly proceed to the place of general interment, where they place the coffins in order, forming a pyramid [21]; and lastly, cover all over with earth, which raises a conical hill or mount. Then they return to town in order of solemn procession, concluding the day with a festival, which is called the feast of the dead.[22]

Romans is much more detailed:

As soon as the deceased is departed, a stage is erected . . . and the corpse is laid on it and covered with a bear skin; if he be a man of note, it is decorated, and the poles painted red with vermillion and bears oil; if a child, it is put upon stakes set across; at this stage the relations come and weep, asking many questions of the corpse, such as, why he left them? did not his wife serve him well? was he not contented with his children? had he not corn enough? did not his land produce sufficient of everything? was he afraid of his enemies? &c. and this accompanied by loud howlings; the women will be there constantly, and sometimes with the corrupted air and heat of the sun faint so as to oblige the by standers to carry them home; the men will also come and mourn in the same manner, but in the night or at other unseasonable times, when they are least likely to be discovered.

The stage is fenced round with poles, it remains thus a certain time but not a fixed space, this is sometimes extended to three or four months, but seldom more than half that time. A certain set of venerable old Gentlemen who wear very long nails as a distinguishing badge on the thumb, fore and middle finger of each hand, constantly travel through the nation (when I was there, I was told there were but five of this respectable order) that one of them may acquaint those concerned, of the expiration of this period, which is according to their own fancy; the day being come, the friends and relations assemble near

---

[21] Some ingenious men, whom I have conversed with, have given it as their opinion, that all those pyramidal artificial hills, usually called Indian mounds, were raised on these occasions, and are generally sepulchres. However, I am of a different opinion.—Bartram.

[22] Bartram, Travels, pp. 514–515, 1792.

the stage, a fire is made, and the respectable operator, after the body is taken down, with his nails tears the remaining flesh off the bones, and throws it with the intrails into the fire, where it is consumed; then he scrapes the bones and burns the scrapings likewise; the head being painted red with vermillion is with the rest of the bones put into a neatly made chest (which for a chief is also made red) and deposited in the loft of a hut built for that purpose, and called bone house; each town has one of these; after remaining here one year or thereabouts, if he be a man of any note, they take the chest down, and in an assembly of relations and friends they weep once more over him, refresh the colour of the head, paint the box red, and then deposit him to lasting oblivion.

An enemy and one who commits suicide is buried under the earth as one to be directly forgotten and unworthy the above ceremonial obsequies and mourning.[33]

Yet Claiborne affirms that suicide was common, assigning " ridicule or disgrace " as the principal cause.[34]

Milfort's testimony comes from a period but a few years subsequent to Romans:

When a Tchacta is dead, his relatives erect a scaffold about twenty or twenty-five feet in front of the doorway of his house, on which they place the corpse wrapped in the skin of a bear or bison, or in a woolen covering, and leave it in that condition for seven or eight months. The nearest female relatives go each morning to weep while they circle the scaffold. When they believe that the body is in a state of putrefaction sufficient to allow the flesh to come away from the bones easily, they (the women) go to inform the priest or medicine man of the canton where the dead man lived, who is entrusted with the dissection, the most disgusting that it is possible to imagine. As all the relatives and friends of the dead man must be present at this ceremony, which is terminated by a family repast, the priest agrees upon a day in order to allow sufficient time to inform everyone; and, on the appointed day all assemble around the scaffold; and there, after having made horrible grimaces as a sign of mourning, they intone sombre chants, in which they express the grief which they feel at the loss they have suffered. When they have finished this horrible charivari, the priest ascends the scaffold, removes the skin or covering which covers the body; and, with his fingernails (he is not permitted to make use of anything else),[34a] he detaches the flesh which may still adhere to the bones, so as to separate the one from the other entirely. When he has finished this disgusting operation, he makes one bundle of the flesh which he leaves on the scaffold to be burned and one of the bones which he carries down on his head to restore to the relatives of the dead man, making them a speech suited to the occasion. As soon as the latter have received the bones, they take great care to examine them, and to assure themselves that the priest has forgotten none of them; afterward they deposit them in a kind of chest, the opening of which they shut with a plank, after which the women kindle torches of pitch pine, and the nearest relatives go in procession to bear this chest into a cabin which serves as the sepulchre of that family alone.

While the priest is on the scaffold occupied with the dissection, all of the others who are present busy themselves on their side in lighting fires, on

---

[33] Romans, Nat. Hist. E. and W. Fla., pp. 89–90.
[34] Claiborne, Hist. Miss., I, p. 495; on suicide see p. 110.
[34a] Adair would seem to imply an exception (see p. 172), but he was probably mistaken.

which they place for the guests great earthen pots full of food. When these viands are cooked, they remove them from the fire in order to allow them to cool without touching them, for the priest alone is permitted to remove the coverings, and he can do so only after having finished his operation.

When the ceremony of inhuming the bones is finished, a great quantity of dry wood is collected about the scaffold where the flesh has been left, the relatives set fire to it, and, while the scaffold burns, they dance around it uttering loud cries of joy; then the priest chooses a suitable place, where all sit about and he remains in the middle, with the vessels holding the viands which are to be served at the feast, and which have been given time to cool. When each has taken his place the medicine man or priest uncovers the vessels, and, without having even washed his hands, which he has merely wiped on some grass, he puts them in the pots in order to draw out the viands and distribute them among the relatives and friends of the dead man, according to their rank; he serves the soup to them in the same manner, as well as the hominy (sagamité) which is their drink.

I have said elsewhere that these people have a particular relish for horse-flesh which they prefer to all other kinds; in consequence if the person whose funeral rites are conducted was rich enough to have horses, as many as three are sometimes killed, which are cooked and their flesh used in doing the honors at the feast. It happens indeed, when the dead man has no horses, that those of the relatives who have them are sacrificed for this ceremony. This reunion of relatives and friends can be dissolved only when there is nothing more to eat; so that after they have had the first meal, and are unable to consume all, they begin to dance. or to indulge in violent exercises in order to acquire an appetite, and be in a condition to finish the feast. When there is nothing more to eat each one returns home.[35]

According to this writer a scaffold was erected and mourning ceremonies gone through for a person who had disappeared and had been declared dead by a doctor.[35a] Next we have a short note by Dr. John Sibley:

The Choctaus in their Town don't bury their dead; but make a Scaffold of forks & Poles of Twelve feet high near their Houses on which they place the Dead body 'till the flesh is so putrid that it will slip off the Bones. This is done by the nearest relation, the flesh is buried, the bones put in a box & deposited in the Bone House.[36]

The Missionary Herald contains this, communicated to the Rev. Cyrus Byington by a white man long resident among these Indians:

When any one died a small scaffold was made in the yard, near the house and high enough to be out of the reach of the dogs. On this the dead body was laid on one side, and then a blanket or bear-skin was thrown over it, and there the body lay until it perished. Then the *bone-pickers*, some old men with long finger nails, came and picked the flesh off and put the bones in a box. The skull was adorned when put away. The bones were then taken to a bone house, (a house set apart to receive the bones of the dead,) standing at the

---

[35] Appendix, pp. 265–267; Milfort, Mémoire, pp. 292–298.
[35a] Ibid., p. 268; see also p. 214.
[36] Letters of Dr. John Sibley of Louisiana to His Son Samuel Hopkins Sibley, 1803–1821 (in The Louisiana Historical Quarterly, vol. 10, No. 4 (Oct., 1927), pp. 499–500.)

edge of a town. When this ceremony was performed, there was a large collection of people. The bone-pickers had some other ceremonies, but I do not recollect them. Twice in each year—spring and fall—the people assembled in numbers near the bone houses, on account of the dead. The two families [i. e. the moieties], into which the nation by the usage of the people is divided, would meet. On one day one family would cry and howl over the bones of the dead, the bones being then brought out of the houses. And while one family cried, the other danced. On the succeeding day, the family that danced on the day before would cry and howl, and the other dance. After this the bones lying in the boxes were deposited again in the bone houses. A small present was made to the bone-pickers. About 38 years since the Choctaws began to bury the dead. At that time an old king died and was buried. He was the first man who was buried.[37]

Coming down to relatively modern times we find in Cushman no less than three descriptions, one by himself, one from a manuscript by a native missionary, Rev. Israel Folsom, and a third quoted from a manuscript by Nathaniel Folsom. These are as follows:

I

In the disposition of their dead, the ancient Choctaws practiced a strange method different from any other Nation of people, perhaps, that ever existed. After the death of a Choctaw, the corpse, wrapped in a bear skin or rough kind of covering of their own manufacture, was laid out at full length upon a high scaffold erected near the house of the deceased, that it might be protected from the wild beasts of the woods and the scavengers of the air. After the body had remained upon the scaffold a sufficient time for the flesh to have nearly or entirely decayed, the Hattak fullih nipi foni, (Bone Picker) the principal official in their funeral ceremonies and especially appointed for that duty—appeared and informed the relatives of the deceased that he had now come to perform the last sacred duties of his office to their departed friend. Then, with the relatives and friends, he marched with great solemnity of countenance to the scaffold and, ascending, began his awful duty of picking off the flesh that still adhered to the bones, with loud groans and fearful grimaces, to which the friends below responded in cries and wailings.

The Bone-Picker never trimmed the nails of his thumbs, index and middle fingers which accordingly grew to an astonishing length—sharp and almost as hard as flint—and well adapted to the horrid business of their owner's calling. After he had picked all the flesh from the bones, he then tied it up in a bundle and carefully laid it upon a corner of the scaffold; then gathering up the bones in his arms he descended and placed them in a previously prepared box, and then applied fire to the scaffold, upon which the assembly gazed uttering the most frantic cries and moans until it was entirely consumed. Then forming a procession headed by the Bone-Picker the box containing the bones was carried, amid weeping and wailing, and deposited in a house erected and consecrated to that purpose and called A-bo-ha fo-ni, (Bone-house) with one of which all villages and towns were supplied. Then all repaired to a previously prepared feast, over which the Bone-Picker, in virtue of his office, presided with much gravity and silent dignity.

As soon as the bone-houses of the neighboring villages were filled, a general burial of the bones took place, to which funeral ceremony the people came from

[37] The Missionary Herald, vol. xxv, No. 11 (Nov., 1829), p. 350.

far and near, and, in a long and imposing procession, with weeping and wailing and loud lamentations of the women, bore off the boxes of bones to their last place of rest, and there depositing them in the form of a pyramid they were covered with earth three or four feet in depth forming a conical mound. All then returned to a previously designated village and concluded the day in feasting.

Thus many of the mounds found in Mississippi and Alabama are but the cemeteries of the ancient Choctaws; since, as often as the bone-houses became filled, the boxes of bones were carried out to the same cemetery and deposited on the previously made heap commencing at the base and ascending to the top, each deposit being covered up with earth to the depth of three or four feet, and thus, by continued accession through a long series of ages, became the broad and high mounds, concerning which there has been so much wild speculation with so little foundation for truth or common sense. Even at the time the missionaries were established among them (1818), many of the mounds were of so recent date that not even bushes were growing upon them, though the custom of thus laying away their dead had become obsolete; still a few Bone-Pickers had survived the fall of their calling, and were seen, here and there, wandering about from village to village as ghosts of a departed age, with the nails of the thumb, index and middle fingers still untrimmed, and whose appearance indicated their earthly pilgrimage had reached nearly to a century, some of whom I personally knew.

Shortly before the advent of the missionaries, the custom of placing the dead upon the scaffolds was abolished, though not without much opposition; and that of burial in a sitting posture was adopted, with also new funeral ceremonies, which were as follows: Seven men were appointed whose duty it was to set up each a smooth pole (painted red) around the newly made grave, six of which were about eight feet high, and the seventh about fifteen, to which thirteen hoops (made of grape vines) were suspended and so united as to form a kind of ladder, while on its top a small white flag was fastened. This ladder of hoops was for the easier ascent of the spirit of the deceased to the top of the pole, whence, the friends of the deceased believed, it took its final departure to the spirit land.[88]

This later form is thus enlarged upon:

When a death was announced, which was made by the firing of guns in quick succession, the whole village and surrounding neighborhood—almost to a man—assembled at once at the home of the deceased, to console and mourn with the bereaved. On the next day a procession was formed headed by seven men called Fabussa Sholih (Pole-bearer), each carrying on his shoulder a long, slender pole painted red, and all slowly and in profound silence marched to the grave, where the poles were at once firmly set up in the ground—three on each side of the grave, and one at the head, on which thirteen hoops were suspended while on its top a small white flag fluttered in the breeze. The corpse was then carefully placed in its last earthly place of rest, the grave filled up, and all returned to the former home of the departed. They had specified cries at the grave of the deceased, which continued for thirteen moons. At the termination of each cry, a hoop was taken off of the pole, and so on until the last one was removed; then a grand funeral ceremony was celebrated called Fabussa halut akuchchih [or fabassa halat akkàchi], (pole to pull down). And the manager of the pole-pulling was called Hattak (man)

---

[88] But regarding this belief see p. 191.

illi (dead) chohpa (meat). That is, meat for the dead man; or, more properly, meat for the obsequies of the dead man.

To this celebration, or last commemoration [of] the dead, when all had assembled, the Fabussa halulli, (the same Fabussa Sholih who had set up the poles) under the command of the Hattak iti i miko (the same who bore and set up the long pole upon which was attached the hoops and flag) slowly and silently marched in solemn procession to the grave and pulled up the poles, and carried them off together with the hoops and concealed them in a secret place in the forest where they were left to return to dust forever undisturbed.

As soon as the Fabussa Hallulli had disposed of the poles and hoops, preparations were begun for the finale—a feast and the grand Aboha hihlah, home dancing; or dancing home of the deceased good man to the land of plenty and happiness, and the bad man to the land of scarcity and suffering.

The festivities continued during the day and the night following the pole-pulling. On the next morning all returned to their respective homes; and from that day he or she of the grave became a thing of the past, whose names were to be mentioned no more. And they were not.[39]

II

The mode of burial practiced by the Choctaws consisted in placing the corpse five or six feet from the ground upon a platform of rough timber made for that purpose, covered with a rough kind of cloth of their own making, or skins of wild animals and bark of trees. After remaining in that condition until the flesh had very nearly or altogether decayed, the bones were then taken down by the bone-pickers (persons appointed for that duty)[40] and carefully put in wooden boxes made for that purpose, which were placed in a house built and set apart for them. These were called bone-houses; whenever they became full, the bones were all taken out and carefully arranged to a considerable height somewhat in the form of a pyramid or cone, and a layer of earth put over them. This custom, which prevailed among many different tribes, is, no doubt, the origin of the Indian mounds, as they are generally called, which are found in various parts of the country, particularly in the states of Mississippi and Alabama, formerly the home of the Choctaws. When the custom of placing the dead upon platforms was abandoned, which met with strong opposition, they buried their dead in a sitting posture in the grave; around the grave they set half a dozen red poles about eight feet high, and one about fifteen feet high, at the top of which a white flag was fastened. The occupation of the bone-pickers having been abolished, it then became their business to make and set up red poles around the graves, and afterwards to remove them at the expiration of the time of mourning, and hence they were called pole-pullers. They were respected by the people, and for less labor being imposed upon them, they were pleased with the change in the burial of the dead. At the pole-pulling, which as stated, was at the expiration of the time of mourning, a vast collection of people would assemble to join in a general mourning. After much food had been consumed they would disperse to their respective homes, and the mourning relations would oil their hair and dress up as usual.[41]

[39] Cushman, Hist. Inds., pp. 225–228; cf. Claiborne, Miss., I, pp. 488–489.
[40] "One Iksa [moiety] piled the bones and buried the dead of another. No Iksa performed these last offices to any of its own Iksa. Each had their bone-pickers—old men being usually chosen for that purpose and were held in high esteem on account of their age and office."—Israel Folsom-in Cushman, p. 367.
[41] Cushman, Hist. Inds., pp. 364–365.

III

When anyone died a scaffold was made in a yard near the house, put high enough to be safe from the dogs. On the top of this the body was laid on its side; and then a blanket or bear skin was thrown over it; and there it remained until it perished. Then the bone-pickers came and picked the flesh off and put the bones in a box, and then the boxes were put away in a bone-house—a house set apart to receive them, and placed at the edge of the town. At this time there was a large collection of people. The bone-pickers had some ceremonies, but I do not recollect them. Twice a year—fall and spring—the people assembled, and had a great gathering over the bones of the dead. The two families would meet. One day one family would cry; and on the next day the other would cry, and then the bones would be brought out in the boxes and buried. A little present was made to the bone-pickers.[42]

Elsewhere Cushman describes the ceremonial wailings for the dead at greater length, as follows:

They had specific cries for the dead, which to us of the present day would appear strange and even bordering upon the romantic, yet could not be witnessed without emotions of sadness. After the death and burial, the time was set by the near relations of the deceased for the cry, and notice was given to the neighboring villages for their attendance, to which all gave a ready response. When assembled, as many as could conveniently, would kneel in a close circle around the grave, both men and women; then drawing their blankets over their heads would commence a wailing cry in different tones of voice, which, though evident to a sensitive ear that the rules of harmony had been greatly overlooked, produced a solemnity of feeling that was indescribable, to which also the surroundings but added to the novelty of the scene: for here and there in detached little groups, were seated upon the ground many others, who in solemn demeanor chatted in a low tone of voice and smoked the indispensable pipe; while innumerable children of all ages and sexes, engaged in their juvenile sports and in thoughtless glee mingled their happy voices with the sad dirge of their seniors; which added to the barking of a hundred dogs intermingling with the tinkling chimes of the little bells that were suspended upon the necks of as many ponies, made a scene baffling all description. At different intervals, one, sometimes three or four together, would arise from the circle of mourners, quietly walk away and join some one of the many little groups seated around, while the vacancy in the mourning circle was immediately filled by others, who promptly came forward, knelt, drew their blankets over their heads, and took up the mournful strain; and thus for several days and nights, the wailing voices of the mourners, the gleeful shouts of thoughtless yet innocent and happy childhood; the howling and barking of innumerable dogs, and the tinkling of the pony-bells of every tone imaginable, in all of which dissonance was a prominent feature, was heard for miles away through the surrounding forests, echoing a wild, discordant note, more incomprehensible than the united voices of a thousand of the different denizens of the wilderness, of which no one, who has not been an eyewitness, can form even the most remote conception. If alone in the silent gloom of the wilderness, the boldest heart would quail, and the strongest nerve relax, unless the course and meaning were known and understood; for he could but believe that all the lost spirits of the lower world had left their dark and dismal abodes, ascended to earth, and, in one mystic concert, brayed the fearful discord. More than once have I wit-

---

[42] Cushman, Hist. Inds., p. 389.

nessed the scene and heard the wailing thereof. Oft, in the calm still hours of a starry night, have I heard the dubious tones of a distant Choctaw Indian cry, and as the disconnected sounds, borne upon the night breeze, floated by in undulating tones, now plainly audible, then dying away in the distance, I must confess there was a strange sadness awakened in my breast, unfelt and unknown before or since. It must be heard to be comprehended. When the time for the cry had expired, the mourning was exchanged for a previously prepared feast; after the enjoyments afforded in the participation of which, all joined in a jolly dance; thus happily restoring the equilibrium so long physically and mentally disturbed. Then each to his home returned, while the name of the departed was recorded among the archives of the past—to be mentioned no more.

The relatives of the deceased, who lived at too great a distance to conveniently [come] to cry over the grave of the dead set up a post a short distance from the house, around which they gathered and cried alternately during a period of twelve months.[43]

Elsewhere he adds:

No people on earth paid more respect to their dead, than the Choctaws did and still do; or preserved with more affectionate veneration the graves of their ancestors. They were to them as holy relics, the only pledges of their history; hence, accursed was he who should despoil the dead.[44]

We find the following regarding the observances in the subsequent period of mourning, on the authority of the Rev. Israel Folsom:

Previous to a spirit winging its flight to the happy hunting ground, or the land of briers and blasted foliage, it was supposed to hover around the place where its tabernacle lay for several days—four at least. They believed that the happy hunting ground was at a distance of many days journey. When a person died, provision was prepared for the journey under the supposition that the departed spirit still possessed hunger. Upon the death of a man, his dog was killed, that its spirit might accompany that of its master. Ponies, after they were introduced, were also killed, that the spirit might ride. They believed that all animals had spirits. During four days a fire was kept kindled a few steps in front of the wigwam of the deceased, whether the weather was cold or hot. They imagined, that if the spirit found no fire kindled in that manner for his benefit, it would become exceedingly distressed and angry, especially when the night was cold, dark and stormy. A bereaved mother, on the loss of her child, would kindle up a fire and sit by it all night. The wife on the loss of a husband performed the same vigil. In either case a rest in sleep was denied. For six months or more, in case of the death of a chief, the sorrowing and mourning relations indicated their grief in many ways. The men, in the early part of their time of mourning, remained silent and subdued, ate very sparingly, and abstained from all kinds of amusements, and from decking themselves out in their usual manner; the women did the same, with this difference, that they remained at home prostrated with grief—their hair streaming over their shoulders, unoiled and undressed, being seated on skins close to the place of burial or sacred fire. They not unfrequently broke the silence of sadness by heart piercing exclamations expressive of their grief. For a long time they would continue to visit the grave regularly morning and evening to mourn and weep.[45]

---

[43] Cushman, Hist. Inds., pp. 203–204.
[44] Ibid., p. 246.
[45] Ibid., pp. 363–364. Consult also the notes on burial in Lincecum's migration legend, p. 20.

Claiborne's notes on this subject indicate, either that the Choctaw whose mortuary rites he happened to observe were influenced by the Chickasaw or Creeks, or that they were rapidly degenerating. Halbert thinks he has confused the earlier and later rites.

The Choctaw, [he says] scaffold their dead until the flesh rots off them; the scaffold being eight or ten feet high and built on the edge of their yard. They then scrape the bones clean, place them in a box or put boards or bark around them and bury them in the ground—burying them sometimes in their yard, sometimes under their house.

"When I assisted," says General Dale, "in moving the first body of Choctaws that went west, there were some of them whose dead were still on scaffolds. They remained to bury the bones and chant the funeral rites the required time, and came afterwards." [46]

The notes which Claiborne took when acting as United States Commissioner, being from personal observation and direct conversations with the Indians, are of more value.

It was formerly the custom to deposit the corpse upon a scaffold; well protected from intrusion, under which a small bark fire was kept. It there lay until decomposition supervened, when a set of men called Iksa-nom-bulla [iksa anumpuli, "speakers for the moiety"], or the Bone-pickers of the Ik-sa, or clan, were sent for, whose duty it was to strip the bones of the remaining integuments. They were an exclusive order of itinerants, with something of the sacerdotal character, and these last ceremonies could only be performed by them. They were painted and tattooed in a peculiar style, and wore their finger-nails like talons, to enable them to perform these revolting rites. The bones were then placed in a deep basket and interred in their cabins or camps. The widow and children sit around the grave twice every day for three months, and weep, chanting a melancholy dirge. Some six months afterward his relatives and friends are invited to lament. They shroud themselves in a blanket and cry. These guests all bring a contribution of provisions, and after the cry, they have a feast, and sometimes a dance, or a ball-play, but the immediate family of the deceased take no part in the festivities. This cry is regarded as the most solemn of obligations, never to be omitted when possible to be performed. To illustrate it, I abridge from my journal now on file in the office of Indian Affairs at Washington:

"No. 72.—*Towah*,[47] full-blooded Choctaw, supposed to be seventy years of age, presented her claim. *An-nu-le-la* deposed that at date of treaty claimant occupied, with her family, three cabins; had a good corn-field; their land was *yock-a-na-chic-a-ma* [yakni achukma] (good land); some time thereafter a white man named Wilkinson, ordered her off, saying that he had bought the land. Claimant had just lost a daughter, and she first remonstrated, and then begged that she might stay until she *cried* over the grave. Wilkinson angrily refused. Witness knew a friendly white man named Johnson. He, the witness, went to him, and he wrote to Wilkinson to let them stay till the *cry* was over. He consented, and when they had *cried* they all moved about a mile off, and built a *cha-pa-chook-cha* [chabli chuka?] (bark house) where they have resided ever since, not wishing to go too far from the dead."

---

[46] Claiborne, Miss., I, p. 493. Other mortuary notes by Claiborne are commented on by Halbert. (See p. 188.)
[47] Towah signifies "a ball."

In very ancient times, a spacious temple, called Tusk-a-chook-a [Táshka chuka], or the House of the Warriors, stood on the verge of the *Kush-tush*, the largest and oldest settlement in the nation, long since deserted. This temple was in the custody of an order of priests, called *Oon-ka-la*. When a great warrior's bones had been prepared for burial by the *Ik-sa-nom-bulla*, they sent for the *Oon-ka-la*, and even from the most remote village they were taken to the temple. The *Oon-ka-la* preceded, chanting a solemn hymn in an unknown tongue, and the relatives and clansmen followed with loud lamentations. Arriving at the temple, the priests purified themselves with lustrations, and administered to the mourners a beverage called the white drink. No bystander was allowed to enter the temple. The priests, holding wands in their hands, passed slowly round it three times, muttering incantations, and then they took the bones within the sacred edifice, singing a hymn in a language unknown to the spectators. This was the practice from remote times, until the French and English traders entered their territory, when the Great Temple was struck by lightning and consumed. This created great alarm throughout the nation; the temple was never re-built, and the city of Kush-osh-ah gradually mouldered away. After this, they began to deposit their dead in the earth. The face of a warrior was painted red and black, the war colors, and his arms and ornaments placed in the grave, that he might be able to resist his enemies or kill his game in the distant shadowy hunting grounds to which he was supposed to have gone.[48]

Claiborne's reference to the ancient common burial temple by the "*Kushtush*" stands entirely by itself, and there is a suspicious resemblance between the story told of the destruction of this temple and the historical destruction of the Taensa temple on the Mississippi in 1700,[49] yet I am inclined to believe that there is a substratum of truth in what he says, though it is now too late to determine certainly how much. The town mentioned is evidently that given in my list as Kashtasha, "place of fleas," which, as we have seen, was once the capital town of the western band of Choctaw. Halbert locates it on the south bank of Custusha Creek, "about 3 miles, a little south of west of West Yazoo town."[50] Perhaps the archeologist may be able to throw light on this matter. The esoteric language mentioned in the narrative need have been nothing more than a peculiar or archaic variety of the common speech. Mention has already been made of the native disinclination to use the names of the deceased.[51]

In referring to the migrations of Indian tribes writers often speak of the regret of the latter at abandoning "the bones of their ancestors," and this expression has been used so frequently that it is generally taken to be rather a product of the romantic imagination of the white man than answering to any very profound native feeling. However, in the subjoined note Claiborne seems to indicate a certain service which these "ashes of the dead" performed in fixing property rights, family as well as tribal, which throws some light on the origin of the much used phrase.

[48] Claiborne, Miss., I, pp. 517–518.
[49] See Bull. 43, Bur. Amer. Ethn., pp. 266–268.
[50] See p. 62.
[51] See pp. 120–121.

Their devoted love of country may be traced to their traditions and customs. No people cherished more reverence for the dead. If a member of a family died from home, no matter how far, it was the ancient usage to carry his body back; or if that was impracticable, his ashes or his bones. To prove that a man had been buried in or adjacent to the house that he occupied, was considered conclusive proof of occupancy and domicile; a custom that prevailed so long and universally in the tribe, the Commissioners adopted it in their adjudications.[52]

In Hodgson's time (1820) the pole-pulling ceremony had already replaced scaffolding and bone-picking. His information is based in part on direct observation.

As soon as it appeared to be twelve o'clock by the sun, three of the Indian women covered themselves with blankets, and approached a little spot in the garden, enclosed by six upright poles, on the highest of which were suspended several chaplets of vine leaves and tendrils: here they either sat or kneeled (the blankets preventing our seeing which) for about twenty minutes, uttering a low monotonous wailing. This mournful ceremony they repeat, at sunrise, noon, and sun-set, for ninety days, or three moons, as the Egyptians mourned for Jacob threescore and ten days. I have since been informed by a very intelligent Indian, that the period of mourning is sometimes extended to four or five moons, if the individual be deeply regretted, or of eminent rank; and that it is occasionally determined by the time occupied in killing the deer and other animals necessary for the great feast which is often given at the pulling up of the poles.

At the celebrated ceremony of the " pole-pulling," the family connexions assemble from a great distance; and, when they are particular in observing the ancient customs, they spend two or three days and nights in solemn preparation and previous rites. They then all endeavour to take hold of some part of the poles, which they pluck up and throw behind them without looking, moving backward toward the East. They then feast together, and disperse to their several homes. . . .

Till within ten or fifteen years, the Choctaws generally killed the favourite horses or dogs of the deceased, and buried them, with his gun and hatchet, in his grave. They still sometimes bury the gun; but it is too frequently stolen: and they now satisfy themselves with believing that the spirits of the horses and dogs will rejoin that of their master at their death.[53] The settlement of White people among them, and occasional intermarriages, have undermined many of their customs. The Choctaws formerly scaffolded their dead, in a house appropriated for the purpose, in their different towns; and in these houses, the various families were kept distinct. Sometimes they bury them in their dwellings, like the ancient Egyptians.[54]

The Missionary Herald gives the following account of the pole-pulling ceremony just before the Choctaw emigration:

The ceremony of *pole-pulling*, mentioned in the preceding letter, has prevailed in all parts of the Choctaw nation, and is attended with great rioting and dissoluteness. Perhaps no one thing tends so much to debase the people,

---

[52] Claiborne, Miss., I, p. 517.
[53] At an earlier date articles were placed on the scaffold where the body was first laid. The disposition then made of the horse and dog is not clear.
[54] Hodgson, Travels, pp. 270–271.

or presents so powerful temptations to those who are somewhat disposed to give up to dissipation. It is connected with their mourning for the dead. When a Choctaw dies, his friends set up a number of poles around the grave, on which they hang hoops, wreaths, &c., for the spirit to ascend upon. Around these poles the survivors of the family gather each day, at sunrise, noon, and sunset, and there prostrating themselves, and uttering convulsive cries, mourn for the deceased. This is continued during 30 or 40 days: then all the neighboring people assemble, the poles are pulled up, and the mourning is ended with feasting, drinking, and great disorder.[55]

Christian opposition to this institution took form in the western district in July of the same year in a public enactment by which the custom was abolished "by a unanimous vote."[56] But it did not come to an end even after the removal of the Choctaw west of the Mississippi, as is shown by Gregg, who says:

In burials, the civilized Choctaws follow the customs of the whites, but the ruder classes still preserve their aborignial usages. According to these, a painted pole with a flag is stuck up at the grave, which usually remains three months. During this period they have regular mourning exercises every morning and evening; and are always prompt to avail themselves, at any hour of the day, of the assistance of any friend who may visit them to help them to weep. At the end of the prescribed term, the friends of the bereft family attend a feast at their house, and, after dancing all night, the next morning visit the grave and pull down the pole; which is called "the pole-pulling." After this all mourning ceases, and the family is permitted to join in the usual amusements and festivities of the tribe, which was not allowable before.[57]

Henry C. Benson, a Methodist missionary, who was in the Choctaw country between 1843 and 1845, gives the following "brief account" of the burial rites at that period.

When the husband dies the friends assemble, prepare the grave, and place the corpse in it, but do not fill it up. The gun, bow and arrows, hatchet and knife are deposited in the grave. Poles are planted at the head and the foot, upon which flags are placed; the grave is then inclosed by pickets driven in the ground. The funeral ceremonies now begin, the widow being the chief mourner. At night and morning she will go to the grave, and pour forth the most piteous cries and wailings. It is not important that any other member of the family should take any very active part in the "cry," though they do participate to some extent.

The widow wholly neglects her toilet, while she daily goes to the grave to weep during one entire *moon* from the date when the death occurred. On the evening of the last day of the moon the friends all assemble at the cabin of the disconsolate widow, bring provisions for a sumptuous feast, which consists of corn and jerked-beef boiled together in a kettle. While the supper is preparing the bereaved wife goes to the grave, and pours out, with unusual vehemence, her bitter wailings and lamentations. When the food is thoroughly cooked the kettle is taken from the fire and placed in the center of the cabin, and the friends gather around it, passing the buffalo horn-spoon from hand to hand

---

[55] Miss. Herald, Dec., 1828 (vol. xxiv, No. 12), p. 381.
[56] Ibid., p. 153.
[57] Gregg, Commerce of the Prairies, in Early Western Travels, ed. R. G. Thwaites, vol. 20, pp. 313–315.

and from mouth to mouth till all have been bountifully supplied. While supper is being served two of the oldest men of the company quietly withdraw, and go to the grave and fill it up, taking down the flags. All then join in a dance, which not unfrequently is continued till morning; the widow does not fail to unite in the dance, and to contribute her part to the festivities of the occasion. This is the "*last cry*," the days of mourning are ended, and the widow is now ready to form another matrimonial alliance. The ceremonies are precisely the same when a man has lost his wife, and they are only slightly varied when any other member of the family has died. But at the time of our residence with them those heathenish ceremonies were not generally observed, yet they were occasionally practiced by the most ignorant and degraded of the tribe.[58]

Among the Bayou Lacomb Choctaw the ancient burial customs seem almost to have disappeared even as memories, as appears from the information furnished by Mr. Bushnell.

There appears to have been very little lamenting or mourning on the occasion of a death or a burial. The body was borne to the grave and the interment took place without a ceremony of any sort. In the event of the death of a man of great importance, however, the body was allowed to remain in state for a day before burial. During that time it was decorated with various ornaments and garments, but these were removed before interment. Such objects are said to have been preserved and handed down from one generation to the next, and used whenever required.

Usually a hunter's gun was placed in the grave with the body.

The period of mourning varied with the age of the deceased. For a child or young person it was about three months, but for an older person, as one's mother or father, from six months to one year.

The women cut their hair and "cried" at certain times near the grave.

When a person desired to cease mourning, he stuck into the ground so as to form a triangle three pieces of wood, each several feet in length, about 1 foot apart. The tops of these sticks were drawn together and tied with a piece of bright-colored cloth or ribbon. This object was placed near the door or entrance of the lodge and indicated to all that the occupant desired to cease mourning.

During the next three days the mourners cried or wailed three times each day—at sunrise, at noon, and at sunset. While wailing they wrapped blankets around their heads and sat or knelt upon the ground. During these three days the friends of the mourners gathered and began dancing and feasting. At the expiration of the time they ceased weeping and joined in the festivities, which continued another day.[59]

The few notes which I have myself collected agree with the above, but amplify it in certain particulars. Thus Jackson Lewis, one of my oldest and best Creek informants, who had been much with the Choctaw, told me that in his early years the people of that tribe used to lay the bodies of the deceased out on the ground in the yard of the dwelling and erect a little house over them, and as the body decomposed they would sharpen canes and punch them into the body

---

[58] Henry C. Benson, Life Among the Choctaw Indians and Sketches of the Southwest. Cincinnati, 1860, pp. 294–295.

[59] Bushnell, Bull. 48, Bur. Amer. Ethn., p. 27.

through cracks in the house so as to start the pus running out and cause more rapid decomposition.

Mrs. McCurtain, widow of one of the governors of the Choctaw Nation, had heard of the ancient mortuary customs but had never seen them. She told me that in her time the last funeral ceremonies were about a month after death, a date having been agreed upon in advance. Meanwhile all of the friends of the dead went back and forth to his grave along with the afflicted family, and mourned there without speaking to one another, after which they would visit his former home. In later times on the day of the final ceremonies they always had a man to hold a service at the house, after which he gave out notice that the last ceremony would be at the grave, and when all had assembled there they moaned and sang a hymn, and then prayer was offered. After that they repaired to the house and the feast took place. The food for this, consisting of beef, pork, and various dishes made of corn, was contributed by the different branches of the dead man's family, and a certain person was appointed to collect this. Another person superintended the cooking. All sat down and the food was distributed to them. The feast being concluded, all returned home.

Mr. A. L. Tinsley, of Philadelphia, Miss., who was for many years a near neighbor of the Bok Chito Band of Choctaw, the band least modified by white influence, furnished me the following notes from his own direct observations:

The body of the deceased was extended at full length in the ground, and articles that had belonged to him such as his gun, ballsticks, beaded belts, articles of clothing, or in the case of a woman, pots and kettles, were laid by it. Then part of the earth was thrown in and two strong Indians jumped down on it and trod it down firmly all about. Afterward they procured three poles which they planted at the head, a longer one in the middle, and a shorter one on each side of it. Garlands of leaves, vines, etc., were hung over these. The next morning and for a number of mornings after, just as the sun was rising above the horizon, the relatives of the dead man went to his grave and wailed there, genuine tears running down their faces. After it was over a great number of people were called together and a great cry indulged in which was followed by a feast, and this again by a dance lasting nearly all night. Next day they had a game of ball.

One informant ventured the assertion that poles were planted only at the graves of persons killed in battle. This may have been true anciently, but certainly not in later times, and Halbert seems to have heard nothing about it.

Simpson Tubby contributed the following notes regarding the later ceremony.

When anyone died the families of both parents of the deceased met and mourned until the remains had been put into the ground. They consulted together and decided upon the date of the " cry " and the time when the mourning poles should be set up. Then the father, if living, would inform the captain of his band of the time determined upon. Forthwith the captain stood up and announced the determination to the assembled families in a short speech, saying that at such-and-such a time they would meet, set up the mourning poles, eat together, and mourn. He would inform various individuals as to the nature of their duties on that occasion, detailing certain women to cook beef or bake bread, certain men to buy the beef, certain others to lift the heavy pots and skillets, who should set the table, pour the coffee and so on. When this feast was over they marched to the grave and all wept there as if they had been hurt by some sudden stroke and it was very sad for those who had to listen. Many cried who were not related to the deceased in any way. After that the mourners laid their mourning costume aside and along with it the memory of the deceased. The name was never mentioned in the family, except perhaps by a child who was always quickly silenced. He could be spoken of to, or by, an outsider, but it was almost like another death to breathe it to anyone of the family for they thought, in that case, such a person would also die very shortly.

As already stated, Halbert's narrative, being the most elaborate and the most critical of all attempts hitherto made to treat of these ceremonies, is reserved until the last. After expressing his conviction that the mortuary rites of the Choctaw were not always uniform, a conclusion much reenforced by what we know of other North American peoples, he goes on to speak of the older custom in these words:

The modern Choctaws of Mississippi who are best informed on the ancient usages of their people, state that in the olden time, whenever a Choctaw died, his body, covered with a blanket or bear skin, was placed upon a scaffold about six feet high, which was erected near the house. Benches were then made and placed around the scaffold. Every day the family were wont to seat themselves upon these benches, and with covered heads, for half an hour or more, to bewail the dead. This same sad duty was also performed by any relative or visitor that happened to be present. After some months, when a sufficient number of corpses in the villages of the community have become so thoroughly putrified as to allow a general burial, word to this effect is sent to the " na foni aiowa," " the bone-pickers." This word, which, according to connection, may be singular or plural, properly translated is " bone-gatherer," having reference to this official's *gathering* the bones for burial. Bone-picker, which is here used in deference to general usage, is not the exact translation, and is somewhat misleading. The bone-pickers in all the adjoining towns or communities, on receiving the news that their services are needed, now get together, hold a consultation, and agree upon a day upon which all the corpses, from all quarters, are to arrive at the bone-house. Some of the dead may be only a few hours' walk from the bone-house, others may be one or two days' journey. The bone-pickers now give small bundles of split cane, " oski kauwa," to messengers to be carried and given to all the families, far and near. These pieces of cane are about four inches long and the size of a broom-straw, arranged in a bundle and this tied around the middle with a string. Time is measured by these sticks, the receiver every morning throwing away a stick. The time has been so well set that he throws away the last stick on the morning of the burial day. The old-time Choctaws reckoned time by "sleeps," and by throwing away a stick after each night's sleep, no mistake could be made.

When the bone-picker arrives at the house of the deceased, the family, kindred and visitors seat themselves on the mourning benches and go through with their usual weeping and wailing. They then remove the benches and the bone-picker attends to his office. He first makes the coffin or coffins, ornamenting them to the best of his taste or ability. He then takes down the corpses, with his long finger nails separates the flesh from the bones, scrapes and washes the bones perfectly clean, and puts them in the coffin. Tradition is silent as to the disposition of the decayed flesh and other refuse. According to Bernard Romans' *Florida*, all this was burned. On the contrary, an old Indian countryman, many years ago, informed the writer that it was buried. This last statement seems to be corroborated by the *Journal* of the Rev. Lorenzo Dow, page 220, where under the date of December 24, 1804, he thus writes: "We rode about forty miles through Six Towns of the Choctaws, and whilst we were passing it, I observed where they scaffolded the dead, and also the spot where the flesh was buried when the bone-picker had done his office." The probabilities are that some communities may have buried the flesh, while others burned it. Or, as Dow was a later observer, it may be that in his day the fashion was changed, the flesh being buried instead of being burned. In this connection it may not be amiss to call attention to Claiborne's *Mississippi*, page 489, where there is a confusion of the ancient and the modern ceremonies. He states that "the shrivelled integuments stripped off by the bone-pickers were buried in a separate place over which a pole was planted." The shrivelled integuments may have been buried, according to the evidence just cited, but no pole was ever planted over them, nor was there any "pole-pulling" ceremony, for, as will be seen farther on, the pole-planting business and the pole-pulling ceremony were introduced afterwards as new ceremonies, when the old bone-picking custom was abolished by the Choctaws.

According to the number of corpses the bone-pickers may be one or more days at work on their respective tasks. When the work is finished, from each place a procession is formed, and the coffins are borne to the bone-house, whether situated far or near. As has been stated, it is well known on what day all are to meet at the bone-house, and every procession so manages its business as to arrive there on the appointed day. On their arrival the coffins are placed upon the ground, the mourners crouch down around them, shroud their heads, then weep and wail a long time. When enough tears have been shed, the coffins are placed in the bone-house, and all then take their departure to their respective homes.

After the bone-house has become full in consequence of successive deposits, the tradition says that men are appointed to cover the house all over with earth, which practically makes a burial mound.

As Halbert points out, the tradition which he recorded differs from other narratives at this point. It also differs in stating that the bones of the dead were synchronously brought to the burial scaffold. He suggests that these discrepancies may be accounted for by variations in usage, but to the present writer it looks as though the tradition had substituted a synchronous collection of bones on the scaffold for the synchronous burial of them in a mound. Occasionally deaths might have taken place near enough together for the bone pickers to treat a number at the same time, but from other narratives it seems that the time allowed to lapse in each case was relatively fixed, and this would have prevented synchronous bestowal of the bones in the cantonal ossuary. Let us hope that the family of a deceased Choctaw were not subjected to the close neighborhood of the remains of their beloved relative longer than was absolutely necessary to enable the " buzzard man " to perform his functions satisfactorily. Halbert continues his discussion by an inquiry into the time when the use of ossuaries became obsolete. He says:

As a result [of an examination of] all the obtainable sources of information, it may be safely stated that the custom fell into disuse in the early days of the nineteenth century. The custom may have lingered longer in some localities than in others. From the passage quoted above from the Rev. Lorenzo Dow's *Journal*, it seems certain that this custom still prevailed in 1804 among the Six-Towns Choctaws. The anonymous author of a little work, published in 1830, entitled Conversations on the *Choctaw Missions*, practically states, on page 211, that the bone-picking custom became obsolete about 1800. Writers describing Choctaw customs subsequent to 1812, make no mention of the bone-picking custom, thus showing that by this time it had passed away. Colonel Claiborne, in his *Life and Times of Sam Dale*, pp. 175–6, has somehow drifted into a strange mistake in stating that the custom still existed in 1832. The Rev. Israel Folsom, in his manuscript, does not give the date of the abolition of the bone-picking custom ; but makes the following statment in regard to the new custom : " When the custom of placing the dead upon platforms was abandoned, which met with strong opposition, they buried their dead in a sitting posture in the grave; around the grave they set up half a dozen red poles, about eight feet high, and one about fifteen feet high, at the top of which a white flag was fastened. The occupation of the bone-pickers having been abolished, it then became their business to set up red poles around the graves, and afterwards to remove them at the time of mourning, hence they were called ' pole-pullers.' They were respected by the people, and far less labor being imposed upon them they were pleased with the change in the burial of the dead." The above statement from Mr. Folsom seems to corroborate the Choctaw tradition that the bone-pickers of the olden time were not looked upon with much respect. Their office was doubtless considered necessary, but not very elevating.

We now pass from the Choctaws of the early years of the nineteenth century down to the remnant of the same people still living in Mississippi in the last half and in the closing years of the same century. Notwithstanding the seemingly impassive nature of our Mississippi Choctaws, upon the death of a member of the household, the family and relatives often give vent to such a passionate outburst of grief that it is almost appaling to a white person unfamiliar with Indian life. The frequent and long-drawn out exclamations of grief uttered by the women, " aiyenaheh " [or aiehnahe] and " ikkikkeh " [or ikikki], fall upon the ear with a wild and mournful sound. During these agonizing scenes the sympathizing friends present are sometimes wont to rub the heads of the mourners with horsemint so as to relieve the headache that is so often caused by excessive grief. Meanwhile preparations are made for the burial. This duty is supervised by the two oldest men in the community, officially called " hattak in tikba," which term may be translated " headman."

The two iksa are represented in these headmen, one of them belonging to the Kashapa Okla, the other to the Okla in holahta.[60] The two headmen now appoint six men as "pole-planters," each headman appointing three from his own iksa. The pole-planters go to work, make the poles from small pine saplings, stripping off the bark and painting or rather daubing the poles with red clay. Two of the poles are about ten or twelve feet high, the other four about eight. A series of grapevine hoops, which are about two feet in diameter, are fastened to the two tall poles. The hoops are made by coiling the vines around two or more times, so that the body of each hoop is made exactly the same size, and then the coil kept securely in its place by being tied with strings. The hoops are tied, about six inches apart, hard and fast to the pole, at the upper and lower edges of their circumference. The number of the hoops is a matter of no consequence, whether many or few.

Every thing being ready for the burial, all repair to the grave, which is generally made very near the house, sometimes even in the yard. The body, enclosed in a coffin, is lowered into the grave. A few years ago, such articles as the deceased most valued in life were deposited with him in the grave or coffin. A gun was a favorite article deposited in the grave of a man, Beads, gorgets and other female paraphernalia in the grave of a woman. Sometimes, especially in the case of children, a pair of shoes was placed in the coffin. These usages are now entirely abandoned. When the last clods of earth have been cast upon the grave and boards placed over it, the six pole-planters come forward and plant their poles, three being set up by the pole-planters of one iksa on one side of the grave, and three set up by the pole-planters of the opposite iksa on the other side. The two tall poles adorned with hoops are in the center of each side, the hoops being on the sides of the poles farthest from the grave. The lowest hoop on each pole is about two feet from the ground. To the tops of the tall poles small streamers are fastened, these streamers being generally small strips of white cloth, though occasionally red handkerchiefs are used. The object of these streamers is to show to the passer-by that it is a grave, and he is expected to halt and show his respect for the dead by weeping a while over it. White strings are tied around the tops of the other poles. If the deceased is male, sometimes a pair of ball sticks is suspended from one of the poles. If, owing to some untoward circumstances, the pole-planters cannot plant their poles at the time of burial, it is expected that they do this work as soon afterwards as possible. Sometimes a child is buried under the house. In such a case, and also in the case of any one dying far from home, a place near the house is selected for the planting of the poles, thus making a kind of cenotaph, where the funeral obsequies are performed. After the pole-planting work is finished, every one on the ground, male and female, assemble around the grave, kneel down, cover their heads, then weep and wail a long time. After indulging in a certain amount of grief, all arise and gradually disperse to their homes.

As a digression, some observations may here be made in regard to the hoops on the two tall poles. The fastening of hoops to the poles fell into disuse about thirty years ago. The Choctaws expressly say that these hoops had no significance whatever. They were simply ornaments to the grave, and were never taken off from the poles. They say that the white man's statement, as recorded in Claiborne's Mississippi, page 489, that these hoops were designed as a ladder for the spirit to ascend at the last cry is simply a fiction created by the white man's fancy, and that no such idea ever existed among the Choctaws. To

[60] See pp. 76–79.

repeat, the hoops were an ornament, that and nothing else. The statement in Colonel Claiborne's History, relative to this " spirit-ladder " business, must then be taken with many grains of salt; in fact, must not be taken at all. The Choctaws are certainly better judges of this matter than any white man can possibly be.[61] In addition to this, as has already been stated, there was no special number of hoops. The "thirteen lunar months" symbolism, as mentioned in Colonel Claiborne's book, is something that was unknown to the Choctaws, and had its origin only in the white man's imagination. A reference to another matter in this same connection. There never was any "dancing-the-spirit home" ceremonies, as likewise recorded on the same page of Colonel Claiborne's History. This is another specimen of the white man's fancy. Farther on in this paper will be given an account of the dances that are danced at the last cry.

Returning from this digression, the cry at the pole pulling is merely the beginning of the many things that are to be done before the final closing of the funeral ceremonies. The family and the near relatives now go into deep mourning, which the men manifest by letting the hair remain unshorn and the women by going barefoot, and neither sex wearing any kind of ornaments, such as plumes, silver bands, sashes, gorgets, beads, bracelets, finger rings, earrings; in short, any ornament peculiar to either man or woman. Under all circumstances the mourners preserve a grave and dignified demeanor. They converse in low tones, and the men never even so far forget themselves as to shout at a dog. They indulge in no jests, laughter, revelry, or merrymaking of any kind. If approached and asked to participate in a dance, for instance, the invariable response is, " Hihla la hekeyu Tabishi sia hokat "—" I can not dance. I am a mourner." Twice a day—early in the morning and late in the afternoon—they go to the grave, cover their heads, kneel down, and weep over it. If a friend comes to see them they even go oftener, the visitor accompanying them and doing his share of weeping. Etiquette also requires that the visitor himself must always approach the grave and weep a while over it before he enters the house. While the immediate family go, as it were, into conventional mourning by the observances mentioned above, as regards letting the hair grow, going barefoot, and wearing no ornaments, this matter is entirely optional to those of more distant relationship. A first cousin, for instance, can use his own pleasure whether or not, by following these observances, he shall be included in the mourning family.

Meanwhile the two headmen confer with each other and appoint the most expert hunters out of the two iksa to go out into the woods, kill as many deer as they can, and barbecue their flesh for "the last cry," or, as it is called by the Choctaws, "yaiya chito"—"the big cry." After a while the mourning family appoint a day for "the little cry"—"yaiya iskitini"—which, of course, is held at the grave. Quite a company generally go to the little cry. The headmen are generally present. There are no ceremonies at the little cry. While there the family agree upon the time for the big cry. This is a kind of communal cry, in which the entire town or community participate. The time for the cry is determined by many circumstances, as the state of the weather, the labor of the crops, etc. Sometimes several months elapse between the death and the last cry. As soon as the time is settled upon, the two headmen, just as in the olden time, send around the small bundles of split cane to all the families, far and near, thereby notifying them of the appointed day.

---

[61] Yes, as to current beliefs, but it is quite possible for beliefs to change. And indeed it is more than possible. It is common. There may or may not have been grounds for Claiborne's statement. Note that Cushman says the same thing (see p. 177).

To record this matter accurately, the Choctaws gradually ceased to use these sticks some 30 years ago, when they began to become familiar with the white man's division of time into days and weeks.[62] Since that time it is sufficient to notify the parties by merely sending word as to the day and week in which the cry is to take place.

The great day at last arrives. During the afternoon the Choctaws from far and near begin to make their appearance upon the camping ground, which is generally a hundred yards, more or less, from the grave. As they arrive upon the ground, each one, without greeting anybody, and looking neither to the right nor to the left, walks straight to the grave, there covers his head with a shawl or blanket, kneels down, and indulges in the prescribed cry. Having discharged this duty to the dead, he returns to the camping ground, fixes himself and family comfortably in camp, and then holds himself in readiness for the coming events. The two headmen make their camp fires opposite each other, about 50 feet apart. As the afternoon begins to draw to a close the hunters bring forward their barbecued venison and deposit it on the ground between the fires of the headmen. Some families have brought with them for the common feast large kettles full of hominy. These, too, are brought forward and placed on the ground along with the venison. As night begins to close upon the scene the camp fires are lighted up afresh and the two headmen hold a consultation. They make an estimate of the numbers of their respective iksa present and proportion the food accordingly. The rigid law of Choctaw etiquette at an Indian cry requires that the two iksa must eat separate and distinct from each other. This is a sacred and inviolable law. The venison and hominy are now carried to the various iksa groups, as they are scattered around over the ground. No group is neglected. In the distribution of the food it is customary to give to all the contributors of hominy a small quantity of venison for their private use, which they can carry home with them. This is intended as a remuneration for their contribution of hominy for the public use. When all the venison and hominy have been distributed each headman delivers an oration to his iksa, these orations being the prelude to the coming big feast. The orators are sometimes excessively tedious and prolix, and the hungry auditors become very impatient under the long-winded speeches. The speeches finally come to a close, and without any more ado the solid work of eating begins. Every Choctaw—male and female, big and little, old and young, mourners and all—now feast to their hearts' content. It is best here to state that the iksa separation in public feasting passed away many years ago, the extinction of the deer and other causes having rendered it impracticable. The two iksa at a cry nowadays eat promiscuously at one long table, for the table has superseded the old method of eating in groups on the ground. The speeches of the orators prior to the feast, however, still continue to be the fashion.

After having regaled themselves to satiety, the crowd scatter over the ground. The men, women and children gather around the various camp fires, and every one passes the time in the best manner to suit himself. It is a very social occasion, and there is very little sleep in the camp that night. The men talk, smoke, chew tobacco, or it may be, some engage in the game of "naki luma," "hidden bullet." [63] The women gossip; whilst the children and the numerous dogs contribute their share to the noise and hilarity of the occasion. After about an hour of general sociability, the young men and the young women assemble at the "ahihla," "the dancing ground," a plot of ground about a hundred yards off, which has been previously prepared for this purpose. Here six different kinds of dances are danced in succession, which, being very

<hr>

[62] Halbert's paper was published in 1900.   [63] See pp. 158–159.

long, take up the greater part of the night. These dances are very complicated and almost incomprehensible to a white person. The first dance is "nakni hihla," "the men's dance," which the men alone dance. This dance over, the young women are now masters of the situation. Each woman selects her own man as her partner for the five coming dances. The man selected cannot back out, but must dance with his partner as long as she chooses to dance, no matter how weary he may become. If the woman herself should finally become weary of dancing, she simply says to her partner, "kil issa," "let us quit," whereupon both withdraw and neither dances any more that night. The second dance is "shatanih hihla," "the tick dance." The third, "nita hihla," "the bear dance." The fourth, "yahyachi hihla," "the trotter's dance." The fifth, "ittisanali hihla," "the dance of those that oppose each other." The sixth, "ittihalanli hihla," "the dance of those that hold each other," which dance, after many evolutions, comes to an end by both sexes standing in two lines facing each other, both hands of the men holding the two first fingers of the women's two hands. Sometimes one of these dances is repeated. It is indispensable that they all be finished before daybreak, for at daybreak there must be a short period—about fifteen or twenty minutes—of quietness in the camp. There is a song sung with every dance, occasionally one of these songs being composed on the spot. On a bright moonlight night these dances with their various evolutions have a wonderful fascination to the on-looking white man. The plumes, the sashes and silver bands of the men, the gaudy dresses, the beads, the gorgets and other silver ornaments of the women, the graceful movements of the dancers, the strange, wild Choctaw songs, all unite to make some of the unique attractions of savage life.

About two hours before day, whilst the dancing of the young people is still under full swing, a short cry is made by the mourners. Some one of them, be it man or woman, sitting by a camp fire, suddenly lifts up his voice in a wailing sound. The other mourners approach him, group themselves around him, cover their heads with their blankets, and for about ten minutes the mourners give vent to cries of wailing and lamentation.

It is now broad daylight. Suddenly the loud voices of the two headmen are heard telling their people that the time is now at hand for the last cry over the dead. The headmen have already appointed the six pole-pullers, three from each iksa. The pole-pullers may be the same men as the pole-planters, or they may be entirely new appointees. All, men, women and children, now repair to the grave. The pole-pullers stand, each one near his pole, three from one iksa on one side of the grave, the other three on the other side. All, except the headmen and the pole-pullers, with covered heads, now kneel upon the ground and for a long time the sound of lamentation and weeping and great mourning goes up to high heaven. The crowd may be very great, so that for some distance around the grave the ground is covered with the kneeling forms of the mourning Indians. Many are the exclamations and expressions of grief, especially from the women. It is an affecting scene; for, even though much of the lamentation on the part of some may be a matter of form, still, with the immediate family, the near kindred and the intimate friends of the dead it is a manifestation of genuine and heartfelt sorrow. After a while, the headman of the iksa opposite to that of the deceased begins his funeral oration, in which he expatiates upon the virtues of their departed friend. The oration is usually short. When the speaker comes to a close, he and his brother headman lift up their voices and utter what is called "tashka paiya," "the warrior's call," consisting of the four following exclamations: "Yo, hyu, hyu, hyu," to which the pole-pullers respond with "ho-ee, ho-ee, ho-ee, ho-ee," as noticed, "ho-ee" being said four times. The headmen again utter their exclamations just as at first, and again the pole-pullers respond with their exclamations in both cases, the same number as at first.

All this is repeated by both parties the third time, and then the fourth and last time. The pole-pullers now perform their office. They take up the poles, bear them erect for some distance, then lower them to a horizontal position and deposit them in a thicket or behind a log. As the pole-pullers start off from the grave nearly all the prostrate crowd arise to their feet, their tears cease to flow, and their wailing comes to an end. The mourning family, however, from a sense of propriety, still remain for some minutes longer weeping over the grave. Finally, they, too, arise and the crowd gradually scatter over the ground. After a while, an old woman of the iksa opposite to that of the dead comes forward with a pair of scissors in her hand, and cuts off a single lock of hair from the heads of the women of the mourning family. An old man, likewise of the opposite iksa, in the same manner, approaches the males of the mourning family and trims off their long hair. These are the last ceremonies in the funeral obsequies of the Choctaws. The time of mourning has now passed. All now gradually leave the ground. The mourners on their return home can resume their usual dress and ornaments and take up again their free and easy Indian life. The custom of clipping a single lock of hair from the heads of the mourning women and girls still prevails to some extent, but trimming the hair of the men and boys became obsolete about twenty years ago (i. e., about 1880). Strictly speaking, about the same time, the custom of the men's letting their hair remain unshorn and the women going barefoot during the period of mourning became obsolete. Also, to a great extent, the disuse of ornaments during the mourning season. As stated, the cry over, all return to their homes. There was no breakfast on the ground at the cries of many years ago, but the modern innovation requires that all must leave the funeral ground with a full stomach.

Such is the manner, from beginning to end, in which the Choctaws of Mississippi are wont to perform the funeral obsequies over their dead. But, to be very accurate in these matters, it is best to say that, excepting the barbecued venison feature, the above is a correct description of the Choctaw funeral ceremonies in nearly all the Choctaw communities down to about 1883. Since that year the introduction of Christianity and education have wrought a great revolution in the ideas and usages of the Choctaws. One custom after another has gradually passed out of use. The last pole-pulling that occurred in the Mokalusha clan was in February, 1885. The custom lingered some years longer among the Bogue Chito Indians, but perhaps now has passed out of use everywhere. In some localities poles with streamers attached are still planted around the grave, but there is no pole-pulling. The cry with some of the old ceremonies still prevails to some extent, especially in the non-Christianized communities, notably among the Bogue Chito Indians, who, of all our Mississippi Indians, most closely resemble the old-time Choctaws. In the Christianized communities there are graveyards near their churches, where they bury their dead, or try to bury them, after the manner of white people. Many Choctaws of the Christianized element are very averse to any usage that, to their view, savors of their old time heathenism. The revolution still goes onward.[64]

RELIGION AND MEDICINE

SUPERNATURAL BEINGS

Some early writers, and in later times Cushman and Bushnell, report that the Choctaw believed in a great good spirit and a great

<hr>

[64] Halbert in Pubs. Miss. Hist. Soc., III, pp. 353–366, 1900.

evil spirit, but it is probably significant that Rev. Alfred Wright, who has left us the best account of primitive Choctaw religion, says nothing whatever regarding the latter. True, a native missionary, Israel Folsom, declares that "they also believed in the existence of a devil, whom they designated Na-lusa-chi-to, a great black being, or soul eater, who found full occupation in terrifying and doing all manner of harm to people." [65] He, however, was probably only one of a number of hobgoblins in no way to be compared with the great marplot of orthodox Christianity. Wright says that four terms were applied to God, Nanapesa, Ishtahullo-chito or Nanishta-hullo-chito, Hushtahli, and Uba Pike [Aba Pⁿki]. As he suggests, the last of these, which means "Our Father," was probably adopted from the whites. The word Nanapesa, "director," or "judge," at first seems to indicate a like origin, but, as we shall see presently, the aboriginal solar deity was supposed to have power of life and death, and I am therefore inclined to consider it as purely native. "Ishtahullo or Nanishtahullo is applied," says Wright, "to whatever excites surprise, and also to anything which they conceive to possess some occult or superior power. Hence it is a name they give to witches." By the Chickasaw, at least, it was also bestowed upon priests or any men who could perform wonders, whether good or bad. The term Shilup chitoh osh is used by Cushman but it is merely a translation into Choctaw of the words "The Great Spirit," in agreement with a supposed widely spread Indian conception. Byington gives another term, Chitokaka, "The Great One," which again is probably modern. The only name which we may set down with confidence as aboriginal Choctaw is Hushtahli (Hàsh-tahli), compounded of hàshi, "sun," and tahli, "to complete an action," but Wright could not suggest an explanation for the compound. It may have had the significance of "culminated or noon-day sun" like the word Kutnahīn, applied by the Chitimacha to their own sun god, though tabokoa is the ordinary word for "noon." Byington says that Hàshtahli was applied to "the governor of the world, whose eye is the sun," from which we may perhaps infer that the being so designated was celestial rather than solar. With this reservation, the following remarks by Wright may be accepted as giving us the best extant view of the character of this belief:

That the Choctaws anciently regarded the sun as a deity, is probable for several reasons. 1. To the sun was ascribed the power of life and death. He was represented as looking down upon the earth, and as long as he kept his flaming eye fixed on any one, that person was safe, but as soon as he turned away his eye, the individual died. To the sun, also, they attributed their success in war. An aged native has given me the form of a speech used by the war-leaders after returning from a successful expedition. In this they

---

[65] Cushman, Hist. Inds., p. 363.

acknowledged, that it was through the influence of *Hushtahli,* or the sun, that they were enabled to find the bright path, which led them to victory, and returned them in safety to their homes. 2. In ancient times, *fire,* as the most striking representation of the sun, was considered as possessing intelligence, and as acting in concert with the sun. The fire and sun were supposed to have constant intercourse with each other, and the fire acted the part of an informant to the sun. And it was an ancient saying of theirs, that if one did anything wrong in the presence of the fire, the fire would tell the sun of it before the offender could go *ashatapa,* the length of his extended arms. This intercourse between the fire and sun is also recognized in one of their war songs, which an aged man has repeated to me from memory. This man stated, that anciently, when about to set out on a warlike expedition, after having performed the prescribed ceremonies, the king being seated on the ground and the warriors about him, the principal waiter on the king arose and sang the war song. In this song there is nothing of a religious nature, except in one stanza, in which the warriors are exhorted to rely for success on *the Sun, and the Fire his mate—Hushtali, micha Luak Hushtali itichapa.* Whether by *Hushtali* they intended the same being whom they sometimes called Nanapesa, or *Ishtahullo chito,* is not easy to decide. It seems probable they did, from the consideration that they have no idea of a plurality of gods: for they invariably assert, that they have no traditional knowledge except of one superior being.

It has been already stated, that the Choctaws have no idea of a being purely spiritual. They conceive that the *Ishtahullo chito* possesses a human shape, and, in speaking of him, often call him the *man above.* His dwelling place is regarded as being somewhere on high. The representation of the Choctaw is, that when the Creator had made the earth, and its inhabitants (the red people), and had given them their civil regulations, he returned to his place above, and they saw and heard nothing more of him.

They do not appear to have acknowledged, that a superintending Providence directed their concerns, and controlled all events. The sun was, indeed, supposed to have the keys of life and death, and on him the warrior was taught to rely for success in war. But in regard to other events in which their happiness was concerned, his agency was excluded. In prosperity they exercised no gratitude to him for benefits received, nor in distress, did they apply to him for relief. In time of drought, they applied to their rain-makers who, being well paid, would undertake to make rain. When the earth was surcharged with water, they would apply to their fair-weather makers for sunshine; and in sickness, to their doctors for cure; without acknowledging or even appearing to feel their dependence on the great Ruler of all things.[66]

In a footnote he says: " Fire they term *shahli miko* and *hushi itichapa.* It is difficult to define the name *shahli miko. Shahli* denotes *addicted to, frequent, much of a thing,* and *frequency of action,* and is used in the comparison of adjectives. The other name, *hushi itichapa,* means the sun's mate, or matched together. The oldest son is called *itichapa,* the father's mate." [67]

Thus it seems clear that the aborignal Choctaw entertained a belief in a supreme deity who, if not identical with the sun, was closely associated with and acted through that luminary and that

---

[66] The Missionary Herald, June, 1828, vol. xxiv, No. 6, pp. 179–180.   [67] Ibid., p. 180.

he was represented on earth by fire. The following from Israel Folsom may be added:

They believed in the existence of a Great Spirit, and that he possessed super-natural power, and was omniscient, but they did not deem that He expected or required any form of worship of them. . . . All they felt was a dread of His attributes and character, made manifest to them by the phenomena of the heavens.[68]

The name of God among the Louisiana Choctaw, Aba, " above," is evidently identical with, or abbreviated from, a purely aboriginal designation, almost identical with one term used by the Chickasaw, Creeks, Chitimacha, and Atakapa.

The supreme being did not exist to the exclusion of all other spirits, whether or not his position with relation to them was as distinct as Wright claims. Cushman speaks of spirits good and evil, and has the following to say about them, though how much is unadulteratedly Indian can only be guessed:

The philosophy of the ancient Indian ever taught him to concentrate his mind upon the spirit land; and that the influences which surrounded him in Nature, above, beneath, around, are sent direct by the spirits that dwell in an invisible world above; that there are two kinds of spirits,—the good and the bad, who are continually at war with each other over him, the good directing all things for his prosperity and happiness, the bad directing all things against his prosperity and happiness; that within himself he can do nothing, as he is utterly helpless in the mighty contest that is waged over him by the good and bad spirits. Therefore he exerts his greatest energies of mind and body to the propitiation of the bad spirits rather than the good, since the former may be induced to extend the sceptre of mercy to him, while the latter will ever strive for his good, and his good alone. Therefore, when he is fortunate he attributes it to some good spirit; when unfortunate, to some bad spirit. So, when he said it is "good medicine," he meant that the good spirit had the ascendency; and when he said it is "bad medicine" he meant that the bad spirit had the ascendency.

Therefore, all things in nature, as a natural consequence, indicated to him the presence of the spirits, both good and bad,—as each made known their immediate nearness through both animate and inanimate nature. The sighing of the winds; the flight of the birds; the howl of the lone wolf; the midnight hoot of the owl, and all other sounds heard throughout his illimitable forests both by day and by night, had to him most potent significations; by which he so governed all his actions that he never went upon any enterprise before consulting the signs and omens; then [he] acted in conformity thereto. If the medicine is good, he undertakes his journey; if bad, he remains at home, and no argument can induce him to change his opinion, which I learned from personal experience.[69]

The Chickasaw and Creeks also believed in good and evil spirits, but it is not clear whether the latter were solely spirits of the dead or whether evil spirits of independent origin were numbered among them.

---

[68] Cushman, Hist. Inds., p. 362.   [69] Ibid., pp. 159–160.

The pygmy being or beings of Creek and Chickasaw mythology appear again in that of the Choctaw. Halbert says:

The Choctaws in Mississippi say that there is a little man, about two feet high, that dwells in the thick woods and is solitary in his habits. This little sprite or hobgoblin is called by the Choctaws Bohpoli, or Kowi anukasha, both names being used indifferently or synonymously. The translation of Bohpoli is the "Thrower." The translation of Kowi anukasha is "The one who stays in the woods," or, to give a more concise translation, "Forest-dweller." Bohpoli is represented as being somewhat sportive and mischievous but not malicious in his nature. The Choctaws say that he often playfully throws sticks and stones at the people. Every mysterious noise heard in the woods, whether by day or night, they ascribe to Bohpoli. He takes special pleasure, they say, in striking the pine trees. A young Indian once told me that one night, whilst camped in the woods, he was awakened out of a deep sleep by a loud noise made on a pine tree by Bohpoli. Bohpoli, or Kowi anukasha, is never seen by the common Choctaws. The Choctaw prophets and doctors, however, claim the power of seeing him and of holding communication with him. The Indian doctors say that Bohpoli assists them in the manufacture of their medicines. Most Choctaws say or think that there is but one Bohpoli. In the opinion of others there may be more than one.[70]

Bushnell was told that this spirit occasionally captured a child and imparted to him secrets which enabled him to become a doctor.

In the stories collected by the last-mentioned writer appear some other supernatural beings, as Kashehotapalo, a combination of man and deer who delights in frightening hunters, Okwa Naholo [or Oka Nahullo], "white people of the water," who dwell in deep pools and have light skins like the skins of trout and sometimes capture human beings whom they convert into beings like themselves; Hoklonote'she, a bad spirit who can assume any shape he desires and is able to read men's thoughts; Nalusa Falaya, "the Long Black Being," which resembles a man, but has small eyes and long, pointed ears and sometimes frightens hunters or even communicates its own power of doing harm; and Hashok Okwa Hui'ga, "grass water drop," which seems to have some connection with the will-o'-the-wisp. Its heart only is visible and that only at night, and if one looks at it he is led astray. Ishkitini, the horned owl, was believed to prowl about at night killing men and animals. This sinister character was undoubtedly due to the association of the bird with witchcraft.

Simpson Tubby claimed that the jack-o'-lantern was called "nightmare" by the Indians and was believed to plait up the tails of horses during the night and to ride them about until they could hardly be used next day and many died from the effects. They also upset a horse's stomach so that an Indian doctor had to be called in to treat him.

---

[70] H. S. Halbert, "The Choctaw Robin Goodfellow," in American Antiquarian, vol. XVII, p. 157.

He said that when the horned owl (ishkitini) screeched it meant a sudden death, such as a murder. If the screech owl (ofunlo) was heard, it was a sign that a child under seven among the connections of that family was going to die, because in size this is a baby owl. If a common owl (ōpa) alighted on a barn or on trees near the house and hooted, it foreboded death among the near relatives.

The sapsucker (biskinik) is the "news bird." He brings news both bad and good. If he lights on a tree in your lot early in the morning, some "hasty" news will come before noon. If he does this late at night, the news will come before morning.

They believed that the chicken had been put into their yards to give them a friendly warning of danger. If a chicken crows outside of its usual time, it is because it foresees bad weather. If one comes up to the doorstep or into the gallery and crows, it means hasty news. If a chicken flies up on the roost and crows after reaching it, there will be trouble in the family. If a hen crows, that means that the women of the neighborhood are going to fall out.

The old Choctaw claimed that the male eel acted also as the male of catfish and fish of other kinds. If one had intercourse with a female eel, the offspring would naturally be eels; if with a mud catfish, the offspring would be blue catfish; if with any scale fish, the young would be channel catfish. It was claimed the different species of fish were made by intermarriages.

They claimed that though the blacksnake would not harm anyone, it would try to scare a person. The coachwhip snake would wrap itself around a person and whip him with its tail, and if a hawk tried to carry one of these serpents off, it would whip him until the feathers flew and make him let it go.

The word "Nahullo" (something supernatural or sacred), which appears above, was probably a generic term applied to spirits that had never existed as human beings, although Cushman speaks of them as a race of gigantic hunters who lived in western Tennessee and the northern parts of Alabama and Mississippi at the period of the Choctaw immigration.[71] Later the term was applied to the white people, probably on account of the lightness of their skins.

Cushman also speaks of certain huge animals to which the Choctaw attributed the origin of the prairies along the western banks of the Tombigbee River. Some of these native conceptions owed their origin, or at least their confirmation, to the discovery of mastodon bones.

He speaks again of "a strange and ancient tradition among the Choctaw and Chickasaw hunters, before their exodus to their present place of abode, that, as soon as the horns dropped off, the buck [deer]

---

[71] Cushman, Hist. Inds., p. 207.

at once pawed a hole in the ground with his feet (it being always soft from the frequent rains during the season of shedding) into which he pushed the fallen horns and carefully covered them up." [72]

COSMOLOGY AND MYTHOLOGY

What must have been the primitive Choctaw conception of the world is preserved in the story of Tashka and Walo recorded by Bushnell among the Choctaw of Bayou Lacomb. It is as follows:

Tashka and Walo were brothers who lived long ago. Every morning they saw the sun rise above the horizon, pass high overhead, and late in the day die in the west.

When the boys were about four years old they conceived the idea of following the sun and seeing where he died. So the next day, when he was overhead, they started to follow him; but that night, when he died, they were still in their own country, where they knew the hills and the rivers. Then they slept, and in the morning when the sun was again overhead they once more set off to follow him. And thus they continued for many years to wend their way after the sun in his course through the heavens.

Long, long afterward, when the two boys had become men, they reached a great expanse of water, and the only land they could see was the shore on which they were standing. Late that day, when Sun died, they saw him sink into the water; then they also passed over the water and entered Sun's home with him. All about them they saw women—the stars are women and the moon is Sun's wife. Then Moon asked the brothers how they had found their way so far from their home. They told her how for many, many years, ever since they were mere boys, they had followed Sun in his daily journey.

The Sun told his wife to boil water. Into this he put the boys and rubbed them; this treatment caused them to turn red and their skin to come off.

Sun then asked them whether they knew the way to return to their home, and they said, " No;" so he took them to the edge, whence they looked down to the earth but they could not distinguish their home.

Sun asked why they had followed him, as it was not time for them to reach heaven. They replied that their only reason for following him was a desire to see where he died.

Sun then told them that he would send them home, but that for four days after reaching their home they must not speak a word to any person. If they spoke during the four days they would die, otherwise they would then live and prosper. A large buzzard was then called by Sun and the two boys were placed on its back. Buzzard then started toward the earth. The clouds are midway between heaven and earth; above the clouds wind never blows. As buzzard flew from heaven to the clouds the brothers could easily keep their hold; but from the clouds to the earth the buzzard was blown in all directions. All reached the earth in safety, however, and the boys recognized the trees that stood about their old home.

They rested beneath the trees, and while there an old man passed by who knew the brothers. He continued down the road, and soon meeting the boys' mother, told her the boys had come back. She hastened to see them. When she saw them she began to talk and made them answer her. Then they told her that, as they had spoken during the first four days after their return, they would

[72] Cushman, Hist. Inds., p. 197.

surely die. Knowing she had forced them to speak, on hearing this the mother was greatly worried. Then all went to the mother's home, and the brothers told of all they had seen and how they had followed Sun during many years. After they had told all, they died and went up to heaven to remain forever.[73]

Inquiries made by Wright regarding the Choctaw conception of creation resulted as follows:

The Choctaws state that, at a remote period, the earth was a vast plain, destitute of hills, and a mere quagmire.[74] The word, which they use to express this primitive state, is applied to clotted blood, jelly, &c. which will serve to explain what their ideas were. The earth in this chaotic state, some of them suppose, was produced by the immediate power of the Creator; but others, indeed the majority with whom I have conversed relative to this subject, have no knowledge how the earth was produced in this state; nor do they appear ever to have extended their thoughts so far as to make a single inquiry with respect to it.

While the earth was in this situation, a superior being, who is represented to have been in appearance as a red man, came down from above, and alighting near the centre of the Choctaw nation, threw up a large mound, or hill, called in their language *Nunih waiya*, "stooping or sloping hill." When this was done, he caused the red people to come out of it, and when he supposed that a sufficient number had come out, he stamped on the ground with his foot. When this signal of his power was given, some were partly formed, others were just raising their heads above the mud, emerging into light, and struggling into life, all of whom perished. The red people being thus formed from the earth, and seated on the area of the hill, their Creator told them that they should live for ever. But not understanding him, they inquired what he said, upon which he took away the grant he had given them of immortality, and told them they would become subject to death.

After the formation of man from the ground, the hills were formed, the earth indurated and fitted to become a habitation for man. The hills, they suppose, were formed by the agitation of the waters. While the earth was in its chaotic state, the waters are represented as having been thrown into a state of great agitation, like that of a boiling liquid, and being driven by violent winds, the soft mud was carried in various directions, and being deposited in different places, formed the mountains and hills which now appear on the face of the earth.

When the Creator had formed the red people from the ground, and fitted the earth for their residence, he told them the earth would bring forth spontaneously the chestnut, hickory nut, and acorn for their subsistence. Accordingly, the Choctaws state, that in ancient times, they lived principally upon these productions of the earth. And they suppose it was not till sometime after they had been a people, that the corn, which now forms no inconsiderable part of their food, was discovered by means of a crow.

They state, that at their first creation, both males and females went entirely naked. After some time, though from what cause they do not know, they began to use some covering. At first, the long moss, which abounds in southern climates, tied round their waists, formed their only covering. At some later period, after the invention of the bow and arrow, when they had

---

[73] Bushnell, The Choctaw of Bayou Lacomb, Bull. 48, Bur. Amer. Ethn., p. 35.
[74] Probably this followed a still earlier stage when water covered all things; see below, p. 202.

acquired skill in hunting wild beasts, they began to use the skins of animals for clothing.[75]

Their social and civil institutions were, according to the same sources of information, given to the Choctaw at Nanih Waiya, and all of these events were supposed to have been of very recent occurrence. "The Choctaws," says Wright, "do not place their formation at any very remote period of time. The old men, who are now seventy or eighty years of age, say that their grandfathers and great-grandfathers saw and conversed with the first race of men formed at *Nunih waiya*, and they reckon themselves to be only the fourth or fifth generation from them." [76]

Wright also recorded a version of the origin legend of the Choctaw, bringing them from the west, which has been given elsewhere.[77]

Cushman lets in some light on the native view regarding the origin of the various races of mankind:

In regard to the origin of man, the one [view] generally accepted among the Choctaws, as well as many other tribes was that man and all other forms of life had originated from the common mother earth through the agency of the Great Spirit; but believed that the human race sprang from many different primeval pairs created by the Great Spirit in the various parts of the earth in which man was found; and according to the different natural features of the world in which man abode, so their views varied with regard to the substance of which man was created; in a country of vast forests, they believed the primeval pair, or pairs, sprang from the trees; in a mountainous and rocky district of country, they sprang from the rocks; in valleys and prairies, from the earth; but [regarding] their views as to the time [when] this creation of man took place, whether at the same time throughout the various inhabited regions or at different periods, their traditions are silent.[78]

Bushnell obtained a creation legend which incorporates episodes from the Biblical story of the Tower of Babel.[79]

Flood legends were naturally of interest to missionaries and therefore no less than three versions of the Choctaw story are given by Cushman, two collected directly by himself and a third from the manuscript notes of Israel Folsom. The Choctaw called this event Oka Falama, "The returned waters," which would indicate that they believed water to have covered everything at the first creation. Following are the three versions just mentioned:

I

In ancient time, after many generations of mankind had lived and passed from the stage of being, the race became so corrupt and wicked—brother fighting against brother and wars deluging the earth with human blood and carnage—the Great Spirit became greatly displeased and finally determined to

---

[75] The Missionary Herald, 1828, pp. 182–183.
[76] Ibid., p. 215.
[77] See p. 11.
[78] Cushman, Hist. Inds., pp. 255–256.
[79] Bull. 48, Bur. Amer. Ethn., p. 30.

destroy the human race; therefore sent a great prophet to them who proclaimed from tribe to tribe, and from village to village, the fearful tidings that the human race was soon to be destroyed. None believed his words, and [they] lived on in their wickedness as if they did not care, and the seasons came again and went. Then came the autumn of the year, followed by many succeeding cloudy days and nights, during which the sun by day and the moon and stars by night were concealed from the earth; then succeeded a total darkness, and the sun seemed to have been blotted out; while darkness and silence with a cold atmosphere took possession of the earth. Mankind, wearied and preplexed, but not repenting or reforming, slept in darkness but to awake in darkness; then the mutterings of distant thunder began to be heard, gradually becoming incessant, until it reverberated in all parts of the sky and seemed to echo back even from the deep center of the earth. Then fear and consternation seized upon every heart and all believed the sun would never return. The Magi of the Choctaws spoke despondently in reply to the many interrogations of the alarmed people, and sang their death-songs which were but faintly heard in the mingled confusion that arose amid the gloom of the night that it seemed would have no returning morn. Mankind went from place to place only by torch-light; their food stored away became mouldy and unfit for use; the wild animals of the forests gathered around their fires bewildered and even entered their towns and villages, seeming to have lost all fear of man. Suddenly a fearful crash of thunder, louder than ever before heard, seemed to shake the earth, and immediately after a light was seen glimmering seemingly far away to the North. It was soon discovered not to be the light of the returning sun, but the gleam of great waters advancing in mighty billows, wave succeeding wave as they onward rolled over the earth destroying everything in their path.

Then the wailing cry was heard coming from all directions, Oka Falamah, Oka Falamah; (The returned waters). Stretching from horizon to horizon, it came pouring its massive waters onward. "The foundations of the Great Deep were broken up." Soon the earth was entirely overwhelmed by the mighty and irresistible rush of the waters which swept away the human race and all animals leaving the earth a desolate waste. Of all mankind only one was saved, and that one was the mysterious prophet who had been sent by the Great Spirit to warn the human race of their near approaching doom. This prophet saved himself by making a raft of sassafras logs by the direction of the Great Spirit, upon which he floated upon the great waters that covered the earth, as various kinds of fish swam around him, and twined among the branches of the submerged trees, while upon the face of the waters he looked upon the dead bodies of men and beasts, as they rose and fell upon the heaving billows.

After many weeks floating he knew not where, a large black bird came to the raft flying in circles above his head. He called to it for assistance, but it only replied in loud, croaking tones, then flew away and was seen no more. A few days after a bird of bluish color, with red eyes and beak came and hovered over the raft, to which the prophet spoke and asked if there were a spot of dry land anywhere to be seen in the wide waste of waters. Then it flew around his head a few moments fluttering its wings and uttering a mournful cry, then flew away in the direction of that part of the sky where the new sun seemed to be sinking into the rolling waves of the great ocean of waters. Immediately a strong wind sprang up and bore the raft rapidly in that direction. Soon night came on, and the moon and stars again made their appearance, and the next morning the sun arose in its former splendor; and the prophet looking around saw an island in the distance toward which the raft was slowly drifting, and before the sun had gone down seemingly again into the world of waters, the raft had touched the island upon which he landed and encamped, and being wearied and lonely he soon forgot his anxieties in sleep; and when morning came, in looking around over the island, he found it covered with all varieties of animals—excepting the mammoth which had been destroyed. He also found birds and fowls of every kind in vast numbers upon the island; among which he discovered the identical black bird which had visited him upon the waters, and then left him to his fate; and, as he regarded it [as] a cruel bird, he named it Fulushto (Raven) [80]—a bird of ill omen to the ancient Choctaws.

With great joy he also discovered the bluish bird which had caused the wind to blow his raft upon the island, and because of this act of kindness and its great beauty he called it Puchi Yushubah (Lost Pigeon) [pàchi yoshoba, the turtle dove].

After many days the waters passed away; and in the course of time Puchi Yushubah became a beautiful woman, whom the prophet soon after married, and by them the world was again peopled.[81]

II

Another Choctaw version of their traditional flood (Oka falama) is as follows: In the far distant ages of the past, the people, whom the Great Spirit had created, became so wicked that he resolved to sweep them all from the earth, except Oklatabashih (People's mourner) and his family, who alone did that which was good. He told Oklatabashih to build a large boat into which he should go with his family and also to take into the boat a male and female of all the animals living upon the earth. He did as he was commanded by the Great Spirit. But as he went out in the forest to bring in the birds he was unable to catch a pair of biskinik (sapsuckers), fitukhak [or fituktàk] (yellow hammers), bakbak [or bàkobàk] (large red-headed woodpeckers); these birds were so quick in hopping around from one side to the other of the trees upon which they clung with their sharp and strong claws, that Oklatabashih found it was impossible for him to catch them, and therefore he gave up the chase, and returned to the boat; the door closed, the rain began to fall increasing in volume for many days and nights, until thousands of peoples and animals perished. Then it suddenly ceased and utter darkness covered the face of the earth for a long time, while the people and animals that still survived groped here and there in the fearful gloom. Suddenly far in the distant north was seen a long streak of light. They believed that, amid the raging elements and the impenetrable darkness that covered the earth, the sun had lost its way and was rising in the north. All the surviving people rushed towards the seemingly rising sun, though utterly bewildered, not knowing or caring what they did. But well did Oklatabashih interpret the prophetic sign of their fast abandoned him to his fate upon the waters, and, as it was a wicked they saw, in utter despair, that it was but the mocking light that foretold how near the Oka falama was at hand, rolling like mountains on mountans piled and engulfing everything in its resistless course. All earth was at once overwhelmed in the mighty return of waters, except the great boat which, by the guidance of the Great Spirit, rode safely upon the rolling and dashing waves that covered the earth. During many moons the boat floated safely o'er the vast sea of waters.

---

[80] This story seems to have been obtained from a Chickasaw Indian. The Choctaw word for raven is fàla chito, "big crow," and the Chickasaw equivalent of this would be fàla ishto.

[81] Cushman, Hist. Inds., pp. 282–284.

Finally Oklatabashih sent a dove to see if any dry land could be found. She soon returned with her beak full of grass, which she had gathered from a desert island. Oklatabashih to reward her for her discovery mingled a little salt in her food. Soon after this the waters subsided and the dry land appeared; then the inmates of the great boat went forth to repeople another earth. But the dove, having acquired a taste for salt during her stay in the boat continued its use by finding it at the salt-licks that then abounded in many places, to which the cattle and deer also frequently resorted. Every day after eating, she visited a salt-lick to eat a little salt to aid her digestion, which in the course of time became habitual and thus was transmitted to her offspring. In the course of years, she became a grand-mother, and took great delight in feeding and caring for her grand-children. One day, however, after having eaten some grass seed, she unfortunately forgot to eat a little salt as usual. For this neglect, the Great Spirit punished her and her descendants by forbidding them forever the use of salt. When she returned home that evening, her grand-children, as usual began to coo for their supply of salt, but their grand-mother having been forbidden to give them any more, they cooed in vain. From that day to this, in memory of this lost privilege, the doves everywhere, on the return of spring, still continue their cooing for salt, which they will never again be permitted to eat. Such is the ancient tradition of the Choctaws of the origin of the cooing of doves.

But the fate of the three birds who eluded capture by Oklatabashih, their tradition states: They flew high in the air at the approach of Oka falama, and, as the waters rose higher and higher, they also flew higher above the surging waves. Finally, the waters rose in near proximity to the sky, upon which they lit as their last hope. Soon, to their great joy and comfort, the waters ceased to rise, and commenced to recede. But while sitting on the sky their tails, projecting downward, were continually being drenched by the dashing spray of the surging waters below, and thus the end of their tail feathers became forked and notched, and this peculiar shape of the tails of the biskinik, fitukhak and bakbak has been transmitted to their latest posterity. But the sagacity and skill manifested by these birds in eluding the grasp of Oklatabashih, so greatly delighted the Great Spirit that he appointed them to be forever the guardian birds of the red men. Therefore these birds, and especially the biskinik, often made their appearance in their villages on the eve of a ball play; and, whichever one of the three came, it twittered in happy tones its feelings of joy in anticipation of the near approach of the Choctaws' favorite game. But in time of war one of these birds always appeared in the camp of a war party, to give them warning of approaching danger, by its constant chirping and hurried flitting from place to place around their camp. In many ways did these birds prove their love for and friendship to the red man, and he ever cherished them as the loved birds of his race, the remembered gift of the Great Spirit in the fateful days of the mighty Oka falama.[83]

This second narrative seems to contain a slight trace of missionary influence but the greater part of it is plainly aboriginal.

III

The tradition, as related by wise men of the Nation, about the flood, is as follows: A long continued night came upon the land, which created no small

---

[83] Cushman, Hist. Inds., pp. 285–287.

degree of fear and uneasiness among the people. Their fears were increased at seeing the terrible buffaloes, and the fleet deer making their appearance, and after them the bears and panthers, wolves, and others approaching their habitations; suspicious at first of their intentions, they thought of placing themselves beyond the reach of the more dangerous animals, but instead of exhibiting any disposition of ferocity, they seemed rather to claim protection at their hands. This presented an opportunity of having a jubilee of feasting, and they therefore indulged themselves to the fullest bent of their propensity and inclinations by an indiscriminate massacre of the animals. Having thus feasted for some time, they at last saw daylight appearing. But what surprised them much, was, they saw it coming from the north. They were at a loss what to think of it. They, however, supposed that the sun must have missed his path, and was coming up from another direction, which caused the unusual long night, or perhaps he had purposely changed his course, to rise hereafter in the north instead of the east. While such conjectures were making, some fast runners arrived as messengers coming from the direction of the supposed day light, and announced to them that the light which they saw was not the day light, but that it was a flood slowly approaching, drowning and destroying everything. Upon this report the people fled to the mountains, and began to construct rafts of sassafras wood, binding them together with vines, believing this expedient would save them from a watery grave. But alas, delusive hope! for the bears were swimming around in countless numbers, [and] being very fond of vine twigs gnawed them through, thereby setting loose the materials of the raft, and bringing the people under dark waters. Their cries, wailing and agony, were unheard and unseen. But there was one man who prepared and launched a strong peni or boat, in which he placed his family and provisions and thus floated upon the deep waters. For days the Penikbi (boat builder) strained his eyes looking all around for the purpose of discovering the existence of some animal life, and a place at which to anchor his vessel.

Nothing met his sight save the cheerless waste of waters. The hawks, eagles and other birds of the same class, had all, when they found that the tops of the mountains could not render them a lighting place from the flood, flown to the sky and clung on to it with their talons, and remained until the flood abated, when they returned to their old haunts and resumed their natural propensities and habits. An indication of the disappearing of the flood thus manifested itself. A crow made its appearance and was so much delighted to see the boat, that it flew around and around it. The Penikbi, overjoyed beyond measure, addressed the sable bird, wishing to elicit some information from it as to their whereabouts, and whether or not the flood was subsiding any, but it heeded him not, seeming to be determined to consult its own safety before that of anyone else; but scarcely had the crow winged away from the peni before a dove was descried flying toward it, and on reaching it, the Penikbi with joy perceived a leaf in its bill. It flew several times around but did not alight; after doing so [it] took its course slowly flying toward the west, but seemingly anxious that Penikbi would steer in the direction [which] it [pursued], which he did, faithfully following the course. In this way many a weary mile was traveled, before seeing a place to land. At length a mountain became visible, and never did a benighted mariner hail the sight of land as Penikbi did, when its summit became visible. When he had safely landed, the dove flew away to return no more.[83]

[83] Cushman, Hist. Inds., pp. 365–366.

The Genesis borrowings are very evident here, but it is still uncertain whether the mention of birds in connection with the Choctaw Noah is entirely borrowed or has some substratum of native origination.

Catlin has an insignificant note regarding this myth,[84] and Charles Lanman, an admirer and imitator of Washington Irving, gives a version in would-be Irvingesque fashion which he had obtained from Peter Pitchlynn. After ages of peace and happiness:

In process of time the aspect of the world became changed. Brother quarreled with brother, and cruel wars frequently covered the earth with blood. The Great Spirit saw all those things and was displeased. A terrible wind swept over the wilderness, and the red men knew they had done wrong, but they lived as if they did not care. Finally a stranger prophet made his appearance among them, and proclaimed in every village the news that the human race was to be destroyed. None believed his words, and the moons of summer again came and disappeared. It was now the autumn of the year. Many cloudy days had occurred, and then a total darkness came upon the earth, and the sun seemed to have departed forever. It was very dark and very cold. Men laid themselves down to sleep, but they were troubled with unhappy dreams. They arose when they thought it was time for the day to dawn, but only to see the sky covered with darkness deeper than the heaviest cloud. The moon and stars had all disappeared, and there was constantly a dismal bellowing of thunder in the upper air. Men now believed that the sun would never return, and there was great consternation throughout the land. The great men of the Choctaw nation spoke despondingly to their fellows, and sung their death songs, but those songs were faintly heard in the gloom of the great night. It was a most unhappy time indeed, and darkness reigned for a great while. Men visited each other by torch-light. The grain and fruits of the land became mouldy, and the wild animals of the forest became tame and gathered around the watchfires of the Indians, entering even the villages.

A louder peal of thunder than was ever before heard now echoed through the firmament, and a light was seen in the North. It was not the light of the sun, but the gleam of distant waters. They made a mighty roar, and, in billows like the mountains, they rolled over the earth. They swallowed up the entire human race in their career, and destroyed everything that had made the earth beautiful. Only one human being was saved, and that was the mysterious prophet who had foretold the wonderful calamity. He had built him a raft of sassafras logs, and upon this did he float safely above the deep waters. A large black bird came and flew in circles above his head. He called upon it for aid, but it shrieked aloud, and flew away and returned to him no more. A smaller bird, of a bluish color, with scarlet eyes and beak, now came hovering over the prophet's head. He spoke to it, and asked if there was a spot of dry land in any part of the waste of waters. It fluttered its wings, uttered a sweet moan, and flew directly towards that part of the sky where the newly-born sun was just sinking in the waves. A strong wind now arose, and the raft of the prophet was rapidly borne in the same direction which the bird had pursued. The moon and stars again made their appear-

[84] Geo. Catlin, The North Am. Inds., vol. II, p. 145. Philadelphia, 1913.

ance, and the prophet landed upon a green island, where he encamped. Here he enjoyed a long and refreshing sleep, and when morning dawned he found that the island was covered with every variety of animal, except the great Shakanli,[85] or mammoth, which had been destroyed. Birds, too, he also found here in great abundance. He recognized the identical black one which had abandoned him to his fate upon the waters, and, as it was a wicked bird, and had sharp claws, he called it Ful-luh-chitto,[86] or bird of the Evil One. He also discovered, and with great joy, the bluish bird which had caused the wind to blow him upon the island, and because of its kindness to him and its beauty, he called it Puch che-yon-sho-ba,[87] or the soft-voiced pigeon. The waters finally passed away, and in process of time that bird became a woman and the wife of the prophet, from whom the people now living upon the earth are all descended. And so endeth the story of The Overflowing Waters.[88]

The origin of corn is connected with a myth called by Cushman the story of Ohoyo Osh Chisba [or Ohoyo osh chishba], "The Unknown Woman." With Cushman's usual emotional setting this runs as follows:

In the days of many moons ago, two Choctaw hunters were encamped for the night in the swamps of the bend of the Alabama river. . . . The two hunters having been unsuccessful in the chase of that and the preceding day, found themselves on that night with nothing with which to satisfy the cravings of hunger except a black hawk which they had shot with an arrow. Sad reflections filled their hearts as they thought of their sad disappointments and of their suffering families at home, while the gloomy future spread over them its dark pall of despondency, all serving to render them unhappy indeed. They cooked the hawk and sat down to partake of their poor and scanty supper, when their attention was drawn from their gloomy forebodings by the low but distinct tones, strange yet soft and plaintive as the melancholy notes of the dove, but produced by what they were unable to even conjecture. At different intervals it broke the deep silence of the early night with its seemingly muffled notes of woe; and as the nearly full orbed moon slowly ascended the eastern sky the strange sounds became more frequent and distinct. With eyes dilated and fluttering heart they looked up and down the river to learn whence the sounds proceeded, but no object except the sandy shores glittering in the moonlight greeted their eyes, while the dark waters of the river seemed alone to give response in murmuring tones to the strange notes that continued to float upon the night air from a direction they could not definitely locate; but happening to look behind them in the direction opposite the moon they saw a woman of wonderful beauty standing upon a mound a few rods distant. Like an illuminated shadow, she had suddenly appeared out of the moon-lighted forest. She was loosely clad in snow-white raiment, and bore in the folds of her drapery a wreath of fragrant flowers. She beckoned them to approach, while she seemed surrounded by a halo of light that gave to her a supernatural appearance. Their imagination now influenced them to believe her to be the Great Spirit of their nation, and that the flowers she bore were representatives of loved ones who had passed from earth to bloom in the Spirit-Land; . . .

---

[85] Shak'anli, "making a noise by gritting the teeth."

[86] Fála, "crow"; fála chito, "raven." See p. 204.

[87] Páchi yoshoba, "turtle dove."

[88] Adventures in the Wilds of the United States and British American Provinces, by Charles Lanman, vol. II, pp. 429–431, Philadelphia, 1856.

The mystery was solved. At once they approached [the spot] where she stood, and offered their assistance in any way they could be of service to her. She replied she was very hungry, whereupon one of them ran and brought the roasted hawk and handed it to her. She accepted it with grateful thanks; but, after eating a small portion of it, she handed the remainder back to them replying that she would remember their kindness when she returned to her home in the happy hunting grounds of her father, who was Shilup Chitoh Osh—The Great Spirit of the Choctaws. She then told them that when the next mid-summer moon should come they must meet her at the mound upon which she was then standing. She then bade them an affectionate adieu, and was at once borne away upon a gentle breeze and, mysteriously as she came, so she disappeared. The two hunters returned to their camp for the night and early next morning sought their homes, but kept the strange incident to themselves, a profound secret. When the designated time rolled around the mid-summer full moon found the two hunters at the foot of the mound but Ohoyo Chishba Osh was nowhere to be seen. Then remembering she told them they must come to the very spot where she was then standing, they at once ascended the mound and found it covered with a strange plant, which yielded an excellent food, which was ever afterwards cultivated by the Choctaws, and named by them Tunchi (Corn.).[89]

Lanman's version, from the same source as his legend of the flood, runs thus:

It was in olden times, and two Choctaw hunters were spending the night by their watch-fire in a bend of the river Alabama. The game and the fish of their country were with every new moon becoming less abundant, and all that they had to satisfy their hunger on the night in question, was the tough flesh of a black hawk. They were very tired, and as they mused upon their unfortunate condition, and thought of their hungry children, they were very unhappy, and talked despondingly. But they roasted the bird before the fire, and proceeded to enjoy as comfortable a meal as they could. Hardly had they commenced eating, however, before they were startled by a singular noise, resembling the cooing of a dove. They jumped up and looked around them to ascertain the cause. In one direction they saw nothing but the moon just rising above the forest trees on the opposite side of the river. They looked up and down the river, but could see nothing but the sandy shores and the dark waters. They listened, and nothing could they hear but the murmur of the flowing stream. They turned their faces in that direction opposite the moon, and to their astonishment, they discovered standing upon the summit of a grassy mound, the form of a beautiful woman. They hastened to her side, when she told them that she was very hungry, whereupon they ran after their roasted hawk, and gave it all into the hands of the strange woman. She barely tasted of the proffered food, but told the hunters that their kindness had preserved her from death, and that she would not forget them when she returned to the happy grounds of her father, who was Hoshtal-li,[90] or Great Spirit of the Choctaws. She had one request to make, and this was, that when the next moon of midsummer should arrive, they should visit the spot where she then stood. A pleasant breeze swept among the forest leaves, and the strange woman suddenly disappeared.

[89] Cushman, Hist. Inds., pp. 276–278.
[90] Corn woman was therefore daughter of the solar or celestial deity. See pp. 194–197.

The hunters were astonished, but they returned to their families, and kept all that they had seen and heard, hidden in their hearts. Summer came, and they once more visited the mound on the banks of the Alabama. They found it covered with a new plant, whose leaves were like the knives of the white man. It yielded a delicious food, which has since been known among the Choctaws as sweet toncha or Indian maize.[91]

An entirely different story is preserved by Halbert, whose notes contain two versions, in both Choctaw and English. The translations are as follows:

I

A long time ago a child was playing in the yard. Just then a crow flying over dropped some corn. The child found a single grain of the corn and said "What is this?" His mother then said, "It is really tanchi (corn)." His mother then planted it in the yard and the corn grew up and ripened. So a child was the finder of corn. In this way the forefathers of the [Choctaw] got their seed corn.

II

A long time ago thus it happened. In the very beginning a crow getting a single grain of corn from beyond the great waters, brought it to this country and gave it to an orphan child who was playing in the yard. The child named it *tanchi* (corn), and planted it in the yard. When the corn grew up high, the child's elders merely had it swept around. But the child wishing to have it a certain way, hoed it, hilled it up and laid it by. When this single grain of corn ripened, it made two ears of corn. And it was really in this way, that the Choctaw discovered corn.

Solar eclipses were attributed to black squirrels, or a black squirrel, supposed to be eating the luminary, and they must be driven off if mankind were still to enjoy heat and light. Cushman says:

The Choctaw . . . attributed an eclipse of the sun to a black squirrel, whose eccentricities often led it into mischief, and, among other things, that of trying to eat up the sun at different intervals. When thus inclined, they believed, which was confirmed by long experience, that the only effective means to prevent so fearful a catastrophe befalling the world as the blotting out of that indispensable luminary, was to favor the little, black epicure with a first-class scare; therefore, whenever he manifested an inclination to indulge in a meal on the sun, every ingenuity was called into requisition to give him a genuine fright [so] that he would be induced, at least, to postpone his meal on the sun at that particular time and seek a lunch elsewhere. As soon, therefore, as the sun began to draw its lunar veil over its face, the cry was heard from every mouth from the Dan to the Beersheba of their then wide extended territory, echoing from hill to dale, "Funi lusa hushi umpa! Funi lusa hushi umpa," according to our phraseology, The black squirrel is eating the sun! Then and there was heard a sound of tumult by day in the Choctaw Nation for the space of an hour or two, far exceeding that said to have been heard by night in Belgium's Capital, and sufficient in the conglomeration of discordant tones terrific, if heard by the distant, little, fastidious squirrel,

[91] Adventures in the Wilds of the United States and British American Provinces, by Charles Lanman, vol. II, pp. 463–464. Philadelphia, 1856.

to have made him lose forever afterward all relish for a mess of suns for an early or late dinner. The shouts of the women and children mingling with the ringing of discordant bells as the vociferous pounding and beating of ear-splitting tin pans and cups mingling in " wild confusion worse confounded," yet in sweet unison with a first-class orchestra of yelping, howling, barking dogs gratuitously thrown in by the innumerable and highly excited curs, produced a din, which even a " Funi lusa," had he heard it, could scarcely have endured even to have indulged in a nibble or two of the sun, though urged by the demands of a week's fasting.

But during the wild scene the men were not idle spectators, or indifferent listeners. Each stood a few paces in front of his cabin door, with no outward manifestation of excitement whatever—so characteristic of the Indian warrior—but with his trusty rifle in hand, which so oft had proved a friend sincere in many hours of trial, which he loaded and fired in rapid succession at the distant, devastating squirrel, with the same coolness and calm deliberation that he did when shooting at his game. More than once have I witnessed the fearful yet novel scene. When it happened to be the time of a total eclipse of the sun, a sufficient evidence that the little, black epicure meant business in regard to having a square meal, though it took the whole sun to furnish it, then indeed there were sounds of revelry and tumult unsurpassed by any ever heard before, either in " Belgium " or elsewhere. Then the women shrieked and redoubled their efforts upon the tin pans, which, under the desperate blows, strained every vocal organ to do its utmost and whole duty in loud response, while the excited children screamed and beat their tin cups, and the sympathetic dogs (whose name was legion) barked and howled—all seemingly determined not to fall the one behind the other in their duty—since the occasion demanded it; while the warriors still stood in profound and meditative silence, but firm and undaunted, as they quickly loaded and fired their rifles, each time taking deliberate aim, if perchance the last shot might prove the successful one; then, as the moon's shadow began to move from the disk of the sun, the joyful shout was heard above the mighty din Funi-lusa-osh mahlatah! The black squirrel is frightened. But the din remained unabated until the sun again appeared in its usual splendor, and all nature again assumed its harmonious course.[92]

This is very graphic, but one wonders how many total eclipses of the sun Mr. Cushman had been able to observe in order to form an opinion of the average Choctaw behavior on such occasions. His second account of this is quoted from Folsom's manuscript.

When the sun began to get less in his brightness, and grow dark and obscure, they believed that some ethereal black squirrels of large size, driven by hunger, had commenced eating him and were going to devour him. With this belief they thought it was their duty to make every exertion they could to save the great luminary of day from being consumed by them. Therefore every person, both men, women and children, who could make a noise, were called upon to join in the effort to drive the squirrels away. To do this they would begin in the same manner as persons generally do in trying to start a squirrel off from a tree. Some would throw sticks towards the declining sun, whooping and yelling, at the same time shooting arrows toward the supposed black squirrels.[93]

---

[92] Cushman, Hist. Inds., pp. 290–291.   [93] Cushman, Hist. Inds., p. 368.

A different explanation was given Bushnell by the Choctaw of Bayou Lacomb.

The Choctaw say that since the sun works every day he becomes dirty and smoked from the great fire within. It is necessary therefore for him to rest and clean himself, after doing which he shines the brighter. During the eclipse he is removing the accumulated dirt. A similar explanation applies to the dark of the moon.[94]

Hence the solar eclipse was known as "sun dark or dirty," and the lunar eclipse as "moon cleaning itself."

The last-mentioned writer has the following on thunder and lightning and the comet:

Thunder and lightning are to the Choctaw two great birds—Thunder (*Heloha*), the female; Lightning (*Mela'tha*), the male. When they hear a great noise in the clouds, Heloha is laying an egg, "just like a bird," in the cloud, which is her nest. When a tree is shattered the result is said to have been caused by Mala'tha, the male, he being the stronger; but when a tree is only slightly damaged, the effect is attributed to Heloha, the weaker.

Great trouble or even war was supposed to follow the sight of a comet.[95]

PRAYER, SACRIFICE, DREAMS, ETC.

An old Choctaw informed Wright that, before the arrival of the missionaries, they had no conception of prayer. However, he adds, "I have indeed heard it asserted by some, that anciently their *hopaii*, or prophets, on some occasions were accustomed to address the sun; but whether in the way of prayer or not I do not know." [96] Nor must we forget the invocations to various powers in nature which were contained in the medical formulæ.

At a later time Simpson Tubby claims that the head chief of the Choctaw was wont to kindle a fire on a still day when the smoke would go straight upward, and bend over it in prayer to some unknown power.

Romans gives us this description of a hunting taboo which is suggestive of sacrifice:

When a deer or bear is killed by them, they divide the liver into as many pieces as there are fires, and send a boy to each with a piece, that the men belonging to each fire may burn it, but the women's fires are excluded from this ceremony, and if each party kills one or more animals, the livers of them are all treated in the same manner.[97]

Adair says that the Indians of his acquaintance believed the time of a man's death to be fated, and the following item regarding

---

[94] Bull. 48, Bur. Amer. Ethn., p. 18.
[95] Ibid.
[96] The Missionary Herald, op. cit., p. 181.
[97] Romans, Nat. Hist. E. and W. Fla., p. 83.

Choctaw doctors would seem to indicate that this fate was revealed to and consummated through the medical fraternity:

> The Choctah are so exceedingly infatuated in favour of the infallible judgment of their pretended prophets, as to allow them without the least regret, to dislocate the necks of any of their sick who are in a weak state of body, to put them out of their pain, when they presume to reveal the determined will of the Deity to shorten his days, which is asserted to be communicated in a dream.[96]

Since a doctor who lost a patient might be in jeopardy of his life while he was permitted to put an end to the existence of one whose death he had prophesied, it might be thought that the scales would be weighted heavily against the patient. This lends credibility to the following story reported by Milfort:

> The Tchactas revere greatly the priests or medicine men of whom I have just spoken, and in whom they have a blind confidence which the latter often abuse. These doctors exact high payments for their labors over a sick man, and almost always in advance. Their avarice is such that, when illness lasts for a long time, and the patient has nothing left with which to pay the doctor, the latter calls a meeting of the sick man's family and informs them that he has given their relative all possible care, that he has employed all of the resources of his profession, but the sickness is incurable and it can end only in death. The family thus forewarned decides that, the patient having already suffered a long time and being without hope of recovery, it would be inhuman to prolong his sufferings further and it is right to end them. Then, one or two of the strongest of them go to the sick man, ask him, in the presence of the entire family, how he is, and while the latter is replying to this question, they throw themselves upon him and strangle him.
>
> In 1782 one of these savages, who had been sick for a long time and who had nothing more to give to his doctor, found himself in danger of being strangled in the manner I have just described. As he was suspicious and was on his guard, he watched for the moment when his family was assembled to hear the report of the doctor and decide to put an end to his sufferings by putting him to death. He took advantage of this moment to flee and escape the ceremony which awaited him. He dragged himself, as well as he was able, as far as a forest, which fortunately was near his dwelling. He was not able to carry with him provisions of any kind, and found himself reduced to the necessity of living on the flesh of wood rats, known under the name of "opossum," which are very appetizing and very healthful. His flight caused all his family great astonishment, but the doctor persuaded them that he had gone away only to conceal his inevitable death.
>
> While this unfortunate savage was wandering in the forest, he remembered that he had frequently visited the Creeks in order to carry thither the belts or strings of beads which serve them as records. He determined to take refuge with them and inform them of his reasons for fleeing from his own country, not doubting that he would find help and protection in a nation with the generosity of which he was acquainted. He then sought out McGillivray, who was at that time head chief, and explained to him the reasons for his journey. He reminded him that he had visited him many times on behalf

---

[96] Adair, Hist. Am. Inds., p. 129.

of his chiefs. McGillivray received him kindly though he was unable to
recognize him for he looked like a skeleton. Food was given him and, as
he was still sick, some days later he had him take some emetic [i. e., cassina]
diluted with sassafras water. This medicine was sufficient to cure his sickness,
but as this savage had suffered much and had been ill for a long time, he
remained four or five months with McGillivray in order to become wholly
restored to health; I saw him often and he related his adventure to me
himself. When he felt entirely restored, he returned to his own nation.
About eight months had then elapsed since his escape, and his family had
raised a scaffold and performed all the ceremonial rites preceding and accompanying funerals which I have described above. The doctor had so strongly
persuaded the relatives of this savage that he could not recover from his ill-
ness that, when he appeared in their midst, they looked upon him as a ghost,
and all fled. Seeing that he was left alone, he went to the house of one of his
neighbors who, seized with the same terror, threw himself on the ground, and,
persuaded that this was only a spirit, spoke to him as follows:

"Why have you left the abode of souls if you were happy there? Why do
you return to us? Is it in order to be present at the last feast which your
family and your friends hold for you? Go! return to the country of the dead
lest you renew the grief which they have experienced at your loss!"

The other, seeing that his presence caused the same fright everywhere,
determined to return to the Creeks, where he saw again, in course of time, many
of his relatives, since these were in the habit of coming there every year. It
was only then that he was able to disabuse them and persuade them that
the doctor had deceived them. They, angered at such a piece of rascality,
sought out the doctor, heaped upon him the most violent reproaches, and
afterwards killed him so that he might deceive no one else. They then made
all possible representations to this savage in order to induce him to return
to them, but he refused steadily and married a woman of the Taskiguys by
whom he had three children, and he lives today at the place where Fort
Toulouse formerly stood.[99]

The subjection of human life to "fate" is also affirmed by Cushman.
"The ancient Choctaws believed," he says, "and those of the present
day believe, and I was informed by Gov. Basil LeFlore, in 1884, . . .
that there is an appointed time for every one to die."[1]

We have already had one reference to native faith in the significance of certain dreams. Speaking of the Choctaw of Bayou Lacomb, Louisiana, Bushnell says:

The Choctaw hold that it is possible for the "spirit" to leave the body
even during life, and by that belief explain dreams thus:

At night when a person is resting and all is quiet the "spirit" steals away
from the body and wanders about the country, seeing many people and things,
which are known to the individual when he awakes. If, during its wanderings, the spirit meets large animals of any sort, the person will surely suffer
misfortune before many days have passed.[2]

At a conference between the Choctaw and French, held in 1751,
one of the Choctaw speakers augured ill for the lives of the French-

[99] Appendix, pp. 267–269; Milfort, Mém., pp. 298–304.
[1] Cushman, Hist. Inds., p. 246.
[2] Bushnell, Bull. 48, Bur. Amer. Ethn., p. 29.

men because on the night before one of his people had dreamed that all of them had been killed. To dream of seeing a ghost presaged sickness or death and a nightmare was thought to be occasioned by a disembodied soul who had come to get the dreamer.[3]

The following regarding " mesmerism " and ventriloquism may have little value but at least it was from the pen of a native Choctaw, Israel Folsom, already several times quoted.

Mesmerism was known among them, though they regarded it with wonder and dread, and it was looked upon as injurious and hurtful in its results; while those who practiced this curious art had often to pay very dearly for it, for they were frequently put to death. Ventriloquism has also been found among them, and used solely for vain, selfish and evil designs, but to the great danger of the life of the person practicing it, for the Choctaws believe that whatever appears supernatural, is suspicious and likely at any time to be turned to evil purposes.[4]

CHARMS

Charms or fetishes were carried by each Choctaw man, and Cushman says that there was one tribal fetish or medicine, but probably we are to understand a fetish belonging to a town or a local group; otherwise more would have been reported regarding it. Very likely this collective charm was of the same nature as that which a war party carried.[5]

What we have called a charm or fetish Cushman designates a " totem " in the following quotation:

. . . every warrior had his totem; i. e. a little sack filled with various ingredients, the peculiarities of which were a profound secret to all but himself; nor did any Indian ever seek or desire to know the contents of another's totem, it was sacred to its possessor alone. I have more than once asked some particular warrior friend concerning the contents of his totem but was promptly refused with the reply: " You would not be any the wiser thereby." Every warrior kept his Totem or " Medicine " about his person, by which he sincerely believed he would be enabled to secure the aid of the Good Spirit in warding off the evil designs of the Evil Spirit, in the existence of which they as sincerely believed, and to whom they attributed the cause of all their misfortunes, when failing to secure the aid of the Good Spirit.[6]

PNEUMATOLOGY

The narrative by Alfred Wright is again our best guide to an understanding of prehistoric Choctaw beliefs regarding the soul. He says:

The present generation of Choctaws believe that the soul, which they call *shilup*, survives the body; but they do not appear to think that its condition

[3] See p. 217.
[4] Cushman, Hist. Inds., p. 368.
[5] See p. 165; Romans, Nat. Hist. E. and W. Fla., pp. 75–76.
[6] Cushman, Hist. Inds., p. 38.

is at all affected by the conduct in this life. They suppose it remains some time about the place where the body is buried. After that, it goes off, but whether it then perishes, or what becomes of it, they say they do not know, nor do they manifest any concern to know. In former times, however, they believed that there was another state of existence, to which the soul went at death. They supposed, that somewhere in the earth there was a delightful land, not unlike the Elysium of the ancients, which they call *shilup i yokni* [shilup i"yakni], the land of ghosts. To this land of delight, ever warm, ever illumined by the beams of a vernal sun, and ever spontaneously pouring forth its varied productions in rich profusion, the soul went as soon as released from the body. Death was a transition from one state to another; the throwing off or shedding of the external covering of the shilup, as the snake sheds his skin. So the shilup having cast off its envelop, and left its imperfections behind, retaining the human shape, entered this land of happiness. When it arrived there, it experienced no more the sorrows and vicissitudes of life. The aged exchanged the grey head and the decrepitude of old age for the beauty, vigor, and sprightliness of youth. The young were confirmed in a state of perpetual youth, nor knew nor feared the encroachments of time. Here they regaled themselves with melons and other delicious fruits, and feasted on the spontaneous productions of the earth. Here was a continued succession of dancing, games, and plays, and thus their time glided sweetly away in one continued scene of festivity and mirth. To enter this land of delight, no spiritual qualifications, no purification of the heart, no amendment of the life, was necessary, and none were excluded from a participation of its pleasures, except those who had committed murder of the most aggravated kind. All others, however polluted and debased, found pleasures suited to their taste and capacity.

Close upon the borders of this happy land, and within sight of it, was the place to which ghosts of murderers went at death. By some uncontrollable destiny, they were unable to find the bright path, which led to the land of the blessed, but were compelled to take another road, that conducted them to the place of their destination. Here, though in view of the happy land, they had no share in its pleasures and enjoyments. Not being permitted to have a participation in those enjoyments they were supposed of course to be unhappy. Some, in speaking of their condition, have imagined, that being a prey to their ungovernable passions, they must necessarily be extremely miserable. An old man, in describing their condition, used the expression, *atuklant illi*, which signifies *the second death;* but though he said their ancestors used that word, and believed that such died the second death, yet he could not tell what was intended by the expression. The misery which the ghosts of murderers thus endured, was not considered as a punishment inflicted by a righteous ruler and judge; nor was the happiness enjoyed by those who reached the good land, a reward of their obedience. They were rather considered as matters of course, taking place in the order of nature, without the interposition of a superior power.

It was their ancient belief, that every man had *shilombish*, the outside shadow, which always followed him, and *shilup*, the inside shadow, or ghost, which at death goes to the land of ghosts. The shilombish was supposed to remain upon the earth, and wander restless about its former habitation, and often, especially at night, by its pitiful moans, so to affrighten its surviving friends, as to make them forsake the spot, and seek another abode. It is also supposed frequently to assume the form of a fox, or owl; and, by barking like the one, and screeching like the other at night, causes great consternation, for the cry is ominous of ill. They distinguish between its note and that of the animals it imitates, in this way. When a fox barks, or an owl screeches, another fox or owl replies. But when the shilombish imitates the sound of either animal, no response is given.

The knowledge of this distinction between the outside and inside shadow, appears in a measure lost by the present generation. And I hear none but aged men speak of the land of ghosts, or of the departed ghost going to this land after death. The present generation seem to suppose that the shilup wanders about some time, and then disappears. The Choctaws have many superstitious fears with respect to ghosts. To see a ghost, is regarded as a certain precursor of death. When a sick person sees one, he despairs at once of recovery, and his doctor ceases to make any further effort for his restoration. Moreover it is customary for the doctor, when he sees his patient will die, in order to save his own reputation to give out that he has seen a ghost, and therefore his recovery is impossible. To dream of seeing a ghost is also ominous of sickness and death, and many pine away with tormenting anxiety, in the fearful looking for death as the inevitable consequence of such dreams. The nightmare is supposed to be occasioned by some restless shilup having come for the person subject to it, and it is believed that the only way to give relief, is to frighten him away by some kind of incantation.[7]

In the main this is undoubtedly a correct statement of ancient Choctaw pneumatology, and it is confirmed in certain of its details by other writers. The association of the ghost with foxes makes clear the following incident in the Choctaw expedition of the French officer De Lusser in the year 1730. He says:

At midnight [Jan. 31] I was awakened by three or four gunshots that were fired near me. I asked what was the matter. The chief [of the Yowanis] replied that it was on account of the barking of foxes which was a bad omen; that that usually happened when one of the band was going to die, and that it was well to fire guns in order to drive them away.[8]

Simpson Tubby said regarding this that they used to be afraid of the howling of a fox until they learned that it was merely caused by the fact that the male and female had gotten separated and they were howling for each other.

The anonymous French Relation informs us that food and drink, a change of shoes, a gun, powder, and balls were placed with a corpse because—

"They say that . . . he is going to another country, and it is right that he have everything he needs in his journey. They believe that the warriors go to make war in the other world, and that everyone there performs the same acts that he did in this."[9] "They say that . . . ghosts (or apparitions) are of people who are dead and have not been given certain effects on dying of which they had need in the other world—as those who are drowned or killed in war— and which they come back to seek."[10]

[7] The Missionary Herald, 1828, pp. 182–183. Byington defines shilombish as "the shadow of a creature, an animal, or a man; the soul, the spirit, a ghost, a shade, a spectre, a sprite." He defines shilup as "a ghost, a spirit, a sprite, an apparition, a fantasm, the painting or picture of a man, manes, a phantom, a shade, a spectre."
[8] Ms. in French Archives.
[9] Appendix, p. 251; Mem. Am. Anthrop. Assn., vol. v, No. 2, pp. 64–65.
[10] Appendix, p. 255; Mem. Am. Anthrop. Assn., v., No. 2, p. 69.

54564—31——15

Simpson Tubby said that he had heard fires used to be lighted where a person had been killed and he thought this might be in order to keep the ghost of another person away.

Almost all of our other informants treat of the two regions of the dead as if they were constituted on the basis of rewards and punishments in a more general sense than Wright indicates, thus Europeanizing what seems to have been the older view. Catlin quotes Peter Pinchlin [Pitchlynn] on this subject as follows:

Our people all believe that the spirit lives in a future state—that it has a great distance to travel after death towards the West—that it has to cross a dreadful deep and rapid stream, which is hemmed in on both sides by high and rugged hills—over this stream, from hill to hill, there lies a long and slippery pine-log, with the bark peeled off, over which the dead have to pass to the delightful hunting-grounds. On the other side of the stream there are six persons of the good hunting-grounds, with rocks in their hands, which they throw at them all when they are in the middle of the log. The good walk on safely, to the good hunting-grounds, where there is one continual day—where the trees are always green—where the sky has no clouds—where there are continual fine and cooling breezes—where there is one continual scene of feasting, dancing, and rejoicing—where there is no pain or trouble, and people never grow old, but for ever live young and enjoy the youthful pleasures.

The wicked see the stones coming, and try to dodge, by which they fall from the log, and go down thousands of feet to the water which is dashing over the rocks, and is stinking with dead fish, and animals, where they are carried around and brought continually back to the same place in whirlpools—where the trees are all dead, and the waters are full of toads and lizards, and snakes—where the dead are always hungry, and have nothing to eat—are always sick, and never die—where the sun never shines, and where the wicked are continually climbing up by thousands on the sides of a high rock from which they can overlook the beautiful country of the good hunting-grounds, the place of the happy, but never can reach it.[11]

Rewards and retributions appear again in the accounts given by Cushman:

Their opinions concerning the departure of the spirit at death were various. Some believed that it lingered for a time near those earthly precincts which it had just left, and it continued still to be, in a certain manner, akin to the earth. For this reason, provisions were placed at the feet of the corpse during the time it lay on its elevated scaffold, exposed to the influence of light or air. The deceased had not as yet entered into the realm of spirits; but when the flesh had withered away from the bones, these were buried with songs and cries, terminating in feasts and dances peculiar to the ceremonies of disposing of the dead. Others believe that when the spirit leaves the body, it lingers for some time before it can be wholly separated from its former conditions; after which it wanders off traversing vast plains in the moonlight. At length, it arrives at a great chasm in the earth, on the other side of which is the land of the blessed, where there is eternal spring and hunting grounds supplied with great varieties of game. But there is no other way of crossing this fearful gulf but by means of a barked pine log that

---

[11] Catlin, N. A. Inds., vol. 2, pp. 145–146.

lies across the chasm, which is round, smooth and slippery. Over this the disembodied spirits must pass if they would reach the land of a blissful immortality. Such as have lived purely and honestly upon earth are enabled to pass safely over the terrific abyss on the narrow bridge to the land of eternal happiness. But such as have lived wickedly, in their attempt to pass over on the log, are sure to lose their footing and fall into the mighty abyss yawning below.[12]

Farther on he elaborates on the subject of the foot log, which has now turned from a pine into a sweet gum:

They also believed that the spirits of the dead . . . had to cross a fearful river which stretched its swirling waters athwart their way; that this foaming stream has but one crossing, at which a cleanly peeled sweet-gum log, perfectly round, smooth and slippery, reached from bank to bank; that the moment the spirit arrives at the log, it is attacked by two other spirits whose business is to keep any and all spirits from crossing thereon. But if a spirit is that of a good person, the guardians of the log have no power over it, and it safely walks over the log to the opposite shore, where it is welcomed by other spirits of friends gone before, and where contentment and happiness will forever be the lot of all.

But alas, when the spirit of a bad person arrives at the log-crossing of the fearful river, it also is assailed by the ever wakeful guards, and as it attempts to walk the slippery log they push it off into the surging waters below, to be helplessly borne down by the current to a cold and barren desert, where but little game abounds and over which he is doomed to wander, a forlorn hope, naked, cold and hungry.[13]

Folsom's testimony, quoted by Cushman, is naturally about the same:

In common with the believers of the Scriptures, they held the doctrine of future rewards and punishments. They differed from them, however, as to the location of heaven and their views of happiness and misery. Heaven, or the happy hunting grounds, in their imagination, was similar to the Elysian fields of the heathen mythology. There the spirits of those who had been virtuous, honest and truthful, while on earth, enjoyed, in common with youthful angels, all manner of games and voluptuous pleasures, with no care, no sorrow, nothing but one eternal round of enjoyment. They believed that angels or spirits seldom visited the earth, and cared but very little about doing so, as being supplied in heaven with everything suitable to their wants, nothing was required from the earth. According to their notion, heaven was located in the southwestern horizon, and spirits, instead of ascending, according to the Christian idea, sped their last journey in a line directly above the surface of the earth in the direction of the southwest horizon. Previous to a spirit's admission into the happy hunting ground, it was examined by the attendant angel at the gate, who consigned it to heaven or hell according to its deeds on earth. Their hell, or place of punishment, as they termed it, was the reverse of the happy hunting ground—a land full of briers, thorns, and every description of prickly plants, which could inflict deep cuts, causing intense pain from which there was no escape; onward they must go—

<hr>

[12] Cushman, Hist. Inds., pp. 31–32.   [13] Ibid., pp. 226–227.

no healing oil for their wounds—nothing but an eternity of pain—no games— no voluptuous pleasures—nothing save an illimitable land of blasted foliage. . . . Previous to a spirit winging its flight to the happy hunting ground, or the land of briers and blasted foliage, it was supposed to hover around the place where its tabernacle lay for several days—four at least. They believed that the happy hunting ground was at a distance of many days journey.[14]

Hence the provisions placed near the grave, the animals killed, the fire kindled there, and the mourning ceremonies as given elsewhere.

Cushman explains aversion to hanging on the ground that the spirit of the person disposed of in this manner would continue to haunt the place,[15] and he informs us that, as was supposed by the Chickasaw and Creeks, " the spirit of the murdered Indian could never take its flight from earth, or find rest anywhere in the eternal unknown, until blood had atoned for blood."[16] Lincecum implies that it was thought the spirits of the dead would resent any indignity offered to their bones,[17] and, like the other southern tribes, the Choctaw believed that the names of the dead should not be uttered.[18]

From the Choctaw of Bayou Lacomb Bushnell obtained the following notes, which in some respects agree remarkably with Wright's statements:

Persons dying by violent deaths involving loss of blood, even a few drops, do not pass to the home of Aba (heaven), regardless of the character of their earthly lives, or their rank in the tribe. . . .

The spirits of all persons not meeting violent deaths, with the exception of those only who murder or attempt to murder their fellow Choctaw, go to the home of Aba. There it is always spring, with sunshine and flowers; there are birds and fruits and game in abundance. There the Choctaw ever sing and dance, and trouble is not known. All who enter this paradise become equally virtuous without regard to their state while on earth.

The unhappy spirits who fail to reach the home of Aba remain on earth in the vicinity of the places where they have died. But Nanapolo [Nan okpulo], the bad spirit, is never able to gain possession of the spirit of a Choctaw.[19]

Thus our latest authority agrees with the one first quoted and neither says anything about the peeled log. Does this mean that there were two different sets of ideas regarding the fate of souls? That souls of the good went to live with the sky spirit was also the belief of the Chickasaw and Creeks, and probably also of the Siouan tribes farther east. That death by violence condemns one to the region of unfortunate souls as well as infliction of death on others is an idea wholly Indian. The immunity of the Choctaw from harm by the evil spirit is evidently a local or, perhaps, rather a personal opinion.

[14] Cushman, Hist. Inds., pp. 362–363.
[15] See p. 108.
[16] Cushman, Hist. Inds., p. 265.
[17] See p. 14.
[18] See pp. 14, 120–121.
[19] Bushnell, Bull. 48, Bur. Amer. Ethn., pp. 28–29.

CEREMONIALS AND DANCES

Every Choctaw town of any size had an open place or square with cabins about it constructed like those in the Creek towns. Councils and ceremonies were held here but we know extraordinarily little about these latter. Our principal French authority states that they held the most of their feasts when the corn was green, by which he means ripe but tender, while in the legends reference is made to a dance held just before clearing the cornfields for planting and a " green corn " or harvest festival lasting five days.[20] But in the absence of details these stray notes mean little or nothing. Some modern Indians assert that the Choctaw formerly had Pishofa dances similar to those of the Chickasaw, but others deny it. The fact seems to be that they had gatherings at times, accompanied by feasts and dances, in the interest of some sick person, but that they were not identical with the ceremonies of the Chickasaw. We seem to gain the impression that the Choctaw were decidedly less given to ceremonialism than almost all the other tribes of the Southeast, and this is confirmed by Wright:

At the time of their formation from the earth, their Maker prescribed no form of worship, nor did he require any homage to be paid him. Nor did he then, or at any subsequent period, make any revelation of his will for the regulation of their conduct. And I cannot think that they ever offered sacrifices, or had any form of public worship, or practiced any of those ceremonies which are common among other tribes, and which are supposed to favor the belief that the Aborigines of this country are the descendants of the lost house of Israel. They state, that they have heard of what is termed the *green corn dance* among the Creeks, but deny having any knowledge that such a practice ever existed among themselves.[21] In some of their dances, they make use of the word *hallelujah*, something in the manner mentioned by Dr. Boudinot, but they aver that is not one of their native songs, and that it was not known in ancient times. It was introduced among them from the Chickasaws, who learned it from the northern Indians.[22]

But what they lacked in ceremonialism they seem to have made up for in social dances and feasts. Bartram says, speaking of the Creeks, " Some of their most favourite songs and dances, they have from their enemies, the Chactaws; for it seems these people are very eminent for poetry and music." [23] The French Relation has the following regarding these:

They have dances among them accompanied by feasts, which are almost alike. Only the names differ; as the dance of the turkey, bison, bear, alligator. In this last they have masks made like the head of this animal, one or

---

[20] Mem. Am. Anthrop. Assn., vol. v, No. 2, p. 58; see p. 247. Consult also the references to ceremonials in Lincecum's version of the migration legend, p. 20.
[21] But see pp. 18–21 and 225–226.
[22] The Missionary Herald, 1828, p. 180.
[23] Bartram, Wm., Travels, pp. 503–504.

two disguising themselves thus, while five or six others take masks of different animals which the alligator commonly eats, and then they make a thousand grotesque antics. [Others are] the dance of the bustard, of the small corn, the war dance, and the dance of the young people, which is danced no longer, the French having made them conceive too great horror for it. When they have these dances, they begin about two hours after midday. They are painted; they put on their finest clothing, and make a belt of about forty pot-metal bells as big as the fist. Others put on little bells, and if they have big bells, and are able to carry them, they take them to these dances, loving the noise extraordinarily. They carry a rattle (chichiquoüa) in the hand, or a war club, or a pistol. They dance around a drummer who has in his hand only one drumstick, with which he strikes a deerskin stretched over an earthen pot or over a kettle. They accompany this sort of noise with a song of five or six words which they repeat continually. These dances last until day, or until they go to sleep.[24]

Folsom remarks:

They had various kinds of dances as well as other people, many of which were, however, insignificant and do not deserve a notice here; but there were others which were considered important and national, such as the ball-play dance, the war-dance, eagle-dance, and scalp-dance, all of which seem to have been the result of rude and savage ideas.[25]

Catlin was very much struck by the eagle dance, of which he made a sketch (pl. 6) and has also left us a description. It was, he says,

. . . a very pretty scene, which was got up by their young men, in honour of that bird, for which they seem to have a religious regard. This picturesque dance was given by twelve or sixteen men, whose bodies were chiefly naked and painted white, with white clay, and each one holding in his hand the tail of the eagle, while his head was also decorated with an eagle's quill. Spears were stuck in the ground, around which the dance was performed by four men at a time, who had simultaneously, at the beat of the drum, jumped up from the ground where they had all sat in rows of four, one row immediately behind the other, and ready to take the place of the first four when they left the ground fatigued, which they did by hopping or jumping around behind the rest, and taking their seats, ready to come up again in their turn, after each of the other sets had been through the same forms.

In this dance, the steps or rather jumps, were different from anything I had ever witnessed before, as the dancers were squat down, with their bodies almost to the ground, in a severe and most difficult posture, as will have been seen in the drawing.[26]

The longest account of the Choctaw dances is that given by Bushnell in his study of the Choctaw of Bayou Lacomb. He says that this band had "one dance ceremony, which is in reality a series of seven distinct dances, performed in rotation, and always in the same order." These were, in the ritual order, the Man Dance, Tick Dance, Drunken-man Dance, Going-against-each-other Dance, Duck Dance, Dance Go-and-come, and Snake Dance. For descriptions of these the reader is referred to Mr. Bushnell's paper.[27] He adds:

---

[24] Appendix, pp. 254–225; Mem. Am. Anthrop. Assn., vol. v, No. 2, pp. 68–69.
[25] Cushman, Hist. Inds., p. 368.
[26] Catlin, N. Am. Inds., pp. 144–145.
[27] Bull. 48, Bur. Amer. Ethn., pp. 20–22.

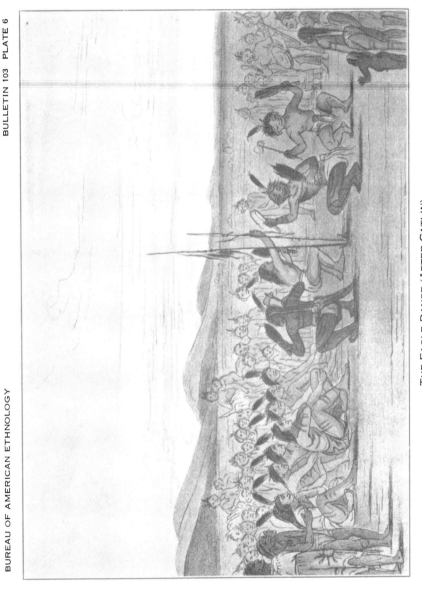

THE EAGLE DANCE (AFTER CATLIN)

" The Bayou Lacomb Choctaw always danced at night, never during the daylight hours, the snake dance, the last of the seven ending at dawn.[28] This agrees with the statement made by Bossu just one and a half centuries ago that ' nearly all the gatherings of the Chactas take place at night.' "[29]

From information furnished by a white man in Mississippi who had lived near the Choctaw it is evident that their dances were similar to those among the Chickasaw and Creeks, and one of these bore the same name as a corresponding Creek dance, the Iskitini hiła or " horned owl dance." These dances were accompanied by feasts to which the men contributed game and the women bread. He said that, like the Chickasaw, they did not dance about a fire, though there were fires near by to furnish light. Sometimes the men would dance by themselves for a while and when they got tired the women would take their places.

Cushman contributes the following observations regarding Choctaw music and dancing:

The ancient Choctaws were as susceptible to all the pleasing emotions produced by the sweet concords of sound as any other people, yet their musical genius, in the invention of musical instruments, never extended beyond that of a cane flute and a small drum, which was constructed from a section cut from a small hollow tree, over the hollow part of which was stretched a fresh deer skin, cleansed from the hair, which became very tight when dried; and when struck by a stick made a dull sound, little inferior to that of our common snare-drum; which could be heard at a considerable distance; and though uncouth in appearance, and inharmonious in tone, as all drums, still its " voice " was considered an indispensable adjunct as an accompaniment to all their national and religious ceremonies; even as the ear-splitting discords of the civilized snare or kettle-drum, united with the deafening roar of the base drum are considered by the white man as indispensable in all his displays of harmony. Yet the ancient Choctaw, in all his solemn ceremonies, as well as amusements and merry-makings, did not depend so much upon the jarring tones of the diminutive drum as he did upon his own voice; which in concert with the monotonous tones of the drum,—to the cultivated and sensitive ear a mere jargon of sound,—was to the Indian ear the most exciting music, and soon wrought him to the highest state of excitement. In all their dances they invariably danced to the sound of the indispensable drum, accompanied with the low hum of the drummer, keeping exact step with its monotonous tone. In the social dance alone were the women permitted to participate.[30]

The Lacomb Choctaw did not use a rattle. Their drum Bushnell describes in the following words:

This [example described by the writer] is 30 inches in height and 15 inches in diameter. It is made of a section of a black gum tree; the cylinder wall is less than 2 inches in thickness. The head consists of a piece of untanned goat skin. The skin is stretched over the open end, while wet and pliable, and is

[28] Bull. 48, Bur. Amer. Ethn., p. 22.
[29] Appendix, p. 263 ; Bossu, Nouv, Voy., II, p. 104.
[30] Cushman, Hist. Inds., p. 215.

passed around a hoop made of hickory about half an inch thick. A similar hoop is placed above the first. To the second hoop are attached four narrow strips of rawhide, each of which is fastened to a peg passing diagonally through the wall of the drum. To tighten the head of the drum it is necessary merely to drive the peg farther in. In this respect, as well as in general form, the drum resembles a specimen from Virginia in the British Museum, as well as the drum even now used on the west coast of Africa. It is not possible to say whether this instrument is a purely American form or whether it shows the influence of the negro.[31]

Cypress knees were also commonly used for the body of the drum. The opening was usually closed with a deerskin but a bearskin is said to have been employed at times.

Simpson Tubby's description of the drum agrees quite closely with that given by Bushnell. He said it was made of a section of black gum or tupelo gum, hollowed out and 12 or 16 inches across, and of about the same length. Over the ends of this deerskins were fitted, each skin being first brought over the outside of a hoop or " cuff " and fastened tight, the cuff being just large enough to fit over the end of the body. After these had been put in place, a larger cuff was made and fitted tight over each and the two outside cuffs were fastened together by means of diagonal cords. Midway of the drum were two other cuffs or hoops fastened to the diagonal cords in such a way that when they were pushed in opposite directions they tightened the heads of the drum. The cuffs were made of white switch hickory, the cords anciently of deer hide, but later of store leather. Two deer-hide strings were allowed to lie across the end of the drum opposite that which was struck. One of these was looser than the other, so that two distinct notes resulted.

Drum sticks were made principally of maple, poplar, or ash. Each had a knob at the end, one made smaller to " beat the seconds," while most of the noise was made with the other. They beat on the end of the drum opposite that across which the strings lay but most of the noise is supposed to have been made by the other end, the compressed air transferring the vibrations across. If they wished to protect the drumhead they wrapped the knobs of the drumsticks with cloth.

It is claimed that no rattle was used except that in the snake dance two sticks were struck against each other. In this dance they gradually spiraled in to the center in the way in which a rattlesnake makes its coils, stopped a minute, and then unwound.

Simpson informed me that feasts were held from time to time throughout the year but that the most important ones were in the fall and early winter, and they were accompanied by ball games and dances. The last feast of the year was near the present Christmas when the Choctaw were summoned from all quarters. It is not clear

[31] Bull. 48, Bur. Amer. Ethn., p. 22.

whether the importance of this feast was due wholly to white influence. Christmas is called in the Choctaw language Nafa iklánna, " middle of winter." In preparation for a feast, when venison was relied upon, hunters were appointed, to each of whom a territory was assigned and he was directed to return in plenty of time so that the cooking could be gotten out of the way and the young people could dance. One of the principal dishes was composed of beef or venison and corn cooked together in the manner elsewhere described.[31a] It was cooked in large pots, of which there might be from three to five on the fire at a time. When the food was ready to serve, certain men appointed for the purpose lifted these pots from the fire and set them down on a table made of split pine logs. Other men then served into each man's plate what was allotted to him, and still others poured out the coffee or tea. Men were also appointed to fan the meat continuously to keep the flies away. However, it is claimed that if it was hung up above a certain height the flies would not bother it.

The band captain now called out the name of each family in turn and the members of it then marched up to the table and seated themselves. In olden times, and occasionally even now, the men ate before the women and children; later men and women sat on opposite sides of the table. If the feast included all of the five bands, the captains called them beginning with that farthest off. While they were eating they preserved perfect order and the captains addressed them all that time. The principal speaker, captain, or head chief, did not eat until after the other men, but before the women and children. After all had had enough, the head chief would call them to order again and make a speech in which he recounted the facts regarding their race and told them what they ought to do and what they should refrain from doing. Every time he made a point they cheered him. When he was through one of the band chiefs addressed both men and women about the dances that were to take place that night, laying down the regulations in accordance with which they were to be conducted. Relatives were not permitted to dance together. No girl was allowed to dance with a boy unless the parents on both sides agreed to it. " Everything was much more harmonious then than now."

He added the following information regarding the green corn dance. This was held in summer, probably in August, and during it laws were made for the ensuing year. They then took time to ferret out the relationship between every two families in order to regulate the marriages properly. The dance lasted three days. As many hunters were told off by the captains and chief as were needed to supply a definite amount of game. The head chief himself

---

[31a] See p. 48.

seldom attended in person but he could easily be reached at the big mound where he commonly stayed, "like the queen of a beehive." It was at the last green corn dance held by the Sukanatcha band, as noted elsewhere, that women are said to have been relieved of the burden of carrying hampers of corn on their backs. The feast proper is said to have been on the last day and while the others were eating the captain spoke to them at length, advising them as to their dealings with one another. He ate last and others then spoke to him and praised him in turn.

MEN HAVING OCCULT POWERS AND DOCTORS

Choctaw who made it their business to deal with the occult belonged to several different classes. We have quoted Claiborne's remarks with reference to "a priestly order" called Oon-ka-la, who had the care of a kind of temple called "the House of Warriors" (Tàshka Tcuka), on the bank of Cushtusha Creek, Neshoba County, Miss., and said to mark the oldest settlement in the Nation. The bones of great warriors were buried there, the Oon-ka-la going at the head of the procession which bore them "chanting hymns in an unknown tongue." I have already noted the apparent confusion between this "temple" and that of the Natchez, and I am suspicious of the information here given, for no one else seems to have been fortunate enough to learn of a similar priesthood, and the word Oon-ka-la does not seem to tally with any known to the Choctaw to-day. Still it has in its favor the fact that Kashtasha was the chief town of the western division of Choctaw, the Oklafalaya.

The Choctaws [says Cushman][32] had several classes of dignitaries among them who were held in the highest reverence: The Medicine Man or Prophet, the Rain Maker, the Doctor.

Folsom, speaking of all classes of doctors, says that they had

As many of the female as of the male sex, who were quite as successful in their practice as the latter. The doctors made use of herbs and roots in various forms, applied and given in different modes—for emetics cathartics, sweats, wounds, and sores; they also made use of cold baths, scarification, cupping and blistered by means of burning punk, and practiced suction to draw out pain; some used enchantment, while others practiced by magic, pretending to have learned the art of healing . . . by special revelation, communicated to them in some retired and unfrequented forest. It was in this way, also, it was said, that the war-prophets were raised up to lead the people to battle. At a high price and much expense the doctors of both sexes learned the mode and manner of the use of herbs and roots. It is a fact worthy of remark, that even now many of them are in possession of some useful and important means of cure. They have, among other things, an effectual remedy for the bite of the rattle-snake, or of any other venomous reptile, the bite of which they consider very easy of cure.[33]

---

[32] Cushman, Hist. Inds., p. 258.   [33] Ibid., pp. 367–368.

The reference to a " special revelation " in the forests suggests the schools of training for doctors among the Creeks,[34] and their existence among the Choctaw seems further indicated by a passage in Cushman.

There was but little difference between the " Indian Magician " and the Indian " Medicine Man," but when a warrior had attained to that high and greatly desired point of communication with the Great and Good Spirit, and had impressed that belief upon his tribe as well as himself, he at once became an object of great veneration, and was henceforth regarded by all his tribe, regardless of age or sex, as a great " Medicine Man," upon whom had been conferred supernatural powers, to foretell coming events, to exorcise evil spirits, and to perform all kinds of marvellous works. But few attained the coveted eminence; yet he who was so fortunate, at once reached the pinnacle of his earthly aspirations. But before entering upon his high and responsible duties, and assuming the authority of a diviner—a graduated Medicine Man, in other words, with a recognized and accepted diploma,—he must have enlisted in his service one or more lesser spirits, servants of the Great and Good Spirit, as his allies or mediators, and to secure these important and indispensable auxiliaries, he must subject himself to a severe and testing ordeal. He now retires alone into the deep solitudes of his native forest and there engages in meditation, self examination, fasting and prayer during the coming and going of many long and weary days, and even weeks. And all that for what end? That he might, by his supernatural power thus attained, be enabled to gratify his ambition in playing the tyrant over his people through fear of him? Or that he might be enabled the better to gratify the spirit of avarice that rankled in his heart? Neither, for both tyrant and avarice were utterly unknown among all Indians [?].

What then? First, that he might ever be enabled, by his influence attained with the Great and Good Spirit, to ward off the shafts of the Evil Spirit, and thus protect himself from seen and unseen dangers, and also be successful in the accomplishment of all his earthly hopes and wishes.

Second. That he might be a benefactor to his tribe, by being enabled to divine future events, and thus forewarn them of approaching danger and the proper steps to take to avoid it successfully; also to heal the sick, etc. True, the fearful ordeal of hunger, thirst, fatigue wrought their part in causing his imagination to usurp the place of reason, filling his fevered mind with the wildest hallucinations and rendering him a fit subject to believe anything and everything. Yet, no doubt, when he left his place of prayer and self-examination and returned to his people, he sincerely believed that he had been admitted to the special favor of the great and Good Spirit and was fully prepared to exercise his newly acquired supernatural attainments for his own benefit and to the interest of his tribe.[35]

Cushman thus enumerates the attainments of the medicine man as distinguished from those of the mere physic doctor.

" The Medicine Man," was a dignitary who swayed his scepter alike among all Indians, but was altogether a very different personage from the common physician. The Medicine Man professed an insight into the hidden laws of Nature; he professed a power over the elements, the fish of the waters and the animals of the land; he could cause the fish to suffer themselves to be caught

---

[34] See Forty-second Ann. Rept. Bur. Amer. Ethn., pp. 617–620.
[35] Cushman, Hist. Inds., pp. 38–39.

voluntarily, and give success to the hunter by depriving the denizens of the forest of their natural fear of man; he could impart bravery to the heart of the warrior, strength and skill to his arm and fleetness to his feet; yea, could put to flight the evil spirits of disease from the bodies of the sick. He could throw a spell or charm over a ball player that would disenable him to hit the post; or over the ball-post that would prevent its being hit by anyone whom he wished to defeat. Such were the professed attainments of the Indian "Medicine Man." But whether he possessed all or any of the supernatural powers, he professed one thing, the power, art, skill, call it what you may, to make his people believe it, and that was all-sufficient for him—even as it is with all humbugs.[56]

It is this type of doctor which the author of the French Relation seems to have in mind in the following paragraphs:

These persons have much to fear when they undertake the case of a sick person who is a chief, for if he dies after they have conjured, his relatives say that he has bewitched him, and if he escapes after he has been condemned to death, they say that he had bewitched him and that fate has erred; so in all ways he runs the risk of being killed. When there is a sick person among them they have the doctor come to the place where he is, who, after having conjured or demanded of their Spirit if the sick person will get well, bleeds him with a piece of flint. Eight or ten incisions are made in the skin in the space of the size of a crown (écu), as when one cups, over which they place one end of a pierced horn and suck it until the horn is full of blood. As these jugglers sometimes wish to hide their ignorance they say that someone has thrown a spell over them (the patients) and then they adroitly put some bison wool or a little piece of wood into the bottom of the horn, and after having sucked the sick man and poured out the blood which is in the horn, they show this wood or bison wool to the parents of the sick man, which they make them believe is a charm; then this juggler passes as a very wise man.

It is certain that these jugglers speak to the devil. I have seen a number of examples of it. I will cite three to you. One day, arriving May third at the house of a man named Fine Teeth, chief of the Naniabas, returning from the Chicachas and being in need of tobacco, I asked some of this chief, who, in order to give me some, hunted in his chest, where he had placed three twists, but could not find them. He thought it was I or some one of the French whom I had with me who had hidden it from him, but when he had learned that it was not, I saw him dress and daub himself as if he were going to a dance, after which, having gone to an open space a gunshot distant from the house, we saw him fill his pipe, strike the flint, light it, and smoke it with many gesticulations, as if he were disputing with someone. When he had smoked it half up it seemed to us that he gave it to someone else to smoke, without, however, our seeing anyone, except that he held his pipe at a distance from himself, and the smoke came out in puffs (peletons) as if someone smoked it. He returned to us immediately and told us, all of a sweat, that he knew who had taken it, and continuing on toward a cabin opposite his own, whither I followed him, he sprang at the throat of a savage, demanding of him the three twists of tobacco which he had taken from him at such an hour in such a manner, in short explaining to him the method which he had employed in accomplishing his theft. The poor savage, all of a tremble, admitted his crime and returned to him his tobacco.

The French, curious regarding his skill, went to find him, and begged him, under promise of recompense, to make the otter dance for them. He took

[56] Cushman, Hist. Inds., pp. 230–231

his tobacco-pouch which was an otter skin in which he kept his pipe and tobacco, which he threw into the middle of an open place where the people were assembled to judge of his skill: after he had uttered a number of obscurely articulated words and thrown himself repeatedly into the fire, from which he came out in a perspiration, and without being burned, this skin was seen to swell out, fill with flesh, and come to life, and to run between the legs of the Frenchmen, some of whom in the company having caressed it and felt of it, found that it was like a true otter. When each one was satisfied it returned to the same place where it had come to life and was seen to diminish in size and return to the form which it had before.

When we were surrounded by the Spaniards in Dauphin Island, and were expecting help from France from day to day, we wished to know whether it was on the point of arriving, which could only be known by means of the savages whom we had with us. They were then made to conjure, and having done this they reported that five vessels would come the next day, three of which were large and two smaller, that they were loaded with soldiers, that one of the little ones would not arrive as soon as the others, because it was separated and was still a long way off, but that all would have arrived the day after that toward evening. This actually took place, for the next day at eight in the morning the first vessel was discovered, and about three or four in the afternoon four were anchored at Dauphin Island, but the fifth did not come in until the day following.[37]

In this quotation we seem to find the practices of the common physician and the performances of Cushman's " Medicine Man or Prophet " somewhat mixed up, but other writers confuse them also, including Bossu and Cushman himself. Bossu, however, dwells most upon the medical side.

The savages generally have a great deal of regard for their medicine men or diviners, perfect charlatans who impose on the common fool so that they may live comfortably at his expense. They also have considerable authority and are turned to for advice on all sorts of occasions as if they were oracles. When a Chacta is sick, he gives all that he has to be treated, but if the sick man dies, his relatives attribute his death to the doctor and not to the condition of the patient. Consequently they kill the doctor if they feel so inclined, but this happens seldom because there is always a back door. Besides, these doctors are acquainted with many plants good to cure the maladies to which one is exposed in this country. They can heal with certainty the bites of rattlesnakes and other poisonous animals.

When savages have been wounded by a bullet or arrows, the jugglers or doctors begin by sucking the patient's wound and spitting out the blood, which is called in France *guérir du secret*. In their dressings they do not make use of lint or of pledgets, but of a powdered root which they blow into the wound to make it suppurate and another which makes it dry up and close. They clear the wounds of gangrene (*cangrène*) by bathing them in a decoction of certain roots with which they are acquainted.[38]

The material side is also principally in evidence in the following from Cushman:

The Choctaws' Materia Medica, like [that of] all their race, was Nature, herbs, and roots furnishing their remedies both externally and internally; and

---

[37] Appendix, pp. 249–251; Mem. Am. Anth. Assn., vol. v, No. 2, pp. 61–63.
[38] Appendix, pp. 260–261; Bossu, Nouv. Voy., vol. 2, pp. 96–98.

the success with which they used those remedies proved their knowledge of the healing properties of the various herbs and roots in which their extensive forests abounded. They had a specific for the bite of the sintullo[39] (rattle-snake). Their doctors relied much on dry-cupping, using their mouth alone in all such cases. Oft have I witnessed the Choctaw physician, east of the Mississippi river, administering to the necessities of his suffering patient through the virtues found in the process of dry-cupping. Stretching the sufferer upon a blanket spread upon the ground, he kneeled beside him and began a process of sucking that part of the body of which the patient complained, or where, in his own judgment, the disease was located, making a guttural noise during the operation that reminded one of [a] dog worrying an opossum; at different intervals raising his head a few inches and pretending to deposit into his hands, alternately in the one and the other, an invisible something which he had drawn from his patient, by a magic power known alone to himself.

After sucking a sufficient length of time to fill both hands, judging from the frequent deposits therein made, with great apparent dignity and solemn gravity, this worthy son of Esculapius arose and stepping to the nearest tree, post, or fence, wiped the secret contents of his apparently full hands thereon; then with an air of marked importance walked away to the enjoyment of his own reflections, while the sufferer, in real or fancied relief, acknowledged the efficacy of the physician's healing powers by ceasing to complain, turned over and sought forgetfulness in the arms of refreshing sleep. If there ensued a change for the better he claimed the honor and praise as due the noble profession of which he recognized himself a worthy and important member; but if the disease proved stubborn and refused to yield to the medicinal virtues of his herbs, roots, and dry-cupping, he turned to his last resort—the Anuka [or anu^nka], (Hot-house). This edifice, an important adjunct in all Choctaw villages, was made of logs rendered nearly air tight by stopping all cracks with mortar. A little hole was left on one side for an entrance. A fire was built in the center of this narrow enclosure, and soon the temperature within was raised to the desired degree, then the fire was taken out and the patient instructed to crawl in; which being done, the little opening was closed. As a matter of course, the patient must bake or sweat; which, however, resulted in the latter; and when, in the opinion of the Alikchi, (doctor) he had undergone a thorough sweating, the entrance was opened, and the patient bidden to come forth; who, upon his exit, at once runs to the nearest water into which he plunges head first; but if not of sufficient amount and depth for the correct performance of that ceremony to its fullest extent, he ducks his head into it several times, thus making practical the wholesome theory of the hygienist: "Keep your head cool, but your feet warm." In case of common intermittent fever, the efficiency of this mode of proceeding (the sweat and cold bath) was truly astonishing, seldom failing to effect a cure.

But if the patient died—ah, then! with that shrewdness peculiar to all quacks the world over, he readily found a cause upon which to base his excuse for his inefficacy to effect a cure; differing somewhat, however, from his white brother alikchi, who attributes the cause of his failure to innumerable "where-as-es and ifs," while he openly acknowledged and emphatically declared the interposition of a hat-tak holth-kun-na [or hatak holhkunna] (witch), which, counteracting the beneficial virtues of his remedies, had caused the death of his patient by thus placing him beyond the reach of mortal skill, nothing more nor less. Sometimes, for the sake of variety, he attributed the death of his patient, if occurring very suddenly, to an Ish tulbih [isht álbi] (witch

---

[39] Sintullo is probably from sinti hullo, "sacred snake," or "sacred mysterious snake."

ball) shot from an invisible rifle in the hands of a witch. At this important juncture of affairs, it now becomes his duty to find the witch that he, she, or it may be brought to pay the penalty of the law in all such cases—death. As a matter of course, the doctor, not very scrupulous in the matter of shifting the blame from his own shoulders to that of another—so natural to all man kind—easily found a witch in the person of some attenuated old woman, whom he designated as the guilty party, and who consequently was immediately slain by the relatives of the deceased.[40]

A white informant of Byington gives the following account of a native medical attempt that failed:

Doctors and Conjurers . . . are a deceitful set of men. Before they commence their operations they sing a song, which expresses a prayer. One came to me once and said he could cure me of my lameness, originating in palsy in the limbs. I told him if he would cure me I would give him a horse, but if he failed I would give him nothing. To this he agreed. He then inquired where the lameness first commenced. I told him that it began in the soles of my feet. He then examined them, and got down on the floor, spit on them, and sucked the instep a long time as though he would draw something out. After a while he got up, and then made a great effort to get something out of his mouth. At length he took out a small piece of deerskin, as I supposed, and said he had drawn that out of my foot. I asked him where the hole was. He said it never makes a hole. I then took the bit of leather and talked to him and told him that *doctors* are the greatest liars in the world. "You never pulled that out of my foot: you cut it off of some deerskin and put it in your mouth. Now stop telling such lies or some one will injure you." He looked very much ashamed and walked off.[41]

Sweat bathing is described not only by Cushman but also by our anonymous French informant and Bossu. The former says:

For this purpose they make a little cabin about four feet in height and eight in diameter, which they cover with bison skin and blankets. They put inside five or six red-hot balls, on which from time to time they throw a little water to stimulate the heat. They enclose in this little space as many as seven persons, and after they have sweat for about a half or three-quarters of an hour they get out of this hole quickly and go with precipitation to throw themselves into the coldest water.[42]

When, on returning from war or a hunt, they are tired and overcome with fatigue [says Bossu] they restore themselves by sweating in a sudatory.[42a] For this purpose they boil in the sudatory all sorts of medicinal and fragrant herbs, the spirits and salts of which carried off by the steam enter by means of the sick man's lungs and the pores in his body and restore his drooping forces. This treatment is as good to calm and drive away all kinds of pains. Besides, gout, gravel, and other infirmities to which we are subject in Europe are not to be found among them, which may be due in part to their constant physical exercise. One sees among them none with big bellies such as there are in Holland nor those big tumors on the throat called goitre such as are found in Piedmont.[43]

---

[40] Cushman, Hist. Inds., pp. 258–260.
[41] Missionary Herald, vol. xxv, No. 11, November, 1829
[42] Appendix, p. 251; Mem. Am. Anth. Assn., vol. v, No. 2, p. 64.
[42a] "These are round cabins, built in the middle of the village in the form of an oven. These sudatories are cared for by an Alekxi or public doctor."—Bossu.
[43] Appendix, p. 261; Bossu, Nouv. Voy., vol. 2, pp. 98–99.

Mrs. McCurtain, widow of a former chief of the Choctaw Nation in Oklahoma, remembered that when a doctor was treating the sick, he danced, sang, and beat upon a drum, calling sometimes on the four quarters of the earth, the sun and the moon. The neighbors were summoned to witness this and afterwards they had a feast supposed to be for the benefit of the patient. She remembered that for biliousness the medicine used was called " thunder medicine " (hilo'ha ikhin'sh).

Cushman was made personally aware of a native belief that white twins " possessed the magic power of dispelling all depredating worms and insects from cornfields, gardens, etc." This was undoubtedly only one of several peculiar beliefs regarding twins whom primitive people usually credit with having peculiar power for good or evil. In the case above mentioned Mr. Cushman's parents were persuaded to allow the use of himself and his twin brother to secure immunity to the Choctaw gardens from the attacks of corn worms.

At once we galloped off in the direction of their village three miles distant called Okachiloho fah [oka chilofa]. (Water falling, or Falling Water.)[44] When we arrived in sight, their success [in obtaining the use of the twins] was announced by a shrill whoop to which the villagers responded their joy by another. As soon as we rode into the village, we were immediately surrounded by an admiring throng, and being tenderly lifted from our positions on the horses, we were handed over to the care of several old men, who took us in their arms and with much gravity carried us into a little cabin, which had previously been set in order for our reception, where we found prepared a variety of eatables, to us seemingly good enough to excite the appetites of the most fastidious twin epicures; after which the venerable old seers of the village instructed us in the mystic rites and ceremonies of their tribe, preparatory to calling into requisition the magic power of our twinship in all its bearings upon the duties of the day. Then they showed us our weapons, which consisted of iron, wood and fire, the two former in the shape of a frying-pan, in which we were to burn the worms after picking them from the corn, and a blazing chunk of fire, two stout and straight sticks about six feet in length, with the proper instructions in regard to the manner of using them effectually. Having been thoroughly drilled in these preliminaries, the line of march was taken up toward the field where the enemy were said to be strongly entrenched; in profound silence and with unfeigned gravity, the Palokta Tohbi [Polukta tohbi], (Twins White, or White Twins) led the van, borne upon the shoulders of two powerful warriors closely followed by three others bearing the arms, while the villagers, headed by the veteran seers, brought up the rear presenting an imposing appearance with a considerable smack of the ridiculous. . . .

When the field was reached a halt was made, and two venerable looking old men, whose hoary locks and wrinkled faces bespoke their earthly pilgrimage had extended many years beyond their allotted three score years and ten, came to the front and, with solemn mien, lifted us from our perches

---

[44] This name does not appear in my list. It evidently belonged to one of the smaller villages.

and gently placed us over the fence into the field; then handing the frying pan, chunk of fire, and sticks, our weapons, to us, with a word of encouragement whispered in our ears to prove ourselves valiant and worthy of our traditional fame, they bade us charge the foe. The plan of the campaign was to attack the enemy first in the center; there build a hot fire with the dry wood, previously prepared by the thoughtful Choctaws, upon which place the frying pan and into which throw all prisoners without discrimination, as our flag bore the motto "Neither giving nor asking quarter;" and likewise also at the four corners of the field. The centre was gained, the fire made, and upon it placed the pan; then we made a vigorous attack upon the strongholds of the enemy dislodging them and at the same time taking them prisoners of war; then hurrying them to the centre hurled them *hors de combat* into the frying pan heated to a red heat, and with our ready sticks stirred them vigorously, while the wreaths of smoke that ascended from the scene of carnage and floated away before the summer breeze, together with the odor, not as fragrant to the sensitive nose, however, as the lily or the rose, gave undisputed evidence of our victories; while our waiting Choctaw friends, acknowledged their approval from the outside of the field, (since the tradition forbade them sharing in the dangers of the conflict—the Paloktas must fight alone) filling our hearts with heroic emotions unfelt before or afterwards.

After we had immolated two or three panfulls of the enemy at the center and at each corner of the field, nor lost a man, we returned in triumph to our waiting friends, by whom we were received with unfeigned manifestations of affection and pride. Thence we were borne as before to other fields, where were enacted the same prodigies of valor, with similar results until the declining sun gave warning of their promise not being fulfilled if the Paloktas were not returned ere the sun went down. Therefore we were carried from our last field of slaughter back to the village in "glorious triumph," where never were offered to frail mortality more sincere homage and unfeigned devotion than were bestowed upon the Paloktas by those grateful Choctaws. They seemed only to regret not being able to manifest a still greater degree of gratitude, and to do more for us as a manifestation of their appreciation of the great favor we had conferred upon them. With zealous care they watched over us while under their care, that no harm might befall us. As we came so we returned, and safely reached home ere the sun sank behind the western horizon. We were afterwards frequently called upon, much to our gratification and delight, it was fun for us, to bring into requisition our mysteriously delegated power in behalf of their cornfields; and we became the special favorites of that kind-hearted and appreciative people; and woe to him or them who should impose upon or attempt to injure their little pets, the pale-face Paloktas.[45]

The feast for the sick reminds one of those indulged in by the Chickasaw at their Pishofa dances.

The anonymous Frenchman says that the Choctaw took medicines internally consisting of herbs and the roots of trees boiled together, "and to make themselves vomit they run feathers down their throats." [46] It seems that the majority were in his time suffering from a kind of debility "with pains over the entire body."

---

[45] Cushman, Hist. Inds., pp. 273–275.
[46] Appendix, p. 251; Mem. Am. Anthrop. Assn., vol. v, No. 2, p. 64.

The diseases from which they suffered and the commoner methods of treating them are thus described by Cushman:

Diseases, they believed, originated in part from natural causes, therefore their doctors sought in nature for the remedies. Graver maladies, to them, were inexplicable, and for their cures they resorted to their religious superstitions and incantations. They were very skillful in their treatment of wounds, snake bites, etc. Their knowledge of the medicinal qualities of their various plants and herbs, in which their forests so bountifully abounded, was very great. 'Tis true they were powerless against the attacks of many diseases—importations of the White Race, such as smallpox, measles, whooping-cough, etc.; yet, they did not exhibit any greater ignorance in regard to those new diseases, to them unknown before, than do the doctors of the White Race, who have had the experience of ages which has been handed down to them through the art of printing, manifest in regard to the new diseases that so oft attack their own race. The art of blood-letting and scarifying was well understood and practiced by many of their doctors, as well as the virtue of cold and warm baths; and in many of the healing arts they fell not so far below those of the White Race as might be supposed, though many white doctors imagine themselves perfect in the healing art, since forsooth their dipolmas boast the signatures of the medical faculties in the world.

In cases of bowel affections they use persimmons dried by the heat of the sun and mixed with a light kind of bread. In case of sores, they applied a poultice of pounded ground ivy for a few days, then carefully washing the afflicted part with the resin of the copal-tree which proved very efficacious; to produce a copious perspiration, a hot decoction of the China root swallowed, had the desired effect. They possessed an antidote for the bite and sting of snakes and insects, in the root of a plant called rattle snake's master, having a pungent yet not unpleasant odor. The root of the plant was chewed, and also a poultice made of it was applied to the wound, which at once checked the poison and the patient was well in a few days. The medical properties of the sassafras, sarsaparilla, and other medicinal plants, were known to them. They possessed many valuable secrets to cure dropsy, rheumatism, and many other diseases, which, no doubt, will ever remain a secret with them, proving that their powers of observation, investigation and discrimination, are not, by any means, to be regarded as contemptible; while their belief, that the Great Spirit has provided a remedy in plants for all diseases to which poor humanity seems an heir, and never refuses to make it known to those who seek the knowledge of it by proper supplications, is praiseworthy in them to say the least of it.[47]

The greatest mortality among them was generally confined to the younger children; while longevity was a prominent characteristic among the adults. After the age of six or eight years the mortality of disease among them was less than among the white children of the present day after that age. But after those baneful diseases, scarlet fever, measles, mumps, whooping-cough, diseases unknown to them before, had been introduced among them, the fatality among the children was distressing, frequently destroying the greater number of children in a village or neighborhood;—being wholly ignorant as they were of the proper mode of treatment was a great cause of the fearful fatality. Mental or nervous diseases were unknown to the ancient Choctaws; and idiocy and deformity were seldom seen. But of all the "diseases" intro-

[47] Cushman, Hist. Inds., pp. 228–229.

duced among them by the whites, the most pernicious and fatal in all its features, bearings, and consequences, to the Choctaw people, was, is, and ever will be, Okahumma (red water or whiskey) ; which, when once formed into habit, seemed to grow to a species of insanity equal even to that so often exhibited among the whites.[48]

In 1730, when the French officer De Lusser was traveling through the Choctaw country, he was seized with a violent attack of nosebleed, which an Indian doctor stopped by the application of an herb. De Lusser also records the case of a Frenchman named Tarascon who was ill with " a sort of leprosy which afflicts him from head to foot and which had made him blind." He had recovered his sight " by means of the fire with which the Indians treated him and with which they maintain that they are curing him." [49]

For late forms of medical practice in the Bayou Lacomb band of Choctaw, a list of 25 medicine plants, and the manner of using them, the reader is referred to Mr. Bushnell's bulletin.[50]

According to Simpson Tubby, it was a common Choctaw belief that people got diseases from the food they ate, and therefore before killing a chicken it was shut up and fed by the owner until what it had foraged for itself was out of it. On the other hand, it was thought that animals gathered their own medicine. The hog roots in the ground for his medicine and a dog should not be shut up or he will not be able to find his own proper remedies. This was one of the reasons advanced by Mashulatubbi in opposing allotment. He maintained that in time the stock would be enclosed so that they could not get to their natural medicine and that the same thing would sooner or later happen to the Indians. The old Choctaw doctors are said to have held, like the Creeks, that animals caused diseases.

The same informant averred that the head chief appointed from one to three doctors from each of the five Choctaw bands, and that he and the doctors together appointed medicine givers who were later to be appointed doctors themselves. After their appointment the doctors and medicine givers were placed in charge of the band captains who had to see that they carried out their instructions. Since it is said that medicine could be given only in the presence of one of these people, and that a man had to be present to see that a male patient took the medicine and a woman to see that a female took it, it would seem that the medicine givers at least were of both sexes. Medicine was administered by " swallows," " fractions of swallows," and " drops." He also said that no one was allowed to

[48] Cushman, Hist. Inds., p. 230.
[49] Ms. in French Archives.
[50] Bull. 48, Bur. Amer. Ethn., pp. 23–25.

take medicine except in the presence of a medicine giver, but it seems evident that only certain medicines were administered in this official manner.

Mention has been made of the readjustment of the pillow in response to certain symptoms. If one complained of a dead feeling in the legs and thighs, the doctor would reduce the height of the head end of the pallet so that the blood would flow less readily toward the feet.

If a person had lived some time in one place and had had much sickness, he would move. This was often at the direction of the doctor, and if the latter told him to move at a certain time he would do so, perhaps living in a tent until there was time to erect a house. Sometimes a man would move a dozen times on 40 acres of land.

Simpson also described what might be called fractional sweat-bathing. In preparation for this a hole was dug in the floor big enough to hold a large pot. Over it crosswise were laid a number of sticks sufficient to hold up a quilt. A kettle containing water and medicines was then put over the fire and, after the contents had been heated, it was placed in this hole, and the affected part laid over it, the whole being covered with the quilt. If the doctor prescribed it, a second kettle of medicine might be used after the first had become cool. After the steaming was over, the patient shut himself in his room and stayed there until the right temperature was restored, or as long as the doctor prescribed.

The use of cow horns, as mentioned above, was universal in the Southeast. Simpson says of it that in the first place the doctor took a sort of punch consisting of a piece of glass fastened on the end of a stick in such a manner that it could enter the flesh only a certain distance, placed the point of it on a small vein over the afflicted part and drove it in with a little mallet. Then he clapped the wide end of the horn over the spot and sucked at the small end until most of the air had been removed, when he closed the hole by means of a bit of cloth previously lodged in his mouth. After waiting a certain time he drew the horn away and examined the blood it contained in order to diagnose the ailment. Another reason was probably to remove a foreign object which some wizard might have injected. This has been mentioned already. They also extracted from a patient such objects as lizards, snakes, terrapin, millipedes, or earwigs, which it was claimed were " aggravating him to death."

For grinding medicines the doctor used a little mortar made out of a hard yellow or white flint which was worked out by beating very carefully with another stone. In dimensions these varied from the size of the fist to the size of a plate. If the workman was in a hurry he heated the rock, but in doing so he was liable to break and ruin it. Sometimes two or three hollows were made in one piece of flint. A kind of sandstone was also employed but grit was apt to come off of it. The pestle was of the same material as the mortar and both were developed together by constant and long continued grinding so that the two exactly fitted. Such flints are found in the entire section but Tallapoosa River was particularly resorted to for them. Simpson has seen his father make these mortars, the last made in the Choctaw country.

Medicinal roots were dug in the fall of the year when they were purer and most of the poison had gone out of them. They were steamed to the boiling point but were not allowed to boil hard. A medicine is said to have been named most often for the insect or animal which attends it. The following notes were obtained regarding specific remedies:

Rabbit tobacco, also called by the whites " life everlasting " (Choctaw, báshûchak), was made into an infusion and drunk in cases of fever. It was also used as a tobacco substitute.

Boneset (Choctaw, hōwē cháche [hobechechi?]) was used in the steaming process mentioned above to make one throw up " cold and bile."

Jerusalem oak, or rather wormseed, called in Choctaw àlà imokhi^{n}sh, or àlà bàlo^{n}tàchi [àlà ibàlhtochi?], " children's medicine," was made the basis for a kind of candy and fed to small children who had worms.

The " pink root " was also called by the Choctaw àlà imokhi^{n}sh sometimes. Just enough whisky was put with this to keep it. It is a system builder, and when one has it he needs no doctor. It makes one very sick at first but afterwards thoroughly well. It drives out fever and is a good tonic for old and young. When it was to be given to children it was weakened and in later times sugar was added.

They used scurvy grass (Choctaw, nuti kishōche [nuti kashoffichi?]) to clean the teeth.

Sampson snake root (Choctaw, nipi lapushkichi) is a poison to any other poison and was therefore used in cases of snake bite. They used to go to the region where Noxubee and Oktibbeha Counties came together, southeast of Starkville, to gather this.

The mayapple (Choctaw, fàla imisito, " crow pumpkin ") is a fine medicine. The fruit is given to children as a purgative. In cases of biliousness they powdered the root, put half an ounce of this into a pint of water, boiled it down to about an ounce, and mixed it with whisky. One swallow, or as much as a person could stand, was a dose. It is a sure cure and " you can hear the cold and the bile tearing out." It received its name from the fact that the crow, which is a wise bird, feeds upon the mayapple.

The wild cherry (Choctaw, iti alikchi) is looked upon as one of the best medicines for young girls. In winter, if cherry wine has not been put up, a tea may be made of the leaves which is given internally to stop pain and cause perspiration. If enough is taken it will purify the blood. If the leaves are gone, the outside bark may be peeled away and the inside bark used in the same way and for the same purposes. It was an axiom never to kill a cherry tree if it could be helped.

The prickly ash (Choctaw, nuti alikchi) is good in cases of toothache. A piece of bark may be cut off to hold in the cavity of the tooth, or it may be powdered and made into a poultice.

Modoc weed (Choctaw, akshish lakna, "yellow root") was used for a weak stomach, in cases of fainting or when the nerves give way. The roots were boiled in water and taken along with whisky.

Golden rod (Choctaw, okhiⁿsh bàlàli) and the puccoon root were sold to the whites for medicinal purposes but not employed by the Choctaw.

The pottage pea (Choctaw, bàlōngtiàchi tapàchi) is an onion-like root with a sweetish taste used in cases of diarrhea.

The butterfly root (Choctaw, hàtapushik okhiⁿsh, "butterfly medicine") was used for human beings in cases of colds. The tops could be employed as well as the roots. However, it seems to have been more often employed as a medicine for horses, being given when they had the blind staggers or seemed physically broken down. It was also given them in the fall to protect them from such sickness the following spring.

When they gave up their old out-of-doors life and came to live in poorly ventilated houses of poles and split logs daubed with mud the Choctaw were attacked by tuberculosis and suffered severely. It was suggested that they move out into the forest until they got well and those who did so saved a part of their families but most of the others died. Some white families were no better off. While the white people remained in one place and kept cleaning that, the Indians waited until the house became too filthy for them and then moved and put up another.

The following experience with a medicine man was given me by Simpson Tubby and is illustrative of the nature of later Choctaw practice. Simpson was once sick and sent for a native practitioner. When the latter came in where Simpson was lying, head to the east, he stood on the north side of him, passed along to his head, fanning him all the way and then round to the south side in the same manner. After that he doubled up his hands and blew through them three times, looking north and toward the top of the house. Then he said to the people in the house, "This man was dreaded by many men, not for things that were reasonable but on account of what he was called to do. He was called for great things in this world and the time has come when he must do them. When he is able to stand it I will separate the impure part of his blood from the right blood and he will be a well man." Then he said to him, " Seven days from to-day come to my house and I will do the work for you." After that he told one of the children to dip up a pail of water at the spring and bring it straight to him without playing with it. As soon as this was provided, he dipped his fingers into it and sprinkled Simpson's face and head with it and it gave Simspon a peculiar sensation. Then he went to his feet and sprinkled them and he sprinkled his hands in the same manner, rubbing the joints of his hands and fingers as well. Then he said, " You may have one more spell like this, but that will be about all you will ever have." And in fact he did have one more attack of the kind and it was the last for a long time.

Belief in witches, which seems to have been an overshadowing horror to so many peoples, was equally rampant among the Choctaw. The native name for them (hatak holhkunna) has already been given.[51] In 1731 Du Roullet records that the Choctaw believed the English and Chickasaw had killed many of their people " by means of a medicine which they had spread among them." [52]

In 1742 " the chief of the Mobiliens [a small tribe closely related to the Choctaw] had two of the warriors of his village killed, one of them a medicine man who had treated a Choctaw who had afterward died. An accusation of sorcery was given as the reason for sacrificing them." [53]

Bossu says:

The Chactas have great faith in sorcerers or wizards, and when they discover one, they knock off his head without ceremony.[54]

I saw a savage belonging to this nation who had been baptized a short time before, and who, because he did not succeed in the chase as well as his comrades, imagined that he had been bewitched. This new proselyte went at once to Father Lefévre, a Jesuit, who had converted him and told him that his medicine was worth nothing and that, since he had received it, he had killed neither stags nor roebucks. He adjured him to take away his medicine, and the Jesuit, to escape the resentment of the savage, made a pretence of unbaptizing him. Some time afterward this pretended debaptized savage having killed a deer by chance or by skill, believed himself disenchanted and was satisfied.[55]

---

[51] See p. 230.
[52] French Archives, MS.
[53] Miss. State Arch., French Domin. MS.
[54] " When I was at Mobile in 1752, I saw a person killed with blows of an ax because he professed to be a sorcerer. The savages attributed to him the misfortunes which happened to come upon their nation."—Bossu.
[55] Appendix, p. 261 ; Bossu, Nouv. Voy., vol. 2, pp. 99–100.

This story shows that some exceptions must be made to Cushman's statement that they never accused anyone of indulging in the black art except old and decrepit women.[56]

What Simpson related regarding the animals sent into a person's body by witchcraft has already been given. The same informant called wizards bad doctors as opposed to prophets or good doctors. He said that a man would sometimes sacrifice four or five dollars worth of property, in the shape of money, silver ornaments, medicine, and so on, at one spring or well into which it was believed a wizard had put an active spirit or "hant," in order to weaken the spell. A wizard held himself in much esteem and was often employed to injure others. They were accepted at ball games because there they had to fight other wizards but not at other times officially. This was Simpson's statement, but it seems to the writer unlikely that in ancient times one who had such a reputation would have been given a position of such importance.

Regarding rainmakers I will quote the following from Cushman:

In the matter of rain, the Choctaw Rainmaker truly swayed the sceptre of authority in that line of art, undisputed, and was regarded with reverential awe by his people. In all cases of protracted drouth, which was quite frequent at an early day in their ancient domains, the Hut-tak Um-ba Ik-bi, (man rain maker) was regarded as the personage in whom alone was vested the power to create rain; therefore to him they went with their offerings and supplications, the former, however, partaking more of a persuasive nature than the latter, in the judgment of the Umba Ikbi, as an effectual means to bring into requisition his mysterious power in the matter of rain. He without hesitation promised to heed their solicitations, though gently hinting that, in his judgment, the offerings were not in as exact ratio to their importunities as they should have been. However, he now assumes an air of mysterious thoughtfulness and, "grand, gloomy and peculiar wrapped in the solitude of his own imagination," strolled from village to village, gazing at the sun by day and the stars by night, seeming to hold communion with the spirits of the upper worlds; finally he ventured his reputation by specifying a certain day upon which he would make it rain. The day arrived, and if haply came with it a rain the faith of his dupes was confirmed, his mystic power unquestioned, and the Umba Ikbi made comfortable. But if otherwise, he did not as the Alikchi, attribute his failure to the counteracting influence of a witch in the person of an old woman, but to that of a brother Umba Ikbi living in some remote part of the nation, with whom he was just then at variance. He now informs his unfortunate but not faithless people that an Umba Ikbi's mind must be free of all contending emotions while engaged in the mystic ceremonies of rain making; that he was now angry, too much mad to make it rain. Upon which announcement, the now despairing people earnestly solicited to know if they, in any way could assuage his wrath. He replied in the negative; but promised, however, to consider the matter as soon as his anger abated. He now became more reserved; sought solitude where undisturbed he might scan the sky and perchance discern some sign of rain. Sooner or later, he discovers a little hazy cloud stretched along the distant western horizon; attentively and care-

---

[56] Cushman, Hist. Ind. Tribes, p. 255.

fully watches it as broader and higher it ascends, until he feels sure he can safely risk another promise; then leaves his place of secret and thoughtful meditation, and, with countenance fair as a summer morn, presents himself before his despairing people and announces his anger cooled and wrath departed; that now he would bring rain without delay, yet dropping a casual hint as to the efficiency of a coveted pony, cow, blanket, etc., being added, as a surer guarantee, since " the laborer was worthy his hire."

The hint was comprehended and fully complied with in hopeful expectation. Anon the low muttering thunder vibrates along the western horizon in audible tones, and the lightning flash is seen athwart the western sky heralding the gathering and approaching storm; soon the sky is overcast with clouds of blackest hue while the lightning's flash and the thunder's roar seem to proclaim to the people their wonderful Umba Ikbi's secret power in the affair of rain; and, as the vast sheets of falling water wet the parched earth they sing his praise; which he, with assumed indifference, acknowledged with an approving grunt; then, with measured steps, sought his home, there to await another necessity that would call him forth to again deceive his credulous admirers.[57]

Romans mentions a rain-making herb.

Many among them are well acquainted with plants of every kind, and apply them judicially [judiciously?] both externally and internally; to others again they attribute supernatural virtues; for instance, there is one which they make use of to procure rain; for this purpose they have a number of people in their nation called rainmakers; these assemble in a deserted field, and they boil this plant in a large pot, dancing and singing around it with numberless awkward gestures; then if it should happen to rain soon after, the jugglers boast the virtue of the plant; but should no rain follow, they say the physick was not strong enough; they take care however not to employ this rain compelling herb unless a cloudy day forebodes rain. The plant is very singular, and I believe a nondescript; I saw two species of it, but could not ascertain the genius [!]; the savages call it *Esta Hoola* [isht ahollo] or the most beloved.[58]

Finally Wright informs us, in a paragraph already quoted. that there was a class of fair-weather makers.[59] This was true also of the Creeks and probably all of the other southeastern Indians.

---

[57] Cushman, Hist. Inds., pp. 260–261.
[58] Romans, Nat. Hist. E. and W. Fla., pp. 85–86.
[59] See p. 196.

APPENDIX

The original texts of the three most important French authorities are given below. They are reproduced exactly with all of their archaisms and peculiarities of spelling and composition unmodified and uncorrected except for some few verbal duplications. The first constitutes chapters 7 and 8 of an unpublished work, the original of which, or at all events a copy, is preserved in the Ayer collection of Americana in the Newberry Library, Chicago. A photostatic reproduction of this was kindly furnished the Bureau of American Ethnology some years ago by the custodians of the collection, at the solicitation of Mr. Hodge, then ethnologist-in-charge. There seems to be no clue to the author of this Relation except the word, or fragment of a word, " Kened," on the back of the binding. He seems, however, to have been a French officer of some prominence. I have conjecturally dated the composition about the year 1755, but the information it contains belongs to a somewhat earlier time, subsequent, nevertheless, to the Natchez uprising of 1729–1731. The other texts are from the narratives of Bossu and Milfort, published at Paris in 1768 and 1802, respectively.

Relation de La Louisiane

Les Chaquetas sont esloignée de la Mobille de cent lieux du costé du nord, ils sont enuiron quatre mil portant les armes. les françois les diuisent en trois quantons, celuy de l'est se nomme Ougoula annalé, le chef de ce quanton a les mesmes prerogatifs que le grand chef. celuy de l'oüest se nomme ougoulatanama. Celuy du midy se nomme Taboka c'est la ou demeure le grand chef.

Cette nation est gouuernée par un grand chef dont le pouuoir n'est absolu, qu'autant qu'il sçait se seruir de son auctorité, mais comme on ne punit pas chez eux la desobeïssence et quils ne sont d'ordinaire ce que lon leurs commende, que quant ils le ueullent bien : on peût dire que c'est un gouuernement mal dissipliné.

Dans chaque uillage, outre le chef, et le chef de guerre, il ya deux Tascamingoutchy qui sont comme Lieutenants du chef de guerre : un tichou mingo qui est comme le major, c'est luy qui ordonne par toutes les ceremonies, les festes, les dances, il porte la parolle du chef, fait fumer les guerriers, et les estrangers. ces Tichou mingos uiennent ordinairement chefs du uillage. Ils se distinguent en quatre ordres, sçauoir les grands chefs, chefs du uillage et chef de guerre. le second se sont les Atac oulitoupa ou les hommes de ualleur.

Le troisiemme est composé de ceux quils appellent simplement tasca, ou guerriers.

Le quatrieme et dernier est atac emitta ce sont ceux qui n'ont pas fait coup ou qui n'ont tué qu'une femme ou un enfant. cette nation est guerriere contre de ses semblables, et dans les bois les françois ayant eu tousjours besoin d'auoir recours a eux dans les guerres, les à rendus si insolents, qu'ils meprisent le françois et uoudroint receuoir les Anglois chez eux. ils se sont si bien accountumés a receuoir des presents des francois, qui autrefois estoint fort peu de chose, ne se montant alors qu'a huit mil liures, et qui augmentant tous les ans reuiennent apresent à plus de cinquante mil franc. ils s'imaginent que c'est un droit que les françois leurs payent pour leurs terres qu'ils occupent, c'est ce qu'ils taschent de faire entendre, dans les harangues qu'ils font aux commendants des postes ou ils uont, en disant, Autrefois nos encestres occupoint l'endroit ou tu demeure a present et y uenoint chasser; ills te l'ont cedé comme à des gens qui uouloint estre de leurs amis, en concideration de quoy tu leurs as promis une certaine quantitée de marchandise, dont la longueur du temp n'a pas aboli la continuation de ce don, et de l'amitiée qui ayant regné parmy nos encestres auec les françois regne encore auec toy et nous. tu sçay que toutes les fois que tu nous as demendé pour tirer uengence de tes ennemis qui t'auoint insulté, nous auons eû pitiée de ce qu'estant peû de monde, nous ne pouuiez pas aller en guerre, et que nous regardant comme uos freres nous auons abandonné nos femmes, enfans, maisons, uillages, (?) ,[1] et temp de chasse pour courir sur uos ennemis, et teindre nos bras de leurs sang, que nous y auons souuent perdu des nostres. tu scay que nombre de fois de retour de guerre nous t'auons fait credit des marchandise que tu nous auois promis et gaigné au prix de notre sang, parce qu'il n'estoit point encore arriué de uesseaux de france. tu sçay que les Anglois sont tous les jours à nos portes à nous perse-cutter de faire allience auec eux, et leurs traiter nos peaux de cheureüil à de plus justes prix que tu ne fais. nous auons donc esperence qu'en concideration de toutes ces choses, tu nous regarderas en pitiée, et que tu nous partageras comme tes freres; affins[2] que nous nous en retournions à notre uillage chargés des presents que tu nous auras fait. uoila àpeû pres une de leurs harangue et les autres ne different guerre de celle la. ils repetent souuent la mesme chose, et pour faire une harangue, ils sont d'ordinaire deux heures a parler.

---

[1] The word *maisons* seems to be repeated here.   [2] Or *attins*.

Lors qu'il en arriue une bande à la Mobille dans le temp des presents qui est ordinairement au mois de mars, ou auril, ils s'arrestent à trois lieux de la uille, et enuoyent un courier aduertir le comdendant de leurs arriuée, et demendent du pain et de leau de uie: on leurs enuoie selon la quantitée qu'ils sont ce qui leurs faut. le lendemain ils arriuent en habit de ceremonie qui consiste, en un capot sans doublure, une chemise tres salle, et un mauuais brayer: la pluspart n'ont qu'une peau de cheureüil, d'ours, ou de Bœuf sur le corps. dans cet equipage l'interprete les conduit chez le commendant, ou ils commencent par luy secoüer la main l'un appres l'autre, uous pouuez croire qu'elle luy sait mal lors que la bande est longue, ils fument ensuitte donnent à fumer au Commendant, et aux officiers qui sont au tour de luy, en signe de paix appres quoy ils font la harangue. on les renuoye dans le bois, on leurs fait raccomoder leurs armes, on les nourit jusqu'a ce qu'ils partent, et on leurs fait leurs presens. toutes ces dessentes de sauuages coutent infiniment. au commendant en ayant tres souuent ou à sa table, ou qui uniennent pendant qu'il mange, aux quels il ne peut se dispenser de donner à boire et à menger pour entretenir l'union ayant esté mis sur ce pied la depuis plusieurs année. a peine sont-ils partis qu'il en reuient d'autres et ce trin dure ordinairement trois sepmaines, quelques fois jusqu'a six. on les nourit pendant ce temp auec du ris, du mahi, des pattates, un peu de pain et de leaudeuie par fois. Lors qu'un françois ueut aller traiter chez eux, il prent ordinairement le temp qu'ils s'en retournent auec leurs presents, il demende au chef de la bande la quantitée de sauuages qu'il a besoin pour porter ses marchandises, car on y uat par terre, et tous les soirs il faut coucher a la belle etoïlle et sur la terre. pour tout lit on à une peau d'ours et une petite couuerture, on uit sur la route de uiande, lors que les sauuages en peuuent tüer, auec du blé de turquis, que lon apelle mahy, qui est boüilli dans l'eau. lors que lon est arriué au uillage, on uous conduit chez le chef ou estant entré sans dire mot, on uous fait asseois sur un lit de canne, esleué de terre d'enuiron trois ou quatres pieds, de peur des puces; on uous jette une pipe, nommée calumet auec la blague pleine de tabac que uous fumé remarqué que tout cela se fait sans parler; appres quoy le chef uous dit, te uoila donc arriué? appres luy auoir repondu que oüi, on luy dit le sujet de son uoyage et lespece de marchandise que lon à apporté pour traiter auec ses guerriers. le lendemain il fait aduertir tout le monde de l'arriuée du francois chez luy, de ce qu'il à apporté et de ce qu'il demende. chaqu'un uient à sa boutique, luy enleue sa marchandise, et lors qu'il à enuie de s'en retourner il aduertit le chef qui luy fait apporter les payements dont il est conuenu auec ses guerriers. il prent de rechef des porteurs, et s'enuat au uillage françois. ces

uoyages sont ordinairement de deux ou trois mois et lon y gaigne
les deux cent pour cent: mais il faut bien sçauoir leurs langue.

Leurs maison n'est autre chose qu'une cabanne de morceaux de
bois gros comme la jambe, enfoncée en terre, attachés ensemble auec
des liannes, qui est un espece de liens fort souple, ces cabannes sont
entourée de torchi sans fenestre, et dont la porte n'a que trois à quatre
pieds de haut, elle sont couuertes d'ecorse d'arbre, de cipre, ou de
pin, on laisse un trou au hault de chaque pignon, pour y laisser
passer la fumée, car ils font leurs feû dans le milieu de leurs cabanne,
qui sont escartée les unes des autres d'une portée de fusil. le dedans
est entouré de lits de canne esleués de trois a quatre pieds de terre
acause des puces qui y regnent en quantitée, prouenant de la mal-
propreté. les sauuages lors qu'ils sont couchés ne se leuent point
pour faire de l'eau, mais la laissent aller à trauers les cannes de
leurs lit. pour se coucher ils ont une peau de cheureüil ou d'ours
dessous eux, et une peau de Bœuf, ou une couuerture dessus. ces
lits leurs seruent de table et de siege. ils n'ont pour meuble qu'un
pot de terre pour faire cüire leurs menger, quelques terrines pour
le mesme office, et quelques uents ou tamis, et paniers pour accomoder
leurs mahy qui est leurs nouriture ordinaire. ils le concassent dans
une pile, ou mortier de bois, qu'ils font d'un tronçon d'arbre
creusé auec de la braize, dont le pilon a quelques fois jus qu'a dix
pieds de haut et menu comme le bras, le bout d'enhaut est une masse
informe qui sert à apesentir et à donner de la force à ce pilon en
retombant, de casser plus facilement le mahy, appres qu'il est ainsi
cassé, ils le sassent pour en separer le plus menu, ils font boüillir le
gros dans un grand peau qui tient enuiron trois ou quatre sceau
d'eau, y meslent parfois de la citroüille, ou des feues, ou des
fœuilles de feues, lors que ce ragoust est presque cüit ils jettent
dedans le plus menu du mahy qu'ils auoint reserué pour epaisir l'eau,
et pour assaisonnement, ils ont un pot suspendu en lair dans lequel
il ya de la cendre de cottons de mahy, de cossas de feue, ou enfin
de cendre de chesne, sur laquelle ayant jetté de l'eau ils prennent
cette laissiue qui est tombée dans un uaze preparé dessous, et en
assaisonnent leurs ragoust qui se nomme sagamité. c'est ce qui
leurs sert de principalle nouriture, comme aux françois qui sont
dans la colonie qui n'ont pas le moyen de uiure autrement.

Ils en font quelques fois du pain sans leuin, mais rarement,
parceque cela depense trop de blé, et qu'il est penible a faire, n'estant
qu'a forces de bras qu'ils le redüisent en farinne, appres qu'il est
petri ou ils le font boüillir dane l'eau, ou l'entortillent de fœuïlle,
et le font cüire dans la cendre, ou enfin ayant applati la paste de
l'epaisseur de deux ecus, et de la grandeur des deux mains en rond,
ils le font cüire sur un morceau de pot sur la braize. ils en font

auec du gland appres auoir redüi le gland en farinne ils le laissent
dans un tamis de canne au bord d'un rüisseau, et de temp en temp
jettent de l'eau dessus, par cette laissiue ils font perdre l'amertume
qu'il a; appres quoy ils mettent cette pâste à lentour d'un morceau
de bois qu'ils font cüire au feu. lors qu'ils ont de la uiande ils la
font boüillir dans l'eau tant salle qu'elle soit sans la lauer, disans
que cela luy feroit perdre son goust. lors qu'elle est cüitte ils mettent quelques fois de cette farinne de gland dans le boüillon. ils
font aussi cüire du mahy sans estre cassé auec leurs uiande, et lors
quelle est seche, ils la pillent et la mettent comme de la charpie, ils la
meslent en boüillant auec ce blé, cela n'a aucune saueur et il faut estre
sauuage pour en manger.

Tant que le blé est uerd c'est la le temp ou ils font le plus de regals
et qu'ils l'accomodent en differentes sortes de facons, premierement
ils le font griller au feû et le mangent demesme, bien des françois en
mangent ainsi. lors qu'il est fort tendre ils le pillent et en font de la
boüillie, mais le plus estimé parmi eux cest la farinne froide. c'est
du blé a un degré de maturité qu'ils font boüillir, ensuitte griller,
de la boucanner et puis ils le pillent et cette farine fait le mesme
effet dans l'eau froide, que la farinne de froment dans leau chaude
sur le feu, et a un goust assez gratieux; les françois en mangent auec
du lait. ils ont aussi un espece de mahy qui est plus petit que l'autre
et qui uient en trois mois a maturité, celuy la ils le font boucanner
puis boüillir, sans le casser auec de la uiande, c'est un regal parmy
eux que de ce petit blé boüilli, auec un dinde ou quelques morceau de
uiande grasse.

Ils sont fort malpropres dans leurs maisons, dans leurs boire et
manger, comme sur eux, on ne uoit guere de tortû, ny bossû parmy
eux. ils sont essez bien faits, leurs femmes sont fort laides, elles
sont comme esclaues de leurs maris. elles font tout dans la maison,
labourent la terre, sement et recüillent. les hommes leurs aident
parfois au desert, mais ne uont jamais chercher de leau, ny du feû,
sçitost qu'ils sont reçus guerriers, comptemps que cela les deshonoi-
roit. ils ne s'occupent uniquement qu'à la chasse, ils sont tres
feneants, sournois, ils gardent une rencune par generation, le petit
fils uengera une insulte faite a son bisaÿeul en tuant un des dessen-
dants de celuy pui à fait le coup. ils esleuent leurs enfans dans cet
esprit de uengence auec cela ils ne se mettent jamais en colère, aiment
bien, et se sacrifiroint pour leurs amis; sont fort patients. dans les
souffrances, et endurent le supplice de la mort sans se plaindre,
aucontraire, ils chantent jusqu'au dernier soupir.

Lors qu'une femme se trouue incommodée, de la maladie
ordinaire, aussitost elle sort de la maison, s'en escarte d'une certaine
distence dans un endroit caché, elle y allume du feû auec un briquet,

ils disent qu'ils leurs faut du feû neuf, et que s'ils en prenoint de celuy de la maison, cette maison seroit soüillée, et la femme mourroit par la force de sa maladie qui augmenteroit. ils n'abittent plus auec leurs femmes pendant qu'elles sont en cet estat, elles se cachent de la uûe des hommes: les maris se font a manger euxmesme, alors, ou uont chez leurs uoisins.

Vn jour je me trouuay chez un sauuage qui estoit allé a la chasse pour moy dez la ueille. le matin a mon reueil ne trouuans pas sa femme a la maison, et uoyans du feû dans le desert, je fus l'y trouuer, j'ignorois alors cette ceremonie, et l'ayant prié de me faire de la boüillie de petit blé, ce ne fut qu'a force de prieres que j'obtins ma demende, comme je commençois à menger, son mary arriua, je luy demenday s'il en uouloit, et m'ayant repondu qu'oüy il se mit à en menger auec moy, mais le plat estant à moities il s'auisa de me demender quiesce qui me l'auoit accomodé: notté qu'il auoit reconnu la cause de l'absence de sa femme par quelques meubles qui menquoint à la maison: luy ayant repondu que c'estoit sa femme qui auoit esté ma cüisinniere, le mal de cœur luy prit sur le champ et il fut uomir à la porte, puis rentrant et regardans dans le plat, il remarqua quelque choses de rouge dans la boüillie, qui n'estoit autre que la peau du blé dont il y en a des grains qui sont rouges. il me dit comment as tu le cœur de menger de ce ragoust? es que tu ne uois pas le sang qui est dedans? et alors il retourna uomir jusqua ce qu'il eut rendu tout ce qu'il auoit mengé; et son imagination fut si fort frapée qu'il en fut quelques jours malade. c'est une chose qu'ils ont grand soin d'obseruer que de s'absenter dans ces temps la, et de se bien baigner auans de rentrer dans la maison.

Lors qu'un garçon ueut se marier, il uat trouuer le pere et la mere de la fille qu'ils ont enuie d'auoir, appres auoir fait sa demende, il jette deunans la mere quelques branches de rassade de uere, et un brayer deuans le pere, s'ils prennent le present cest marque du consentement, et alors le garçon emmenne la fille chez luy sans autre ceremonie, dez ce moment la mere ne paroist plus deuans son gendre: si mesme ils sont obligés de demeurer dans la mesme chambre, ils font une petite separation entre eux de peur qu'ils ne se uoyent. lors que leurs femme est grosse et preste d'acoucher tant qu'elle est en trauail ils ne mangent que le soir appres soleil couché, et si c'est une fille ils obseruent ce jeûne encore huit jours appres. ils sont fort jaloux. lors qu'ils trouuent leurs femme en flagrand delict, ils se plaignent à ses parents de ce qu'ils luy ont donné une p. . . . luy coupent les cheueux et la repudient. Quelques fois le uillage prent fait et cause, attrape la femme, et l'amant et luy donnent cent coups de bastons, souuent luy coupoint le nez et les oreilles. ce dernier article ne s'executte plus, a cause de la difformité que cela

cause, outre que souuent ils en mouroint. autrefois lors qu'ils attra-
point une femme en faute, ils l'attachoint à quatre piquets, et l'aban-
donnoint a trois ou quatre cent jeunes gens, dont elle mouroint. lors
qu'une femme est abandonnée de son mary elle est declarée pour ce
qu'elle est, et alors la prent qui ueut, a moins que quelqu'un ne
l'adopte pour sa femme, ce qui est rare, amoins que ce ne soit un
homme d'une autre nation, qui la prent et l'emmenne auec luy sans
quoy elle est obligée d'aller le soir a la brunne du long des ruisseaux,
en chantans des chansons a cet usage, et d'un ton de uoix particulier.
au quel son si quelques jeunes gens en à besoin il la uat chercher,
l'abrie en lemmenans, de sa couuerture pour faire uoir qu'elle est sous
sa protection.   il la garde tant qu'il ueut et la nourit : mais lors qu'il
en est las, elle est obligée de recommencer ces cources pour uiure.
quant mesme elle uoudroit changer de uie ses parants ne la reprennent
pas, n'osans se fiër à ses promesses.   il faut que ce soit un garçon qui
la retire pour en faire sa femme, pour qu'elle soit a labri de l'insulte.
ils peuuent abandonner leurs femmes quant ils ueulent ; et en prendre
plusieurs à la fois, j'en ay uû un qui auoit les trois sœurs : lors qu'ils
se remarient ils prennent la sœur de la defunte, si elle en auoit, sinon
une de la famille. ils ne battent jamais leurs enfans. ils uiuent
amicalement, s'il y en à un qui les uient uoir, ils luy presentent aussitost a manger, desorte qu'un homme qui entre dans trante maisons
dans un jour, c'est trante repas qu'il fait, ils sont fort sobres.[3]

Ils n'ont point de Religion, ils ne recognoissent que le diable,
et ceux qui l'inuoquent parmy eux se nomment jongleurs : ceux la
sont ordinairement medecins. ces gens la ont beaucoup à craindre
quant ils entreprennent un malade, qui est chef, car s'il meure appres qu'ils lont jonglé ; ses parents disent qu'il la ensoncellé, et
s'il en rechappe apprest qu'il l'a condamné à mourir, ils disent qu'il
l'auoit ensorcellé, et que le sort à manqué : ainsi de toutes façons il
cours risque d'estre tüé. lors quil y à un malade parmy eux, on
fait uenir le medecin, qui appres auoir jonglé, ou demendé à leurs
esprit si leurs malade en reuiendra. ils le seignent auec un morçeau
de pierre a fusil, ils luy incizent la peau huit ou dix fois dans la
grandeur d'un ecû. comme lors qu'on donne les uentouzes, sur quoy
ils posent un bout de corne percée et le succent jusqu'a ce que la
corne soit pleine de sang. Comme ces jongleurs ueulent quelques
fois cacher leurs ignorences ils disent que quelqu'un leurs à jetté un
sort ; et alors adroitement ils mettent dans le fond de la corne du
poël de boeuf, ou quelques petit morceau de bois, et appres auoir
succé le malade et renuersé le sang qui est dans la corne, ils font
uoir aux parents du malade ce bois, ou ce poil qu'ils font accroire
estre un sort ; alors ce jongleur passe pour entre tres sçauant.

---

[3] Chapter VII of the *Relation* ends here.   Chapter VIII begins with the next paragraph.

Il est seur que ces jongleurs parlent au demon. j'en ay uû un nombre d'exemples je uous en citeray trois. vn jour arriuans moy troisieme chez un nommé Belles dent chef des Naniabas, reuenant des Chicachas et manquant de tabac, j'en demenday a ce chef, le quel ayant foüillé dans son coffre pour m'en donner, ou il en auoit mis trois endoüilles, il ne les trouua plus: il crut que c'estoit moy ou quelqu'un des françois que j'auois qui luy auoint caché: mais ayant appris que non, je le uis s'abiller et se mâtacher comme si il alloit a une dance, appres quoy estant allé dans une pleine à une portée de fusil de la maison, nous le uîsme charger sa pipe, battre le briquet, l'allumer, et la fumer en gesticulant beaucoup, comme si il disputoit auec quelqu'un. lors qu'il l'eut fumé à moitiee il nous sembloit qu'il donnoit à fumer à quelqu'un, sans cependant que nous uissions rein, si non qu'il tenoit sa pipe loing de luy, et la fumée qui sortoit à pelotons comme si quelqu'un eut fumé. il reuint à nous ausitost, et nous dit tout en süeur, qu'il sçauoit celuy qui luy auoit pris, et continuant ses pas uers une cabanne uis à uis de la sienne, ou je le suiuis, il sautta au col d'un sauuage en luy demendant ses trois endoüilles de tabac, qu'il luy auoit pris à telle heure de telle façon enfin luy expliqua la maniere dont il s'estoit serui pour faire son uol. le pauure sauuage tout tramblant luy auoua son crime, et luy rendit son tabac.

Les francois curieux de son sçauoir furent le trouuer, et le prierent moyenant recompencé de leurs faire dancer la loutre. il prit sa blague qui estoit une peu de loutre dans la quelle il mettoit sa pipe et son tabac, qu'il jetta aumilieu d'une place ou le monde estoit assemblé pour juger de sa sçience: apres qu'il eût proferé quantitée de parolles mal articulée, et s'estre jetté a plusieurs reprises dans le feû, d'ou il sortoit en süeur, et sans l'estre brulé: on uit celle peau se gonfler, et se remplir de chair et prendre uie, courir entre les jambes des françois, dont quelques uns de la compagnie l'ayant caressée et tastée, la trouua comme si s'auoit esté une ueritable loutre. lors qu'un chaqu'un fut comtent elle retourna à la mesme place ou elle auoit pris uie, et on la uit desenfler et reuenir en la mesme forme quelle estoit auans.

A lisle Dauphine lors que nous estions entourés des espagnols, et attendans de jour en jour du secours de france; on uoulut sçauoir s'il estoit bientost prest d'arriuer, ce que lon ne pouuoit cognoistre que par le moyen des sauuages que nous auions auec nous on les fit donc jongler, ce qu'ayant fait, ils rapporterent qu'il y auoit cinq uesseaux qui arriueroint le lendemain dont il y en auoit trois gros et deux plus petits qui estoint chargés de soldats dont un des petits n'arriueroit pas quant et quant les autres, parce qu'il s'estoit escarté et qu'il estoit encore loing, qu'ils seroint tous arriués le lendemain

sur le soir, ce qui se trouua ueritable, car le lendemain à huit heures
du matin on decouurit le premier uesseau, et sur les trois ou quartre
heures appres midy, tous les quatres moüillerent a l'isle Dauphine, et
le cinquieme ne se rendit que le lendemain. ils se medicamentent
souuent de leurs chef. ils prennent des medecines dherbes, et de
racinne de bois büillie ensemble. qu'ils boiuent, et pour so faire
uomir ils s'en foncent une plume dans le gozier; quelques fois ils se
font süer: pour cet effet ils font une petite cabanne de quatre pieds
de haut et de huit de tour qu'ils couurent de peau de bœuf et de
couuerture, ils mettent dedans cinq ou six boulets rouges, sur les
quels de temp en temp ils jettent un peu d'eau pour exciter la chaleur,
ils s en ferment dans ce petit espace jusqu'a sept personnes, et lors
qu'ils ont süé enuiron demy heure, ou trois quarts d'heure, ils sortent
uiste de ce trou, et uont auec precipitation se jetter dan l'eau la plus
fraische. je suis seur que ce remede n'a jamais esté ordonné par
aucun descendant d'Esculape. aussi, il est uray que la plus part
de ces gens la meurent en langueur auec des douleurs par tout le
corps.

Lors qu'un malade est prest de mourir le medecin le quitte et en
aduertit ses parents, les asseurant qu'il n'en peut rechaper, alors les
femmes uiennent luy lauer le corps, le peignent, luy matachent le
uisage, l'habillent de toutes les hardes qu'il auoit les plus belles: et le
couchent à terre sur la place qui est deuans sa porte: sa femme se
couche sur son estomac, en pleurant, auec ses plus proches parents
qui se couchent aussi sur luy, et qui l'étouffent, ils luy demendent
douuien esce qu'il a faim de mourir, si il a manqué de quelques chose,
si sa femme ne l'aimoit pas bien, si il n'estoit pas bien concideré dans
son uillage; enfin ce malheureux patient est obligé de mourir malgré
luy, ceux qui sont couché sur luy crient a tüe teste simaginant qu'il
nentend pas, puis qu'il ne repond point outre çà il y a des crieurs
a gage qui pendant ce temp uiennent pleurer, ou plustost heurler en
musique a costé du corps, deuans et appres sa mort. scitost qu'il est
mort ses parents esleuent une espece de cabanne uis à uis sa porte,
à six pieds de terre, sur six piquets, en forme de cercœüil, entouré
de torchy, et couuert d'ecorce dans quoy ils enferment ce corps tout
habillé, et qu'ils couurent d'une couuerture. ils mettent à menger et
à boire à costé deluy, luy donnent des souliers de rechange, son fusil,
de la poudre et des balles, ils dizent que c'est parcequ'il uat dans
un autre païs, et qu'il est juste qu'il aye tout ce qu'il luy faut dans
son uoyage, ils croyent que les guerriers uont faire la guerre dans
lautre monde, et qu'un chaqu'un y fait le mesme exercice qu'il fesoit
dans celuy cy. ce corps reste la dedans cinq ou six mois, jusqu'a ce
qu'ils croyent qu'il soit poury ce qui donne une infection terrible
dans la maison; au bout du quel temp tous les parents s'assemblent

en ceremonie, et la femme de ualleur du uillage, qui à pour son distrique de decharner les os des morts; uient decharner ce cadaure, netoïe bien les os, les met dans un panier de canne fort propre, qu'ils entourent de toille ou d'étoffe, ils jettent la chair dans un champ, et cette mesme decharneuse, sans se lauer les mains uient seruir à menger à l'assemblée. cette femme est tres conciderée dans le uilage. appres le repas on uat porter les os en chantant, et heurlans, dans le charnier du canton qui est une cabanne qui n'a qu'une couuerture, dans la quelle on met ces painers, de rang sur des bastons. aux chef on fait la mesme ceremonie, a la reserue qu'aulieu de mettre les os dans des paniers on les met dans des coffres fermant a clef dans le charnier des chefs.

Lors que quelqu'uns de leurs ennemis leurs à declaré la guerre ils tiennent conseil ensemble sur l'affron qu'ils ont reçeu, et appres auoir resolu de faire le guerre à la nation dont ils sont insultés; ils commencent la dance de guerre, qui dure ordinairement huit jours, qui sert a encourager un chaqu'un des guerriers, qui ne mangent guere pendant ce temp: et qui font des libations de jus d'herbes que le medecin leurs donne, et dont ils se frottent, qui à la uertu disent-ils de leurs donner de la force et du courage; herbe impayable si elle estoit cognüe en Europe; appres quoy ils partent pour la guerre. dans la route lors qu'ils sont obligés d'allumer du feû pour faire a manger, ils le font d'ordinaire dans un uallon de peur d'estre decouuerts par quelques party: car en ce cas le party les suiuroit jusqu'a ce qu'il eût trouué sa belle pour fondre sur eux. ils n'attaquent jamais leurs ennemis lors qu'ils sont esueillés: mais le soir lors qu'ils ont remarqué l'endroit ou ils ueulent passer la nuit. ils taschent de les aller joindre le plus prest qu'ils peuuent: et comme la terre dans le bois est couuerte de fœüille seiche qui font du bruit en marchant, ils ont la patience de les oster une a une auec les doits des pieds dont ils se seruent comme de la main, et si maheureusement ils cassent quelques petites branches, ils contrefont aussitost le crï de quelques oiseaux qu'ils imittent fort bien, pour faire accroire que c'est cet oiseau qui à fait le brüit. s'ils apperçoiuent leurs ennemi endormy, sur tout uers la pointe du jour, ils font le cri de mort, et a linstant ils tirent tous a la fois chaqu'un sur leurs homme, et sauttent dessus le casse teste a la main pour finir de tuer ceux qui ne sont que blessés, a qui ils leuent la cheuelure, s'ils ont le temp ils les depoüillent et s'en retournent à leurs uillage, a la uûe du quel ils font le cri de guerriers qui ont fait coup, et qui apportent des cheuelures, chaqu'un uient au deuant d'eux, en ceremonie et on les introdüit demesme. sur la place. ils font des dances en marque de rejoüissence de leurs uictoire et si quelques uns du party à quelques enfant ou neueu qui ne se soit pas trouué encore dans l'occasion ils

luy partage la moitiee de la cheuelure qu'il a leué et le fait receuoir
guerrier: cette ceremonie est, que celuy qui se fait receuoir, souffre
deux cent coups de collier, qui est un morceau de cuir de cinq on six
brasses de long, large d'un doit, ployé en plusieurs double, dont les
guerriers le frappent a tours de bras, sur le dos, et sur le uentre:
pour luy faire comprendre qu'un guerrier doit tout endurer
patiemment, mesme lors qu'il est pris par ses ennemis, et chanter
pendant qu'on le fait souffrir, et mourir, il doit souffrir ces coups
en chantant, car s'il pleuroit, il ne seroit jamais reçeu, et passeroit
pour une femme, et indigne d'estre aggregé dans le corps des
guerriers. lors qu'ils font ces dances de ceremonie, ils portent sur
leurs teste une couronne faite, d'un morceau de peau de loutre à la
quelle sont attachée autant de plumes blanches cassée, qu'ils ont
tüé dhomme dans leurs uie. chaque famille à ses armes piquée sur
l'estomac, et sur les bras, ils les mettent aussi sur le manche de leurs
casse teste, et lors qu'ils ueulent se joindre dans le bois ils font une
marque aux arbres, ou ils placent leurs armes, par ou on connoist
celuy qui a fait la marque, le chemin quil à pris, et ou il est allé.

Lors qu'ils attrapent quelques jeunes gens, filles fammes, ou jeune
garçons, uiuans, ils les enmennent a leurs uillages et les font esclaues.
il y a des nations qui les adoptent pour leurs chien; alors ils luy font
faire toutes les fonctions d'un chien, de garder la porte, de gronder
quant il entre ou sort quelqu'un de manger les restes des plats,
et ronger les os. lors qu'ils peuuent amener quelques prisonniers, ils
le font bruler à leurs uillages, et c'est une grande joie pour eux lorsque cela arriue.

Lors que les françois sont arriués chez eux ils ne uouloint manger
ny poules ny cochons parceque disoint-ils ces animeaux mangoint
des ordures: mais ils s'y sont accoutumés auec les francois, et
mangent de tous leurs ragoust. lors qu'ils ueulent regaler de leurs
amis ils tuent un chien dont ils ont quentitée, et leurs en seruent.

Lors qu'ils n'ont point de battefeu dans le bois, et qu'ils ueullent
en allumer, ils le font facillement par la contraction de deux
morceaux de bois qu'ils frottent auec uitesse lun contre l'autre et
font prendre de l'amadou qui est aupres. cet amadou est faite auec
des champignons qui uiennent aux chesnes.

Lors qu'ils ont fait la promesse de conclure une paix ils uiennent
cinq ou six principeaux de la nation, portent un calumet, ou pipe,
fait d'une pierre rouge comme du corail qui se trouue, en rochers
aux Illinois. ce Calumet a un tuyau d'enuiron deux ou trois pieds
de long entouré de plumes rouges artistement trauaillé, et ou pendent
huit ou dix plumes noires et blanches qui leurs sert comme d'estandar
a la guerre. de seau [4] dans les alliances, de continuation de fidelité

---

[4] Sceau.

parmy les amis, et de signe de guerre auec ceux auec qui ils ueulent rompre; il est uray que l'un est Calumet de paix et l'autre de guerre, ils sont faits semblablement tous deux. ˙quant ils ont conclu la paix le mestre des ceremonie allume ce calumet et fait fumer deux ou trois gorgées, a tous ceux qui sont dans l'assemblée, alors le traité est fini et inuiolable. ils liurent ce Calumet au chef auec qui ils contractent qui est comme un ottage de leurs bonne foy, et de la fidelité auec la quelle ils ueulent obseruer les articles dont ils sont conuenus.

Ils ne font aucun ouurage de curieux sinon ces calumets dont je uiens de parler et de la laine de Bœuf que les femmes fislent dont elles font des jartierres quelles teignent en diuerses couleurs et qui ne changent jamais. elles font aussi un dissu, partie de cette laine, et partie de pitre, herbe tres forte quelles filent. ce tissu est double comme ces mouchoirs a deux fasces et epais comme de la toile de uoile de demy aulne de large et de trois quarts de long, cela leurs sert de jupe. elles font aussi des paniers de canne de diuerses couleur, fort jolis.

Ils sont fort fainéants de leurs naturel, plus long temp couché que debout, fort grands joüeurs de plottee qui est comme la longue paume. ils se mettent une uingtaine d'un uillage, contre autant d'un autre, et font des gageures ensemble assez conciderables pour eux: ils gagent un fusil neuf contre un uieux que ne uaut rien, aussi facilement comme s'il estoit bon; et disent pour raison que s'ils ont a gagner, ils gagneront esgalement contre une mauuaise chose comme contre une bonne, et qu'ils aiment mieux parïer contre quelques chose que de ne point parier du tout. ils ont aussi un jeu, auec quatre morceaux de canne, ou lors qu'ils sont bien acharnés, ils joüent tout ce qu'ils ont, et quant ils ont tout perdu, ils jouent leur femmes, pour un certin espace de temp, et apres se jouent eux mesme, pour un temp limité.

Ils comptent par nuits, et lors qu'ils ueulent jouer auec un autre uillage, ils enuoyent un deputé, qui porte la parolle, et qui liure au chef un nombre de petites buchettes, tous les jours on en jette une, et la derniere qui reste, fait uoir que c'est le lendemain le jour assigné. ils font des dances entre eux, accompagnés de repas, qui sont à peu pres les mêsmes, il n'y à que les noms de difference; comme la dance du dinde, du Bœuf, de l'ours, du Crocodille, a celle cy, ils ont des masques faits comme la teste de cet animal dont un ou deux se deguisent ainsi, et cinq ou six autres prennent des masques de differents animeaux que la Crocodille à coutume de manger, et alors ils font mil singeries crotesques: la dance de l'outarde, du petit blé, la dance de guerre, et la dance des jeunes gens, qui ne se dance plus les françois leurs en ayant fait conceuoir trop d'horreur: lors qu'ils font ces dances, c'est sur les deux heures appres midy qu'ils commencent. ils sont matachés. ils mettent leurs plus beaux habits. se font une cinture d'une quarantaine de grelots de potin gros comme le poing, d'autres mettent des clocettes, et s'ils auoint des cloches, et qu'ils les pussent porter, ils en porteroint a ces dances aimant extrahordinairement le brüit: ils ont un Chichiquoüá a la main ou un casse teste, ou un pistolet, ils dancent en rond autour d'un tembour qui n'a en main qu'une baguette dont ils frappent une peau de cheureüil qui esttendüe sur un pot de terre, ou sur une marmitte ils accompagnent cet espece de son dune chanson de cinq ou six parolles qu'ils repetent continuellement. ces dances durent jusqu'au jour, ou alors ils uont dormir. ils ont des connoiscences de simples tres curieuses.

Ils croyent qu'il y'a des reuenants et font plusieurs histoires à ce sujet qui n'ont pas de uraisemblances. ils disent que ces reuenans ce sont des gens qui sont morts. a qui on n'a pas donné quelques effets en mourant dont ils auoint besoin, dans l'autre monde, comme ceux qui sont noyé ou tüé à la guerre, et qu'ils uiennent le rechercher.

Leurs païs est tres beau, pas si fourny de bois qu'au band de la mer. il y a des plaines fort grandes entrecoupée de petits rüisseaux qui les arrosent; dedans ces plaines il ya des herbages excelents pour la pasture des bestiaux, qui uiennent de la hauteur d'un homme. il n'y à qu'une riuierre qui passe pres de cette nation à un uillage nommé youanny que lon ne peut monter que lors que l'eau est à demy haute parceque quant elle est tout à fait haute le courant est trop rapide: et tout à fait basse il n'y a pas assez d'eau pour faire passer les uoitures. elle uat se decharger dans la riuiere des Pascagoula qui donne dans la mer, uis à uis lisle Ronde à huit lieux du Biloxy. c'est par la que lon porte les marchandises au detachement qui est aux youanny. il n'y à que quelques année qu'il y en a un que lon à enuoyé, parce que les sauuages auoint demendé d'auoir des francois chez eux: ils uouloint aussi y auoir un magazin, allegant pour raison la difficulté de porter leurs peaux de cheureüil à la Mobille, ou a la Nouuelle Orleans, et que la facilité de trouuer des marchandises chez eux leurs donneroit courage a s'adonner plus uoluntiers à la chasse. il y à aussi une raison qui y deuroint engager c'est que cette facilité qu'ils auroint à trouuer des marchandise dans leurs uillages, les empescheroit de porter les leurs à d'autres nations, ne les receuroint point ches eux, et s'attacheroint dauantage aux françois. mais il faudroit aussi que ces magazins, ne menquassent jamais de marchandise. ce qui arriue souuent par le retardement des uesseaux. on a uoulu donner le priuilege exclusif de cette traite a trois ou quatres personnes comme cela ce fait en Canada, qu'il ne uat qu'un certin nombre de personne traiter auec le sauuage, par

congé, qu'ils acheptent; mais la Colonie de la Loüisianne n'est pas
assez bien establie pour en agir de mesme: il y'a un nombre de gens
hors d'estat de faire aucun metier, n'en scachant point, et hors d'estat
de trauailler à la terre n'ayant point les forces, ny les moyens dauoir
des negres, mais qui uiuant par le moyen de la traite. à leurs
retour des sauuages dispersent dans la uille leurs pelletrie, ou denrée
qu'ils rapportent en payement à ceux chez qui ils ont emprunté de
quoy faire leurs traite: ce qui fait qu'un chaqu'un se sent de ce
commerce au lieu qu'estant exclusiuement a trois ou quatres personnes, qui s'enrichissent pendant que les autres meurent de faim dedans un establissement, on doit plutost regarder le general que le
particulier.

Le païs des Chiquachas est plus fourny de plaines que celuy des
Chaquetas et le terrein plus beau, la terre beaucoup meilleure: il
est aussi plus froit. plus on monte auans dans le païs, plus on le
trouue beau, gratieux, fecond et propre à y bastir des uilles. ils y
a des montaignes toutes de pierre. il y a de toutes sortes de bois
pour constuire, mais la riuiere de la mobille ne condüit pas jusqu'au
uillage.

Lors que les Chiquachas ou Chaquetas ueulent apporter quelques
chose à la Mobille en hiuer, du produit de leurs chasse, ils font un
cajeux, se mettent dessus auec leurs marchandises et se laissent aller
au courant qui les menne au uillages sauuages pres des françois: où
ayant uendu leurs marchandise, ils s'en retournent chez eux par terre
à pied, quoy qu'ils ayent beaucoup de cheuaux pres que tous Anglois
ou Espagnols.

Comme les Anglois y portent toutes leurs marchandises sur des
cheuaux, souuent ils leurs en uollent et les gardent. a lesgard des
Chaquetas la plus part de ceux qu'ils ont uiennent des françois a la
derniere guerre des Natchés ils se firent donner une juman par chaque
esclaue françois, et noir qu'ils auoint retiré. c'est ce qui les en à
fourny, et bientost ils en pouroint uendre aux françois. ils les
laissent uiure dans le bois, et lors qu'ils en ont besoin, ils uont les y
chercher: j'ay remarqué que ces sortes d'animaux accoutumés à uiure
dans le bois lorsque lon uouloit les garder chez soy ils deperissoint
à uüe. d'œüil, il est uray que lon ne les nourit pas comme on Europe
et qu'ils ne sont pas estrillés demesme, ils reuiendroint bien cher, si
on uouloit faire la depence de les auoir toute l'année chez soy: n'y
ayant point de fourage conuenable a garder long temp. ils sont fort
uif sortant du bois et ceux qui les montent uont a perte d'halenne.
les femmes et les filles uont naturellement a cheual dans toutes les
isles comme les hommes. comme les cheuaux ne sont pas communs,
on se sert des Bœuf pour la charette, et pour les charües.

Noms des Uillages Chaquetas

	Nombre d'hommes
Ceux de l'est sont six uillages	
Chicachæ	150
Osquæalagna	400
Tala	60
Nachoubaoüenya	40
Bouctouloutchy	30
Youanny	30
Ceux du midy sont quatre uillages	
Conchats	150
Yanabé	100
Oqué loüsa	80
Coït chitou	80

Ce nom la ueut dire, une grande lieux; ils disent qu'autrefois ce uillage auoit une grande lieux de tour c'est la ou demeure le grand chef.

Ceux de l'oüest sont 35 uillages	
Bouctoucoulou	60

Celuy qui doit succeder a la couronne est toujours chef de ce uillage. et le grand chef y demeure aussi, fort souuent.

Pinté	50
Abissa	40
Boucfalaya	70
Itéchipouta	40
Filitamon	60
Conchabouloucta	100
Pouscouchetacanlé	50
Ectchanqué	30
Ougoulabalbaa	100
Oqué oüiloü	60
Mongoulacha	150
Otouc falayá	100
Boucfouca	80
Castacha	80
Yachou	40
Abeca	200
Cafétalaya	70
Outapacha	40
Toüalé	40
Achouq ouma	30
Bisacha	80
Scanapa uillage du chef	30
Eb¹toupougoula	60
Bouctoucoüloü	90
Abeca	60
Oulitacha	40
Loucféatá	50
Mongoulacha	60
Yachoü ou Achouq loüá	70
Ité opchaqüo	100
Osapa issa	50
Ouatonaoülá	80
Epitoupougoula	80
Ougoula tanap	150

ce uillage est prest des Chiquachas sur le chemin des Alibamons
et il y a un fort parceque ces deux nations sont tres souuent en
guerre ensemble. il y en à comme uous uoyé plusieurs du mesme
nom. outre ces quarante cinq uillages il y en a encore plusieurs
petits dont je ne sçay pas le nom, qui ont cependant leurs chef
particuliers comme les grands mais comme ces uillages sont fort
reculés et fort petits les françois ne les pratiquent guere et n'en
ont de connoiscence que par ce qu'en disent les sauuages eux mesme.
ils rapportent qu'au dessus de chés eux ils ont uû quelques fois
passer des sauuages errants: il les nomment ainsi parceque ces
gens la ne font point de uillages, parconsequent ne plantent, ny
ne sement, et ne uiuent que de uiande; ils süiuent les bandes de
Bœufs, et ces animaux leurs seruant de nouriture, leurs fait changer
de sejour autant de fois qu'ils en changent eux mesme. le soir
ils couchent dans des arbres de peur des serpents ou bestes
uenimeuses. ces sauuages la se sauuent a l'aspect d'autres creatures
qui leurs ressemblent.

M. Bossu, Nouveaux Voyages aux Indes Occidentales, Paris, 1768,
Vol. 2, pp. 88–106

Cette Nation peut mettre sur pied 4000 guerriers qui marcheroient
volontiers. . . .

Les *Chactas* aiment la guerre, & ont entr'eux de bonnes ruses.
Ils ne se battent jamais de pied ferme; ils ne font que voltiger;
ils narguent beaucoup leurs ennemis, sans pour cela être fanfarons;
car, lorsqu'ils en viennent aux mains, ils se battent avec beaucoup
de sang froid. Il y a des femmes qui portent une telle amitié à
leurs maris, qu'elles les suivent à la guerre. Elles se tiennent à
côté d'eux dans les combats, avec un carquois garni de flèches, &
les encourageant en leur criant continuellement qu'ils ne doivent
pas redouter leurs ennemis, qu'il faut mourir en *véritables hommes*.

Les *Chactas* sont extrêmement superstitieux; losqu'ils vont en
guerre, ils consultent leur Manitou, c'est le Chef qui le porte.
Ils l'éxposent toujours du côté où ils doivent marcher à l'ennemi;
des Guerriers font sentinelle autour. Ils on tant de vénération
pour lui, qu'ils ne mangent point que le Chef ne lui donne la
premiere part.

Tant que la guerre dure, le Chef est exactment obéi; mais dès
qu'ils sont de retour, ils n'ont de considération pour lui, qu'autant
qu'ils est libéral de ce qu'il posséde.

C'est un usage établi parmi eux, que lorsque le Chef d'un parti
de guerre a fait du butin sur l'ennemi, il doit le distribuer aux
Guerriers, & aux parents de ceux qui ont été tués dans les combats,
pour *essuyer*, disent-ils, *leurs larmes*. Le Chef ne se réserve rien
pour lui, que l'honneur d'être le Restaurateur de la Nation. . . .

Si le Chef d'un parti de *Chactas* ne réussit pas dans la guerre qu'il a entreprise, il perd tout son crédit; personne n'a plus de confiance à son commandement, & il est obligé de descendre au rang de simple guerrier. Cependent admirez la variété des opinions dans les différentes Nations. Il n'y a point de honte pour ceux qui lâchent le pied parmi ces peuples guerriers. Ils attribuent leur désertion à un mauvais rêve; si le Chef même d'un grand parti, ayant rêvé le nuit qu'il perdra du monde, assure à ses Guerriers qu'il a fait un mauvais rêve, ils se replient tout aussitôt sur leur village; Dès qu'ils s'y sont rendus, ils font la médecine; car ils l'employent en toutes sortes d'affaires; puis ils retournent à l'ennemi; si dans leur route, ils le rencontrent, ils lui tuent 5 ou 6 des siens, & ils reviennent alors sur leurs pas, aussi contents que s'il savoient subjugue un grand Empire.

Un Général qui remporteroit une victoire avec une perte de beaucoup de monde, seroit très mal reçu de sa Nation, parceque ces Peuples comtent pour rien la victoire quand elle est achetée au prix du sang de leurs parens & de leurs amis: aussi les Chefs de parti, ont grand soin de conserver leurs Guerriers, & de n'attaquer l'ennemi, que lorsqu'ils sont surs de vaincre, soit par le nombre, ou l'avantage & la position des lieux; mais comme leurs adversaires ont la même ruse, & qu'ils sçavent aussi bien qu'eux, éviter les piéges qu'on veut leur tendre, c'est le plus fin qui l'emportera; pour cet effet, ils se cachent dans les bois le jour, & ne marchent que la nuit; s'ils ne sont point découverts, ils attaquent au point du jour. Comme ils sont ordinairement dans des Pays couverts, celui qui marche le premier porte quelque fois devant lui, un buisson fort touffu, & comme ils se suivent tous à la file, le dernier efface les traces des premiers, en arrangeant les feuilles ou la terre sur laquelle ils passent, de manière qu'il ne rests aucun vestige qui puisse les déceler.

Les principales choses qui servent à les faire découvrir de leurs ennemis, sont la fumée de leurs feux qu'ils sentent de fort loin, & leurs pistes qu'ils distinguent d'une maniere presqu'incroyable; un jour un Sauvage me montra dans un endroit où je n'avois rien apperçu, l'empreinte des pieds de François, de Sauvages & de Negres qui avoient passé, & le tems qu'il y avoit; j'avoue que cette connoissance me parut tenir du prodige: ou peut dire que les Sauvages, lorsqu'ils s'appliquent à une seule chose y excellent.

L'art de la guerre, chez eux, comme vous voyez, consiste dans la vigilence, l'attention à éviter les surprises, & à prendre l'ennemi au dépourvu, la patience & la force pour supporter la faim, la soif, l'intemperie des saisons, les travaux & les fatigues inséparables de la guerre.

Celui qui a fait coup, porte en trophée la chevelure du mort, s'en fait piquer ou calquer la marque sur son corps, puis en prend le deuil, pendant lequel tems, qui dure une lune, il ne peut se peigner, ensorte que si la tête lui démange, il ne lui est permis de se gratter qu'avec une petite baguette, qu'il s'attache exprès au poignet.

Les *Chactas*, & leurs femmes sont très-malpropres, habitant la plûpart des lieux éloignés des rivières. Ils n'ont aucun culte; ils prennent le tems comme il vient, sanssouci pour l'avenir, & croyent cependant l'ame immortelle; ils ont une grande vénération pour leurs morts qu'ils n'enterrent point; losqu'un *Chactas* est expiré, on expose son cadavre dans une bierre faite exprès, d'ecorce de cyprès, & posée sur quatre fourches d'environ quinze pieds de haut. Quand les vers en ont consumé les chairs, toute la famille s'assemble; le désosseur vient qui démembre le squélêtte: il en arrache les muscles, les nerfs & les tendons qui peuvent être restés, puis ils les enterrent, & deposent les os dans un coffre, après en avoir vermillionné là tête. Les parents pleurent pendant toute la cérémonie qui est suivie d'un repas qu'on fait aux amis qui sont venus faire leur compliment de condoléance, après quoi on porte les reliques du deffunt au cimetiere commun, dans l'endroit où sont déposés celles ses ancêtres. Pendant qu'on fait ces cérémonies lugubres, on observe un morne silence; on n'y chante ni ne danse; chacun se retire en pleurant.

Dans les premiers jours de Novembre, ils célébrent une grande fête qu'ils appellent la fête des morts ou des ames; chaque famille alors se rassemble au cimetiere commun, & y visitent en pleurant, les coffres funébres de ses parens, & quand elles sont de retour, elles font grand festin qui termine la fête.

On peut assurer, à la louange de ces Amériquains, que l'amitié entre les parens, si rare parmi les Européens, mérite d'être imitée; j'en ai rapporté quelques traits pui l'emportent sur ceux de l'antiquité; L'amour que les Sauvages, ont les uns pour les autres, les porte humainement à se secourir mutuellement lorsqu'ils sont infirmes.

On reconnoit cet amour sincere par les derniers devoirs qu'ils rendent à leurs proches & à leurs amis, par leurs pleurs & leurs regrêts, lors même qu'ils n'existent plus.

Les Sauvages en général ont beaucoup vénération pour leurs Médecins ou Devins, vrais Charlatans qui en imposent au sot vulgaire, pour vivre gracieusement à ses dépens. Ils ont aussi beaucoup d'autorité, & c'est à eux qu'ils s'adressent en toute sorte d'occasion pour receivoir leurs avis, ils les consultent comme l'oracle. Losqu'un *Chactas* est malade, il donne tout ce qu'il a pour se faire traiter; mais si le malade meurt, ses parents attribuent sa mort à la médecine, & non à la disposition du malade: en conséquence ils tuent le médecin s'ils le veulent; mais ce cas n'arrive gueres, parce qu' ils ont toujours une porte de derriere; au reste, ces Médecins ont la connoissance de plusieurs plantes excellentes pour la guérison des maladies aux quelles on est sujet dans ce pays; ils sçavent guérir surement la morsure des Serpens à sonettes, & des autres animaux vénimeux.

Lorsque les Sauvages sont blessés d'un coup defeu ou de flèches, les Jongleurs ou les Médecins commencent par succer la playe de malade, & en crachent le sang, ce qu'on appelle en France guérir du secrêt; ils ne se servent dans leurs pansemens ni de charpie, ni de plumaceaux; mais de la poudre d'une racine qu'ils soufflent dans la paye, pour la faire supurer, & d'une autre qui la fait sécher & cicatriser; ils garantissent les playes de la cangrêne, en les bassinant avec une décoction de certaines racines qu'ils connoissent.

Lorsqu'au retour d'une guerre ou d'une ou d'une chasse, ils sont las & excédés de fatigues, ils se restaurent en se faisant suer dans des étuves[1] ; ils font bouillir pour cet effet dans l'étuve toutes sortes d'herbes médicinales, & odoriférantes, dont les esprits & les sels enlevés avec la vapeur de l'eau, entrent par la respiration & par les pores dans le corps du malade, qui recouvre ses forces abbattues. Ce remede n'est pas moins bon pour calmer & dissiper toutes fortes de douleurs; aussi ne voit—on chez eux ni goutte, ni gravelle, & autres infirmités auxquelles nous sommes sujets en Europe: ce qui peut aussi venir en partie des leurs fréquents exercices du corps. On n'y voir point de gros ventres comme en Hollande, ni de grosses tumeurs à la gorge appellés goëtres comme en Piedmont.

Les *Chactas* croyent beaucoup aux sorciers ou enchanteurs, & lorsqu'ils en découvrent, ils leur font sauter la tête[2] sans autre forme de procès.

J'ai vu un Sauvage de cette Nation, qui s'étoit fait baptiser depuis peu; comme il ne réussissoit pas à la chasse, ainsi que ses camarades, il s'imagina qu'il étoit ensorcelé; ce nouveau prosélite fut aussitôt trouver le Pere Lefévre Jésuite, qui l'avoit converti, & lui dit que sa médecine ne valoit rien, que depuis qu'il l'avoit reçue, il ne tuoit ni cerfs ni chevreuils. Il le conjura de vouloir bien lui ôter sa medécine; le Jésuite, pour éviter le ressentiment du Sauvage, fit semblant de le débaptiser. Quelques tems après ce prétendu débaptisté ayant tué par hazard ou par adresse un chevreuil, se crut désorcelé, & fut content.

L'esprit de cette Nation est en général fort brute & fort grossier. On a beau leur parler des mysteres de notre Religion, ils répondent toujours que ce qu'on leur dit, est audessus de leur connoissance. Ils sont au surplus fort pervers dans leurs mœurs: la plupart étant adonnés à la sodomie. Ces hommes corrompus, portent de grands

---

[1] Ce sont des cabanes rondes, construites en forme de four au milieu du village, ces étuves sont entretenues par un Alekxi ou Médecin public.

[2] En 1752, lorsque j'étois à la Mobile, j'en vis un que l'on assomma a coups de hâche, à cause qu'il se disoit sorcier. Les Sauvages lui attribuoient les malheurs qui arrivoient par hazard à leur Nation.

cheveux, & une petite jupe comme les femmes, dont ils sont en revanche souverainement méprisés.

Les *Chactas* sont très-alertes & très-dispos. ils ont un jeu semblable à notre longue paume, auquel ils sont fort adroits; ils y invitent les villages voisins, en les narguant de mille propos agaçans, les uns plus que les autres. Les hommes & les femmes s'assemblent dans leurs plus belles parures; ils passent la journée a chanter & à danser; on danse même toute la nuit au son du tambour & du chichikois. Chaque village est distingué par un feu particulier qu'il allume au milieu d'une grande prairie; le jour qui suit est celui du jeu; ils conviennent d'un but qui est éloigné de 60 pas, & désigné par deux grandes perches entre lesquelles il faut faire passer la balle. La partie est ordinairement en 16. Ils sont 40 contre 40, & tiennent chacun en main une raquette longue de deux pieds & demi: elle est à-peu-près de la même forme que les nôtres, faite de bois de noyer, ou de châtaigner, & garnie de peau de chevreuil.

Un vieillard jette en l'air, au milieu du peu, une balle ou ballon fait de peau de chevreuil, roulées les unes sur les autres. Les joueurs alors courent aussitôt à qui attrapera la balle avec sa raquette; c'est un plaisir de voir ces joueurs, le corps nud, peint de toutes sortes de couleurs, ayant une queue de tigre attachée au dirriere, & des plumes aux bras & sur la tête, qui voltigent en courant, ce qui fait un effet singulier; ils se poussent, se culbutent les uns les autres; celui qui a l'adresse d'attraper la balle, la renvoye à ceux de son parti; ceux du parti opposé courent contre celui qui a saisi la balle, la renvoyent au leur, à qui on la dispute, & ainsi réciproquement parti contre parti, ce que les uns & les autres font avec tant d'ardeur, que quelquefois il y a des épaules démises. Ces joueurs ne se fachent jamais: des vieillards qui assistent à ces jeux, se rendent les médiateurs, & concluent que le jeu n' est que pour se recréer, & non pour se quereller. Les paris sont considérables; les femmes parient contre d'autres femmes.

Quand les joueurs ont cessé, les femmes s'assemblent éntr'elles pour venger leurs maris perdans. La raquette dont elles se servent différe de celle des hommes, en ce qu'elle est recourbée; elles ont beaucoup de dexterité; elles courent les unes contre les autres avec une grande vitesse, & se collettent comme les hommes, étant également mises, à l'exception de ce que la pudeur veut qu'on couvre. Elles ne se mettent du rouge qu'aux joues seulement, & du vermillion sur les cheveux au lieu de poudre.

Après avoir bien joué de part & d'autre toute la journée, chacun se retire chez soi avec sa gloire ou sa honte; mais sans rancune, se promettant de jouer une autre fois à qui mieux; c'est ainsi que tous les Sauvages, tant hommes que femmes, s'exercent à la course, aussi sont-ils fort alertes; j'en ai vu courir avec autant de vitesse qu'un cerf.

Les enfants s'exercent à tirer des prix entr'eux avec l'arc; celui qui tire le mieux remporte le prix de louange que lui donne un vieillard, qui le nomme apprentif guerrier; on les prend par les sentimens, sans les battre; ils sont très adroits à la sarbacane; elle est faite d'un roseau d'environ sept pieds de long, dans lequel ils mettent une petite fléche garnie de bourre de chardon, & en visant les objets, ils soufflent dedans, & tuent souvent de petits oiseaux.

Presque toutes les assemblées des *Chactas* se tiennent pendant la nuit. Quoi qu'ils soient barbares & féroces, il faut pour se concilier leur confiance, avoir grand soin de leur tenir parole quand on leur a fait quelques promesses, sans quoi ils vous traitent avec le dernier mépris, en vous disant fiérement que vous êtes un menteur, épithéte que ces Sauvages ont donne au Gouverneur actuel qu'ils appellent *Oulabe-Mingo*, c'est-à-dire, le Chef menteur.

Quand les femmes sont enceintes, leurs maris s'abstiennent de sel, & ne mangent point de cochon, dans la fausse opinion où ils sont que ces alimens pourroient faire tort à leurs enfants. Les femmes ne font jamais leurs couches dans la cabane; elles vont accoucher dans les bois sans recevoir aucun secours de personne.

Aussitôt qu'elles sont délivrées, elles lavent elles-mêmes leurs enfans; les meres leur appliquent sur le front une masse de terre pour leur applatir la tête, & à mesure qu'ils prennent des forces, elles augmentent la charge; c'est une beauté parmi ces Peuples d'avoir la tête plate; elles n'emmaillottent point leurs enfans, ni ne les garotent point dans des linges avec des bandes.

Elles ne les sévrent que lorsqu'ils se dégoûtent du sein maternel. J'en ai vû d'assez forts qui disoient à leur mere, assied-toi, que je téle, & la mere, aussi-tôt s'asseioit. Leur berceau est fait de roseaux, les meres y couchent les enfans de maniere qu'ils ayent la tête de trois ou quatre doigts plus basse que le corps; c'est pourquoi l'on ne voit jamais parmi les Sauvages de tortus ni de bossus. Elles quittent aussi la cabane dans leurs flux périodiques, que les Sauvages disent *être de valeur;* elles sont obligées, pendant ce tems de crise, d'apprêter elles-mêmes leur boire & leur manger, & ne reviennent parmi les hommes qu'après s'être bien purifiées. Ces Peuples croient que s'ils s'approchoient d'une femme en cet état, ils en tomberoient malades, & que s'ils alloient à la guerre cela leur porteroit malheur.

Quoique les Sauvages ne considérent leur origine que du côté des femmes, elles n'ont cependant pas la liberté de corriger les garçons, elles n'ont d'autorité que sur les filles. Si une mere s'avisoit de frapper un garçon, elle recevroit de vives reprimandes, & seroit frappée a son tour; mais si son petit garçon lui manque, elle le porte à un vieillard qui lui fait une marcuriale, puis lui jette de l'eau fraiche sur le corps.

Si une femme fait une infidélité, il la fait passer par la prairie, c'est-à-dire, que tous les jeunes gens, & quelquefois même les vieillards satisfont sur elle leur brutalité tour à tour. Telle est la punition de l'adultere chez les *Chactas.* Quelquefois la coupable a la ressource, après une telle infamie, de trouver un lâche qui la prend pour sa femme, en disant pour excuse qu'elle doit être dégoûtée du commerce criminel qui lui a attiré cette punition, & qu'ainsi elle sera plus sage à l'avenir. Quoi qu'il en soit, elle n'en est pas moins regardée comme une femme depravée & sans mœurs.

Gen. Milfort, Memoire ou Coupe-d'Oeil Rapide sur mes différens voyages et mon séjour dans la nation Crèck, Paris, 1802, pp. 288–310

La nation des Tchactas est encore assez considérable; elle est partagée en deux sections ou provinces, dont une est au midi et l'autre au nord; et il existe une si grande différence dans les habitudes et le caractère des habitans de ces deux provinces, que l'on pourroit les prendre pour deux peuples différens, quoique ce soit absolument la même nation, parlant la même langue.

Les Tchactas du nord sont très-braves et très-guerriers; ils sont habillés, et portent leurs cheveux coupés à la manière des Crècks.

Les Tchactas du sud, qui habitent à l'ouest de la Mobile, et au nordouest de Paskagoula, sont peu guerriers; ils sont lâches, paresseux et mal-propres: quoiqu'ils habitent une terre assez bonne, ils, négligent la culture et préfèrent la vie de mendians. Ils descendent plusieurs fois chaque année à la Mobile et à la Nouvelle-Orléans, pour y faire des quêtes. Lorsqu'ils y arrivent, le gouverneur leur fait délivrer *gratis* des vivres pour trois jours, et ne leur permet pas d'y rester plus long-temps. Cette gratification de vivres, quoique volontaire de la part du gouverneur espagnol, est dégénérée en habitude, qu'ils regardent adjourd'hui comme obligatoire; et, si le gouverneur s'y refusoit, ils se livreroient au pillage et à toutes sortes d'excès. Au bout de ces trois jours, ils se disposent á repartir, et reçoivent encore des vivres pour huit jours, temps suffisant pour retourner dans leur patrie, quoiqu'ils en mettent beaucoup plus. Ils partent ordinairement sur-le-champ, et s'en retournent par le lac Pont-Chartrain; mais ils s'arrêtent souvent dans la baie St.-Louis et à Paskagoula, où ils mendient auprès des habitans, qui leur donnent du bled de Turquie, avec lequel ils font de la bouillie, de la sagamité et du pain, qu'ils mangent avec le poisson qu'ils prennent dans la baie de la Mobile ou dans les rivières des environs, qui sont très-poissonneuses. Ils aiment beaucoup la chair de cheval; et, lorsqu'ils en trouvent quelques-uns morts même naturellement, ils les préfèrent au bœuf et à toute autre viande. Ces Sauvages sont si paresseux et si mal-propres, qu'ils ne se nétoient jamais aucune partie du corps, qui, étant presque nu, est couvert d'une crasse, à laquelle le temps donne la couleur de suie. Ils ne portent pour vêtemens qu'une bande d'étoffe de laine ou des peau de daim, qu'ils passent entre leurs cuisses, et dont les deux bouts, attachés avec des cordes, leur servent de ceinture. Les femmes portent une espèce de jupon de même étoffe, qui les couvrent depuis la ceinture jus-qu'aux genoux; le reste du corps est nu. Quelques-unes d'entr'elles, plus riches que les autres, parce qu'elles sont femmes de bons chasseurs, portent sur leurs épaules des couvertures de laine blanche, rouge ou bleue.

Ils aiment beaucoup à porter des grelots semblables à ceux que l'on attache aux colliers des chiens en Europe. Lorsqu'ils peuvent s'en procurer par quelques échanges, ou pour de l'argent, ils les fixent à une espèce de jarretière faite de peau de chevreuil, et les attachent au-dessous des genoux. Les jeunes gens qui ont cette parure, en sont fiers, et croient être plus agréables aux jeunes filles, qui, de leur côté, pour paroître jolies, se percent la partie inférieure de la cloison du nez, et y passent un anneau, où est attaché un pendant en forme de poire, et semblable à nos pendans d'oreilles.

Il est nécessaire d'observer ici que tous les Sauvages de l'Amérique septentrionale aiment beaucoup cette parure, et ont l'habitude de la porter. J'ai été moi-même obligé de me faire percer le nez pour porter des pendans tels que ceux des Sauvages, lorsque je marchois à leur tête.

En passant dans cette nation, j'ai été témoin de la manière dont ils en usent envers leurs morts; elle m'a paru si extraordinarie, que le lecteur ne sera fâché que je lui en donne ici une idée.

Lorsqu'un Tchactas est mort, ses parens élèvent à une distance d'environ vingt à vingt-cinq pas, directement en face de la porte d'entrée de sa maison, un échafaud, sur lequel ils déposent le mort enveloppé d'une peau d'ours ou de bufle, ou dans une couverture de laine, et le laissent ainsi pendant sept ou huit mois. Les femmes des plus proches parens, vont chaque matin, pleurer, en fesant le tour de l'échafaud. Lorsqu'elles jugent que le cadavre est dans un état de putréfaction suffisant pour que les chairs quittent aisément les os, elles vont en prévenir le prêtre ou médecin du canton où habitoit le mort, qui est chargé de la dissection la plus dégoûtante qu'il soit possible d'imaginer. Comme tous les parens et amis du mort doi-vent être présens à cette cérémonie, qui se termine par un repas de

famille, le prêtre prend jour pour laisser le temps de prévenir tout
le monde; et, le jour indiqué, chacun se rend autour de l'échafaud;
et là, après avoir fait d'horribles grimaces en signe de deuil, ils
entonnent des chants lugubres, où ils expriment les regrets qu'ils
ressentent de la perte qu'ils ont faite.   Lorsqu'ils ont fini cet épou-
vantable charivari, le prêtre monte sur l'échafaud, il ôte la peau ou
couverture qui couvre le cadavre; et, avec ses ongles (il ne lui est pas
même permis de se servir d'autre chose), il détache les chairs qui
peuvent encore être adhérentes aux os, de manière à séparer absolument l'un d'avec l'autre.   Lorsqu'il a terminé cette dégoûtante
opération, il fait un paquet des chairs qu'il laisse sur l'échafaud
pour être brûlées, et un des os qu'il descend sur sa tête pour les
remettre aux parens du mort en leur fesant une harangue analogue
à la circonstance.   Aussitôt que ceux-ci ont reçu les os, ils ont grand
soin de les visiter, et de s'assurer que le prêtre n'en a pas oublié;
ensuite ils les déposent dans une espèce de coffre, dont ils ferment
l'entrée avec une planche; après quoi les femmes allument des torches
de bois gras, et les plus proches parens vont en procession porter ce
coffre dans une cabane qui sert de sépulture à la famille seule.

Pendant que le prêtre est sur l'échafaud occupé à la dissection,
tous les assistans s'occupent, de leur côté, à allumer des feux, sur
lesquels ils mettent de grands pots de terre pleins de viandes, pour
les convives.   Lorsque ces viandes sont cuites, ils les retirent du feu
pour les laisser refroidir, et sans y toucher; car il n'est permis qu'au
prêtre d'en lever les couvercles, et il ne peut le faire qu'après avoir
terminé son opération.

Lorsque la cérémonie de l'inhumation pour les os est terminée, on
approche une grande quantité de bois sec autour de l'échafaud où
sont restées les chairs; les parens y mettent le feu; et, pendant que
cet échafaud brûle, ils dansent en rond autour, en poussant de grands
cris de joie; ensuite le prêtre choisit un emplacement convenable, où
chacun s'assied en rond, et il reste au milieu, avec les vases où sont
renfermées les viandes qui doivent servir au festin, et auxquelles on
a donné le temps de refroidir.   Quand chacun a pris sa place, le
médecin ou prêtre découvre les vases; et, sans même s'être lavé
les mains, qu'il a seulement essuyées avec de l'herbe, il les met dans
les marmites pour en tirer les viandes et les partager entre les parens
et amis du mort, suivant leur rang; il leur sert le bouillon dans la
même proportion, ainsi que la sagamité, qui est leur boisson.

J'ai dit ailleurs que ce peuple a un goût particulier pour la chair
de cheval, qu'il préfère à toute autre; il en résulte que si la personne
dont on fait les funérailles est assez riche pour avoir des chevaux, on
en tue quelquefois jusqu'à trois, que l'on fait cuire, et c'est avec leur

chair que l'on fait les honneurs du festin. Il arrive même, lorsque le mort n'a pas de chevaux, que ceux des parens qui en ont les sacrifient pour cette cérémonie. Cette réunion de parens et d'amis ne peut se dissoudre que lorsqu'il n'y a plus rien à manger; ensorte que lorsqu'ils ont fait le premier repas, et qu'ils n'ont pu tout consommer, ils se mettent à danser ou se livrent à des exercices violens pour gagner de l'appétit, et être en état terminer le festin. Lorsqu'il n'y a plus rien à manger, ils s'en retournent chacun chez eux.

Cette bizarrerie n'est pas la seule que j'aie remarquée, il en est une autre que je vais rapporter, et qui ne paroîtra pas moins étonnante que la première.

Les Tchactas révèrent beaucoup les prêtres ou médecins dont je viens de parler, et dans lesquels ils ont une confiance aveugle, dont ceux-ci abusent souvent. Ces médecins se font payer chèrement les peines qu'ils prennent auprès d'un malade, et presque toujours par avance. Leur avarice est telle, que lorsqu'une maladie dure long-temps, et que le malade n'a plus de quoi payer le médecin, celui-ci convoque une assemblée de la famille du malade, et lui expose qu'il a donné à leur parent tous les soins possibles; qu'il a fait usage de toutes les ressources de son art, mais que la maladie est incurable, et qu'il n'y a que la mort qui puisse y mettre fin. La famille ainsi prévenue, décide que le malade ayant déjà souffert long-temps, et ne pouvant point espérer de guérison, il seroit inhumain de prolonger encore ses souffrances, et qu'il est juste de les terminer. Alors, un ou deux plus forts d'entr'eux vont trouver le malade, lui demandent, en présence de toute la famille, comment il se trouve; tandis que celui-ci répond à cette question, ils se jettent sur lui et l'etranglent.

En 1782, un de ces Sauvages, qui avoit été long-temps malade, et qui n'avoit plus rien á donner à son médecin, se trouvoit exposé à être étranglé, ainsi que je viens de le dire. Comme il s'en doutoit, et qu'il étoit sur ses gardes, il épia le moment où sa famille étoit assemblée, pour entrendre le rapport du médecin, et décider de mettre fin à ses souffrances, en lui donnant la mort. Il saisit cet instant pour s'échapper, et se soustraire à la cérémonie qui l'attendoit. Il se traîna, comme il put, jusqu'à une forêt, qui heureusement étoit proche de son habitation. Il n'avoit pu emporter avec lui aucune espèce de provisions; et se trouva réduit á vivre de la chair de rats de bois, connu sous le nom d'*opossum*, qui est trés-agréable au goût, et très-saine. Sa fuite cause un grand étonnement à toute la famille, à laquelle le médecin persuada qu'il n'avoit disparu que pour cacher sa mort, qui étoit inévitable.

Tandis que ce malheureux Sauvage étoit ainsi à errer dans la forêt, il se rappela qu'il avoit été plusieurs fois chez les Crëcks, pour porter,

de la part des chefs de sa nation, les banderoles ou chapelets, qui
servent d'archives. Il prit la résolution de s'y réfugier, et de faire
connoître les motifs qui l'obligeoient à fuir sa patrie; ne doutant
pas qu'il ne trouvât secours et protection chez une nation dont il
connoissoit la générosité. Il fut donc trouver Maguilvray, qui étoit
alors grand chef, et lui exposa les motifs de son voyage. Il lui
rappela qu'il étoit venu plusieurs fois auprès de lui, de la part de ses
chefs. Maguilvray le reçut avec bonté, quoiqu'il ne pût le recon-
noître; car il avoit l'air d'un squelette. Il lui fit donner les alimens
qui lui etoient nécessaires; et, comme il étoit encore malade, il lui
fit prendre, au bout de quelques jours, de l'émétique délayé dans de
l'eau de sassafras. Cette médecin suffit pour guérir sa maladie; mais,
comme ce Sauvage avoit beaucoup souffert, et qu'il avoit été long-
temps malade, il resta quatre à cinq mois chez Maguilvray, pour
rétablir parfaitement sa santé; j'ai eu souvent occasion de le voir, et il
ma'a raconté lui-même son aventure. Lorsqu'il se sentit parfaitement
rétabli, il retourna dans sa nation: il y avoit alors environ huit mois
que son évasion avoit eu lieu; et sa famille avoit élevé un échafaud,
et fait toutes les cérémonies d'usage, qui précèdent et accompagnent
les funérailles, ainsi que je les ai décrites plus haut. Il arriva
précisément le jour de la fête de ses funérailles, et trouva sa famille
assemblée, et son bûcher en feu, comme si son corps eût été dessus.
Le médecin avoit si fortement persuadé les parens de ce Sauvage,
qu'il ne pouvoit revenir de sa maladie, que, lorsqu'il parut au milieu
d'eux, ils le regardèrent comme un revenant, et prirent tous la fuite.
Se voyant seul, il alla chez un de ses voisins, qui, frappé de la
même terreur, se jeta par terre; et, dans la persuasion que ce n'étoit
qu'une ombre, lui parla en ces termes:

"Pourquoi as-tu quitté le séjour des ames, si tu y étois heureux?
pourquoi reviens-tu parmi nous? Est-ce pour assister à la der-
nière fête que font pour toi ta famille et tes amis? Va! retourne
au pays des morts, dans la crainte de renouveler la douleur qu'ils
ont ressenti de ta perte!"

Celui-ci voyant que sa présence causoit par-tout le même effroi,
prit le parti de retourner chez les Crëcks, où il revit, par la suite,
plusieurs de ses parens, qui avoient l'habitude d'y venir tous les ans.
Ce ne fut qu'alors qu'il parvint à les désabuser, et à les persuader que
le médecin les avoit trompés. Ceux-ci, irrités d'une telle fourberie,
furent trouver ce médecin, lui firent les plus violens reproches, et
finirent par le tuer, pour qu'il ne trompât plus personne. Ils firent
ensuite toutes les instances possibles auprès de ce Sauvage, pour l'engager à retourner parmi eux; il s'y refusa constamment, et épousa
une femme de la nation des Taskiguys, avec laquelle il eut trois

enfans; et il demeure encore aujourd'hui sur la place où étoit le fort Toulouse. C'est devant sa porte que sont les quatre pièces de canon laissées sans oreillons par les Français, lors de leur retraite, dont j'ai parlé plus haut.

Avant de quitter l'histoire de ce peuple, je rapporterai ici une anecdote dont j'ai été témoin, et qui m'a paru si extraordinaire, que je n'hésite pas à la mettre sous les yeux du lecteur.

Lorsqu'une femme Tchactas est reconnue adultère, son mari a le droit de la répudier; mais cette répudiation est précédée d'une étonnante cérémonie. Le mari, avant de pouvoir répudier sa femme, assemble, sans l'en prévenir, ses amis, quelques parens de la femme, et autant de jeunes gens qu'il peut en trouver. Lorsqu'ils sont tous réunis, ils détachent un d'entre eux, pour s'assurer si la femme est chez elle; lorsqu'ils ont cette certitude, ils entourent la maison; le mari entre avec deux des parens de la femme; là, ils se saisissent d'elle, et l'emmènent dans une prairie ou les Sauvages ont coutume de jouer à la paulme (tous les Sauvages aiment beaucoup cet exercice); ils s'arrêtent sur le bord de cette prairie, et envoient aussitôt deux des jeunes gens couper un petit arbre, en ôter l'écorce, et le planter en terre à environ un quart de lieue de distance du lieu de l'assemblée. Ce poteau blanc ainsi planté, est apperçu de loin. Les deux jeunes gens qui l'ont planté, étant de retour, donnent un signal; alors chacun des témoins s'assied par terre, les jambes croisées. Losqu'ils sont tous dans cette posture, le mari prend sa femme par la main, et la conduit à environ vingt-cinq pas en avant de l'assemblée; là, il lui ôte son jupon, et la met toute nue; il lui montre ensuite l'endroit ou est planté le poteau, et lui dit: "part; si tu peux toucher le poteau, avant d'être attrapée, ton divorce est fini, sans autre formalité; si, au contraire, tu es prise dans ta course, tu connois la loi."

La femme part aussitôt, et court avec toute la vîtesse dont elle est susceptible, pour atteindre le but, avant que les coureurs ne l'aient atteint elle-même; car, au signal qu'elle reçoit pour commencer sa course, les témoins, qui, comme je l'ai dit, sont assis par terre, les jambes croisées, se lèvent, et partent après elle pour l'attraper; et, comme les Tchactas sont tres-bons coureurs, il est rare qu'elle parvienne au but avant eux.

Lorsqu'elle parvient au poteau blanc la première, le mari n'a plus de droit sur elle, et son divorce est prononcé par ce seul fait; mais, lorsqu'elle est atteinte par les témoins qui courent après elle, elle est condamnée à se soumettre aux volontés érotiques de tous ceux qui l'exigent d'elle. C'est ordiairement celui que l'a attrapée dans sa course qui exerce, le premier, ses droits a cet égard; il est ensuite imité par tous successivement, s'ils le jugent à propos: ils en sont absolument .les maîtres. Comme il n'existe peut-être pas sur le globe un peuple dont les habitudes soient plus dégoûtantes que celles des Tchactas, il en résulte que la femme adultère est presque toujours forcée de subir le peine jusqu'au bout, et d'assouvir la brutale lasciveté de ceux que son mari a choisis pour la déshonorer. Lorsque chacun a exercé ses droits, le mari se présente a la femme, lui dit: "Tu es libre maintenant, tu peux t'associer l'homme avec lequel tu m'as outragé." La femme est alors libre de s'en retourner chez ses parens, ou de se remarier sans le consentement de sa famille. Si elle a des enfans, les filles lui restent, et les garçons appartiennent a la famille du pere.

Je fus un jour, par l'effet du hasard, témoin de cette extra-ordinaire et choquante cérémonie; voici comment. J'avois traversé, en revenant des souterrains de la rivière Rouge, avec mes deux cents jeunes guerriers, un village des Tchactas, et j'avois fait camper mes guerriers dans une plaine peu distante de ce village, où j'étois resté pour prendre quelques refraîchissemens. Je fus invité à assister à cette cérémonïe, dont je n'avois jamais ouï parler. Je me rendis à l'endroit ou elle devoit avoir lieu, et j'y trouvai environ une trentaine d'hommes assemblés et une femme au milieu d'eux. Aussitôt que je fus arrivé, l'homme qui m'avoit invité prit cette femme par la main, et la conduisit à une distance de vingt-cinq pas environ, comme je l'ai dit, et lá, lui ôta son jupon, seul vêtement qu'elle eût; à un signal qu'il fit, elle partit avec une rapidité qui m'étonna, mais qu'elle ne put soutenir; car elle fut attrapée dans sa course, et le vainqueur vint me faire hommage de ses droits, que l'on m'avoit fait connoître, mais je n'étois pas jaloux de les exercer; alors il usa de son droit devant toute l'assemblée, qui suivit son ex-emple. Peu curieux d'assister a un spectacle qui me causoit autant d'horreur, je retournai au village, où je vis peu d'instans après cette même femme, qui ne me parut pas très-affectée de l'humiliation à laquelle elle venoit d'être soumise.

BIBLIOGRAPHY

ADAIR, JAS. The history of the American Indians. London, 1775.

BARTRAM, WM. Travels through North and South Carolina, Georgia, east and west Florida, the Cherokee country, the extensive territories of the Muscogulgees or Creek Confederacy, and the country of the Chactaws. Philadelphia, 1791. London, 1792.

BENSON, HENRY C. Life among the Choctaw Indians. Cincinnati, 1860.

BOSSU, M. Nouveaux Voyages aux Indes Occidentales. Vols. I–II. Paris, 1768.

BROWN, CALVIN. Archeology of Mississippi. Miss. Geol. Surv. University, Miss., 1926.

BUSHNELL, DAVID I., JR. The Choctaw of Bayou Lacomb, St. Tammany Parish, Louisiana. Bulletin 48, Bur. Amer. Ethn., Washington, 1909.

——— Myths of the Louisiana Choctaw. Amer. Anthrop., n. s. vol. XII, pp. 526–535, Lancaster, Pa., 1910.

BYINGTON, CYRUS. A dictionary of the Choctaw language. Edited by John R. Swanton and H. S. Halbert. Bulletin 46, Bur. Amer. Ethn., Washington, 1915.

CATLIN, GEORGE. Letters and notes. London, 1841.

——— North American Indians. Vols. I–II. Philadelphia, 1913.

CLAIBORNE, J. F. H. Mississippi as a Province, Territory, and State. Vol. I (only one volume printed). Jackson, 1880.

COLLINS, HENRY B., JR. Potsherds from Choctaw village sites in Mississippi. Jour. Wash. Acad. Sci., vol. 17, pp. 259–263, Baltimore, 1927.

CULIN, STEWART. Games of the North American Indians. Twenty-fourth Ann. Rept. Bur. Amer. Ethn., Washington, 1907.

CUSHMAN, H. B. History of the Choctaw, Chickasaw, and Natchez Indians. Greenville, Tex., 1899.

DE CRENAY, LE BARON. Map of the territory between the Chattahoochee and Mississippi Rivers. In Hamilton, Colonial Mobile, New York, 1910, p. 196. Also in Bull. 73, Bur. Amer. Ethn., Pl. 5, Washington, 1922.

DE LUSSER, M. Journal of a visit to the Choctaw Nation made in 1730. In the Archives Nationales, Colonies; Correspondence Générale, Louisiane. Copy in the Library of Congress, Manuscripts Division, Washington, D. C.

DE VILLIERS, MARC. Documents concernant l'histoire des Indiens de la région orientale de la Louisiane. Jour. Soc. Amér. de Paris, n. s. vol. XIV, pp. 127–140, Paris, 1922.

——— Notes sur les Chactas d'après les journaux de voyage de Régis du Roullet (1729–1732). Journ. Soc. Amér. de Paris, n. s. vol. XV, pp. 223–250, Paris, 1923.

DONALDSON, THOMAS. The George Catlin Indian gallery in the U. S. National Museum (Smithsonian Institution) with memoir and statistics. Ann. Rept. Smithson. Inst. for 1885, pt. II, Washington, 1886.

DU PRATZ. See LE PAGE DU PRATZ.

DU ROULLET, RÉGIS. Journal of a visit made to the Choctaw nation in 1732. In the Archives of the Naval Hydrographic Service, Paris. Copy in Library of Congress, Manuscripts Division, Washington, D. C.

——— See DE VILLIERS, MARC.

BUREAU OF AMERICAN ETHNOLOGY [Bull. 103]

FOREMAN, GRANT, ed. A traveler in Indian Territory. The journal of Ethan Allen Hitchcock, late Major-General in the United States Army. Edited and annotated by Grant Foreman. Cedar Rapids, Iowa, 1930.

GATSCHET, ALBERT S. A migration legend of the Creek Indians. Vol. I, Philadelphia, 1884 [Brinton's Library of Aboriginal American Literature, No. 4]. Vol. II, St. Louis, 1888 [Trans. Acad. Sci. St. Louis, vol. v, nos. 1 and 2].

GREGG, JOSIAH. Commerce of the prairies. Pt. II. In Early Western Travels, Reuben Gold Thwaites, editor, vol. xx, Cleveland, 1905.

HALBERT, HENRY S. Courtship and marriage among the Choctaws of Mississippi. Amer. Naturalist, vol. xvi, pp. 222–224, Philadelphia, 1882.

——. The Choctaw Achahpih (Chungkee) game. Amer. Antiq., vol. x, pp. 283–284, Chicago, 1888.

—— Pyramid and Old Road in Mississippi. Amer. Antiq., vol. xiii, pp. 348–349, Chicago, 1891.

—— A Choctaw migration legend. Amer. Antiq., vol. xvi, pp. 215–216, Chicago, 1894.

—— The Choctaw Robin Goodfellow. Amer. Antiq., vol. xvii, p. 157, Chicago, 1895.

—— Nanih Waiya, the sacred mound of the Choctaws. Publs. Miss. Hist. Soc., vol. ii, pp. 223–234, Oxford, Miss., 1899.

—— Funeral customs of the Mississippi Choctaws. Publs. Miss. Hist. Soc., vol. iii, pp. 353–366, Oxford, Miss., 1900.

—— The Choctaw creation legend. Publs. Miss. Hist. Soc., vol. iv, pp. 267–270, Oxford, Miss., 1901.

—— District divisions of the Choctaw nation. Publs. Ala. Hist. Soc., Misc. Colls., vol. i, pp. 375–385, Montgomery, Ala., 1901.

—— ed. See BYINGTON, CYRUS.

HAMILTON, PETER J. Colonial Mobile. Boston and New York, 1910.

HITCHCOCK, ETHAN ALLEN. See FOREMAN, GRANT, ed.

HODGSON, ADAM. Remarks during a journey through North America. New York, 1823.

INDIAN AFFAIRS, U. S. Office of Indian Affairs (War Department). Reports, 1825–1848. Reports of the Commissioner (Department of the Interior), 1849–1856.

LANMAN, CHARLES. Adventures in the wilds of the United States and British American Provinces. Vols. I–II. Philadelphia, 1856.

LE PAGE DU PRATZ, ANTOINE S. Histoire de la Louisiane. Tomes I–III. Paris, 1758.

LINCECUM, GIDEON. Choctaw traditions about their settlement in Mississippi and the origin of their mounds. Publs. Miss. Hist. Soc., vol. viii, pp. 521–542, Oxford, Miss., 1904.

MILFORT [LE CLERC]. Mémoire ou coup d'œil rapide sur mes différens voyages et mon séjour dans la nation Crěck. Paris, 1802.

MISSIONARY HERALD, THE. Vols. xxiv–xxv, Boston, 1828–1829.

MISSISSIPPI PROVINCIAL ARCHIVES. See ROWLAND, DUNBAR.

MISSISSIPPI STATE ARCHIVES. Manuscripts and copies of manuscripts in the Mississippi State Department of Archives and History. Jackson, Miss.

MORGAN, LEWIS H. Ancient society, or researches in the lines of human progress from savagery through barbarism to civilization. New York, 1877. (Same, 1878.)

PICKETT, ALBERT JAMES. History of Alabama and incidentally of Georgia and Mississippi. Sheffield, Ala., 1896.

ROMANS, BERNARD. A concise natural history of East and West Florida. Vol. I. (Only one volume printed.)   New York, 1775.

ROWLAND, DUNBAR, ed. Mississippi Provincial Archives, 1763–1766. English Dominion. Vol. I. Nashville, Tenn., 1911.

SCHERMERHORN, JOHN F. Report respecting the Indians inhabiting the western parts of the United States. Colls. Mass. Hist. Soc., 24 ser., vol. II, pp. 1–45, Boston, 1814.

SIBLEY, JOHN. Letters of Dr. John Sibley of Louisiana to his son Samuel Hopkins Sibley, 1803–1821. La. Hist. Quar., vol. 10, no. 4, pp. 498–507, New Orleans, 1927.

SWANTON, JOHN R. An early account of the Choctaw Indians. Mem. Amer. Anthrop. Asso., vol. V, no. 2, Lancaster, Pa., 1918.

—— Early history of the Creek Indians and their neighbors. Bull. 73, Bur. Amer. Ethn., Washington, 1922.

—— Social organization and social usages of the Indians of the Creek Confederacy. Forty-second Ann. Rept. Bur. Amer. Ethn., pp. 23–472, Washington, 1928.

—— Social and religious beliefs and usages of the Chickasaw Indians. Forty-fourth Ann. Rept. Bur. Amer. Ethn., pp. 169–273, Washington, 1928.

——, ed. See BYINGTON, CYRUS.

WADE, JOHN WILLIAM. The removal of the Mississippi Choctaws. Publs. Miss. Hist. Soc., vol. VIII, pp. 397–426, Oxford, Miss., 1904.

INDEX

O